Presidential Elections

PRESIDENTIAL ELECTIONS
Strategies and Structures of American Politics

FOURTEENTH EDITION

**Nelson W. Polsby, Aaron Wildavsky,
Steven E. Schier, and David A. Hopkins**

ROWMAN & LITTLEFIELD
Lanham • Boulder • New York • Toronto • Plymouth, UK

Published by Rowman & Littlefield
4501 Forbes Boulevard, Suite 200, Lanham, Maryland 20706
www.rowman.com

10 Thornbury Road, Plymouth PL6 7PP, United Kingdom
Copyright © 2016 by The Polsby Family Trust, Steven E. Schier, David A. Hopkins

British Library Cataloguing in Publication Information Available

Library of Congress Cataloging-in-Publication Data
Polsby, Nelson W.
  Presidential elections : strategies and structures of American politics / Nelson W. Polsby, Aaron Wildavsky, Steven E. Schier, and David A. Hopkins. — Fourteenth edition.
    pages cm
  Includes bibliographical references and index.
  ISBN 978-1-4422-5365-0 (cloth : alk. paper) — ISBN 978-1-4422-5367-4 (pbk. : alk. paper) — ISBN 978-1-4422-5366-7 (electronic) 1. Presidents—United States—Election. I. Wildavsky, Aaron B. II. Schier, Steven E. III. Hopkins, David A. IV. Title.
  JK528.P63 2016
  324.973—dc23

♾™ The paper used in this publication meets the minimum requirements of American National Standard for Information Sciences—Permanence of Paper for Printed Library Materials, ANSI/NISO Z39.48-1992.

Printed in the United States of America

By Nelson A. Polsby and Aaron Wildavsky—

To our grandchildren
Benjamin Polsby Stern
Eva Miriam Wildavsky
Aaron Alexander Wildavsky
Edward Polsby Stern
Saul Abraham Wildavsky

By Steven E. Schier—
To my family
Mary, Anna and Teresa Schier

By David A. Hopkins—
To my family and friends

Contents

Tables, Figures, and Boxes

TABLES

FIGURES

BOXES

Preface

NELSON W. POLSBY and Aaron Wildavsky first met as graduate students at Yale University in the mid-1950s and soon became close friends as well as professional collaborators. As Polsby later remembered, they hatched the idea for this book during a long conservation over the Thanksgiving holiday in 1960, a few weeks after John F. Kennedy's narrow election to the presidency. *Presidential Elections* first appeared in 1964 and revised editions have proceeded at regular four-year intervals ever since, reflecting the continuing evolution of American electoral politics while educating generation after generation of readers.

Aaron Wildavsky died on September 4, 1993 and Nelson W. Polsby passed away on February 6, 2007. We hope their vitality, imagination, wit, and commitment to fair and accurate political science are still as visible to readers of these pages as they are to us as we prepare this new edition, even as the march of events and the progress of scholarship in the years since they wrote this book together have continued to unearth many additional matters deserving significant consideration. Though the 2012 election produced the usual number of new issues, questions, and milestones, we believe that the basic theoretical foundation established in the first edition of *Presidential Elections* and further elaborated in subsequent volumes remains as sound as ever. Put simply, the pages that follow argue that the institutional rules of the presidential nomination and election processes, in combination with the behavior of the mass electorate, structure the strategic choices faced by politicians in powerful and foreseeable ways. We can make sense of the decisions made by differently situated political actors—incumbents, challengers, Democrats, Republicans, consultants, party officials, activists, delegates, journalists, and voters—by understanding the ways in which their world is organized by incentives, regulations, events, resources, customs, and opportunities.

This new fourteenth edition of *Presidential Elections* is the second to be produced via collaboration between Steven E. Schier and David A. Hopkins. Dave, one of Nelson W. Polsby's last PhD students in the Department of Political Science at the University of California, Berkeley, also assisted in the creation of two previous editions. We sought to maintain the high quality and original arguments that characterized earlier versions of this book while updating the text to reflect the contemporary political environment.

The theoretical perspectives of Polsby and Wildavsky, developed especially in the volume's final two chapters, remain of central importance to the study of presidential elections despite the ongoing changes in campaign strategies, technologies, and processes accounted for in this newly revised edition.

It is a great honor for us to continue the publication of *Presidential Elections*, allowing future students of American politics to benefit from the insights of its two founding authors. We are especially indebted to Linda O. Polsby and Mary Wildavsky, and to Lisa, Emily, and Dan Polsby, for their faith in our ability to take up the mantle. Thanks also to Jon Sisk at Rowman & Littlefield for his encouragement, support, and enthusiasm. We express our gratitude to Marissa Marandola for her research assistance and to Jonathan Bernstein for his invaluable contributions to previous editions. We also benefit from much constructive kibitzing by the colleagues and students who have sustained our morale every day at Carleton College and Boston College.

Steven E. Schier
Northfield, Minnesota

David A. Hopkins
Chestnut Hill, Massachusetts

PART I

The Strategic Environment

THE STRATEGIES of all the participants in presidential elections are to a certain extent constrained, and to a certain extent driven, by the ways in which actors are situated with respect to conditions that are for them given and hard to manipulate. Here are some examples: the rules governing how votes are counted, the sequence in which primary elections occur, the accepted practices of campaign journalism, whether candidates are incumbents or challengers, and the habits of voters. All these conditions need to be taken account of by participants and need to be understood by observers.

CHAPTER 1

Voters

MORE THAN 130 million Americans voted in the 2012 presidential election. Millions more who were old enough to vote—about 110 million in 2012—did not. Parties and candidates depend on their supporters to turn out on Election Day. And so it is important for them to know why some people show up at the polls and why others do not. In two respects, Americans are different from citizens of other democratic nations. A smaller proportion of Americans will usually vote in any given election than the citizens of most other democracies, but Americans collectively vote much more often, and on more matters, than anyone else.[1] Voting behavior is one of the most carefully studied political activities. Who votes? Who doesn't vote? Who votes for which candidate and why? Each of these questions is the subject of extensive study.

WHY PEOPLE DON'T VOTE

A lot of elections, not just presidential contests but also congressional, state, and local elections, take place in the United States. Americans are noted for their lukewarm levels of participation as compared with voters in most world democracies, especially those of Western Europe. Table 1.1 compares the voting turnout rate of Americans in the most recent election for president, when participation is highest in the United States, to the most recent turnout figures in the national elections of other democratic countries. Why don't Americans vote more, or at least more like Europeans? In some respects, to be sure, the elections being compared are not exactly the same. Parliamentary elections in many places—for example, the United Kingdom—require voters to do only one thing: place a single X on a ballot to fill an office more or less like that of a U.S. representative in Congress. Who ends up running the government in these countries depends on how many parliamentarians of each political party are elected (from over six hundred constituencies in the U.K.), and so most voters cast party-line votes and do not much care about the identity of individuals on the ballot.[2] Ballots in U.S. presidential elections are longer and more complex: they require voting for president and vice president, members of the House of Representatives, senators (two-thirds of the time), various state and local offices, ballot propositions, and so on. American

TABLE 1.1. Voter Turnout in Selected World Democracies

Country	Turnout of Voting Age Population	Compulsory Voting	Eligible Required to Register
Belgium	87.2	Yes	Automatic
Sweden	85.8	No	Automatic
Denmark	81.8	No	Automatic
Iceland	80.0	No	Automatic
Australia	79.7	Yes	Automatic
Norway	77.9	No	Automatic
Israel	73.2	No	Automatic
France	71.2	No	Automatic
Netherlands	71.0	No	Automatic
Finland	70.1	No	Automatic
New Zealand	69.8	No	Yes
Greece	69.4	No	Automatic
Italy	68.3	No	Automatic
Germany	66.0	No	Automatic
Ireland	63.8	No	Automatic
Spain	63.3	No	Automatic
United Kingdom	61.1	No	Automatic
Japan	59.7	No	Automatic
Portugal	56.9	No	Automatic
Canada	54.2	No	Yes
United States	*53.6*	*No*	*Yes*
Switzerland	40.0	No	Automatic

Sources: International data from International Institute for Democracy and Electoral Assistance, http://www.idea.int/vt/. U.S. data from Michael P. McDonald, George Mason University, http://www.electproject.org/2012g.

Note: The percentage listed for each country is the proportion of the voting-age population casting ballots in the most recent national election as of 2014.

ballots therefore demand quite a lot of knowledge from voters. In general, Americans do not invest their time and energy in becoming knowledgeable about all the choices they are required to make.[3]

But American voters do turn out for presidential elections more conscientiously than for midterm congressional elections, so the complexity of presidential elections is clearly not a deterrent to voting (see table 1.2). To the contrary, the added publicity of a presidential campaign obviously helps turnout, as do the greater sums of money spent by candidates and the increased level of campaign activity in presidential elections by political activists and interest groups.[4]

An often-heard explanation of low turnout in the United States (low by the standards of other Western democracies) is that Americans are unusually disaffected from politics and that abstention from voting is their method of showing their disapproval of, or alienation from, the political system. Scholars have been deeply interested in the subject of political alienation, but they have shown that this explanation of low turnout is at best incomplete.

TABLE 1.2. Turnout of Eligible Voting-Age Population in Presidential and Midterm Elections, 1952–2014

Year	Presidential Elections	Year	Midterm Elections
1952	62.3	1954	43.5
1956	60.2	1958	45.0
1960	63.8	1962	47.7
1964	62.8	1966	48.7
1968	62.5	1970	47.3
1972	56.2	1974	39.1
1976	54.8	1978	39.0
1980	54.2	1982	42.1
1984	55.2	1986	38.1
1988	52.8	1990	38.4
1992	58.1	1994	41.1
1996	51.7	1998	38.1
2000	54.2	2002	39.5
2004	60.1	2006	40.3
2008	61.7	2010	41.0
2012	58.2	2014	35.9

Sources: Harold W. Stanley and Richard G. Niemi, *Vital Statistics on American Politics, 2013–2014* (Washington, DC: CQ Press, 2010), pp. 4–5; Michael P. McDonald, "2014 General Election Turnout Rates," http://www.electproject.org/2014g.

There are several elements to their demonstration. First, scholars note that the constellation of sentiments associated with alienation—disaffection, loss of trust in government, and so on—are more prevalent, on the whole, in many countries where turnout is relatively high. Citizens of the United States increasingly voice negative feelings about government.[5] Americans, however, rank comparatively high in other forms of political participation: expressing interest in politics, discussing politics with others, trying to persuade others during elections, and working for candidates or parties of their choice.[6] Within the United States, people who don't like or don't trust government vote about as frequently as people who do.[7]

A better explanation for what really distinguishes Americans from their more participatory counterparts elsewhere is the existence of stringent voter registration requirements in the United States. While most other democratic nations either consider all of their citizens to be automatically registered to vote, requiring no special initiative on the part of the prospective voter, or combine voter registration with enrollment for government benefits such as health insurance or pension programs, every American state except North Dakota requires citizens to apply to their city, town, or county government specifically in order to participate in elections, including presidential elections. In most states, registration must be completed at least thirty days before the election, when political interest among the public has yet to peak.

Moreover, American citizens must register all over again each time they change address, even when they move within the same state or city. Because the United States is an unusually mobile nation—in any given two-year period, roughly one-third of the American public will have moved at least once—a lot of reregistering is required in order to maintain voting rights.[8] Most states also have laws permitting or requiring regular purges of the voting rolls to remove citizens who have not voted for a certain number of years or who are believed—sometimes incorrectly—to have moved, died, or become ineligible to vote due to a criminal conviction; if they are indeed still among the eligible living, these individuals must register again in order to resume electoral participation.[9] Unsurprisingly, the costs imposed by this system of voter registration depress American participation rates relative to those in Europe. The turnout of *registered* voters in the United States is, in fact, comparable to that of other democratic nations; about 80 percent of active registered voters participated in the 2012 presidential election.[10]

Voting itself takes place not on a national holiday, as in some countries, or over a weekend, but on a regular weekday—for presidential elections, the Tuesday after the first Monday in November.[11] Presidential primaries (electoral events that play a major role in nominating presidential candidates) take place, state by state, on a series of dates, usually but not always on Tuesday, stretching from January or February to June of a presidential election year. These primary dates can be, and often are, changed every four years and may or may not be combined with a state's primary elections for other offices. History, geography, and custom thus play a significant part in determining contemporary patterns of turnout.

While the United States now lags behind the performance of most Western democracies in overall levels of voter participation, there was once a time—in an era when the impact of the federal government was remote, mass communication absent, and electronic voting equipment unheard of—when more than 70 percent of potential (not just registered) voters participated in presidential elections: the late nineteenth century, or "Gilded Age," when partisan mobilization in the United States reached extremely high levels. In the election of 1876, for example, 82 percent of the eligible electorate (which at the time consisted only of men) turned out in the nation as a whole. Soon thereafter, however, nearly every state introduced strict registration requirements, cloaked in rhetoric about reducing fraud and corruption but aimed at keeping down the vote of "undesirable elements" (code words for immigrants and blacks). As Stanley Kelley and his collaborators observed, turnout "may have declined and then risen again, not because of changes in the interest of voters in elections, but because of changes in the interest demanded of them. . . . [Not only are] electorates . . . much more the product of political forces than many have appreciated. But also, . . . to a considerable extent, they can be political artifacts. Within limits, they can be constructed to a size and composition deemed desirable by those in power."[12]

Until relatively recently, the ease of voter registration in a particular jurisdiction could be manipulated by local political figures in an attempt to give an advantage to their electoral supporters.[13] The most extreme examples of this practice were the measures taken in the South in the late 1800s by white segregationists to prevent black participation, including poll taxes and literacy requirements, which were outlawed by the Twenty-Fourth Amendment to the Constitution in 1964 and the Voting Rights Act of 1965. But even after the civil rights era, state laws varied considerably on such details as the length of residence required before one could legally vote, and registration might well require a trip to the county courthouse several months before the election. In a nation noted for the geographic mobility of its population, a majority of states required, as recently as 1972, a residence of at least one year within the state, three months within the county, and thirty days within the precinct in order to vote in any election, including for president. That year, the Supreme Court ruled that thirty days was an ample period of time for the state of Tennessee to register its voters and declared its existing six-month state residency requirement an unconstitutional denial of equal protection. In two subsequent per curiam decisions, the court held that an extension to fifty days was permissible under certain conditions, but that this time period represented the absolute limit.[14]

Declining national turnout rates from the 1960s to the 1990s prompted a series of public initiatives intended to reduce the burdens of registration and participation on prospective voters. In 1993, Congress enacted the National Voter Registration Act, commonly known as the "motor voter" law. This legislation required voter registration forms to be available at the Department of Motor Vehicles and other government offices in every state, allowed registration by mail-in form, and compelled states to allow citizens to register up to thirty days before an election. The "motor voter" law was widely expected to benefit Democrats, whose popular constituencies (especially low-income citizens and ethnic minorities) tended to be underrepresented on the voting rolls; in fact, Republican President George H. W. Bush had vetoed an earlier version of the legislation in 1992. In practice, however, though the law appeared to have a minor positive impact on turnout rates, it produced no significant effect on the partisan affiliation of the American electorate.[15]

Several states took additional measures to encourage voter turnout. Minnesota, Wisconsin, and a few other states introduced same-day voter registration, under which an unregistered citizen may go to a polling place on Election Day, register to vote, and immediately cast a ballot. The turnout rate in these states is noticeably higher (see table 1.3).[16] Other states loosened eligibility requirements for absentee ballots, which were once reserved for those unable to vote in person due to travel or illness. For example, California now allows any voter to register as a "permanent absentee" and receive a ballot automatically by mail before each election; fully 51 percent of the state's vote in 2012 was cast by absentee ballot.[17] Oregon has dispensed with the traditional polling place altogether, conducting its elections entirely by mail. And thirty-three states in 2012, including California, Texas, Florida, New Jersey, North Carolina, Arizona, Colorado, Georgia, and Tennessee, offered early voting, allowing voters to cast ballots in person at designated places in the weeks before Election Day.

These reforms may have helped to produce a rebound in the national turnout rate in the presidential elections after 1996, when it reached a modern nadir of slightly over 50 percent of the eligible adult population (see table 1.2), although a series of closely fought elections and renewed voter mobilization efforts by political parties and interest groups have also likely contributed to the recent rise in mass participation. In any case, voters clearly welcome the opportunity to escape the hassles and long lines of Election Day polling places in states where alternative voting procedures are available. In the 2012 election, an estimated thirty-two million citizens, or 24.5 percent of the national electorate, cast their ballots via absentee or early voting (as compared to only 7 percent in 1992); in ten states, more than half of all votes were cast in advance of the nominal date of the election.[18] Candidates and campaigns must compete in an electoral world in which voting increasingly occurs in stages over a period of several weeks rather than on a single day nationwide.

Still, many potential voters are kept out of the electorate. Noncitizens are not allowed to vote, whether legal or illegal aliens. Most states strip convicted felons of their

TABLE 1.3. Turnout in States with Same-Day Voter Registration, 2012

	Turnout of Eligible Voting-Age Population
Minnesota	76.4 %
Wisconsin	72.9
New Hampshire	70.9
Maine	69.3
North Carolina	65.4
Montana	63.5
Connecticut	61.4
Idaho	61.0
North Dakota	60.4
Wyoming	59.0
United States Total	58.6

Source: Michael P. McDonald, "2012 General Election Turnout Rates," http://www.electproject.org/2012g.
Note: North Dakota does not require voter registration.

voting rights while incarcerated or on parole; in eight states, this disenfranchisement may stand for life even if the sentence is completed.[19] These groups are not insignificant in size. Michael P. McDonald has estimated the number of ineligible voting-age residents as roughly nineteen million people as of 2012, about one-thirteenth of the adult population of the United States.[20]

There is no convincing evidence that the basic human nature of Americans differs from that of citizens of other democratic lands. But the United States has organized itself differently—state by state rather than as a unitary nation—to do political business. The right to vote is administered in a more decentralized fashion than in most democracies, and its exercise requires more initiative on the part of the prospective voter (in the form of registration before the election at each new residential address). That seems better than any other explanation to account for much of the difference in turnout between American presidential elections and parliamentary elections in comparable nations.

WHY PEOPLE DO VOTE:
A THEORY OF SOCIAL CONNECTEDNESS

These findings still leave open why the millions of Americans who vote in presidential elections bother to do so. This question is a matter of some interest to candidates and their advisers. Even though in recent years some congressional elections have turned on a handful of votes, and the outcome of the 2000 presidential election was determined by a disputed 537-vote margin in the state of Florida, it cannot possibly be the case that millions of voters have convinced themselves to turn out in presidential elections because each of them believes that he or she will likely cast the deciding vote. Oddly enough, the more votes being aggregated in an election and the more voters expected at the polls, the larger is the proportion of those eligible who actually show up, so that presidential elections regularly inspire higher turnout than midterm elections for

Congress. But as the psychologist Paul Meehl once noted, the probability of casting the decisive vote in a national election is smaller than the likelihood of being killed in an accident en route to the polling place.[21]

The decision to vote is best understood less as the result of a coldly rational analysis, in which citizens weigh the cost of time and energy involved against the miniscule chance that their single ballot will determine the outcome, than as an activity that provides social or psychological benefits to those who participate.[22] Many Americans view voting as a civic duty, an opportunity for personal expression or group solidarity, or an act that gives them the moral standing to complain about politics or politicians until the next election. Others vote to please or impress family or friends. One experiment conducted on the online social network Facebook demonstrated that users who were notified that people they knew had voted were more likely to vote themselves than members of a control group who were not exposed to such messages.[23]

Above all, voting is a habit that citizens fall into as they adopt other forms of social participation in the course of becoming integrated into public life.[24] In general, voters are people connected in various ways to the larger society or to their local community, and nonvoters are not. Thus people who are settled in one place vote more than people who move around. Married adults vote more frequently than the unmarried. People who belong to civic organizations or interest groups vote more than nonjoiners. Citizens who follow current events and have strong opinions on policy matters vote more than the politically indifferent. Voting participation generally increases with age until late in life when social participation of all sorts drops away—frequently as the result of declining health or the loss of a spouse. The young, many of whom are unsettled and unmarried, vote much less than their elders, but as they settle down, they begin to vote. The better-educated vote more than the less well-educated. And people who identify with one or another political party vote more than those who claim no party affiliation or loyalty.[25]

Residence, family ties, education, civic participation in general, and party identification all create ties to the larger world, and these ties evidently create social habits that include turning out to vote. Families of government workers—a special sort of interest group—also participate at extremely high levels.[26] Perhaps these voters are voting because they perceive a monetary incentive to do so. Typically, however, their votes have little or no direct impact on their salaries. But they may feel keenly the centrality of civic involvement in their lives.

If voting were in general a rationally calculated activity, we conjecture that large numbers of the most well-educated and sophisticated citizens would become free-riding nonvoters, since showing up at the polls or filling out an absentee ballot is hardly worth the effort given the next-to-zero probability that any single vote will decide the outcome of an election. Yet it is precisely those citizens best equipped to see the logic of the free ride—the well-educated—who vote the most conscientiously.

This reasoning also gives a basis for the view that political life is significantly organized according to the social identities of voters. Foremost among the group affiliations that matter are the political parties, organizations that specialize in political activity. Two such organizations, the Democratic Party and the Republican Party, more or less monopolize the loyalties of American voters. Either the Democratic or the Republican nominee has won every presidential election since 1852, and only twice during this time (1860 and 1912) has the candidate of the other party not finished second in both the popular vote and the electoral college. Over the long term, the two major parties are evenly matched. In the twenty-two presidential elections since 1928, the Democrats have won twelve times and the Republicans ten (see table 1.4).

PARTY IDENTIFICATION AS SOCIAL IDENTITY

Most Americans vote according to their habitual party affiliation.[27] In other words, because they consider themselves Democrats or Republicans, many people will have made up their minds how to vote in an election before the candidates are even chosen.[28] These party identifiers are likely to be more interested and active in politics and have more political knowledge than people who call themselves political "independents."[29] Party regulars rarely change their minds. They tend to listen mostly to their own side of political arguments and to agree with the policies espoused by their party. They even go so far as to ignore information that they perceive to be unfavorable to the party of their choice.[30]

Thus party identification is important in giving a structure to voters' pictures of reality and in helping them choose their preferred presidential candidate. But where do people get their party affiliations? There seems to be no simple answer. Every individual is born into a social context and consequently inherits a social identity that may contain

TABLE 1.4. Presidential Election Results, 1928–2012

Year	Winning Candidate	Elect. Votes	Pop. Vote Pct	Losing Candidate	Elect. Votes	Pop. Vote Pct
1928	Herbert Hoover (R)	444	58.2	Al Smith (D)	87	40.8
1932	Franklin D. Roosevelt (D)	472	57.4	Herbert Hoover (R)*	59	39.6
1936	Franklin D. Roosevelt (D)*	523	60.8	Alf Landon (R)	8	36.5
1940	Franklin D. Roosevelt (D)*	449	54.7	Wendell Willkie (R)	82	44.8
1944	Franklin D. Roosevelt (D)*	432	53.4	Thomas E. Dewey (R)	99	45.9
1948	Harry Truman (D)*	303	49.5	Thomas E. Dewey (R)	189	45.1
1952	Dwight D. Eisenhower (R)	442	54.9	Adlai Stevenson (D)	89	44.4
1956	Dwight D. Eisenhower (R)*	457	57.4	Adlai Stevenson (D)	73	42.0
1960	John F. Kennedy (D)	303	49.7	Richard Nixon (R)	219	49.5
1964	Lyndon Johnson (D)*	486	61.1	Barry Goldwater (R)	52	38.5
1968	Richard Nixon (R)	301	43.4	Hubert Humphrey (D)	191	42.7
1972	Richard Nixon (R)*	520	60.7	George McGovern (D)	17	37.5
1976	Jimmy Carter (D)	297	50.1	Gerald Ford (R)*	240	48.0
1980	Ronald Reagan (R)	489	50.7	Jimmy Carter (D)*	49	41.0
1984	Ronald Reagan (R)*	525	58.8	Walter Mondale (D)	13	40.6
1988	George H. W. Bush (R)	426	53.4	Michael Dukakis (D)	111	45.6
1992	Bill Clinton (D)	370	43.0	George H. W. Bush (R)*	168	37.4
1996	Bill Clinton (D)*	379	49.2	Bob Dole (R)	159	40.7
2000	George W. Bush (R)	271	47.9	Al Gore (D)	266	48.4
2004	George W. Bush (R)*	286	50.7	John Kerry (D)	251	48.3
2008	Barack Obama (D)	365	52.9	John McCain (R)	173	45.6
2012	Barack Obama (D)*	332	51.0	Mitt Romney (R)	206	47.1

Note: Asterisk denotes incumbent.

a political component. People are Democrats or Republicans, in part, because their parents and the other people with whom they interact are Democrats or Republicans.[31] Most individuals come into close contact predominantly with members of only one party.[32] And just as people tend to share social characteristics with their friends and families, such as income and educational level, ethnic identification, religious affiliation, and area of residence, they also tend to share party loyalties with them.[33]

Of course, we all know of instances where this is not so, where people do not share some of these status-giving characteristics with their parents and at least some of their friends. In these circumstances, we would expect political differences to turn up when there are other kinds of differences. But by and large, voters retain the party loyalties of the primary groups—people they interact with directly—of which they are a part.

PARTIES AS AGGREGATES OF LOYAL VOTERS

As a result of this tendency, each of the major political parties maintains a reservoir of voting strength among the public that it can count on from election to election (see table 1.5). Since the 1850s, when the Republican Party was organized, Republicans traditionally have done well in the small towns and rural areas of the Northeast, Midwest, and interior West. Over the last fifty years, the GOP has also found increasing electoral success in the South. Republican candidates draw their support from people who are more prosperous than Democratic supporters, occupy managerial or professional positions or run small businesses, and are predominantly Protestant (evangelical Protestants in particular tend to be strong Republican supporters). Democratic candidates traditionally draw substantial numbers of votes from large urban areas outside the South—Boston, New York, Philadelphia, Chicago, Los Angeles. Wage earners, union members, Catholics, African Americans and Latinos, and many of the descendants of the great waves of immigrants entering this country in the latter half of the nineteenth century—Jews, Irish, Poles—all contribute disproportionately to the Democratic vote.[34]

But why did these particular social groups come to have these particular loyalties? We must turn to history to find answers to this question. Enough is known about a few groups to make it possible to speculate about what kinds of historical events tend to align groups with a political party.

Here are a few examples. From the end of Reconstruction in 1877 until the rise of the civil rights movement nearly a century later, the historically "Solid South" perennially supported Democratic candidates for president as an expression of lingering sectional bitterness at the outcome of the Civil War and at northern Republicans' postwar rule over the former Confederate states. Yet closer inspection reveals substantial geographic variation in these sentiments. In much of the Old South—largely rural territory—there were two kinds of farms: plantations on the flat land, which grew cash crops, used slaves, and, in general, prospered before the Civil War; and subsistence farms in the uplands, which had a few or no slaves and, in general, were run by poorer white people who had little or no stake in the Confederacy and mostly opposed secession. The prevalent pro-Union sympathy in the mountain South translated after the war into substantial support for Republican presidential candidates in western Virginia and North Carolina, eastern Tennessee and Kentucky, and southeastern West Virginia, in sharp contrast to the strong Democratic loyalties of the plantation territory. This pattern persisted well into the twentieth century, even after the

TABLE 1.5. Party Identification by Social Group, 2012

	Democrat	Independent	Republican
Nationwide	33 %	43 %	24 %
Men (48)	29	47	22
Women (52)	36	40	25
18–24 years (13)	32	52	17
24–34 years (16)	34	49	17
35–44 years (18)	34	43	23
45–54 years (17)	31	41	28
55–64 years (17)	37	37	27
65 years and older (18)	30	41	29
White (71)	23	47	30
Black (12)	73	26	1
Hispanic/Latino (11)	51	38	11
No college education (41)	36	45	19
Some college (30)	30	47	23
College graduate (29)	31	38	31
Union household (16)	40	46	14
Income under $12,500 (15)	35	36	19
Income $12,500–25,000 (14)	48	41	16
Income $25,000–50,000 (22)	33	48	18
Income $50,000–100,000 (30)	31	40	28
Income $100,000 and over (20)	25	43	32
No religion (25)	33	53	14
White fundamentalists, evangelicals (20)	17	42	43
South (37)	31	42	22
Non-South (63)	34	45	22

Sources: All adult respondents, National Election Study, 2012. Percentages in parentheses indicate the percentage of the total sample in each category.
Note: Party "leaners" are treated as independents.

Civil War and Reconstruction had faded from living memory.[35] From the 1950s and 1960s forward, the political division between the upland and lowland South finally began to diminish as conservative southern whites from the plantation belt who were previously staunch Democrats started to support Republican candidates at increasing rates, a trend that accelerated after the civil rights movement and the mobilization of socially conservative evangelical Protestants into the Republican Party beginning in the 1970s.[36]

The voting habits of African American citizens, when and where they have historically been permitted to vote, have also been shaped by several large events. The Civil War freed them from slavery and prompted the vast majority to become Republicans, the party of Abraham Lincoln and U. S. Grant. But the southern reaction to Reconstruction disenfranchised them once again, because most blacks at the time lived in the rural South well within the reach of Jim Crow laws preventing them from voting.[37] The growth of American industry brought many African Americans north in the first half of the twentieth century, taking them away from the most severe legal impediments to political participation but not always lifting their burden of economic destitution or racial discrimination.[38] The effects of the Great Depression of the 1930s on African American voters in the North unmoored them from their traditional Republican loyalties and brought them into Democrat Franklin D. Roosevelt's New Deal coalition; northern blacks have remained overwhelmingly Democratic ever since.[39] In the South, especially after the Voting Rights Act of 1965 was enacted by bipartisan congressional majorities during the Democratic presidency of Lyndon Johnson, newly enfranchised African Americans also voted Democratic. As these voters have observed Democratic politicians (in increasing numbers themselves black)[40] espousing causes in which they believe, they have maintained their high levels of support.

If the historical events of the Civil War in the 1860s and the Great Depression of the 1930s shaped the political heritage of some people, for others the critical forces seem less dramatic and more diffuse. It is possible to see why the poor become Democrats, for the Democratic Party since the 1930s has been in favor of social welfare programs, but why do the rich lean toward the Republicans? Undoubtedly, in part, wealthy voters have reacted negatively to the redistributive aspirations of some New Deal initiatives and the inclination of Democratic presidents to expand the role of government in the national economy. But they have also been attracted to the Republican Party by its long-standing record—dating back to the nineteenth century—in favor of measures benefitting business interests.[41] Recent Republican presidents and congressional leaders have upheld the party's traditional advocacy of policies that disproportionately appeal to affluent voters, such as income tax cuts for high earners, reduction or repeal of the federal estate tax, and the relaxation of government regulations of private corporations.

Sometimes party affiliation coincides with ethnic identification because of the political and social circumstances surrounding the entry of ethnic groups into the country. A dramatic example is the rapid influx since the 1960s of Cuban refugees from the Communist regime of Fidel Castro—many of them well-to-do and solidly middle class or above—into southern Florida. For these Cuban émigrés and their families opposition to Communism was extremely salient, and most favored the Republican Party. In recent years, though, children of these refugees are voting increasingly Democratic.[42] The descendants of the Cuban cigar makers who settled many decades ago in the Tampa area, on Florida's west coast, vote more according to their pocketbooks and their union loyalties and have been predominantly Democratic for decades.[43] The vast majority of Hispanics/Latinos in the southwestern states of California, Arizona, and Texas are of Mexican descent, while Puerto Ricans are more numerous in New York, New Jersey, and the rest of the northeastern United States. Members of both of these nationalities have long voted overwhelmingly for Democrats, who are the traditional party of immigrants and lower-income voters. Republican leaders, mindful that Hispanic or Latino voters comprise a growing share of the American electorate, have increasingly attempted to court this voting bloc in recent years, achieving some limited success during the presidency of George W. Bush; these efforts, however, are made more difficult by the Republican Party's traditional advocacy of restrictions on immigration.[44]

In the decades following the Civil War, politics in most major northern cities was dominated by the Republican Party and by "Yankees" (Protestants of British ancestry) of substance and high status. During this time, thousands of Irish people—many of them fleeing the potato famine of the mid-nineteenth century and rule in Ireland by the English and Scots-Irish cousins of Yankee Americans—streamed into Boston, New York, and other large population centers in the eastern United States. The Democratic Party welcomed them; the Republicans did not. In due course, the Democratic percentage of the two-party vote began to increase, and Irish politicians, who uniquely among newer immigrants already knew the English language, took over the Democratic Party nearly everywhere they settled.[45] In the Midwest, events such as American involvement in two world wars against Germany under Democratic auspices in many cases shaped the political preferences of Americans of German descent toward the more isolationist Republicans.[46] These are a few examples of the ways in which group membership and historical circumstances have given voters special ties with particular parties.

Party identification may also be shaped by the identity of the politicians in power when citizens come of political age. The generation of Americans who reached adulthood during the 1930s, for example, became socialized into national politics during the administration of a popular Democratic president, Franklin D. Roosevelt. As a result, most of these voters became Democrats themselves; even sixty years later, the now-elderly "New Deal generation" was still more likely to support the Democratic Party than voters who first became involved in politics during the 1950s, when Republican Dwight D. Eisenhower was president. Similarly, voters who entered the electorate during Ronald Reagan's presidency in the 1980s remain, even today, significantly more Republican than their slightly younger counterparts who reached adulthood in the 1990s during the Democratic administration of Bill Clinton.[47] In the 2012 election, 44 percent of voters under the age of thirty identified as Democrats, compared to just 26 percent who considered themselves Republicans.[48] This wide Democratic advantage among the youngest generation of voters was due in part to the personal popularity of incumbent president Barack Obama among this age cohort. If these voters continue to take a positive view of Obama's presidency, their initial preference for the Democratic Party may, for many, solidify into lifelong identification.

Once voters form psychological ties to a political party, a great deal follows. Merely to list the functions that party identification performs for voters—reducing their costs of acquiring political information, telling them what side they are on, organizing their political knowledge by ordering their preferences, letting them know what is of prime importance—is to suggest the profound significance of parties for voting behavior. Politics is complex; there are many possible issues, relevant political personalities, and decisions to be made on Election Day. Voters who follow their party identification can simplify their choices and reduce to manageable proportions the time and effort they spend on public affairs simply by voting for their party's candidate. Voters with strong party identifications need not puzzle over each and every issue. They can, instead, listen to the pronouncements of their party leaders, who inform them what issues are important, what information is most relevant to those issues, and what positions they ought to take. Of course, citizens with greater interest in public affairs may investigate matters for themselves. Even so, their party identification provides them with important guidance in learning about the issues that interest them as well as the many matters on which they cannot possibly be well informed. All of us, including full-time participants in politics such as the president and other leading politicians, must find ways to cut our information costs on some issues.[49] For most of the millions who vote, identification with one of the two major political parties performs that indispensable function most of the time.

IDEOLOGIES, CANDIDATES, AND ISSUES
IN THE MINDS OF VOTERS

Another method of reducing the costs of information may be for voters to have or acquire a more or less comprehensive set of internally consistent beliefs, sometimes known as an *ideology*. How do ideologies structure political beliefs? Voters or party activists may be conscious of having an ideology and thus adopt views consistent with their position; they can use ideological labels as a shortcut in making decisions, or at least they can think of one issue as related to another. There is some evidence that only small numbers of voters are fully consistent in their ideological thinking; a larger minority makes use of various forms of group references when expressing preferences for a particular candidate, and a still larger group makes use of ideological labels.[50] This segment of the electorate has grown in recent years, perhaps due to rising education levels.[51]

Labels such as left and right and liberal and conservative, while commonly used in political discourse, sometimes work and sometimes do not in structuring attitudes. If we talk about social welfare or economically redistributive issues, these labels serve reasonably well in sorting people out: left for, right against. But some issues are harder to fathom. What would be the "conservative" position on abortion, for example, when conservative libertarians are pro-choice and other conservatives pro-life?[52]

Specific candidates with special attractiveness or unattractiveness may under certain circumstances sway voters to desert their habitual party in a presidential vote. The landslide victories of Dwight D. Eisenhower in 1952 and 1956 are examples of this appeal. Though a Republican, Eisenhower enjoyed remarkable popularity among Democrats, who perceived him less as a partisan figure than as a national military hero of the recently concluded World War II (1941–1945). It is not surprising, then, that Eisenhower's personal following did not greatly aid Republican candidates for other offices who ran with him, or the Republican Party itself once he no longer headed the ticket. The unpopular candidacy of George McGovern in 1972 had the opposite effect; it prompted many Democrats to desert their party's nominee in favor of Republican opponent Richard Nixon.[53] In recent presidential elections, both parties have managed to choose nominees who appeal strongly to the voters of their own party but are viewed much less positively by members of the opposition, leading to relatively high rates of party loyalty in the electorate.

Particular issues have much the same occasional effect as candidates on voters' loyalties.[54] This is true because for an issue to change a voter's habitual party preference, it has to reach a high degree of salience for the voter. Voters must know about the issue, they must care about it at least a little, and they must be able to distinguish the positions of the parties and their candidates on the issue. Data from public opinion polls tell us that most people are not well informed about the details of issues most of the time.[55] All but major public issues are thus eliminated for most people as important in influencing their vote. And even these major issues may enter the consciousness of most people in only the most rudimentary way.

Once voters have some grasp of the content of a public policy and learn to prefer one outcome over another, they must also find a public leader to espouse their point of view. Discerning differences on policy issues between parties is not always easy. Party statements on policy may be vague because leaders may deliberately obfuscate an issue

BOX 1.1. In the Arena: 2012 Obama and Romney Voters Speak on Issues, Ideology, and Candidates

Issues

"Romney's plan just doesn't add up. How do you increase military spending, cut taxes, and balance the budget? He's either going to raise middle-class taxes, cut your grandmother's healthcare and social security drastically, or increase the deficit."

"Obama is cutting our military, therefore weakening America in the world. Also, he took away "work for welfare" so now, that person with six kids gets to live off of your tax dollars and never hold a job because they are financially dependent on government. Romney has the business experience to fix our problems."

Ideology

"Our founding fathers designed our country to be free from government intervention and not be a socialist nation. If Obama is reelected, he will push this nation closer to becoming an entitlement state."

"Romney is the candidate for the rich people. As we know from his remarks, he sees the only important people as the business owners and the rich. Obama is in tune with the working and middle class."

Candidates

"I am not going to trust Romney, some heigh-ho millionaire to know what is good for me and the people I care about. I'm sure he is a nice guy, but I really don't see him doing anything good for me."

"Obama doesn't know how to handle an economy. He is inexperienced, indecisive, and hypocritical, and he has failed as a president of the United States."

Source: Posted comments to the question: "Who should I vote for—Obama or Romney?" Located at https://answers.yahoo.com/question/index?qid=20121027224533AArHlkf

for fear of alienating interested publics. They also may try to hold divergent factions in their parties together by glossing over disagreements on many specific issues. Even when real party differences on policy exist, many voters may not be aware of them. The subject may be highly technical, or the time required to master the subject may be more than most people are willing to spend. By the time we get down to those who know and care about and can discriminate between party positions on issues, we usually have a small proportion of the electorate. The proportion of politically sophisticated voters appears to be no larger than 30 percent.[56]

What can we say about these people? Their most obvious characteristic is interest in and concern about issues and party positions. These are precisely the same people who are most likely to be strong party identifiers. Party loyalty thus works against the possibility that voters will shift allegiance just because of a disagreement on one or two issues.[57] Voters who pay only a moderate amount of attention to politics are most likely to be affected by new information on issues. This is because the most attentive are generally committed to a party and that party's position, whereas the least attentive are unavailable to persuasion: since they don't take in political information, they cannot be influenced by it. This leaves the middle group as most open to persuasion. Not being intensely partisan, they are not previously committed, but they learn enough so that it is possible for them to be swayed by new information about issues and by campaigns.[58] The number of issue-oriented "independents"—voters who care about public issues but have no consistent party preference—is very small. Knowledgeable citizens are more likely to have strong opinions about politics, and therefore almost always consider themselves either Democrats or Republicans. Most people who call themselves independents actually lean toward one or another of the two major parties.[59] So purely issue-oriented voters may be distributed on both sides of major policy questions in such a way that gains and losses balance out and the total number of votes gained or lost by the impact of any specific issue is minute. This is even true of such issues as the Vietnam War, which from 1968 to 1972 was of tremendous salience to many Americans.[60]

Even these changes may not amount to much if other issues are also highly salient to voters and work the other way. For if voters were willing to change their votes on one particular issue, why should they not switch their support back because of another? There usually are many issues in a campaign; only if all or most of the issues pointed voters in the same direction would they be likely to switch their votes. What is the likelihood that candidates will arrange their policies along a broad ideological front, forcing large numbers of weak party identifiers or "independent" voters from or into the fold? It is low, but not nonexistent. In 1964 the Republicans, led by extreme conservative Barry Goldwater, did so. And in 1972 the Democratic candidate, George McGovern, "was perceived as so far left on the issues that his Republican opponent, Richard Nixon, was generally closer to the electorate's average issue position on 11 out of 14 separate issues."[61] Supporters of the Goldwater and McGovern campaigns argued that enthusiasm for their candidates' more ideologically extreme positions would inspire a massive increase in turnout among disaffected citizens who previously declined to participate in politics (a claim known as the "hidden vote" theory). Instead, Goldwater and McGovern merely alienated large numbers of Americans who already vote regularly, including many members of their own party, resulting in landslide victories for the opposition.

Issues that arouse deep feelings can alter longer-term voting patterns, but this usually occurs when one party gets very far out of step with the preferences of voters. In the 1930s and 1940s this happened to the Republicans on the issue of social welfare programs.[62] When voters perceive a vast chasm separating them from one of the candidates, as they did with Goldwater and again with McGovern, the importance of issues relative to party is bound to grow. In short, when voters disagree with a candidate on key issues and know that they disagree, they are likely to vote against him or her. Candidates and their campaigns therefore work hard to inform voters about potentially unpopular positions taken by their opponents, efforts that have reached a new intensity in recent years. The 2012 contest between President Obama and Mitt Romney featured a record proportion of negative television ads.[63] Negative campaigning, however, works uphill against party habits and the disinclination of voters to pay much attention to the content of campaigns.

FIGURE 1.1. The Effect of Income Growth on Incumbent Party Success, 1932–2012

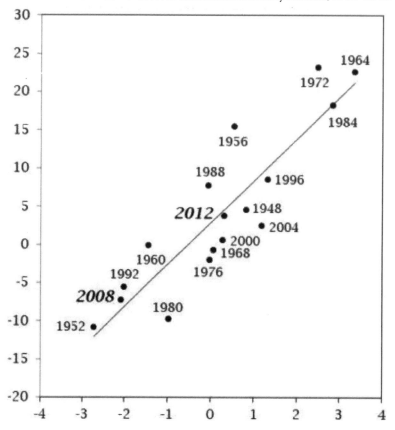

When voters wish to reject the current presidential administration, yet they are not sure that the other party's policies are better, they may nevertheless decide to take a chance on the challenging candidate. Stung by "stagflation," a politically deadly combination of high inflation and high unemployment, and dismayed over what they perceived to be President Jimmy Carter's lack of leadership, voters in 1980 chose Republican nominee Ronald Reagan despite uneasiness about Reagan's conservative issue positions. They may have thought that under then-current conditions of uncertainty about the economy, a new administration would do better. When unemployment rose in 1981 and 1982, President Reagan's popularity dropped, and Republican congressional candidates suffered. Economic recovery brought Reagan renewed support and a resounding victory in 1984. Figure 1.1 shows how closely the vote for the president's party tracks the performance of the economy.[64]

News of an economic turnaround came too late to save George H. W. Bush in 1992. He lost his bid for reelection despite his tremendous popularity two years earlier at the time of the Desert Storm operation (January 1991) when he orchestrated the defense of Kuwait against Iraqi aggression. By the fall of 1992, however, Americans were more concerned with the state of the national economy than with the nation's military successes. Bush fell victim to negative retrospective evaluations of his performance on domestic matters and to popular feelings that he demonstrated insufficient concern about an economic recession occurring on his watch, receiving only 37 percent of the vote in a three-way race.[65]

George W. Bush's unpopular economic stewardship in 2008 created serious political problems for his fellow Republican, John McCain, who was running to succeed him as president. An unprecedented financial crisis, threatening the survival of several prominent private investment banks and insurance companies, erupted just weeks before the November election in the midst of an existing recession. This development made the management of the national economy the dominant issue of the fall campaign. McCain's career-long focus on national security concerns did not position him well to address this matter, allowing his Democratic opponent Barack Obama to charge that McCain would simply continue Bush's policies if elected. Obama's solid victory, by a popular margin of 53 percent to 46 percent, reflected voters' historical tendency to hold the incumbent party responsible for poor economic conditions. Even so, Republican voters remained loyal to their party, casting 90 percent of their votes for McCain.

Obama's reelection campaign in 2012 also faced the problem of a sluggish economy that had recovered from the depths of the prior recession but still suffered from historically high rates of unemployment and low economic growth. His opponent, former Massachusetts governor Mitt Romney, failed to capitalize on this issue. The Obama campaign successfully portrayed him as a wealthy "out of touch" multimillionaire, an image reinforced by Romney's maladroit comments during the fall campaign. This candidate "framing," combined with the then relatively quiet international scene and the successful assassination of terrorist mastermind Osama bin Laden by the administration, allowed Obama to achieve a 51 to 47 percent victory. The election featured heavily negative messaging by each candidate's campaign and produced record party loyalty in presidential voting by both Democrats and Republicans. As Figure 1.1 suggests, the tentative economic recovery was just enough to help facilitate Obama's reelection.

So while candidates matter sometimes, and issues matter sometimes, and both are capable of affecting who wins, for most voters, party matters almost all the time. Activating party loyalties is the most important electoral strategy at the disposal of candidates.

CHANGES IN PARTY IDENTIFICATION: SOCIAL HABIT VERSUS CONTEMPORARY EVALUATION

Thus far we have considered factors that cause voters to deviate in voting from their underlying party allegiance. Under what conditions do they actually change their party identification?

The prevailing model of party identification holds that it is a strong social habit. It begins early in life, is remarkably stable, resists short-run political forces, and changes only through reaction to long-lasting and powerful political events, such as the Great Depression of the 1930s. This view was authoritatively propounded in 1960 by the authors of *The American Voter*. At its core is the idea that party identification constitutes a strong emotional bond and is therefore "firm but not immovable."[66] This leaves at least a little room for candidate and issue-related changes and for a more active evaluative role on the part of voters. One classic study shows that those who change party from one election to the next generally are sympathetic to some key policies of their new party. "Standpatters," in contrast, tend to agree with major policies of their existing party.[67]

It is often difficult to determine whether citizens choose a party in accordance with their preexisting political beliefs or instead adopt a party's positions after affiliating with it for other reasons, such as ethnic, religious, or class identity or affinity for a particular political leader. Almost certainly, both processes are having an impact on the electorate. One synthesis that combines long-term habit with more contemporaneous evaluations concludes that "there is substantial continuity in partisanship from one point in time to the next" and that party identification "can be interpreted as the individual's accumulated evaluation of the parties."[68]

In addition to extremely rare tidal waves that change the party preferences of large groups of voters, there are also more common squalls that affect the life experiences of smaller numbers of individuals and from time to time lead a relatively few voters to alter their party identifications. Since these eddies in the larger flow of events lack a common origin, they usually cancel one another out in their net effects. Thus the big picture of relatively stable aggregate partisanship in the overall electorate can be reconciled with a more complicated picture of occasional individual change.[69] Both the thinking and feeling individuals who change parties once in a while and the large masses of people who are caught up in infrequent movements away from or toward certain parties are galvanized by their reactions to shared experiences.[70] Thus people whose partisanship was not firmly fixed early in life, perhaps because politics was seldom discussed in the home, may develop party identifications in their twenties or thirties. They adjust their party loyalties to their policy preferences or to the views of the groups with which they associate. But they do not make these adjustments often. As Charles Franklin tells us, "citizens remain open to change throughout life, though as experience with the parties accumulates, it is accorded greater weight."[71]

Is party identification a durable standing decision to vote a certain way, as the authors of *The American Voter* put it, or, as Morris Fiorina argues, a "running tally of retrospective evaluations of party promises and performance" subject to significant change based on unfolding political events?[72] Scholars find that citizen assessment of party performance on major dimensions of public policy—war and peace, employment, inflation, race relations—do matter.[73] Nevertheless, most changes of party identification involve switching in and out of the independent category rather than between the parties.[74] This seemed to happen in 2008, as Republican identifiers decreased as the number of independents grew. Donald Kinder sums up:

> So party identification is *not* immovable; it is influenced by the performance of government, by policy disagreements, and by the emergence of new candidates. The loyalty citizens feel for party is at least partially a function of what governments and parties do, and what they fail to do. . . . I do not mean to press this too hard, however. Although party identification does respond to political events, it does so sluggishly. It is one thing for Republicans to feel less enthusiastic toward their party after a period of sustained national difficulty presided over by a Republican administration; it is quite another to embrace the opposition. The latter seldom happens.[75]

Has there been an overall decline in party identification in the United States? From 1952 to 1964, the level of party identification among voters remained stable. From 1964 onward, many more Americans identified themselves as independents. By the late 1990s, more Americans classified themselves as independents than identified with each of the two major parties. In 2012, a declining number of Republicans (then 24 percent) resulted in fewer Democrats (32 percent) than independents (38 percent) in a survey by the Pew Research Center for the People and the Press.[76] These trends have prompted some observers to claim that parties do not affect the behavior of voters nearly as much as they once did.[77] However, more than two-thirds of nominal independents acknowledge that they "lean" toward either the Democratic or Republican Party.[78] These partisan independents are far more knowledgeable and participate much more actively in politics than "pure," non-leaning independents; they also show a far greater tendency to vote, and they nearly always vote for the party toward which they lean. In short, independents who lean toward a party behave almost the same as partisans and not at all like truly independent voters. By separating party identification into seven categories rather than three, table 1.6 shows that the number of pure independents is closer to 10 percent than to the 35 percent often cited.[79]

People are a lot more stable in their party identifications than in the policy preferences that are sometimes held to underlie party allegiances.[80] But lifelong identification with a party does not ensure that a voter will always support that party's nominees for public office; in the past, there have often been significant defections of partisan identifiers to the other party's candidate in presidential elections. From 1952 to 1968, Democrats defected, on average, about twice as often as Republicans (19 percent to 10 percent). After 1972, Republican defection rates stayed about the same, but Democratic defections increased, averaging 25 percent from 1976 to 1988.

Recent elections, however, have been different. Bill Clinton, after losing about a quarter of Democratic voters in 1992 to Republican George H. W. Bush and independent candidate Ross Perot, received 85 percent of the Democratic vote in 1996. For the first time in many years, Republicans were slightly less loyal than Democrats, with defections totaling 27 percent in 1992 and 20 percent in 1996. Both major candidates received overwhelming support from their parties' identifiers in the closely fought 2000, 2004, and 2008 elections, reflecting the highly polarized nature of contemporary electoral politics. In 2000, 91 percent of Republicans voted for George W. Bush, while 86 percent of Democrats backed Al Gore. Four years later, Bush received 93 percent of the Republican vote, while 89 percent of Democrats supported their party's nominee,

TABLE 1.6. Party Identification, 1952–2012

	Democrats			Pure	Republicans		
Year	Strong	Weak	Independent	Independent	Independent	Weak	Strong
1952	22 %	25 %	10 %	6 %	7 %	14 %	14 %
1962	23	23	7	8	6	16	12
1972	15	26	11	13	10	13	10
1982	20	24	11	11	8	14	10
1992	18	18	14	12	12	14	11
2002	16	17	15	8	13	16	14
2012	20	15	12	14	12	12	15

Source: Harold W. Stanley and Richard G. Niemi, *Vital Statistics on American Politics, 2013–2014* (Washington, DC: CQ Press, 2014), based on data from the National Election Studies.

John Kerry—the highest combined level of party loyalty in the American electorate since the advent of modern survey research over fifty years ago.[81] This result was virtually replicated in 2008, when Barack Obama gained the support of 89 percent of Democrats and John McCain won 90 percent of self-identified Republicans.[82] In 2012, partisan loyalty in presidential elections reached a new modern peak. Obama received the votes of 92 percent of Democrats, while Mitt Romney gained the support of 93 percent of Republicans.[83]

So party as an orientation point is still very important. Most people, especially most voters (since those without any party preference are much less likely to vote), identify with or lean toward one party or the other. There are always defections, however, and the parties cannot automatically count on all their identifiers to give them unqualified support in every election. Party identification does not translate automatically into party-line voting. Voters may tend to be loyal, but they can also be driven away.

A CENTRAL STRATEGIC PROBLEM: THE ATTENTIVENESS OF VOTERS

A remarkably consistent picture emerges from the study of American voters over the past several decades:

1. Most voters (about 70 percent, or more than 90 percent if independent "leaners" are included) have a party allegiance, which determines their vote most of the time. The strategic implication for presidential candidates is that there is such a thing as a party base. Major-party candidates must mobilize this base so that the party faithful turn out, and they must strive to minimize defections; the overwhelming evidence is that efforts in this direction will be rewarded.
2. In any election, the number of voters making a judgment to desert their customary party of preference will ordinarily be small. If there is a tide of such evaluations in a single direction, this can be decisive for the outcome. Mostly, these tides are expressed as decisions to move from partisan loyalty to weaker loyalty, from weak loyalty to neutrality or to a weakened resolution to vote at all.
3. Most citizens do not pay much attention to politics or keep well informed about the substantive details of current events. The world inhabited by politicians, a world full of public policy and of contention over complex issues, is only dimly perceived by ordinary voters. A strategic implication is that politicians must expend resources and work very hard to give meaning to the choices that voters ordinarily make according to party habit. For a candidate to become visible as an individual to voters is a difficult task. Much of the activity during an election campaign is understandable in the light of the fact that voters are not attentive to the specifics of public affairs, ideologically consistent in their views, or spontaneously eager to change their habitual orientations to politics. Politicians must therefore strive to capture their attention.
4. Voters participate in politics often in accordance with their social loyalties and involvements. They retain and sometimes exercise their capacity to make contemporary judgments on issues. Partisanship and ideological convictions increasingly overlap in the American electorate. Voters' behavior is importantly influenced by the ways in which they are organized into social groups, especially political parties.

In the heat of a fall presidential campaign, voters are not always coolly rational in their choices. That makes presidential candidates and parties all the more eager to find a way to reach and influence them. "Persuadable" voters, those not anchored by ideology or party identification and less attentive to politics, become a central campaign focus. Larry M. Bartels notes that recent studies offer abundant evidence that election outcomes can be powerfully affected by factors unrelated to the competence and convictions of the candidates. But if voters are so whimsical, choose the candidate with the most competent-looking face or most recent television ad, how do they manage to sound so sensible? Most people seem able to provide cogent-sounding reasons for voting the way they do. However, careful observation suggests that these "reasons" often are merely rationalizations from readily available campaign rhetoric to justify preferences formed on other grounds.[84]

Discovering the true reasons why citizens vote the way they do—retrospective performance, issue positions, perceptions of candidates, party identification—and attempting to influence these decisions is the central objective of presidential campaigns.

CHAPTER 2

Groups

THE PRESIDENTIAL VOTE AS AN AGGREGATION OF INTEREST GROUPS

IN EACH ELECTION, members of the various social groups that make up the American voting population turn out to vote, dividing their loyalties in varying ways between the major parties. Turnout varies enormously among different groups in the population, rising with income, occupational status, education, and age. Since Republicans are disproportionately located in the high-turnout groups and Democrats in the low, this tends to give Republicans electoral advantages that in some measure, varying from election to election, counteract the overall preponderance of Democrats in the total adult population.

The two major parties are somewhat differently constituted as voting blocs of interest groups. Democrats appeal especially to identifiable segments of society—notably, disadvantaged minorities—that have specific programmatic interests. That is the Democratic base, and Democrats win presidential elections by activating these interest groups and persuading them to turn out. This is not always easy, since among the groups that characteristically turn out at lower rates—recent immigrants, the young, the poor, the less well-educated, the less well socially integrated—many tend to favor the Democratic Party when they do vote.

Republicans win presidential elections by doing slightly better than Democrats and better than usual for Republicans among the big battalions: aggregates of voters not necessarily organized as self-conscious groups, such as white voters (72 percent of the electorate in 2012), voters in their middle years or older, those with at least some college education, and Protestants. In years when Republicans do slightly less well among these very large segments of the population, Democrats win (see table 2.1).

Democrats maintain a strong electoral base among groups that for one reason or another have historically felt disadvantaged in American society: black and Latino voters, union members, religious minorities, gay voters. Even in years when Democrats lose the presidency, they tend to do well with these groups (see table 2.2). Note, for example, the strong Democratic vote of blacks and union members even in 1984, when

TABLE 2.1. Republicans Win by Doing Well with Large Groups

Groups	Percentage of 2012 Electorate	Percentage of Group Voting Republican								
		2012	2008	2004	2000	1996	1992	1988	1984	1980
Whites	72	59	55	58	54	46	40	59	64	56
White Protestants	39	69	65	67	63	53	47	66	72	63
Married	60	56	52	57	53	46	41	57	62	62
Suburbanites	47	50	48	52	49	42	39	57	61	61
All Voters	100	47	46	51	48	41	38	53	59	59

Sources: Marjorie Connelly, "How Americans Voted: A Political Portrait," *New York Times*, November 7, 2004, sec. 4, p. 4; for 2008, "CNN Presidential Exit Poll," http://www.cnn.com/ELECTION/2008/results/polls/#val=USP00p1; for 2012 "CNN Presidential Exit Poll," https://web.archive.org/web/20130102104436/http://www.cnn.com/election/2012/results/race/president.

Republican Ronald Reagan won a landslide victory. No large interest group votes as overwhelmingly Republican as African Americans vote Democratic. And several other groups vote nearly as lopsidedly for Democrats.

The differences in the ways the two major parties are constituted as voting coalitions give a clue as to differences in the ways they approach public policymaking. Democrats are more overtly distributive in their concerns, Republicans more concerned with overall principles that apply in a blanket way to the entire population.[1] Republicans figure, rightly, that policies that yield evenhanded opportunities for all will not greatly disadvantage their well-situated clientele; Democrats figure, rightly, that their relatively disadvantaged constituencies will be less well served by blanket policies that take no special account of them.

For most of the twentieth century, the Democrats held a significant advantage in aggregate party identification in the general public; according to the National Election Studies, 39 percent of Americans identified as Democrats compared to only 25 percent who reported membership in the Republican Party as late as 1990. But significant fractions of Democratic voters crossed over to support Republican presidential candidates with some regularity during this era, while Republicans usually remained strongly united behind their own party's nominees. This asymmetric party loyalty allowed the Republican Party to win the presidency in seven of the ten elections between 1952 and 1988 despite being outnumbered among the American public. Since the 1980s, Democratic voters have become more likely to remain faithful to their own party's presidential ticket, with defection rates falling to become comparable with those of Republicans. Unfortunately for the Democratic Party, this trend has occurred at the same time as an erosion in the formerly significant Democratic numerical advantage in party identification. Whereas Democratic identifiers outnumbered Republicans among all adult citizens by 47 percent to 28 percent in 1952's National Election Study, by 2014 this gap had declined to just five percentage points (31 percent to 26 percent), according to data from the Gallup Poll. However, the national Democratic edge in party identification can still prove decisive. In both 2008 and 2012, Democrats benefitted from record high turnout among a reliably partisan group, African Americans excited about Barack Obama's

TABLE 2.2. The Democratic Party Base: Smaller, Loyal Groups

Groups	Percentage of 2012 Electorate	Percentage of Group Voting Democratic								
		2012	2008	2004	2000	1996	1992	1988	1984	1980
Blacks	13	93	95	88	90	84	83	86	90	85
Latinos	10	71	67	56	67	72	61	69	62	59
Jews	2	70	78	74	79	78	80	64	67	45
Union Household	18	58	59	59	59	59	55	57	53	49
Family Income Under $30,000*	20	63	63	65	61	55	49	55	46	50
Big City Residents	11	69	70	60	71	68	58	62	63	–
Gays, Lesbians, Bisexuals	5	76	70	77	71	71	72	–	–	–
All Voters	100	51	53	48	48	49	43	45	40	41

Sources: Marjorie Connelly, "How Americans Voted: A Political Portrait," *New York Times*, November 7, 2004, sec. 4, p. 4; "Exit Polls," MSNBC, available at http://www.msnbc.msn.com/id/5297138/; for 2008, "CNN Presidential Exit Poll," http://www.cnn.com/ELECTION/2008/results/polls/#val=USP00p1; for 2012, "CNN Presidential Exit Poll," https://web.archive.org/web/20130102104436/http://www.cnn.com/election/2012/results/race/president.

*This income category is $25,000 annually or lower for elections 1988 or earlier.

candidacy, and a large identification advantage among voters under the age of thirty. Partisans on both sides were overwhelmingly loyal to their party's nominee. The national exit poll reported that Democrats comprised 39 percent of the 2008 electorate and 38 percent of the 2012 electorate, compared to 32 percent who identified as Republicans in each election. This partisan advantage allowed Obama to win reelection in 2012 despite losing the independent vote to Romney by a margin of 50 percent to 46 percent.[2]

To determine the contribution that a particular social group makes to the electoral coalitions of the parties, it is necessary to know three things: how big the group is, how many of its members actually vote, and how devoted its members are to one party or another. For example, consider the voting preferences of poor people—defined as those whose household incomes are in the bottom one-sixth of the total population. As table 2.3 shows, the proportion of the total Democratic vote supplied by poor voters has ranged from 12 to 19 percent in presidential elections over the past five decades.[3] At the same time, often over 90 percent (and 96 percent in 2012) of the Republican vote comes from the nonpoor—voters whose incomes place them in the top five-sixths of the population. Poor voters therefore regularly constitute a higher proportion of the Democratic electoral coalition (about 15 percent, on average) than the Republican coalition (10 percent or less and about 7 percent in 2012).

Most people have overlapping characteristics. Thus a single individual can be white, female, Catholic, and a union member all at the same time. It would be useful to try to identify the contribution of each attribute alone. By separating subjective identification

TABLE 2.3. The Parties as Coalitions of Social Groups, 1952–2012

	Democratic Coalition						Republican Coalition					
Year	P	NW	U	CJO	F	C	NP	W	NU	Pro	M	SR
1952	15	8	37	40	50	39	86	99	79	76	48	71
1956	12	6	37	38	48	28	88	98	78	75	46	77
1960	12	8	33	46	49	28	87	97	81	90	45	82
1964	17	13	32	36	56	31	88	100	87	79	48	76
1968	13	20	29	41	58	33	89	98	80	80	44	79
1972	19	25	31	41	60	35	87	96	77	72	47	81
1976	13	20	31	39	56	30	93	96	82	73	44	76
1980	19	29	33	35	59	39	90	96	79	68	48	82
1984	15	29	31	46	61	32	94	92	83	66	47	84
1988	15	34	26	42	59	32	91	92	84	70	48	83
1992	15	31	21	46	59	33	92	90	86	69	48	81
1996	15	33	27	46	60	31	94	92	87	66	55	79
2000	12	31	19	48	60	36	94	89	87	59	49	83
2004	13	38	27	48	55	–	90	86	85	59	51	–
2008	13	35	15	49	59	–	92	95	88	68	45	–
2012	17	41	20	51	57	–	96	90	86	64	45	–

Source: National Election Studies and 2012 CNN exit polls. Measures adapted in part from Robert Axelrod, "Presidential Election Coalitions in 1984," *American Political Science Review* 80 (March 1986): 281–84.

*Note*s: Figures represent the percentage of each party's votes supplied by each social group in each presidential election.

P/NP	Poor (household income in lowest sixth of national population)/Nonpoor
NW/W	Nonwhite (Black, Latino, Asian, Native American)/White
U/NU	Union member in household/Nonunion
CJO/Pro	Catholic, Jewish, Other, or No Religion/Protestant
F/M	Female/Male
C/SR	City/Suburb or Rural Area

with the working class from belonging to a union, scholars have shown that living in a household with at least one union member creates a strong push toward Democratic allegiance. Being female, nonwhite, or non-Protestant also makes Democratic identification more likely.[4]

Black voters and other racial minorities have established themselves as a substantial component of the Democratic coalition over the past fifty years. During this time, blacks have remained a relatively constant 12 to 13 percent of the total population. African American voters' vastly increased contribution to the Democratic vote since the 1960s has been the result of a near doubling of their turnout throughout the nation (thanks largely to the Voting Rights Act of 1965, which allowed many southern blacks to vote for the first time), of their high loyalty to the Democratic Party (85 to 95 percent of black voters consistently support Democratic candidates), and of fluctuations in Democratic voting by white voters. The growing Hispanic or Latino population, less heavily Democratic than African Americans but still significantly more so than whites, has also contributed an increasing number of votes to the Democratic coalition in recent elections. Voters of Asian descent, while less numerous, have voted Democratic at a slightly higher rate than whites in the last several elections, while the Native American population, also small nationwide but electorally important in a few western states, tends to be heavily Democratic as well. In 2012, a record high 41 percent of the votes for the Democratic presidential candidate came from nonwhite voters, while the Republican coalition remained overwhelmingly white (see table 2.3).

Members of labor unions and their families have also historically been an important source of electoral support for the Democratic Party. But as the proportion of American workers affiliated with a union has declined since the 1950s, the labor vote has become a smaller component of the Democratic electoral coalition. Whereas union households contributed four times as many votes as African Americans and other minorities to the Democratic Party in 1960 (33 percent of the total), by the 1990s Democratic candidates had begun to receive more total votes from nonwhites than from union members and their families (see table 2.3). In 2012, more than twice as many Democratic votes came from nonwhites as from union households.

Roman Catholic voters represent another traditional source of support for Democratic candidates that has weakened in recent decades. Catholic loyalty to the Democratic Party dates back to the mid-nineteenth century and was cemented by the advent of the New Deal in the 1930s. Even in 1952, when Republican Dwight D. Eisenhower defeated Democrat Adlai Stevenson by 55 to 44 percent nationwide, Stevenson won 56 percent of the Catholic vote. In 1960, when the Democrats nominated a Catholic candidate, Senator John F. Kennedy of Massachusetts, they captured 78 percent of the vote among Catholics.[5]

But as anti-Catholic prejudice in society has declined and Catholics have become less socioeconomically distinct from other Americans, they have started to vote more like the rest of the nation. Though white Catholics remain a significantly more Democratic group than white Protestants, the once enormous gap between them has narrowed, and Democratic candidates can no longer count on automatic Catholic support. For the first time since 1960, the Democrats nominated a Catholic politician for president in 2004, but unlike Kennedy, John Kerry did not benefit from strong loyalty among his co-religionists. In fact, he lost the Catholic vote to George W. Bush by 52 to 47 percent.[6] At the same time, the smaller populations of Jews, members of other religions, and the nonreligious have either maintained or increased their high levels of support for Democratic candidates since the 1970s and 1980s. In 2012, Barack Obama received half of his votes from non-Protestants, while almost two-thirds of Romney voters were Protestant (see table 2.3).

An even more dramatic change in partisan preferences has occurred among southern whites. In 1952 and 1956, southerners voted about 10 percentage points more Democratic than the rest of the country. Republicans began to make inroads among this group in the 1960s and 1970s, though southern voters moved back to the Democrats in 1976 and 1980, when former governor Jimmy Carter of Georgia headed the Democratic ticket. Since 1984, the Republicans have consistently received very strong support from southern whites; according to the National Election Studies, Mitt Romney outpolled Barack Obama by a roughly two-to-one margin among these voters in 2012.

What about the voting habits of young people, those under thirty years of age? Until 1972, they were not consistently a significant component of either party's coalition and their comparatively low turnout reduced any impact that their 18 percent share of the voting-age population might have given them. After the voting age was lowered in 1971 from 21 (in most states) to 18 nationwide, and because of the baby boom after World War II, the proportion of the voting-age population under the age of thirty increased to 28 percent, and in the 1970s there was much talk of young people as a separate, presumably more liberal, voting bloc. Since then, as the baby boomers have aged, young people have decreased as a proportion of all voters, representing 17 percent of the total electorate in 2004. With the much touted appeal of the Obama candidacy to younger voters in 2012, their proportion of the electorate only increased slightly, to 19 percent. Are they now making a big difference?

"Whatever else young voters are," Raymond Wolfinger tells us in a well-advised note of caution, "they are not harbingers of future outcomes."[7] The reason is that most of the time people under thirty do not divide their vote much differently from the rest of the population. The belief that the youth vote was pro-Democratic began in 1972, when it was close to being true, but it has not been consistently true since 1976. A similar tale, only in the opposite, Republican direction, has been told of the allegedly big youth vote for Ronald Reagan in 1984. Actually, as table 2.4 shows, the youth vote did not differ from other age groups in that year, while in 1988 and 1992 Democrats Michael Dukakis and Bill Clinton both received their strongest support from both the youngest and the oldest groups of voters. Since 1992, the young have demonstrated a modest pro-Democratic tilt that exploded in 2008 into an overwhelming Democratic advantage. Though Obama's appeal did not greatly increase turnout among voters under thirty, he won 66 percent of their votes to 32 percent for McCain—the largest pro-Democratic margin in this age group since the Johnson landslide of 1964. Though Obama's advantage in the youth vote declined slightly in 2012, voters under thirty still preferred him to Romney by a substantial margin of 60 percent to 37 percent.

What is the Republican electoral coalition? White people, who constitute about three-quarters of all voters, usually vote anywhere from 5 to 7 percent more Republican than the total electorate, though that margin rose to 12 percent in 2008 and 2012. Historically, the overwhelming majority of Republican votes came from whites: 98 percent, on average, between 1952 and 1980. Since the 1980s, nonwhites have become a slightly larger component of the Republican vote, but whites still constituted 90 percent of Mitt Romney's electoral coalition in 2012. If one can conceive of nonunion families and Protestants as "social groups" in the usual sense, they made up about 82 percent and 53 percent of the 2012 population, respectively, and vote 5 to 10 percent more Republican than the nation as a whole.

TABLE 2.4. Vote for Democratic Presidential Candidate by Age Group, 1968–2012

Age	2012	2008	2004	2000	1996	1992	1988	1984	1980	1976	1972	1968
18–29	60	66	54	48	53	43	47	40	44	51	47	38
30–44	52	52	46	48	48	41	45	42	36	49	34	47
45–59	51	49	48	48	48	41	42	40	39	47	31	37
60+	56	47	56	51	48	50	49	39	41	47	29	40

Sources: For 1964–1972, National Election Studies; for 1976–2004, Marjorie Connelly, "How Americans Voted: A Political Portrait," *New York Times*, November 7, 2004, sec. 4, p. 4; for 2008, "CNN Presidential Exit Poll," http://www.cnn.com/ELECTION/2008/results/polls/#val=USP00p; for 2012, "CNN Presidential Exit Poll," http://www.cnn.com/election/2012/results/race/president.

The Republican Party gets its votes, then, predominantly from white people, middle- and upper-income earners, non-union members, and Protestants, especially evangelical Protestants, outside large cities. Republicans received majorities of 60 percent or better from all these groups in their landslide victories of 1972 and 1984. In 1992 and 1996, defections to Democrat Bill Clinton and independent candidate Ross Perot held Republicans to under 50 percent of the vote in most of these groups, making victory impossible. George W. Bush improved his party's standing among these voters in 2000 and 2004, winning 54 and 58 percent of the white vote, respectively, including about two out of every three votes among southern whites and white Protestants.[8] John McCain in 2008 and Mitt Romney in 2012 also won a majority of the white vote but did not perform well enough to offset Obama's much larger electoral margin among nonwhites.

The 2012 election also revealed demographic trends among three groups that augur well for Democrats in the future. The Latino proportion of the electorate grew by about two-thirds in eight years—from 6 percent in 2004 to 10 percent—and the Democratic advantage among Latino voters rose to 71 percent Democratic–27 percent Republican from 56 percent–44 percent in 2004.[9] Also increasing was the percentage of Americans claiming no religious affiliation, which grew from 9 percent in 2000 to 12 percent in 2012. Seculars awarded Democrats 70 percent of their 2012 votes, up from 67 percent in 2004 and 61 percent in 2000. Americans with postgraduate degrees, a growing share of the electorate in the last three presidential elections, have also regularly cast majority votes for Democrats: 58 percent in 2008, 55 percent in 2004 and 2012, and 52 percent in 2000. All three groups bring distinct advantages to Democrats in presidential elections. Latinos promise to continue to grow as a percentage of the electorate, and secular Americans may well increase as well in accord with recent trends. Secular Americans in recent years have demonstrated increased activism by forming national interest groups.[10] An increasing Democratic margin among those with postgraduate degrees also pays dividends because such people are disproportionately likely to contribute to candidates and serve as campaign volunteers.

To sum up, while there has been no case of abrupt partisan realignment in the years since 1932, the coalitions of both parties have evolved substantially since the New Deal era. Roman Catholics, union members, and southern whites have become less important components of the Democrats' electoral base over time, while the party is increasingly dependent on votes from nonwhites, non-Christians, younger voters, and well-educated professionals. The Republican Party has maintained its long-term advantage among the business class, adding substantial support over the past several decades from religiously observant white Protestants—especially in the South—and Catholics. Since 1992, these partisan coalitions of social groups have translated into relatively stable geographic bases in presidential elections for both parties, with the Democrats holding an advantage within the Northeast, urban Midwest, and Pacific Coast while Republicans predominate across most of the South, Great Plains, and Rocky Mountains.[11]

VARIATIONS AMONG INTEREST GROUPS

Interest groups are collections of people who are similarly situated with respect to one or more policies of government and who organize to do something about it. The interest groups most significant for elections in our society are those having one or more of the following characteristics:

1. They have a mass base, that is, they are composed of many members.
2. They are concentrated geographically, rather than dispersed thinly over the entire map.
3. They represent major resource investments of members—such as sugar cane growers, whose entire livelihoods may be tied up in the industry involved, as compared to the consumers of sugar, for whom government policy on the issue is not anywhere near as important.
4. They involve characteristics that give people status in society, such as race or ethnicity.
5. They evoke feelings about a single issue that are so intense as to eclipse the concerns of their members about other issues.
6. They are composed of people who are able to participate actively in politics; that is, people who have time or money to spare.

Interest groups having these characteristics matter most in presidential elections because these characteristics are most likely to claim the loyalties of large numbers of voters and form the basis for the mobilization of their preferences and their votes. Moreover, they reflect the fact that America is organized into geographic entities—states, congressional districts—as the basis of political representation.

Interest groups may be more or less organized and more or less vigilant and alert on policy matters that concern, or ought to concern, them. They are not necessarily organized in ways that make them politically effective; very often, the paid lobbyists of interest groups spend more time trying to alert their own members to the implications of government policies than they spend lobbying politicians.[12]

In American politics, interest group activity is lively and can be found nearly everywhere, even when it is not particularly effective or meaningful for policy outcomes. Three characteristics of interest groups are especially important for presidential elections. First, membership in these groups may give voters a sense of affiliation and political location. In this respect, interest groups act much the way parties do, helping to fill in the voter's map of the world with preferences, priorities, and facts. Interest groups act as intermediary agencies that help voters identify their political preferences quickly by actively soliciting their members' interest in behalf of specific candidates and parties and, more important, by providing still another anchor to voters' identities. This helps voters fix their own position quickly and economically in what otherwise would be a confusing and contradictory political environment. Second, interest groups frequently undertake partisan political activities; they may actively recruit supporters for candidates and aid materially in campaigns.

Third, interest groups may influence party policy by making demands of candidates with respect to issues in return for their own mobilized support. The extent to which interest groups can "deliver" members' votes, however, is always a problem; to a great degree interest group leaders are the prisoners of past alliances their group has made. This means that they may not be able to prevent their followers from voting for their traditional allies even when group leaders fall out with politicians. In 1993, labor union leaders vowed revenge on Democratic members of Congress who voted for the North American Free Trade Agreement (NAFTA),[13] but in the 1994 election, 63 percent of union families still voted Democratic in elections for the House of Representatives, as they had in 1980, 1986, and 1988. This was only one point worse than in 1984 when

BOX 2.1. In the Arena: 2012 Group Endorsements for Obama and Romney

For Obama

Sierra Club—"The president has demonstrated exceptional leadership in standing up to big polluters, implementing historic mercury protections, and strengthening the clean energy economy. If President Obama is reelected, he will have a clear mandate to protect Americans' air, water, land and health, creating momentum for progress on the issues we care so deeply about for generations to come."

AFL-CIO—"President Obama honors the values of hard work, of mutual respect and of solving problems together—not every person for himself or herself. He believes that together we will get through the most challenging economic crisis in memory and restore opportunity for all. Each of the Republican presidential candidates, on the other hand, has pledged to uphold the special privileges of Wall Street and the 1% that have produced historic economic inequality."

For Romney

National Rifle Association—"Today, we live in an America that is getting harder to recognize every day led by a President who mocks our values, belittles our faith, and is threatened by our freedom. . . . There is only one choice—only one hope— to save our firearms freedom and our way of life. Help take back our country and protect our freedom. On November 6, vote freedom first—Vote Romney-Ryan!"

Association of Builders and Contractors—"The election of Mitt Romney as president is a top priority for the commercial and industrial construction industry and the millions of Americans it employs. He has articulated a clear position on issues important to ABC members, including . . . returning the National Labor Relations Board to a neutral arbiter of labor disputes and supporting the free-market, merit shop philosophy."

Sources:
http://www.huffingtonpost.com/mary-anne-hitt/sierra-club-obama-endorsement_b_1434130.html
http://www.aflcio.org/Blog/Political-Action-Legislation/Citing-Shared-Values-AFL-CIO-Unions-Vote-to-Endorse-Obama-for-Second-Term
https://www.nrapvf.org/articles/20121004/nra-pvf-endorses-romney-and-ryan
http://www.abc.org/NewsMedia/NewsReleases/tabid/144/entryid/163/ABC-Endorses-Mitt-Romney-For-President.aspx

Walter Mondale, a conspicuous friend of labor, headed the Democratic presidential ticket.[14]

Various ethnic and religious votes, the farm vote, the labor vote, the youth vote, the consumer vote, and many other "votes" are sometimes discussed as though they were political commodities that interest group leaders could manipulate easily in behalf of one or another candidate. This is not as easy as it sounds. Fifty years ago or more, when the analysis of election statistics and opinion polls was an esoteric discipline, most politicians could only evaluate intuitively claims to guarantee group support or threats to withdraw it, and no one could tell with any certainty whether interest group leaders maintained sufficient influence among their constituents to deliver on their promises. The development of the craft of public opinion analysis now makes it easier to assess these political claims.

The usual argument is that if one or another candidate captures the allegiance of a particular bloc, that bloc's pivotal position or large population in a key state will enable the fortunate candidate to capture all of the state's electoral votes and thus win the election. Many big Electoral College states contain large populations of traditional Democratic voting blocs: racial minorities, union members, those with postgraduate degrees and seculars. During the hard-fought 2008 Democratic primary campaign between Barack Obama and Hillary Clinton, the candidates and their advisers regularly traded competing claims of superior interest-group mobilization capacity. Obama argued that his selection as the Democratic standard-bearer would inspire high rates of participation and support in the general election among racial minorities, young voters, and political independents, while Clinton countered that her nomination would generate particular enthusiasm for the party among women and working-class voters. Of course, no one combination of states totaling more than a majority of electoral votes is more critical, valuable, or pivotal than any other such combination. In a fairly close election the shifting of any number of combinations of voting blocs or states to one side or the other could spell the difference between victory and defeat.

There is little doubt that under certain conditions and at particular times some social characteristics of voters and candidates may have relevance to the election results. Finding the actual conditions under which specified social characteristics become relevant to voter choice is difficult. We know that in a competitive political system various participants (parties, political leaders) back candidates with the hope of capturing the allegiance of various social groups. It is rarely wise to appeal to one group alone; in a very large electorate, the support of only one group will not be enough to win. Many different groups exist, with all sorts of policy preferences, and each individual voter has many social characteristics that are potentially relevant to his or her voting decision. While some people may be so single-minded that they have only one interest that is important in determining their vote—their race, religion, ethnic background, income, feelings about gun control or abortion or the State of Israel or the environment—most of us have multiple interests. Sometimes these interests conflict. Environmental organizations, for example, may have less success in mobilizing voters in areas where environmental regulation is believed to reduce employment opportunities than in areas where the two do not compete. The worse the economic conditions, the sharper the perceived conflict. Concern about increasing unemployment may influence how some voters feel about governmental support of the unemployed. Much depends on the tides of events, which may bring one or another issue to the forefront of the voters' consciousness and incline them toward the candidate they believe best represents their preferences on that particular matter.[15]

One of the largest social groups of all, women, provides an example of a group membership whose political importance has changed significantly since the 1980s. At one time gender could not be shown to have a strong effect on partisanship or voting habits; what weak tendency existed at the time of *The American Voter* (1960) showed women to be slightly more Republican than men.[16] In 1980, however, women were substantially less supportive of Ronald Reagan's candidacy than were men and thus made up a much larger part of the Democratic than of the Republican coalition (see tables 2.3 and 2.5).[17] Throughout President Reagan's first term, differences between men and women appeared in public opinion polls that asked about party identification, and it became commonplace to refer to Reagan's "gender gap."[18] In 1984, women voted 6 to 9 percent less for Reagan than did men, depending on the survey. By 1992, 58 percent of Bill Clinton's vote came from women, but only 52 percent of Bush voters were women. In 1996 the gender gap widened. Among women, Clinton won a sixteen-point landslide, but Bob Dole actually maintained a slim plurality among men. The 2000 election produced a record gender gap: Al Gore carried the women's vote by eleven percentage points, but lost among men to George W. Bush by the same margin. In 2004 and 2008, however, the difference between the sexes appeared to narrow a bit, with exit polls showing only a seven-point gap in the presidential vote between men and women. By 2012, the gap was back up to ten points.[19]

TABLE 2.5. The Gender Gap: Votes in Presidential Elections by Sex, 1960–2012

	Men			Women		
Year	Democrat	Republican	Independent	Democrat	Republican	Independent
1960	52	48		49	51	
1964	60	40		62	38	
1968	41	43	16	45	43	12
1972	37	63		38	62	
1976	50	48		50	48	
1980	36	55	7	45	47	7
1984	37	62		44	56	
1988	41	57		49	50	
1992	41	38	21	45	37	17
1996	43	44	10	54	38	7
2000	42	53	3	54	43	2
2004	44	55		51	48	
2008	49	48		56	43	
2012	45	52		55	44	

Sources: For 1960–1972, Harold W. Stanley and Richard G. Niemi, Vital Statistics on American Politics, 2005–2006 (Washington, DC: CQ Press, 2005), p. 122; for 1976–2004, Marjorie Connelly, "How Americans Voted: A Political Portrait," New York Times, November 7, 2004, sec. 4, p. 4; for 2008, "CNN Presidential Exit Poll," http://www.cnn.com/ELECTION/2008/results/polls/#val=USP00p1; for 2012 "CNN Presidential Exit Poll," http://www.cnn.com/election/2012/results/race/president
Note: Independent candidates were George Wallace in 1968, John Anderson in 1980, Ross Perot in 1992 and 1996, and Ralph Nader in 2000.

But the case of the "women's vote" should also alert us to some of the complexities of group interest. Generalizations about social groups, especially groups—like women—that encompass a majority of the electorate, may obscure important internal differences among their members. For example, richer women tend to identify as Republicans and poorer women as Democrats, just like men. Group memberships do not necessarily organize voters along a single dimension; the "interests" of a given group may be of greatest interest to only a subset of members. While organized interest groups claiming to represent women's preferences concentrate much of their lobbying activity on pressuring policymakers to maintain or expand legal access to abortion in order to protect "a woman's right to choose," Karen M. Kaufmann reports that public opinion surveys find "few, if any, significant differences between women and men on abortion attitudes and issues of female equality" within the American electorate.[20]

Instead, recent research indicates a growing political divide between older, married, traditionalist, religiously observant women and younger, single, secular, more highly educated women, with the first group becoming more ideologically conservative and pro-Republican over time and the latter more liberal and Democratic.[21] As Barbara Norrander and Clyde Wilcox point out, the gender gap "is as much one of divisions among women as differences between the sexes."[22] In addition, though the rise of the gender gap over the past several decades is usually portrayed in news media accounts as the result of a movement among women toward the political left and the Democratic Party, evidence also exists of increasing conservatism (and Republicanism) among men during the same period.[23]

Democratic candidates have a problem attracting white men and Republicans have a problem attracting women in general. There is no doubt about the numbers, only about the explanation. It is possible that the egalitarian bent of the Democratic Party has appealed to women and repelled men. The argument for this view would be that Democrats include women among the deprived minorities for whom affirmative discrimination is in order, leaving white males above the poverty line as the residual category who must help all the rest. The Republican Party's emphasis on opportunity rather than on more equal outcomes, by contrast, leaves the existing status or privileges of white and more affluent men untouched. In a corresponding manner, white women of low income may see the Democratic Party as providing them with concrete benefits, while middle- and upper-middle-income women, many of them influenced by the feminist movement, may see Republicans as opposed to their views on cultural matters.[24] Women are also more concerned with egalitarian or "compassion" issues—fairness to the poor, unemployment—and tend to be less likely than men to support increased defense spending and the use of military force.[25] Thus women differ from men on specific issue positions as well as on party identification and candidate choice, though not necessarily on the stereotypical "women's issues" commonly assumed to account for the contemporary gender gap.

"SPECIAL" INTERESTS, CAMPAIGN SPENDING, AND PUBLIC INTEREST GROUPS

Is there any difference between interest groups, as we have described them here, and the "special" interests that attract so much criticism from politicians and the news media? Not as far as we can tell. Americans have always organized themselves into interest groups. Groups may have interests that are broad or narrow, but it is hard to see why interests that are narrow, and therefore presumably more "special," are any less legitimate than broad interests, which presumably require more common resources to satisfy. The language of political competition in American elections frequently requires political actors to disparage the claims of others by labeling them "special" interests and therefore somehow not worthy of consideration. "We" are presumably "the people" and "they" are "special interests." But of course the "people" have interests too. In a democracy, leaders are supposed to inform themselves about and sympathize with the policies that people want. Paying attention to these concerns of the people looks to us very much like attending to the needs of special interests.

The rise of rhetoric stigmatizing interests as "special" interests is in part the result of the rise of vocal and deeply concerned groups claiming to represent the "public" interest rather than the private or pecuniary interests of their members. Although interest groups in the past have differed over policy, they have not (at least since the acceptance of industrial unions in the 1930s and African American organizations in the 1960s) denied the rights of opponents to advocate their policy preferences. But, in one significant respect, that is no longer true. "Public interest" lobbies have attacked the legitimacy of "private interest" groups. Political parties, labor unions, trade associations, and religious groups are examples of such private interest groups, intermediary organizations that link citizens and their government. Many are indeed "special interest" groups—groups, that is, with special interests in public policy. Part of the program of public interest groups such as Common Cause or Ralph Nader's various organizations is to reduce the power of private, special interests and substitute their own services as intermediary organizations. Typically, public interest groups have fewer—sometimes vastly fewer—members than private interest groups.[26] They rely on journalists, newsletters, and the Internet to carry their messages to the population at large, and their success is an indication of the extent to which American voters now rely on mass media rather than group membership to obtain their political orientations and opinions.

A remarkable example of the ways in which the mass media have to a certain extent transformed the interest-group environment of elections is the rise of radio talk shows as instruments for the crystallization of political opinions. Radio talk show hosts with compelling personalities—exemplified by conservative mainstay Rush Limbaugh—can over a relatively short period of time mobilize strong expressions of opinion by many listeners and callers, in effect creating interest groups out of thin air by giving voice mainly to exasperated antigovernment and other negative sentiments. Limbaugh has an estimated thirteen million listeners each week. His books have sold millions of copies.[27] Political leaders and opinion leaders who write for the news media are increasingly persuaded that he and others like him have touched a chord of real feeling in the American populace. The large population of political blogs and websites—such as Daily Kos and Talking Points Memo on the left and Townhall and Redstate on the right—on the Internet also remain an important source of campaign information and analysis and influence more mainstream media outlets.

Laws have been passed and constitutional amendments proposed by public interest groups that restrict the amounts of money unions and corporations can contribute to political campaigns and use in lobbying. On the whole, however, these laws have been unsuccessful in curbing interest-group activity. What has happened is that interest groups have found new ways within the law to advance their interests. The history of campaign finance since the 1970s is a story of interests finding new ways to legally spend unlimited funds in election campaigns.

A long-standing device for group spending is the political action committee (PAC), an organization devoted to the disbursement of campaign money from interest groups to candidates. From 1974 to 1982 the number of political action committees organized by business and unions more than quadrupled, increasing from 608 to 2,601; in the next six years, PACs of all types (including those unconnected to business and unions) rose to a total of 4,268 in 1988, remaining relatively stable ever since. (See table 2.6.) The bulk of the original increase was accounted for by the rise in corporate PACs from only 89 in 1974 to 1,816 in 1988, but the number of these corporate PACs has slightly declined in the last twenty years, reaching a total of 1,652 in 2012.[28]

PACs are created to collect and disburse political contributions. They must contribute to more than one candidate, and the amount they may give to any one candidate is limited. In 1976, amendments to the Federal Election Campaign Act enabled individual companies or labor unions to establish multiple PACs, thus multiplying the amount of money they could funnel to any single candidate. Surprisingly, corporate PACs did not originally favor Republican campaigns as much as might be expected. Corporate PACs usually support incumbents over challengers, and for much of the 1970s and 1980s Democratic officeholders outnumbered Republicans at both the federal and state levels. Accordingly, they reaped contributions from corporate PACs.[29] After the Republican Party gained a majority in both houses of Congress in the 1994 election, corporate PAC contributions favored the GOP, but shifted back to the Democrats when they retook control of the legislative branch from 2006 to 2010.[30]

The Supreme Court decision in *Buckley v. Valeo* (1976) removed any contribution restrictions from PACs. Thus, "a corporate or union political action committee can collect donations and contribute an unlimited sum of money to unspecified numbers of

TABLE 2.6. The Rise of Political Action Committees (PACs), 1974–2012

Year	Corporate	Labor	Professional Groups	Cooperatives	Corporation Without Stock	Nonconnected	Total
1974	89	201	318	–	–	–	608
1976	433	224	489	–	–	–	1,146
1980	1,206	297	576	42	56	374	2,551
1984	1,682	394	698	52	130	1,053	4,009
1988	1,816	354	786	59	138	1,115	4,268
1992	1,735	347	770	56	142	1,145	4,195
1996	1,642	332	838	41	123	1,103	4,079
2000	1,548	318	844	38	115	972	3,835
2004	1,538	310	884	35	102	999	3,868
2008	1,601	273	925	38	97	1,300	4,234
2012	1,652	280	985	35	104	1,601	4,657

Source: Harold W. Stanley and Richard G. Niemi, *Vital Statistics on American Politics, 2013–2014* (Washington, DC: CQ Press, 2014), Table 2.9.

Note: Nonconnected PACs do not have a sponsoring organization.

candidates or committees so long as no single contribution exceeds $5,000."[31] In addition, once a PAC "contributes to five or more federal candidates, [it] can make unlimited independent expenditures on behalf of candidates or parties" (e.g., advertising on behalf of a candidate independent of that candidate's campaign in print or electronic media).[32] Not surprisingly, prospective presidential candidates themselves now organize PACs as a way of developing political alliances.

The rise of PACs to prominence is an ironic result of misplaced idealism. In the 1950s, reformers thought that it would be a good idea if local parties, which were held together mostly through jobs and sociability, were employed for more idealistic uses. It was thought that the replacement of a politics of patronage with a politics of issues would lead to a form of responsible party government in which informed activists could hold public officials accountable for their policy positions.[33] As government grew, however, two things happened. Business corporations, concerned about what government was doing to them, founded or reinvigorated their own interest groups, and other citizens formed and joined new groups to press their particular concerns. Instead of the integration and strengthening of parties that result in party government, parties were weakened. The weakening of parties facilitated fragmentation into a system dominated by what are called "single-issue special interest groups," groups such as those concerned to support or oppose issues like gun control or abortion. The emphasis on issues has led to fragmentation, manifested in the explosive growth of political action committees.

A second irony is that the PACs, now a leading source of political finance, were created in response to congressional efforts to restrict the role of money in elections. Government intervened in 1971, 1974, and 1976 with the passage of the Federal Election Campaign Act (FECA) and subsequent amendments. By limiting the amount of money any individual or company could contribute, FECA reduced the role of large contributors and at the same time gave incentives for the formation of groups of small contributors. Once the courts decided that money raised and spent in politics was protected under the First Amendment as a necessary means to facilitate political speech and expression, the way was open for committees to proliferate, all concentrating on the issues and candidates of their choice.[34] A decision of the D.C. District Court of Appeals, *SpeechNow.org v. FEC* (2010), allowed the formation of "super PACs." These PACs can accept previously prohibited amounts and sources of funds, including large individual, corporate and union contributions, as long as the PAC only makes independent expenditures— those not coordinated with a candidate—and does not contribute to candidates. PACs became a rival to political parties in support of candidates but without any obligations to govern or to appeal broadly to electorates.

Interests and individuals now maintain a variety of legal organizations to deploy unlimited cash in elections, including presidential contests. In the decades since the 1970s reform legislation, crafty operatives have found provisions in federal law that allow for the formation of organizations than can engage in unlimited independent spending that is not coordinated with candidate campaigns. These are the so-called "527 groups," named for the federal tax code provision that authorizes them; they have no limits on contributions to them and can spend unlimited funds in elections on explicit behalf of candidates but must disclose to the Federal Election Commission their donors and their amounts donated. Then there are "501(c)(4) groups," which can also raise unlimited contributions but do not have to disclose their donors or the amounts they have donated. They primarily are supposed to lobby, but they can also engage in unlimited independent spending and endorse candidates as long as those campaign activities are not a "substantial" share of the organization's activities—a restriction that in practice has proved hard to enforce.

Groups and wealthy individuals were aided in their efforts to deploy campaign money by two recent decisions by the Supreme Court. In the 2010 case *Citizens United vs. FEC*, a 5–4 majority held that: "No sufficient governmental interest justifies limits on the speech of nonprofit and for-profit corporations."[35] This ruling allowed unlimited independent spending in election campaigns by both corporations and unions. In *McCutcheon v. FEC*, a 2014 ruling, the Court by a 5–4 decision voided aggregate personal contribution limits by individuals to candidates (then $123,200 annually), stating that "the aggregate limits on contributions . . . intrude without justification on a citizen's ability to exercise 'the most fundamental First Amendment activities.'"[36]

A more permissive campaign finance regime permitted a large tide of independent group spending in the 2012 presidential contest. On Obama's behalf, $131,303,352 in independent expenditures by groups occurred, primarily by super PACs created as 501(c)4 organizations. Mitt Romney in 2012 benefitted from $418,635,080 of such spending. In comparison, the Obama campaign itself had operating expenditures of $683,546,548 and the Romney campaign $483,281,516, both record amounts.[37] Total presidential election spending, combining that of the candidates' campaigns, the national parties and independent groups reached record highs: $1.11 billion aiding Obama and $1.24 billion for Romney.

Independent group spending seems here to stay. Both presidential candidates and voters confront new campaign problems as a result. Independent spending produces a clutter of campaign messages that reduces the ability of candidates to dominate campaign discourse. The resulting blizzard of campaign messages also produces accountability difficulties for voters. Who is behind which message? Often contributors are not disclosed and organizations adopt vague and reassuring monikers that reveal little about their aims. The two biggest spenders in the 2012 presidential election were the super PACs "Priorities USA" and "Restore Our Future." The first spent $65,166,859 to reelect Obama and the latter funded efforts on Romney's behalf totaling $142,097,336. Both are 501(c)(4) corporations.

Public interest lobbies since the 1970s have opposed the new avenues of presidential campaign spending. The lobbies represent not direct material interests as corporations and unions do but "issue" interests such as campaign finance reform and tort reform.[38] They have also sought to weaken the power of party leaders and strong party identifiers and to strengthen citizens who are weakly identified with parties and who emerge briefly during a particular election campaign or in response to a current issue. The stress on ease of entry into internal party affairs—more primaries, more conferences, more frequent and more open elections to party bodies—given the fact that party membership occurs in the first place by self-activation, leads to the domination of parties by activists who have time and education and are able to take the trouble to go to meetings. What kinds of people have these characteristics? Among others, they are the middle- and upper-middle-class professionals who predominate in supporting Common Cause, Nader's Raiders, and other public interest lobbies. Thus, among interest groups, if money matters less as a resource, business matters less; if time and talk and education matter more, ordinary workers matter less. As leaders of labor, business, and the parties lose power, organizers of public interest lobbies gain. These public interest lobbies are not necessarily all on one side of the ideological spectrum. People who defend corporate capitalism as well as those who attack it can organize in the public interest. And they do.

Two advantages have helped public interest groups expand their influence. One is a product of modern technology and the other has been generated by government. The use of computerized mailing lists and communication via the Internet has permitted these groups to tap contributions from large numbers of people who do not otherwise participate directly in group activities but receive mail and e-mail and thus become privileged spectators to group leaders' battles over public policy. This opportunity for vicarious participation not only generates ready cash but also simplifies somewhat the tasks of leadership. Instead of having to satisfy an active membership that might make diverse or contradictory demands, only the top leadership of public interest groups need be consulted. Leaders of public interest groups are frequently poorly paid, accepting low income as a sacrifice for their cause, but they exercise strong influence on the groups they lead.

The second advantage is that people who contribute to public interest groups are entitled to count these monies as tax-deductible. When the group wishes to undertake activities incompatible with eligibility for deduction, it often establishes a separate educational or litigating arm that can receive non-tax-deductible contributions. Without tax deductibility, the survival of some of these groups would be in doubt. The tradeoff is that they are required to engage in educational activities rather than overt lobbying, even though this may be a distinction without a difference. In addition, some of these groups achieve a status as legally authorized interveners before regulatory commissions, a role that entitles them to payment for their activity. In this sense, public interest groups are sometimes partially subsidized by government.

POLITICAL PARTIES AS ORGANIZATIONS

A third aspect of the social framework, along with voters and interest groups, that will help us account for the strategies of participants in presidential elections is the nature of political parties in the United States. Here we discuss parties as organizations rather than as symbols for voters.

Party organizations are composed of three basic groups. First, professional employees of the party at the national and state levels staff the party offices and perform tasks on behalf of the party. Second, candidates and elected officials affiliated with the party carry the party label when they run for public office. Third, party activists are involved in party activities such as candidate recruitment, fund-raising, and getting out the vote, but are not themselves candidates or full-time employees of the party. Each group plays a different role in party activities, and sometimes their interests conflict.

The primary goal of party professionals is to run an organization that will maintain or increase the power of the party. We define power in this situation as the ability to influence decisions made by government. Parties obtain this power by helping to elect individuals affiliated with their organization and through control of the appointive jobs (patronage) elected officials ordinarily bestow on members of their own party.[39] For party representatives—candidates and elected officials—and party activists, however, increasing the power of the party as an organization is often a secondary goal; other interests may be more important.

Candidates and elected officials are managing their own careers; their primary goal is most often personal success, both in the campaign and in governing. While party organizations can help nominees with fund-raising, supplying campaign expertise, and mobilizing supporters, individual politicians still retain a considerable amount of autonomy. Candidates for Congress, for example, usually build up their own political bases separate from support for the party and rely on these personal constituencies when running for reelection.[40]

On the national level, the rise of the primary system as a means for selecting presidential nominees (see table 2.7) has meant a corresponding decline in the candidates' reliance on traditional—especially state—party organizations. In order to win a party's nomination at the national convention, presidential hopefuls used to curry favor with the leaders of state party delegations, forging relationships with these party professionals to secure the votes of the state's delegates. In modern campaigns, state party bosses do not decide how their delegations will vote; instead, state delegates are pledged to candidates according to the results of the primary election in their state. Aspiring presidential nominees thus spend time in states courting primary voters, not party officials, and their success is more closely tied to their personal popularity than to the support of the local party leadership. To be sure, candidates still covet the support of party officials and other notables, but now those endorsements are valuable indirectly as tools to raise money (which is used to advertise to primary electorates) and to impress reporters (in order to obtain favorable coverage in the news media, and therefore win votes in primaries).[41]

Thus, party professionals cannot always count on their party's candidates to share the goals of the central organization. What might be the most effective strategy for a candidate to adopt in a given campaign or legislative situation may not fit with the party's overall plan or policy platform. Conflicts are certain to arise. Aware of this, party organizations have developed strategies aimed at keeping candidates and elected officials loyal to their goals.

Most significant is the fund-raising that national party organizations perform in order to spend money on behalf of the party's candidates for the presidency and other federal offices. The Republican National Committee (RNC), under Chairman William Brock, began in the late 1970s to raise large sums of money from a broad network of individual donors to provide aid to state parties and to help candidates and state parties professionalize their operations.[42] The Democratic National Committee (DNC), more haltingly and less successfully, began to follow suit. This process was accelerated when the Supreme Court ruled in the 1996 case of *Colorado Republican Campaign Committee v. Federal Election Commission* that the First Amendment protected the right of political parties to campaign on behalf of their candidates and policy positions. In 2002, Congress raised the limit on individual contributions to national party committees from $20,000 to $25,000 per year, and indexed it to increases over time in the national cost of living (so that the limit on individual contributions to national parties was $32,400 in 2014). As table 2.8 makes clear, the growth in fund-raising by the national party committees (the DNC, RNC, and House and Senate campaign committees on both sides) has increased exponentially over the past few presidential election cycles, nearly doubling between 2000 and 2004 alone.

Parties at times experience tensions between two of their primary goals. On the one hand, they must satisfy their activists and interest-group supporters by committing, or appearing to commit, to policies of concern to them. On the other hand, they are trying

TABLE 2.7. The Growth of Presidential Primaries, 1960–2012

Year	Democrats		Republicans	
	Number of Primaries	Percentage of Delegates Selected in Primaries	Number of Primaries	Percentage of Delegates Selected in Primaries
1960	16	38.3	15	38.6
1964	16	45.7	16	45.6
1968	15	40.2	15	38.1
1972	21	65.3	20	56.8
1976	27	76.0	26	71.0
1980	34	71.8	34	76.0
1984	29	52.4	25	71.0
1988	36	66.6	36	76.9
1992	39	66.9	38	83.9
1996	35	65.3	42	84.6
2000	40	64.6	43	83.8
2004	40	67.5	26	55.5
2008	39	67.4	42	82.2
2012	26	47.2	36	71.3

Source: Harold W. Stanley and Richard G. Niemi, Vital Statistics on American Politics, 2013–2014 (Washington, DC: CQ Press, 2014), Table 1-23.

Note: Some states cancelled their Republican presidential primaries in 2004 and Democratic presidential primaries in 2012 because George W. Bush and Barack Obama were unopposed for their party's nomination.

to lure enough people uncommitted on these policies in order to win the election. In a close election, the ability of a party to increase its support within one critical electoral group from, say, 20 to 30 percent may be crucial, even though that group still votes overwhelmingly for the opposition. The strategic implications of these remarks color all of national campaign politics: when they are trying to win, the parties try to do things that will please the groups consistently allied to them without unduly alienating other voters.

It is even more difficult to predict how these aggregations of actual and potential interest groups might react to shifts in party policy positions, and still more hazardous to prophesy what different policy commitments might do to the margin of votes required for victory. This pervasive problem of uncertainty makes the calculations of gain from changes in policies both difficult and risky and suggests that the interests of parties and candidates frequently are best served by vague, ambiguous, or contradictory policy statements that will be unlikely to offend anyone. The advantages of vagueness about policy are strengthened by the facts that most citizens are not interested in policy or are narrowly focused on a small number of issues and that only a few groups demand many specific policy commitments from their parties and candidates.

Yet, despite all this, political leaders and parties do, at times, make policy commitments that are surprisingly precise, specific, and logically consistent. Thus we must go beyond our consideration of why the parties sometimes blur issues and avoid commitments to ask why they often commit themselves to policies more readily than their interest in acquiring or retaining office would seem to require.

TABLE 2.8. The Rise of National Party Fund-Raising, 1983–2012

	Democratic Party Funds Raised (in millions of dollars)	Republican Party Funds Raised (in millions of dollars)	Total
1983–1984	84.4	289.0	373.4
1987–1988	116.1	257.5	373.6
1991–1992	163.3	264.9	428.2
1995–1996	221.6	416.5	638.1
1999–2000	275.2	465.8	741.0
2003–2004	678.8	782.4	1,461.2
2007–2008	763.3	792.9	1,556.2
2011–2012	805.6	806.9	1,612.5

Source: Harold W. Stanley and Richard G. Niemi, *Vital Statistics on American Politics, 2013–2014* (Washington, DC: CQ Press, 2014), Table 2-6.

Part of the answer may arise from the fact that the parties depend on their party activists and that many of these activists, especially the purists among them, demand specific policy commitments from the party. The activists are the heart of any party organization; they are the volunteers and donors for campaigns, the people who stimulate participation in their communities, and most likely they are the party's strongest supporters and most dependable voters. Unlike most voters, who are otherwise largely disengaged from politics, activists are likely to have elaborate political opinions and preferences and to act on them even when an election is not imminent. Their desires to make these preferences internally consistent and consistent with the preferences of their party certainly lead to demands on the party leadership for policy positions that are reasonably clear and forthright.[43] Demands of this sort have contributed to the ideological polarization of the two political parties in recent decades. The national Democratic Party is now more uniformly liberal in its policy positions and the national Republican Party more thoroughly conservative in its stands than thirty years ago.[44]

Furthermore, the interest groups most closely allied with each party make policy demands that parties must to some extent meet. Even more than voters, who are generally interested at most in only a few specific policies, interest-group leaders and their full-time bureaucracies are manifestly concerned citizens and often party activists as well. If they feel that the interests they represent are being harmed, they may so inform their members or even attempt to withdraw support from the party at a particular election. Should voters find that groups with which they identify are opposed to the party with which they identify, they may temporarily support the opposition party, or, more likely, they may withdraw from participation and not vote at all. Consequently, the party finds that it risks losing elections by ignoring the demands of interest groups, especially those that are part of the party base.

The demands of many of these groups conflict, however. If unions object to party or candidate advocacy of antipollution devices on automobiles because they increase costs and decrease car sales, for example, Democratic leaders will find it impossible to satisfy both labor and environmental groups. If business interests wish immigration levels to be raised to increase the supply of labor while nationalist groups push for greater restrictions, Republican leaders may be unable to choose a side without alienating an important party constituency. Therefore, the parties may attempt to mediate among interest groups, hoping to strike compromises that, though they give no one group everything, give something to as many groups as they can. The increasing number of single-issue groups makes mediation more difficult. Many Democratic candidates have attempted to court Roman Catholic bishops on the basis of their shared commitment to social welfare programs, only to endure sharp criticism for the politicians' opposition to the prohibition of abortion and support for gay marriage. Several bishops announced in 2004 that they would deny Democratic candidate John Kerry, a practicing Catholic, the rite of communion in their dioceses owing to his pro-choice stance.[45]

Party organizations are further divided between state organizations and national organizations, and this division provides additional occasions for conflict and disunity. The national organization concerns itself primarily with national elections, and thus is interested above all in promoting unity and support for national party candidates. State organizations devote themselves primarily to state elections, pursuing state party interests, and may therefore respond to more localized sentiments. Furthermore, state organizations follow no single organizational pattern. Sometimes elected state chief executives run them; sometimes they are run by coalitions of party chieftains representing the local organizations of several large cities or counties. Sometimes party officials and elected officials work cooperatively; sometimes they work at cross-purposes. The best evidence suggests the number of states with permanent party headquarters and professional staff who recruit candidates, raise money, and help campaigns is growing.[46] State party chairs now have seats on the national committees. They mediate between national rules and state practices. They are conduits for the growing services—recruitment, polling, fund-raising, issue development, vote mobilization—provided by the national parties.

What at the national level used to be a loose federation of state parties is slowly being converted, by changes in party rules and by judicial decisions, into a somewhat more centralized structure. Thus our national parties combine elements of both decentralization and centralization. The most obvious indicator of continuing decentralization is that national parties are organized on a geographical basis with the state units as the constituent elements. The party organizations from different states meet formally by sending delegates to national committee meetings, and most important, by coming together every four years at national conventions to nominate a president.

The strongest indicators of nationalization are the guidelines set out at the national level, which, especially for Democrats, are important in determining who these delegates will be.[47] Still, it is the states that choose their representatives to national party bodies; the national committees and conventions do not choose officers of state parties. Both parties' national organizations now have sizable staffs who recommend effective campaign managers, consultants, pollsters, and accountants, going so far as to buy blocks of services that then can be allocated to close races. In addition, they assist state parties and candidate campaigns with fund-raising contacts, political strategy, and media relations.[48] National party committees may also spend unlimited amounts of money on behalf of candidates for the presidency and other offices, as long as the expenditures are formally uncoordinated with the candidates' own campaigns.

On the other hand, when and where they are strong enough, state parties have substantial powers enabling them to claim a share in making national policy and to be influential in the nomination and election of members of Congress. The states have their own sources of patronage, as well as a share in federal patronage through their congressional representatives and senators (when they are of the president's party). The very fact that the states are each separate constitutional entities engenders a drive for autonomy as those who hold places of importance in the state governments and parties seek to protect their jurisdictions, much as the framers of the Constitution hoped they would. This is an example of federalism and it is much more than a legal fact. The states have great vitality because there exist distinct, numerous, and vigorous ethnic, religious, racial, and economic groups that demand separate recognition and that are disproportionately located in specific geographic areas. State organizations, therefore, become infused with the purposes of groups that use their state parties for the recognition and enhancement of their separate identities and needs. Italian Americans in Rhode Island, Jews and African Americans in New York, dairy farmers in Wisconsin, labor unions in Michigan, retirees and Cuban-Americans in Florida, wheat growers in Kansas, gay rights advocates in California, and many others form the building blocks of unique political cultures state by state and make the idea of a decentralized party system a reality.[49]

Each of the state parties is composed of people with somewhat different interests to protect and demands to make. Control over state parties must be exercised from within each state, since the various states do not control one another and the national party exercises only partial control. This is the essence of what is meant by a decentralized party system in which power is dispersed among many independent state bodies.

THIRD PARTIES

While candidates nominated by parties other than the Democrats and Republicans appear on the ballot in every presidential election, most are virtually invisible to the press and public and attract little support from voters. Occasionally, a more prominent third-party or independent candidate emerges. The unusual success of Ross Perot in the 1992 presidential election (he received nearly twenty million votes) added a dimension to the calculations of candidates of the two major parties that year because each had to figure out whom the third candidate hurt the most. It is somewhat misleading to refer to independent candidates such as Perot in 1992 as constituting third parties, since the organizational basis of his candidacy was a membership organization devoted only to him. This differs from a proper political party, which also runs candidates for lesser offices.[50]

In 1992 Perot used his enormous personal financial resources to support only one candidacy, his own, supplemented by a last-minute choice of retired admiral James Stockdale as a vice-presidential running mate. There was no contest among alternatives or any decision-making process that might have led to the selection of somebody other than Perot as the candidate of his front group, United We Stand America. So he was not the founder of a third party so much as a self-promoter. This seems, more often than not, to be the case with third-party candidates; 74 percent of presidential "third parties" have persisted long enough to contest only two elections and over half contest only one, suggesting that they are built around the easily exhausted presidential aspirations of individuals, rather than longer-term party-building activities.[51]

Unlike southern candidates George Wallace in 1968 and Strom Thurmond in 1948, Perot's candidacy had no particular regional base. This precluded the possibility of his winning votes in the Electoral College, which requires candidates to finish first in a state. A Texan, Perot was thought to be just barely plausible as a winner there in a three-way race. This would not have been a negligible achievement, given the size of the Texas electoral vote, but at a maximum it would have spoiled the result for one or the other of the major parties rather than contribute to a likely winning coalition for Perot. It was assumed that the main loser would be Republican incumbent George H. W. Bush, whom Perot gave signs of personally disliking.[52]

Perot ended up with an extraordinary 19 percent of the popular vote in 1992, drawn from disgruntled voters across many segments of the population. Because he took votes about equally from both Bush and Clinton, Perot's presence in the race did not influence the outcome of the election.[53] His vote was not widely interpreted as personal devotion to Perot so much as a conveniently visible place to park the negative feelings that the campaign had generated about both major-party candidates. Perot ran again in 1996 as the standard-bearer of the Reform Party, a party that he had personally founded in the interim, and received only 9 percent of the vote; again, his candidacy did not appear to affect the outcome.

It is frequently asserted, and frequently denied, that voters who vote for third parties are throwing away their vote. What is presumably meant is that voting for a third party means not voting for a potential winner of the election. But third party voters generally understand that they are not backing a winner but rather withholding their vote from a (potential) winner. They may hope that this sends a message of overall dissatisfaction with the main alternatives on offer, and hence this would not necessarily be regarded by the voter as a wasted vote.

Another way of determining whether an individual's vote is wasted is to ask who the voter's first choice is among the major party candidates, or who is the voter's second choice overall. If a third party vote contributes to the loss of that voter's second choice, and the victory of his or her third choice, then the vote has been thrown away. Thus in the 2000 election, Florida voters for Green Party nominee Ralph Nader who preferred Republican George W. Bush to Democrat Al Gore did not throw away their vote; Nader voters who preferred Gore to Bush did throw away their vote.

Most observers believe that a majority of Nader voters would have preferred Gore to Bush. So a Nader vote in any state carried by Gore would therefore not have been thrown away. But in a state like Florida, carried by Bush by 537 votes out of nearly six million cast, and where Nader received 97,488 votes, it is plausible to assume that the Nader vote was instrumental in defeating Gore and electing Bush. This reasoning lies behind the ironic suggestion that when Nader ran again in 2004 as an independent candidate he should have adopted the slogan "Four more years." While Nader received 2.9 million votes nationwide, or 2.7 percent of the total, as the Green Party nominee in 2000, his subsequent independent candidacies in 2004 and 2008 received only 0.4 percent and 0.5 percent of the popular vote, respectively, exerting a negligible impact on the outcome in both years. Nader's performance fits a common general pattern in which candidates outside the two-party system reach an early peak of support and then decline in popularity as their voters return to the major parties or to non-participation.

Third-party candidates have a long record of occasional victories in congressional and gubernatorial elections.[54] In recent years, however, such successes have reflected individual efforts, without long-term consequences for party politics in the United States. Third-party candidacies do play a significant role in presidential elections from time to time. They can act as spoilers if they draw votes disproportionately from one major side or the other. They can focus discontent. They can raise issues.[55] But because candidates must place first in a state to receive electoral votes, the American electoral system is stacked strongly against third-party candidates actually winning the presidency.[56]

CHAPTER 3

Rules and Resources

RULES: THE ELECTORAL COLLEGE

AMERICAN PRESIDENTIAL elections are not decided directly by a national popular vote. Instead, each state casts all of its electoral votes for the candidate placing first in the statewide popular vote. This "winner take all, loser take nothing" approach is called a "unit rule."[1] In chapter 6 we consider whether votes ought to be counted in this manner. For the moment, however, we concentrate on how the electoral college works, and why it matters.

Each state casts as many electoral votes as it has senators and representatives in Congress. Thus all states, no matter how small, have at least three electoral votes. This means that sparsely populated states are numerically overrepresented in the electoral college. In 2012, 249,061 voters in Wyoming influenced the disposition of the state's three electoral votes, a ratio of one electoral vote for every 83,020 voters. In Ohio, on the other hand, 5,590,934 voters went to the polls and voted for 18 electors, a ratio of one electoral vote for every 310,607 voters. One might conclude, therefore, that each voter in Wyoming had more than three times as much influence on the outcome of the 2012 election as each voter in Ohio. But this is not entirely valid.

Why not? Because of the unit rule, which provides that the candidate receiving the most popular votes in a state receives the entire electoral vote of the state. This means that each Wyoming voter was influencing the disposition of all three of Wyoming's electoral votes, and each Ohio voter was helping to decide the fate of all eighteen of Ohio's votes. Ask any politician whether he or she would rather have three votes or eighteen—the answer is immediately apparent. Thus, as long as the outcome in Ohio is in doubt, the Ohioans get more collective attention from the campaigns even though each one of them does not matter so much. In fact, the present method of electing the president encourages candidates to devote most of their attention to populous, politically competitive states; the bigger the state, the more electoral votes are at stake.

The varying strength of states in the electoral college matters a great deal for the strategies of presidential nominees seeking a national majority of 270 electoral votes. Because the unit rule renders the popular margin of victory in a state irrelevant to the allocation of its electors, campaigns direct their resources—such as television advertising, candidate appearances, and voter mobilization efforts—to the subset of states considered winnable by either side, while ignoring states in which the outcome is not in doubt. In 2012, the presidential campaigns of Barack Obama and Mitt Romney targeted ten key states deemed open to persuasion by both parties: Colorado, Florida, Iowa, Nevada, New Hampshire, North Carolina, Ohio, Pennsylvania, Virginia, and Wisconsin. Within this group, the most populous states, casting the most electoral votes, received by far the largest share of candidate attention.[2] Over the final month of the 2012 campaign, the two nominees, running mates, and their spouses made a combined 162 personal visits to Ohio, Florida, and Virginia alone.[3]

In previous elections, other candidates have identified different states as pivotal. But the reason the campaign battleground is concentrated in the big states that might go either way is the unit rule of the electoral college.

THINKING ABOUT RESOURCES

In thinking about resources and their importance, it is necessary to distinguish between conditions that exist for the official candidates of the two major parties after they are nominated and the situation of prospective candidates—politicians seeking the nomination of their party—during the prenomination period. Individual candidates before the nomination do not have the benefit of party support, and the way they look at resources is quite different from the way successful nominees do.

There are many resources that, at any given time, may be disproportionately available to Democrats and Republicans, or to different candidates. Possession of the presidential office, skill in organization, knowledge of substantive policies, a reputation for integrity, facility in speechmaking, ability to devise appealing campaign issues, personal wealth and fund-raising ability, physical stamina—all can be drawn on to good advantage in a presidential campaign. More resources are available to parties and candidates than any one book could deal with exhaustively. But some resources obviously are going to be more important than others, and the importance of different resources varies from occasion to occasion. It would be sensible to regard as especially important those resources that one side monopolizes—such as the presidency—and those resources that can easily be converted into other resources, or directly into public office—such as money, which can be used to buy competent staff, advertising, and so on.

Although political resources are at times distributed unequally between the parties, in a competitive two-party system such as ours the inequalities rarely run all in the same direction. Sometimes Republican candidates reap the benefits; sometimes Democrats do. One result of these inequalities in access to various resources is that different strategies are more advantageous to each of the two parties, as we see when we examine the effects on election strategies of three resources commonly held to be extremely important: money, control over information, and the presidential office.

RESOURCES: MONEY

Presidential campaigns are terribly expensive. The production and airing of radio, television, and Internet advertising; travel for the candidate and campaign staff; mailings of campaign material; the salaries of consultants and advisers; office space and equipment;

lawn signs and bumper stickers; conducting polls and focus groups; registering and mobilizing voters; and raising money itself—all cost a great deal of money.[4] In 2012, Barack Obama's successful reelection campaign cost over $737 million, while his Republican rival, Mitt Romney, spent about $483 million; other candidates who sought the Republican nomination for president spent about $136 million in total. Candidates for the Senate and House of Representatives in 2012 collectively spent another $1.4 billion. In addition, the two major parties spent over $1.5 billion in support of candidates at all levels of government.[5] The total amount of federal campaign spending by candidates and parties exceeded $4.7 billion in 2012 (see table 3.1), not including another $1 billion in independent expenditures made by outside groups.[6] How do candidates for the presidency manage to raise such large sums in their quest for office?

In answering this question, we note the difference between the presidential primary and caucus period, when candidates are on their own and when raising money may prove to be a severe problem for some of them, and the general election campaign, when the mobilization of party-loyal donors, expenditures by party organizations and independent groups, and other factors come into the picture, shrinking the problem of the availability of money to a more manageable size once a candidate has received the nomination of a major party.

The Beverly Hills Primary

The most important source of money for a candidate seeking a party's nomination for president is the individual private contributor, who, under federal law, may donate up to $2,000 in 2002 dollars ($2,500 in 2012) to a candidate's primary campaign. In order to avoid the appearance of playing favorites, national party organizations do not spend money on behalf of any specific candidate as long as the party nomination is still in legitimate doubt. In addition, most political action committees (PACs) prefer to avoid prenomination campaigns and the high-risk politics associated with them. The result is that PAC contributions to presidential candidates are negligible—about $1.8 million in total in 2012, about one-tenth of one percent of the nearly $1.3 billion spent by candidates in the 2012 presidential election.[7]

To fund their campaigns, candidates go where the money is, organizing fund-raising events in areas where large numbers of supporters will attend with checkbooks in hand. One especially well-documented path leads Democrats to southern California, home of the traditionally liberal entertainment industry; a contested Democratic presidential nomination will invariably feature competing slates of celebrity supporters. In 2008, for example, Senator Barack Obama of Illinois enjoyed the backing of such "A list" stars as Oprah Winfrey, George Clooney, Robert DeNiro, Chris Rock, and Scarlett Johansson. Senator Hillary Clinton of New York received endorsements and contributions from Barbra Streisand, Rob Reiner, Maya Angelou, Amber Tamblyn, Ron Howard, Ted Danson, and Magic Johnson. John Mellencamp and Bonnie Raitt backed former senator John Edwards of North Carolina, while Sean Penn supported Representative Dennis Kucinich of Ohio. For Republican candidates, key stops on the fund-raising circuit include New York (home to Wall Street and much of the financial services industry) and Texas (for energy and real estate interests).

Candidates may also enjoy access to valuable home-state constituencies. For example, then governor of Arkansas Bill Clinton used his connections in that state to raise

TABLE 3.1. Federal Campaign Spending, 1972–2012

Election	Spending by Presidential Candidates (Millions of Dollars)	Spending by Congressional Candidates (Millions of Dollars)	Spending by Parties (Millions of Dollars)	Total Federal Election Spending (Millions of Dollars)
1972	127	77	13	217
1976	118	115	46	279
1980	188	239	216	643
1984	194	374	420	988
1988	316	458	424	1,198
1992	323	680	488	1,491
1996	405	765	894	2,064
2000	520	1,006	1,190	2,716
2004	844	1,157	1,408	3,409
2008	1,677	1,375	1,513	4,565
2012	1,360	1,847	1,577	4,783

Sources: Presidential candidate spending data from Herbert E. Alexander, *Financing the 1972 Election* (Lexington, MA: Lexington Books, 1976), pp. 85–87; Herbert E. Alexander, *Financing the 1976 Election* (Washington, DC: CQ Press, 1979), pp. 171–75; Herbert E. Alexander, *Financing the 1980 Election* (Lexington, MA: Lexington Books, 1983), pp. 113–16; Herbert E. Alexander and Brian A. Haggerty, *Financing the 1984 Election* (Lexington, MA: Lexington Books, 1987), pp. 85–87; Herbert E. Alexander and Monica Bauer, *Financing the 1988 Election* (Boulder, CO: Westview Press, 1991), p. 12; Herbert E. Alexander and Anthony Corrado, *Financing the 1992 Election* (Armonk, NY: M. E. Sharpe, 1995), p. 20; Federal Election Commission, "2004 Presidential Campaign Finance Activity Summarized," press release, February 3, 2005, http://www.fec.gov/press/press2005/20050203pressum/20050203pressum.html; Federal Election Commission, "2008 Presidential Campaign Finance Activity Summarized," press release, June 8, 2009, http://www.fec.gov/press/press2009/20090608PresStat.shtml; Federal Election Commission, "FEC Summarizes Campaign Activity of the 2011–2012 Election Cycle," press release, April 19, 2013, http://www.fec.gov/press/press2013/20130419_2012-24m-Summary.shtml. Congressional candidate spending data from Herbert E. Alexander, "Spending in the 1996 Elections," in John C. Green, ed., *Financing the 1996 Election* (Armonk, NY: M. E. Sharpe, 1999), pp. 11–36, at 23; Federal Election Commission, "Congressional Candidates Spend $1.16 Billion During 2003–2004," press release, June 9, 2005, http://www.fec.gov/press/press2005/20050609candidate/20050609candidate.html; Federal Election Commission, "Congressional Candidates Raised $1.42 Billion in 2007–2008," press release, December 29, 2009, http://www.fec.gov/press/press2009/2009Dec29Cong/2009Dec29Cong.shtml. Party spending data from Alexander, *Financing the 1972 Election*, pp. 88–90; Alexander, *Financing the 1976 Election*, pp. 176–177, 360, 403; Alexander, *Financing the 1980 Election*, pp. 305, 311; Alexander and Haggerty, *Financing the 1984 Election*, p. 331; Alexander and Bauer, *Financing the 1988 Election*, p. 41; Federal Election Commission, "FEC Reports Major Increase in Party Activity for 1995–96," press release, March 19, 1997, http://www.fec.gov/press/press1997/ptyye1.htm; Federal Election Commission, "FEC Reports Increase in Party Fundraising for 2000," press release, May 15, 2001, http://www.fec.gov/press/press2001/051501partyfund/051501partyfund.html; Federal Election Commission, "Party Financial Activity Summarized for the 2004 Election Cycle," press release, March 2, 2005, http://www.fec.gov/press/press2005/20050302party/Party2004final.html; Federal Election Commission, "Party Financial Activity Summarized for the 2008 Election Cycle," press release, May 28, 2009, http://www.fec.gov/press/press2009/05282009Party/20090528Party.shtml; Federal Election Commission, "FEC Summarizes Campaign Activity of the 2011–2012 Election Cycle," press release, April 19, 2013, http://www.fec.gov/press/press2013/20130419_2012-24m-Summary.shtml.

Notes: Figures correspond to the two-year federal election cycle ending in the year displayed above. Totals do not include convention costs or independent expenditures by organizations formally unaffiliated with the candidates and parties. Party spending includes expenditures by the national party and congressional campaign committees and federally regulated spending by state and local parties. It also includes "soft money" for the 1980–2000 period.

over $2.5 million in his 1992 presidential campaign, a remarkable harvest from a state with a population of only 2.3 million. One event in Little Rock in late 1991 raised almost $1 million. Many local businesses helped organize Clinton fund-raising events, no doubt mindful of the governor's control over the state's bond market, pension funds, and other regulated businesses. The Worthen National Bank of Arkansas established a credit line worth $3.5 million for the Clinton campaign. This helped tide the campaign over when damaging allegations arose about Clinton's marital infidelity and avoidance of military service.[8]

Barack Obama's 2008 campaign benefited from the strong support of Penny Pritzker, a billionaire businesswoman from his hometown of Chicago whose family owns the Hyatt hotel chain and whose backing had previously helped Obama win the Illinois Democratic primary for the U.S. Senate in 2004. As the chair of the Obama campaign's finance committee, Pritzker used her personal and business connections to raise enough money for Obama to compete effectively against Hillary Clinton in the 2008 Democratic primaries. "Without Penny Pritzker," noted the *New York Times*, "it is unlikely Barack Obama ever would have been elected to the United States Senate or the presidency."[9] Obama later appointed Pritzker as U.S. Secretary of Commerce during his second term in office.

The advent of the Internet has increasingly allowed candidates to raise large amounts of money from supporters across the nation outside of the traditional mechanism of fund-raising events. The first presidential candidate to master online fund-raising was former governor Howard Dean of Vermont, whose outsider bid for the Democratic nomination in 2004 was financially fueled via his campaign website by an enthusiastic cadre of committed "Deaniacs." Obama later built on Dean's model by extending his Internet outreach to new heights. His site hosted "meet ups" for like-minded supporters (an innovation borrowed from Dean), gave supporters "widgets," portable packets of software code, that allowed supporters to set up their own "fundraising pages, goals, progress indicators (i.e., a thermometer), events and lists."[10] Obama, with a background as a community organizer, used the Internet to create a self-sustaining movement behind his candidacy. Former Federal Elections Commission chair Michael Toner explained the new techniques employed by Obama and other campaigns:

> A decade ago, if someone was impressed with what a candidate said at a debate or a rally and wished to make a contribution, he or she needed to find their checkbook, figure out the payee, determine where to send the check, and get the check in the mail. Today, if someone likes what a candidate says, he or she can make an online contribution on [an] iPhone in a matter of minutes. Moreover, presidential campaign websites today provide donors with the option of making recurring monthly contributions on their credit cards in $25, $15 or even $5 amounts. . . . In this way, the Internet facilitates the making of political contributions separate and apart from public interest in presidential races. Which may partially account for the record-breaking amounts of money that presidential candidates have raised in recent years.[11]

The accumulation of money interacts with the events of the nomination process. Successful candidates can expect to reap a windfall of cash within hours of a victory in a key state primary. But as a less fortunate candidate's defeats add up over the course of the election season, visibility and credibility begin to slip, and fund-raising falls even as expenses mount. Tactical considerations become more and more important as dwindling resources limit the number of states that can be contested. For example, by March 3, 1992, the date of several state primaries, Nebraska senator Bob Kerrey was forced by financial desperation to ignore the Maryland primary, to limit expenditures in Colorado to one thirty-second advertisement, to rely on personal appearances in Georgia to generate enough free press coverage to make up for his lack of any paid airtime, and to hope that $6,600 spent on radio ads in Idaho might influence the outcome in the state's low-turnout Democratic caucus. Not surprisingly, none of these tactics paid off, and Kerrey abandoned his campaign two days later.[12]

By the end of 2007, John Edwards had raised $44 million for his campaign for the Democratic nomination, placing him far behind both Clinton and Obama, who had collected over $100 million apiece.[13] In order to compete effectively with his rivals, Edwards decided to concentrate his campaign spending and personal appearances in Iowa, home of the first state caucus in the nation. Edwards hoped that an impressive victory in Iowa would generate a great deal of favorable publicity in the news media that would both compensate for his initial financial disadvantage and stimulate additional contributions. His second-place Iowa finish, eight percentage points behind Obama, doomed this strategy, and he soon withdrew from the race.

While presidential challengers cope with financial shortages and strategic dilemmas, incumbents, who are always well-funded and frequently unopposed for renomination, can use the primary period to stockpile campaign money until a nominee emerges in the other party. George W. Bush, for example, was able to attract to his 2004 reelection campaign some of the most prominent Republican fundraisers. Supporters who solicited, collected, and delivered large donations to the Bush campaign from a network of personal and business associates, a practice known as "bundling," received a special recognized title from the Bush campaign if the total of their bundled contributions exceeded a certain monetary amount—an innovation designed by Bush campaign aides to encourage aggressive fund-raising. The *New York Times* reported in early 2004 that by late 2003,

> Bush had 350 top-level volunteer fund-raisers—Pioneers, who agree to raise at least $100,000 from friends, colleagues, neighbors and anyone else in their phone books, and Rangers, who agree to raise $200,000. That is an increase of more than 100 people over the 2000 Bush campaign. "They've created new networks, and it's given them better results," said one Pioneer based in Washington. "One thing they don't do is just round up all the usual suspects."
>
> There are now Pioneers and Rangers in 43 states and Washington, D.C., records show. Texas has the most, at 43, followed by Florida at 35, California at 34 and New York at 27, according to Texans for Public Justice, a group that tracks campaign finance. Representing all segments of industry, these fund-raisers have gathered at least $48.4 million since Mr. Bush began raising money in May. Mail and phone solicitations brought in $27 million more and the Internet brought in about $3 million, according to the campaign. Fund-raisers paint a picture of an organized operation that encourages friendly competition and makes top campaign officials accessible to those raising money out in the field.
>
> "He's been easier to raise money for than many," said former senator Rudy Boschwitz, a Ranger from Minnesota. "He's extremely well organized. He has the

same people running the show that he had in 2000, and the group has coalesced." Mr. Bush even started a new class of fund-raisers last year, Mavericks, who raise at least $50,000 and are under 40 years old. So far, at least 10 people have raised enough to earn the title and 17 others hold it in addition to Ranger or Pioneer.[14]

An extensive roster of fund-raising bundlers also helped Barack Obama raise a large amount of money in 2011 and 2012 as his Republican opponents fought among themselves for the right to face him in the 2012 general election. The Obama reelection campaign followed the practice of the Bush campaigns in 2000 and 2004 in voluntarily releasing the names of these fundraisers, though Obama bundlers were not given special campaign titles like the "Pioneer" and "Ranger" designations used by Bush. Well-known figures who raised $500,000 or more for Obama's 2012 campaign included the married couple of actor Will Smith and actress Jada Pinkett-Smith, actress Eva Longoria, Hollywood studio executives Jeffrey Katzenberg and Harvey Weinstein, film director Tyler Perry, *Vogue* editor Anna Wintour, and pop musician Gwen Stefani.[15] Obama raised more than $55 million from bundlers between April and October 2011 alone, helping him gain a significant head start in the money race more than a year before his reelection.[16]

Campaign Finance in Presidential Primaries

Responding to the campaign finance scandals that came to light in relation to the Watergate affair, Congress acted in 1974 to create a system of partial public financing for candidates seeking their party's presidential nomination. For more than twenty years thereafter, most serious candidates—and all eventual nominees of both parties—participated in the public funding program. Candidates who establish eligibility (by raising at least $5,000 in contributions of $250 or less from individuals in each of 20 states—$100,000 total) can choose to receive public funds matching all individual contributions up to $250 from a pool created by a voluntary check-off on federal income tax returns. This provision thus doubles the value of individuals' contributions up to $250, encouraging candidates who participate in the matching funds program to seek financial support from large numbers of individual contributors.

In exchange for receiving matching funds from the federal government, however, candidates must abide by two key requirements. The first is a restriction on the amount of money a candidate may spend out of his or her own pocket: candidates accepting matching funds cannot contribute more than $50,000 to their campaigns from their own assets or from those of their immediate families. Candidates accepting matching funds must also observe limits on the money spent by their campaigns in the prenomination period. Congress established an overall spending limit of $10 million in 1974, which is adjusted every four years for increases in the cost of living. For the 2012 election, the nationwide spending limit required for participation in the matching funds program stood at roughly $55 million, not including various fund-raising and compliance costs, which are not counted against the total. In addition, participating candidates must abide by spending limits in each state based on the size of the state's voting-age population.[17]

Beginning with George W. Bush in 2000, presidential candidates have increasingly opted to decline matching funds and the restrictions that come with them, concluding that they could raise far more money by relying solely on private donations and thus escaping the overall and state-by-state spending caps. Unless Congress acts to provide greater financial incentives for participation, it appears that the system of partial public financing for primary elections is virtually defunct. Some dark horse candidates unable to raise large sums on their own may still be willing to abide by the accompanying restrictions in order to receive matching funds. But those in serious contention for their party's nomination will wish to remain free of spending limits, especially since these limits apply, even after a presumptive nominee has emerged, until the nomination is made official at the party's national convention.

Before the primary contests ramp up, politicians considering a bid for the presidency also form pre-candidacy political action committees. Originally, potential candidates founded PACs in order to get around the spending limits in the public financing system. Today, PACs have become just another way to raise money, especially during the early months when prospective candidates have yet to officially enter the race by creating formal presidential campaign organizations. Politicians test the waters by using their personal PACs to fund visits to Iowa, New Hampshire, and other key primary and caucus states, while also disbursing PAC money to party candidates for other offices—who might be expected to return the favor with endorsements or fund-raising efforts later in the primary season.[18]

During the nomination process, presidential contenders may also benefit from the support of outside groups that are formally unaffiliated with their campaigns but spend money on behalf of their candidacies. A series of federal court decisions—most notably *Citizens United v. Federal Election Commission* (U.S. Supreme Court, 2010) and *SpeechNow.org v. Federal Election Commission* (U.S. Court of Appeals for the District of Columbia, 2010)—have found that Congress lacks the constitutional authority to restrict contributions to, and expenditures of, certain independent organizations that spend money in order to influence the outcome of elections, as long as these entities do not coordinate their activities with particular candidates or parties. These judicial rulings have allowed for the increasing prevalence of groups that, unlike candidates' own campaign organizations, can accept unlimited donations from individuals and can receive contributions of any size from corporations and labor unions.

One category of outside groups, officially classified as "independent expenditure-only committees" but more commonly known as "super PACs," has quickly gained influence in presidential nomination politics. During the 2012 Republican presidential primaries, several candidates benefited from the support of nominally independent super PACs that funded advertising campaigns designed to create positive impressions of their candidacies—or, more commonly, to create negative impressions of their opponents. Restore Our Future, a committee founded in 2010 by former aides to Mitt Romney, spent millions of dollars in late 2011 and early 2012 on television advertisements attacking Romney's rivals for the Republican presidential nomination, calling former senator Rick Santorum of Pennsylvania "the ultimate Washington insider" and claiming that former House speaker Newt Gingrich "has more baggage than the airlines."[19] But Romney's opponents had outside help of their own. Santorum's candidacy was bolstered by the Red, White and Blue Fund, a super PAC that ultimately raised and spent more money than the candidate's own campaign organization did (due in large part to contributions totaling more than $2 million from a single patron, Wyoming investor Foster Friess). Meanwhile, the pro-Gingrich super PAC Winning Our Future received over

$20 million in donations from Las Vegas casino magnate Sheldon Adelson and members of his family, which collectively represented about 90 percent of the organization's total budget.[20] Without this considerable indirect financial assistance, both Santorum and Gingrich would have had even more difficulty in competing with Romney's well-funded campaign.

Raising and Spending Money in the General Election

The federal public financing system that provided matching funds to candidates running in presidential primaries and caucuses also granted each major-party nominee $20 million in 1974 dollars—$91 million in 2012—to fund a general election campaign, with the stipulation that candidates who accepted public money had to restrict their spending to this amount and refuse additional contributions from individuals or PACs except to pay the compliance costs incurred in following the law. Just as participation in the matching funds program fell substantially after 2000 as candidates increasingly concluded that they could raise greater sums on their own, presidential nominees have recently declined public funding in the general election in order to remain free of the corresponding spending limits. Relying instead upon his unique fund-raising prowess, Barack Obama became the first major-party nominee since the creation of the public financing program to privately fund his general election campaign in 2008—allowing him to greatly outspend his Republican rival John McCain, who accepted the public funds and accompanying spending cap. In 2012, both Obama and his opponent Mitt Romney declined public financing, setting what will undoubtedly serve as a precedent for future presidential elections. As in the presidential nomination phase, individuals may donate up to $2,000 in 2002 dollars ($2,500 in 2012) to a candidate's general election campaign; donors who already contributed the maximum legal amount to a candidate during the primaries are allowed to give again in the general election.

Once the nomination races are decided, the money spent by the candidates' own campaign organizations is augmented by additional expenditures made by the national parties. Federal law limits the amount that each party committee is allowed to spend in coordination with the presidential nominees ($21.6 million for each party in 2012); however, the parties may spend unlimited additional funds as long as the activity remains independent of the candidates' own campaigns. The Democratic National Committee spent $292 million in the 2012 election, mostly on behalf of Obama's bid for reelection, while the Republican National Committee spent up to $386 million in support of the Romney candidacy.[21] Donations to parties are regulated much the same as those to individual candidates. Corporations and labor unions are not allowed to contribute, and donations by an individual citizen to a party committee may not exceed $25,000 in 2002 dollars per calendar year ($30,800 in 2012). Party committee fund-raising in future presidential elections will be aided by the U.S. Supreme Court's ruling in *McCutcheon v. FEC* (2014) striking down legal restrictions on the total amount of money that individuals may donate to federal candidates and parties in any given election year.

Prior to 2002, party organizations were also permitted to raise "soft money" that was not as tightly regulated by federal campaign finance law as traditional "hard money" contributions. Individuals could donate unlimited amounts of soft money to party committees, and corporations and unions were permitted to contribute as well.

Unlike hard money, soft money could not be legally used to fund advertising that expressly advocated the election or defeat of a political candidate, although it could be used to pay for "issue ads" that attempted to influence voters' evaluations of the two contenders.[22] By the 1990s, parties had become increasingly reliant on soft money; the Democrats and Republicans raised about $120 million each in 1996 and about $250 million apiece in 2000.[23] While advocates emphasized the party-building effects of soft money—which was also used to bolster state and local party organizations—critics viewed it as a loophole exploited by parties to evade regulation and contribution limits.[24] As a result, soft money was outlawed by the Bipartisan Campaign Reform Act (BCRA), also known as the McCain-Feingold law, enacted by Congress in 2002.

The prohibition on soft money hastened the rise of independent groups that raise and spend funds outside the structure of formal candidate campaigns and party organizations. In the wake of the *Citizens United* and *SpeechNow.org* court decisions, independent expenditure-only committees (super PACs) are permitted to accept unlimited donations from individuals, corporations, and unions, and to spend this money on advertising that explicitly advocates the election or defeat of political candidates. However, they are still subject to federal laws requiring them to disclose the source and amount of their donations and the size of their expenditures. Non-profit 501(c)(4) organizations (named after the section of the federal tax code under which they fall) may also fund ads during election campaigns, although the law nominally requires that political activity cannot be the primary purpose of such groups; unlike super PACs and other organizations that are regulated by Section 527 of the tax code (and are therefore called "527 committees"), 501(c)(4) groups are not compelled to publicly disclose the sources of their donations—leading reform advocates to dub their spending "dark money."

Independent expenditures by groups formally unconnected with the candidates and parties now represent a significant fraction of campaign spending in the United States. Traditional PACs, super PACs, 501(c)(4) groups, and other outside entities spent over $500 million on behalf of presidential candidates in 2012. The vast majority of advertising funded by outside groups is negative in tone. For example, the pro-Republican American Crossroads super PAC spent over $84 million attacking Obama in 2012 and just $6.5 million on positive ads supporting Romney, while Priorities USA Action, a super PAC founded by former Obama aides, spent $65 million on anti-Romney communications while making no pro-Obama expenditures.[25] Because these independent groups are not officially tied to the campaigns or parties and may not legally coordinate with them, candidates and party leaders do not bear direct responsibility for these attack ads, even though they are produced for their political benefit.

Does Money Buy Elections?

The billions of dollars spent on American elections inevitably raise serious questions about the relationship between wealth and decisions in a democracy. Are presidential nominating and electoral contests determined by those who have the most money? Do those who make large contributions exercise substantial or undue influence as a result? Is the victorious candidate under obligation to "pay off" major financial contributors? Do those who pay the piper call the tune?[26]

This was certainly the reasoning that inspired the post-Watergate political reforms of the mid-1970s, which attempted to minimize the influence of money on presidential

**BOX 3.1. In the Arena: The Role
of Super PACs in the 2012 Campaign**

**Bill Burton, strategist for Priorities USA
(the largest pro-Obama Super PAC):**

"In the primary the Super PACs made a huge difference. I don't think that Mitt Romney would have been the nominee if it weren't for Restore Our Future [the largest pro-Romney Super PAC]. . . . But if you look at the broad picture, at the hundreds and hundreds of millions of dollars, I understand the confusion about whether or not it made a bit of difference because here you look at the final outcome and it's a 50-50 country, basically. But that's like saying, 'If you were in a war where two countries were firing missiles at each other, did the missiles make any difference?' And if one of those countries isn't firing missiles, you can see what the difference is a lot more than you can if both countries are firing the missiles. So I think that they do make a big difference, and I think that in 2016 you will see a proliferation of outside groups far beyond what you saw this time around."

**Charlie Spies, treasurer, Restore Our Future
(the largest Pro-Romney Super PAC):**

"This is not about *Citizens United*. This is about the McCain-Feingold law that was passed and pushes money away from political parties and pushes money away from candidates and forces the money into the outside groups who have an advantage of being able to take more money. So this is not a *Citizens United* phenomenon. Post McCain-Feingold, in 2004, you saw this with Progress for America, you saw the Swift Vote Veterans, and then you saw it with the George Soros groups after that. Until the McCain-Feingold law is repealed or at least modified, and you're able to get money into political parties and campaigns, you are going to have outside having disproportionate influence."

Source: Institute of Politics, John F. Kennedy School of Government, Harvard University, *Campaign for President: The Managers Look at 2012.* Lanham, MD: Rowman & Littlefield Publishers, 2013, pp. 142–43, 156.

elections.[27] Before these elaborate limitations were established, however, the evidence was slight that presidential elections were unduly influenced, never mind "bought," by moneyed interests. Republicans did spend more than Democrats in most general elections, but the difference was not as overwhelming as some would suppose. The percentage of post-nomination expenditures spent by the Democratic nominee from 1932 to 1980 varied from a low of 33 percent in 1972 to a high of 51 percent in 1960; the average was about 41 percent.[28] Although Lyndon Johnson spent more money in 1964 than John F. Kennedy in 1960, Barry Goldwater's losing campaign spent $17.2 million—significantly more than Johnson's $12 million expenditure—yet received only 38 percent of the national popular vote.[29] Total spending by both parties was high in absolute terms, but outlays per voter per party were quite modest, running in the 1972 election to about $1.31 for each of the 76 million voters.[30]

The most obvious and most important conclusion in our view is that even in the era when the parties were free to spend whatever they could raise and were not subject to the restrictions and regulations established by Congress in 1974, money did not buy election victories. The candidate and party with the most money did not always win. Otherwise, Republicans would have won every presidential election but one between 1932 and 2004, but in fact Democrats won seven of the nine elections from 1932 to 1964 and five more contests since then. Nor does there seem to be a correlation between the amount of money spent and the size of electoral victory in national elections.[31] In 1968, for example, the Republicans outspent the Democrats by more than two to one, yet they won the election by a mere 500,000 out of the 72 million votes cast.

One would expect that money would flow into the coffers of the party believed to have the best chance of victory. That did happen to the Democrats in 2008. Obama greatly outspent McCain—who was subject to the strict spending limits required of participants in the public financing program—in advertising and deployed a much larger network of field offices in the weeks leading up to the election; at times, in fact, it appeared as if the Obama campaign was raising money faster than it could spend it. With television airwaves in the usual battleground states already saturated with Obama campaign commercials by the fall of 2008, the candidate's advisers expanded their campaign activity into states such as Indiana and North Carolina that were not central to their electoral college strategy, funded their own dedicated channel ("Obama on Demand") on residential satellite systems that ran continuous programming produced by the campaign, and even purchased advertising in popular video games such as Guitar Hero.[32] But though his overwhelming financial advantage may have added to his ultimate vote margin, Obama almost certainly would have won the election anyway due to the strongly favorable political environment for Democratic candidates in 2008.

Most likely, the vast sums spent in American presidential elections represent a textbook example of the law of diminishing returns. Candidates, parties, and outside groups on both sides reliably raise more than enough money to hire competent staff, build strong campaign organizations, fund voter registration and mobilization efforts, and blanket the airwaves of battleground states with television advertising for months before the election. By Election Day, the average resident of a key swing state has seen hundreds of campaign ads—the Obama campaign calculated that the typical voter in Cleveland, Ohio, was exposed to 190 different television spots in 2012, aired a total of 1,450 times—and received a constant stream of mailings, telephone calls, and personal visits from representatives of both candidates.[33] It is difficult to believe that additional expenditures by one side or the other would prove decisive in such a saturated communication environment, and indeed much of the current spending in presidential elections is probably well in excess of the levels at which additional money has a measurable effect on the outcome. David Axelrod, chief strategist for Obama's 2008 and 2012 campaigns, believes that television spending in particular is highly inefficient, even arguing that "there was no ad that ran after the [national] conventions that ever in the modern era won a presidential race; paid media becomes largely irrelevant in the general [election] after the conventions" because voters have become so overloaded with campaign messages.[34]

Moreover, voters are influenced by more than just television ads or campaign mailings. The overall economic health and direction of the nation, the personal qualities and policy positions of the candidates, events of the campaign season such as conventions and debates that receive considerable attention from journalists and pundits, and other considerations enter into the calculation of citizens making up their mind in the voting booth. While advertising can play a role in shaping voters' perceptions, it is not necessarily the dominant means by which they form their evaluations of the candidates, parties, and issues—especially in presidential elections, which provide ample alternative sources of information by inevitably attracting extensive coverage from the news media and stimulating frequent conversations among citizens' personal acquaintances.

Money is a more powerful factor in deciding presidential nomination contests than general elections. Candidates embark on aggressive fund-raising efforts well before the first primaries and caucuses; having enough financial resources to compete effectively in the early states helps to raise additional funds to sustain candidates throughout the primary season. A well-funded campaign is necessary both to boost a candidate's name recognition among intermittently attentive primary voters and to signal to the press corps that the candidate should be taken seriously as a contender for the nomination. If a campaign war chest is sufficiently imposing, potential rivals for the nomination might also be dissuaded from jumping into the race.

The dollar amounts necessary for competitiveness have grown greatly over time. Dwight D. Eisenhower and Robert Taft each spent about $2.5 million on their nominating campaigns in 1952.[35] George McGovern spent $12 million in 1972 on the way to his nomination.[36] Jimmy Carter spent $12.4 million in 1976 and, as an incumbent president, $19.6 million in 1980.[37] In 1984, Walter Mondale spent $26.2 million, while Ronald Reagan, despite his lack of serious opposition for the Republican nomination, spent $25.9 million.[38] In 1988, both the winning nominees had more money to work with than their rivals; Bush and Dukakis both spent $28 million, the maximum allowed at the time for candidates participating in the matching funds program.[39]

As of the end of February 2004, the field of Democrats seeking their party's presidential nomination had spent a combined $190 million on their campaigns: former governor Howard Dean of Vermont led the pack with expenditures of $48 million, followed by Senator John Kerry of Massachusetts at $38 million, Senator John Edwards of North Carolina at $26 million, retired General Wesley Clark at $24 million, Representative Richard Gephardt of Missouri at $20 million, and Senator Joseph Lieberman of Connecticut at $18 million.[40] The 2008 spending totals for major nomination contenders far eclipsed even the amounts expended in 2004. Both Hillary Clinton and Barack Obama spent over $200 million in their long primary contest, while John Edwards, who dropped out shortly after New Hampshire, still managed to spend over $50 million. On the Republican side in 2008, Rudy Giuliani, who ended his campaign at the end of January, also spent over $50 million. Mitt Romney, John McCain's main rival until the beginning of February, expended over $100 million in funds. McCain himself, though the certain nominee by early March, still spent $190 million during the primary season.[41] By the time that the 2012 Republican nomination contest was effectively decided at the end of March, Romney (running for a second time in four years) had spent $78 million, compared to $35 million by Ron Paul, $21 million by Newt Gingrich, $20 million by Rick Perry, and $19 million by Rick Santorum; of course, these totals were augmented considerably by independent expenditures from super PACs allied with the candidates.[42]

Money, however, is only one factor affecting the fortunes of potential nominees. Skill and strategy in using resources matters as much as having them; as Howard Dean discovered in 2004, a large war chest manifestly does not guarantee victory in primaries. Though Dean boasted the biggest bank account of all the Democratic candidates, he did not spend his ample funds wisely. In the weeks before the Iowa caucus, Dean's campaign bused thirty-five hundred young volunteers into the state from elsewhere at great expense to knock on doors in support of his candidacy, renting vans, cell phones, and lodging for them to use during their stay. "I had never seen a campaign spend like this one," Dean's Iowa spokeswoman later remarked. Despite the high cost, this mobilization effort did not persuade most Iowans to vote for Dean. One nineteen-year-old volunteer who traveled from Vermont to Iowa for the caucus admitted with hindsight that "many voters . . . may have been insulted by out-of-staters rushing in to tell them how to vote." John Kerry's campaign, in contrast, focused more on courting support from veteran Iowa political organizers who cultivated ongoing personal networks within the state; these efforts paid off when Kerry placed first in the Iowa caucus, setting him on a path to the Democratic nomination.[43] Wesley Clark was also a proficient fundraiser in the weeks before the primary season began, but his decision not to compete in Iowa cost him valuable publicity, and his campaign never recovered despite the money he spent in New Hampshire and subsequent primary states.[44] For Dean, Kerry, and Clark, strategy seemed to weigh more heavily than money in determining their electoral fortunes in 2004.

This was also true during the 2008 primaries for John McCain, who benefited from a careful focus on New Hampshire, South Carolina, and Florida, leading to successes in all three state primaries despite limited campaign funds, especially in comparison to his free-spending, partially self-financing rival Mitt Romney. On the Democratic side in 2008, though Hillary Clinton initially outraised Barack Obama, Obama ran a relatively smooth campaign while Clinton's operation was hobbled by strategic errors and organizational disarray that may well have made the difference in the outcome. For example, Clinton advisers mistakenly assumed that their candidate's electoral strength in the populous states holding primaries on Super Tuesday, February 5, would all but end the race. As a result, they ignored the smaller states holding caucuses on that day (thus allowing Obama to gain a number of delegates from these states without challenge) and failed to plan properly for a longer nomination battle by organizing effectively in states voting later in the month, such as Virginia, Maryland, and Wisconsin, all of which were won easily by Obama.

In addition, the Clinton campaign spent its money far less efficiently than did Obama, requiring Hillary Clinton herself to make several personal loans to her campaign totaling $13 million in order to keep it afloat in the final months of the race—loans that were ultimately never repaid.[45] Obama, meanwhile, benefited from abundant funds, a strong, unified campaign organization, and sound strategy: usually an unbeatable combination. Even so, Clinton's enduring popularity among Democratic voters and Obama's own vulnerabilities as a candidate made the nomination battle unusually close.

It is exceedingly difficult to get reliable information on an event that involves a decision not to act, such as a potential candidate's decision not to run because he or she could or would not attract the necessary funds. There is only a little literature on this subject, mostly news stories announcing early decisions to forego a presidential race. But undoubtedly there have been some prospective candidates whose inability or unwillingness to raise large sums of money has proved fatal to their chances of being considered for the nomination. Whether their failure represents an inability to satisfy the moneyed classes or to convince enough people that their candidacies were serious and worthy is difficult to say in the abstract. A more important question concerns whether there has been a systematic bias in favor of or against certain candidates that consistently alters the outcomes of presidential nominations. We can immediately dismiss the notion that the richest person automatically comes out on top. If that were the case, Mitt Romney would have bested John McCain for the Republican nomination in 2008, while either Hillary Clinton or John Edwards would have defeated Barack Obama in the Democratic side. Nelson Rockefeller would have triumphed over Barry Goldwater in 1964 and Richard Nixon in 1968, and Robert Taft would have beaten Dwight D. Eisenhower in 1952. In 1976, Ronald Reagan's personal wealth eclipsed Gerald Ford's, as, in 1980, Edward Kennedy's did Jimmy Carter's. Nevertheless, in both these instances, the incumbent president beat the challenger.

Perhaps the best test of the proposition that the richest candidate will win was found in the Republican nomination contest in 1996. Rather than relying on a mixture of small contributions and public matching funds, as every major candidate for the nomination had done since the public financing system was created, multimillionaire publisher Steve Forbes decided to spend his own money in an effort to secure the Republican nomination. Under the Supreme Court decision in *Buckley v. Valeo* (1976), candidates may spend as much as they wish from their personal fortune. Many wealthy state-level candidates had taken advantage of that ruling, but Forbes was the first candidate for a major party presidential nomination to do so.[46] Certainly, self-financing helped Forbes. Other than money, the only obvious resource he brought to the campaign was a mild case of name recognition, since his family's name is also the title of his national business magazine. It was his ability and willingness to spend vast sums of money—$37 million, almost as much as eventual nominee Bob Dole and far more than any other candidate for the nomination—that convinced the press to treat Forbes as a serious candidate, despite his late entry, lack of organization in Iowa or New Hampshire, and absence of normal qualifications for the presidency such as previous elected office or substantial public service. His money was not, however, capable of buying Forbes the nomination. In the critical states of Iowa and New Hampshire, he failed to finish among the top three candidates. While he did win two primaries (one, in Delaware, by default since he was the only candidate to campaign there), he never really threatened to win the nomination.[47] After reinventing himself as a social conservative, Forbes ran again for president in 2000. He spent even more (over $42 million) the second time around, but fared no better among the voters, withdrawing from the race on February 10 after receiving just 13 percent of the vote in New Hampshire and finishing third in the Delaware primary.[48]

A similar fate befell Mitt Romney in his 2008 campaign for the Republican nomination. Romney "loaned" his campaign $44 million in personal funds, far more than any other major candidate running for either nomination that year. Yet he was defeated in a series of early primaries by John McCain despite outspending McCain two-to-one on television ads.[49] By the end of February, Romney had spent over $100 million seeking the GOP nomination, as compared to McCain's $50 million, yet McCain had easily outdistanced Romney among pledged delegates. Romney fared better with the voters when he ran a second time in 2012, ultimately capturing the Republican nomination that had eluded him four years before, but this time he did not contribute financially to his own campaign and relied entirely on donations from others.

The ability to raise money is a matter not only of personal wealth but also of being able to attract support from a large network of enthusiastic contributors. Given the legal limits that apply to direct contributions to candidates and parties, presidential campaigns face a strong incentive to build a wide donor base comprised of millions of individuals. In 2012, the Obama reelection campaign raised $233 million from "small donors"—those giving $200 or less—which represented 33 percent of the total amount raised; Romney raised $88 million, or 18 percent of his total fund-raising haul, from small donors.[50]

The advent of the Internet as a powerful fund-raising tool has allowed candidates to cultivate large numbers of financial supporters; those who make a contribution will be targeted by regular solicitations urging them to give again and again. In June 2012, the Obama campaign sent an e-mail message to members of its electronic mailing list signed by Obama himself with the attention-grabbing subject line "I will be outspent," with Obama warning that he would be "the first president in modern history to be outspent in his re-election campaign, if things continue as they have so far." The e-mail turned out to be the most successful single fund-raising message of the race, alone stimulating over $2.5 million in donations to the Obama campaign.[51] However, its prediction was inaccurate; Obama ultimately outspent Romney by roughly $250 million in 2012, although this advantage disappeared when independent expenditures by parties and outside groups were taken into account.

Campaign Finance Reform

The dissatisfaction of many citizens, especially left-of-center political activists, with the current system of financing political campaigns in the United States has led to an ongoing series of proposals for reform, which Congress has occasionally adopted—most notably in the Federal Election Campaign Act, or FECA (1972, amended in 1974, 1976, and 1979) and the Bipartisan Campaign Reform Act, or BCRA (2002)—and which have then received constitutional scrutiny from the federal judiciary. Four broad issues are raised by the ways in which money is acquired and spent in presidential elections. The first is the issue of public disclosure of campaign financing. The contributions to, and expenditures of, federal candidates, party organizations, PACs, and super PACs must be reported to the Federal Election Commission, which makes this information available to the public.[52] The federal courts have upheld the constitutionality of disclosure requirements, rejecting claims that public knowledge of citizens' campaign contributions inhibits political expression by chilling support for socially marginal candidates or parties.[53] The growing role of 501(c)(4) organizations in election campaigns has become an area of concern for advocates of reform; these groups are required to disclose their political expenditures but not the source of their contributions.

Under federal law, political communications such as television advertisements and campaign mailings must contain text identifying the sponsoring candidate, party, or organization. The BCRA included a provision, later upheld by the U.S. Supreme Court in *McConnell v. Federal Election Commission* (2003), that requires every presidential and congressional candidate to appear in all radio and television advertising produced by his or her campaign, stating his or her name and explicit authorization of the ad, usually with the following format: "I'm [candidate name], and I approve this message." Online advertising, however, is not subject to this requirement.

A second issue raised in presidential campaigns is the question of public funding. The 1974 amendments to FECA created a public financing system for presidential (but not congressional) elections, covering both the pre- and post-nomination stages, in an attempt to promote fairness and reduce the opportunity for corruption. However, the Supreme Court has ruled that such programs must be voluntary, with candidates free to choose whether to take public subsidies (and operate under the corresponding restrictions on donations and spending). Public funding programs also inspire debate over eligibility requirements (such as for minor parties), the generosity of the subsidies, and the desirability of using tax dollars to fund political campaigns.

Although a substantial fraction of the increase in the nominal cost of campaigns since 1972 is due to inflation (see table 3.2), the total spending by federal candidates and parties still more than quadrupled in real dollars between 1976 and 2008, even before considering the increasing prevalence of independent expenditures by outside groups. The public financing program established in the 1970s has not kept up with the sharply rising costs of campaigns, as well as the easier access to private dollars enjoyed by today's presidential candidates. As a result, it has been abandoned by serious contenders in both the primaries and the general election, and there seems to be little sentiment among elected officials today for reforming the system to make it more attractive to candidates—which would necessarily involve authorizing more than a billion dollars in public subsidies to the presidential campaigns every four years.

A third unresolved question is the advisability of strict regulations on the money spent by national, state, and local party organizations. The BCRA banned soft money in 2002, under the theory that the absence of contribution limits and lack of restrictions on corporate and union donations meant that soft money could represent a potentially corrupting influence on candidates and party leaders. While the U.S. Supreme Court upheld the soft money ban as applied to parties, it has taken a much less deferential view towards attempts to enforce similar restrictions on outside groups such as super PACs. As a result, certain types of donations that were once given directly to parties have not been removed from the political system but are now directed instead toward less visible organizations with, perhaps, less responsiveness to voters.

Finally, the topic of campaign finance reform raises the question of how the regulation of political money should be balanced against the constitutional rights of Americans to engage in political speech. Since the passage of the BCRA in 2002, which contained several provisions designed to limit the electoral influence of political actors other than candidates' own campaign organizations, parties, and traditional PACs, the Supreme Court has become increasingly willing to strike down legal and regulatory restrictions on the activity of outside organizations such as corporations and super PACs. In the *Citizens United* decision of 2010, Justice Anthony Kennedy wrote that "when government seeks to use its full power, including the criminal law, to command where a person may get his or her information or what distrusted source he or she may not hear, it uses censorship to control thought. This is unlawful. The First Amendment confirms the freedom to think for ourselves."[54]

To the minority bloc of liberal justices, this reasoning obscured what they viewed as the very real danger to the political system posed by the excessive influence of special interests over the outcome of elections. In his *Citizens United* dissent, Justice John

TABLE 3.2. Federal Campaign Spending, 1972–2012 (Adjusted for Inflation)

Year	Actual Spending (Millions of Dollars)	Consumer Price Index (1972 Base)	Adjusted Spending (Millions of 1972 Dollars)
1972	217	100.0	217
1976	279	136.1	205
1980	643	197.1	326
1984	988	248.6	397
1988	1,198	283.0	423
1992	1,491	335.7	444
1996	2,064	375.4	550
2000	2,716	412.0	659
2004	3,409	451.9	754
2008	4,565	515.0	886
2012	4,783	549.3	871

Source: See table 3.1. CPI data from Bureau of Labor Statistics, http://data.bls.gov/cgi-bin/cpicalc.pl.

Paul Stevens argued that the decision "threatens to undermine the integrity of elected institutions across the Nation. . . . While American democracy is imperfect, few outside the majority of this Court would have thought its flaws included a dearth of corporate money in politics." Many Democratic officials and advocates of campaign finance reform echoed this criticism, including Barack Obama, who claimed in his 2010 State of the Union Address that the *Citizens United* case would "open the floodgates for special interests—including foreign corporations—to spend without limit in our elections."

While this debate over the value and constitutionality of campaign finance regulation will no doubt continue, the current state of federal law and judicial precedent has created an increasingly open environment for a variety of politically active groups to engage in voter persuasion efforts during presidential campaigns, and for individuals with the requisite financial means to donate large sums of money to independent organizations involved in producing political communications directed toward the American electorate. What relationships are we observing when we track this money? While some campaign finance reform advocates tend to portray campaign donations, especially those from wealthy individuals, as little more than legalized bribery, it is often difficult to identify examples of politicians changing their policy positions as a result of receiving financial contributions. More commonly, politically engaged citizens donate funds in order to bolster the electoral chances of candidates who already share their views, and the multiplicity of interests within the American public guarantees that political money will be divided among multiple parties and candidates with very different positions on the salient issues of the day. In addition, while adequate financial support is essential to a successful candidacy, it is far from the only valuable resource in presidential elections.

RESOURCES: CONTROL OVER INFORMATION

Political information is so easy to acquire during a presidential election campaign that it is hard to identify anybody in control of its spread. There are, however, features of the overall system by which information is manufactured and distributed in the United

States that materially affect the fortunes of candidates and the ways in which they are perceived by electorates. Campaign professionals generally divide sources of information into free media and paid media. Free media (sometimes called "earned media") consist of publicity that candidates do not have to pay for, as the result of news coverage. Patterns of news coverage matter enormously to candidates, and they spend great effort conforming their campaigns to the professional practices of print, television, and online media.

News organizations customarily assign experienced journalists to campaigns they judge to be "serious" and so in the first instance aspiring candidates must attempt to be taken seriously; those deemed to have no plausible chance at winning their party's presidential nomination will be largely ignored by the press. Usually, to be judged a "serious" candidate requires being a well-known public figure and hiring a staff of campaign professionals recognized by journalists as capable. Thus, even receiving free coverage usually requires money, and sometimes quite a lot of money, since journalists often judge the relative standing of presidential candidates during the early stages of the campaign by the size of their campaign war chests. Pre-nomination debates among candidates are often covered on television and on the Internet. Appearing in debates is one good way for candidates to get publicity while keeping costs down, and being included in debates is a mark of credibility for candidates, a sign that they must be taken seriously.

Paid media refers mostly to television, radio, and Internet advertisements, which candidates produce and place on the air or online. Advertising is a form of information that uninvolved observers, such as a normal American electorate, frequently find credible. Especially during the presidential primary season, when multiple candidates compete for the nomination of each major party, candidates must purchase advertising in order to boost their name recognition and favorability among potential voters.

What constitutes information varies with the various stages of the process, as we discuss in chapter 4. Traditional topics include horse-race information, estimating which candidates are ahead and which are behind, thereby keeping a running tally on the viability and hence the seriousness of different candidacies. The news media also cover what they call "the issues," which may be, variously, public policy proposals brought up or emphasized by one or more candidates, social and political questions of the day, or other topics such as the past voting record or personal behavior of a candidate.

In all these matters, the news media generally maintain a rather close consensus about which candidates are serious contenders (and which are not), who is ahead or gaining ground (and who is stalling or slipping behind), and which issues are important. This agreement arises from the sharply competitive conditions under which individual news organizations operate, from the shared perspective that arises because journalists from different organizations hang around together as they cover the travels of campaigning candidates, and because they keep close track of one another's product. Because television producers watch the other networks and read the newspapers, and print reporters and editors keep an eye on what's on television and the Internet, there is a tendency for their stories to converge.

Sometimes this herd mentality leads the news media astray. Most political journalists, for example, believed that former governor Howard Dean of Vermont had the 2004 Democratic nomination virtually wrapped up even before the first primary events, based in part on Dean's fund-raising advantage and his campaign's confident claims of organizational superiority in key states. Dean's disappointing third-place finish in the Iowa caucus forced an immediate widespread reappraisal of the race. While the "conventional wisdom" is not dependably accurate, it nonetheless exists as a powerful force shaping campaign coverage, due in large part to the work ways of professional reporters and commentators.

Newspapers

Though the onset of the electronic media age has drastically reduced the readership and circulation of most daily newspapers, driving many out of business entirely, print journalism remains a major source of political information for many Americans. Newspaper coverage of current events has maintained its importance even in the Internet era; the websites operated by the *New York Times*, *Washington Post*, and *USA Today* rank among the most popular online sources for information, while the news stories displayed on CNN.com and popular Internet portal sites are chiefly supplied by newspaper wire services such as Reuters and the Associated Press. Candidates realize the influence of newspaper coverage of their activities, and pay close attention to the treatment they receive from print journalists.

Most studies of political reporters confirm that they are a liberal-leaning group.[55] A recent survey of national journalists by the Pew Research Center found that 34 percent described themselves as liberals and just 7 percent as conservatives, with the balance considering themselves ideological moderates.[56] But standards of professional journalistic practice discourage slanted political coverage. As Michael Robinson has shown, while reporters may lean to the left, it is hard to find this bias in their copy.[57] Hard, but not impossible. Overt expressions of partisan bias are regarded as unprofessional in news columns and may even be veiled in articles labeled "analysis." In at least two ways, however, attitudes shared by many journalists influence political coverage in newspapers in ways that may, in practice, systematically advantage some candidates over others, despite their formal neutrality.

In the first place, it is permissible under standard journalistic norms to entertain a general pro-underdog bias. Journalists pride themselves in their calling to "comfort the afflicted and afflict the comfortable." Comforting any sizable body of afflicted persons may be well beyond the capacities of the news media.[58] It is far easier to afflict the comfortable, since this merely entails maintaining a *pro forma* skepticism about the presumably self-interested pronouncements of incumbents of high office. Incumbents escape this presumption only rarely. In the early stages of a foreign crisis, when there is a rally-round-the-flag effect, incumbents are permitted the luxury of being described as speaking on behalf of all the people. As George H. W. Bush discovered in the early stages of the American invasion of Kuwait in 1991, and his son George W. Bush similarly found after the terrorist attacks of September 11, 2001, this does wonders for their public opinion ratings. Ordinarily, however, Americans are instructed by the media to take their leaders' statements with a grain of salt.[59]

Perhaps for this reason, journalists often submit front-running candidates to stricter scrutiny than also-rans. This is particularly true in the presidential primary season, when the candidates are not widely known, making the tone of coverage more influential in shaping voters' opinions—and when reporters have an interest in prolonging the horse race excitement for as long as possible. Thus candidates may emerge from obscurity to pull into contention on the basis of initially positive media coverage, as Howard Dean did in the summer of 2003, only to face an increasingly skeptical press corps once they are anointed as "front-runners." (It didn't help Dean that he had a famously prickly relationship with the correspondents covering his campaign.) In the fall of 2011, a series of Republican presidential candidates each seemed to capture temporary momentum in the nomination contest—Governor Rick Perry of Texas; former House speaker Newt Gingrich; even Georgia businessman Herman Cain, an outsider candidate who had never held elective office—before wilting under the unfamiliar volume of public attention that followed their surge in the polls.

Second, illustrating Bernard Cohen's observation that the news media tell their consumers what to think *about*, there is the issue of "framing." How issues are framed matters over the long run because frames determine the terms within which alternative solutions are debated, and indeed they frequently serve to define the very nature of the problem.[60] Thus whether or not unemployment, inflation, health care reform, education funding, illegal immigration, global warming, violent crime, international famine, or other societal ills are seen as serious problems requiring political solutions at any given time is not entirely dependent on objective measurement of the phenomenon in question.[61] In part, their status as important "issues" of the day is determined by whether people feel that they are important, for whatever reason, and these feelings are in turn partially determined by how, or to what extent, the news media cover them. Thus the very problems our leaders are called on to solve may differ from era to era according to ebbs and flows of public attention to them.[62] Politicians work hard to seize control of this public agenda and have a considerable impact on its contents.[63] So, too, do the decisions of journalists, who give and withhold credibility to leaders according to their own collective judgments about issues and the seriousness with which politicians are addressing them.

Some candidates become personally popular or unpopular with the reporters who cover them—understandably so during a long election season in which members of the press corps travel across the country with the campaigns for weeks at a stretch. Bias based on such evaluations sometimes seeps into the copy sent back home by correspondents on the road. John F. Kennedy's warm relationships with many reporters in 1960 may have given him an advantage over his opponent, Richard Nixon, who repeatedly complained about his own coverage in the newspapers.[64] (At a 1962 press conference announcing his retirement from politics—prematurely, as it turned out—Nixon told the assembled journalists, "You won't have Dick Nixon to kick around anymore.") Nixon, who long had a tense relationship with the press, compensated in his 1972 reelection campaign by largely ignoring national correspondents who might pepper him with hostile questions, benefiting from the norm that anything the incumbent president does constitutes "news."[65] Ronald Reagan, with his affable personality and long experience in show business, cultivated good relations with the news media during his successful 1980 and 1984 campaigns, while Bill Clinton's charm and communication skills similarly earned him generally if not uniformly positive coverage during the 1992 and 1996 elections.[66] George W. Bush's folksy demeanor, on display in the documentary film *Journeys with George*, appears to have largely won over the traveling press corps during his successful 2000 and 2004 campaigns, especially when compared to his earnest, less outgoing opponents Al Gore and John Kerry. Barack Obama may have benefited in

2008 from many journalists seeking to "vote the story" in their coverage because they considered the nomination and election of the first African-American president to be the news event of a lifetime.

Just as norms of proper journalistic practice in most cases prevent overt bias from coloring campaign coverage, other considerations discourage the slanting of straight news stories. In a time of declining circulation and mounting costs for the newspaper industry, owners can ill afford to offend half their potential readership. Budget constraints have also led to consolidation among newspapers and have forced the reduction of resources devoted to the coverage of current affairs. Today, most newspapers do not maintain their own news bureaus in Washington or generate a great deal of original coverage of national politics. They increasingly rely on stories supplied by wire services or purchase content from the news services maintained by larger newspapers such as the *New York Times*, *Washington Post*, and *Los Angeles Times*. These news-gathering agencies serve a wide clientele with a broad spectrum of opinion, and therefore endeavor to prepare stories that appear objective and impartial.[67] While every story will not be completely fair to all sides, the final product is much closer to the canons of neutrality than would be the case if each paper prepared stories in accordance with its own editorial positions.

For these reasons, newspaper coverage of campaigns is, on the whole, not consistently slanted in favor of a particular political viewpoint. One meta-analysis of fifty-nine separate studies over fifty years concluded that "across all newspapers and all reporters, there is only negligible, if any, net bias in the coverage of presidential campaigns. To the extent that there are newspapers whose coverage is biased in favor of Democrats, they are offset by newspapers whose coverage is biased in favor of Republicans."[68] Barack Obama received unusually favorable press coverage in 2008, according to a study by the Project for Excellence in Journalism (now the Pew Research Center Journalism Project), receiving reportage much less negative in tone during the fall campaign than his rival John McCain.[69] However, this could have reflected less a strong pro-Obama bias among reporters than a reflection of the horse race during the weeks before the 2008 election, when Obama consistently led in the polls and the McCain campaign grappled with the travails of controversial vice presidential nominee Sarah Palin.

In 2012, both Obama and Romney received press coverage that was more negative than positive. Romney was the target of more negative stories than Obama during the month of September, when he lagged the incumbent narrowly in the race and faced widespread criticism due to several verbal gaffes committed on the campaign trail. After Romney bested Obama in the first presidential debate on October 3, however, the tone of news stories shifted, with Obama receiving more negative coverage than his opponent over the subsequent weeks.[70] This pattern strongly suggests that journalistic perceptions of electoral momentum have a decided effect on the positive or negative cast with which the press portrays each candidate at any given time.

The potential effect of media bias, ideological or otherwise, on the attitudes of readers has decreased over the years, simply because the volume of political coverage in newspapers is itself on the decline. The era of crusading editors who used their papers primarily as a vehicle for advancing political causes has given way to a modern industry dominated by corporations devoted primarily to maximizing shareholder profit.[71] Extensive attention to the world of politics attracts fewer subscribers than does coverage of crime, sports, human-interest stories, and the hijinks of celebrities; especially outside the major metropolitan areas, political news, though it does have a place, is given secondary consideration simply because most newspaper readers are not terribly interested.[72]

Even if a particular news source or coverage in a particular election is biased, are ordinary citizens actually influenced in their opinions and voting choices by the newspapers that enter their homes? The fact that a newspaper arrives on the doorstep is no guarantee that its political news and editorials will be read. Most people pay little enough attention to politics; they often read nothing or just scan the headlines without carrying away much of an impression. Even if the content is perused with some care, a reader's perception of what has been written may differ markedly from the writer's intentions. An editorial may not be clear in intent, particularly if it is hedged by qualifications or watered down to minimize offense, as it often is. Readers with existing opinions on the subject may well conclude that the item supports their views, whether it was meant to or not.

Opinion studies have demonstrated the remarkable capacity of people to filter out what they do not wish to hear and come away with quite a different impression than an objective analysis of an editorial or article would warrant. Indeed, the reader may interpret the story to mean precisely the opposite of what it intends. A criticism of Harry Truman for being vituperative, for example, could be taken—as it now generally is, with the hindsight of history—as a commendation of his fighting spirit. A condemnation of Jimmy Carter for being obstinate could emerge as praise for his high principles.[73] Ronald Reagan's "detachment" could be seen by some observers as incompetence, by others as floating benignly above politics. Conservative criticism of Bill Clinton for being "slick" and "calculating" simply mirrored his supporters' regard for his charm and political skills, while George W. Bush's frequent malapropisms and lack of interest in the details of public policy simultaneously inspired contempt in liberals and admiration in conservatives, who saw him as plain-spoken and a strong leader. John McCain struck some observers as an admirable maverick and others as erratic and headstrong; Obama seemed mature and steady to his fans, distant and arrogant to his opponents.

News stories or editorials may be interpreted correctly and still rejected as invalid. There is a great deal of suspicion of the press in the United States.[74] Party identification is so powerful that for many readers it would overwhelm almost anything a paper says. Obviously millions of citizens have no difficulty voting Republican while reading Democratic newspapers or vice versa. Many people derive their political opinions from sources other than the news media; the influence of family members, friends, coworkers, ethnic and religious organizations, and other social forces can ordinarily be expected to far outweigh anything written in a newspaper.[75]

Whatever role the press plays in influencing presidential elections varies enormously with circumstances. Against popular incumbents with publicity resources of their own, the impact of the media may be negligible. Less well-known candidates, such as many challengers, may be more dependent on positive (or at least not dismissive) press coverage in order to make their case to voters, especially during the nomination stage. The sheer number of different issues that may become relevant during a presidential campaign may either neutralize or intensify the influence of the press, depending on whether they are "pocketbook" issues that are grasped with relative ease by voters or "style" issues that owe their existence as issues to the attention paid them by the mass media.

BOX 3.2. In the Arena:
Newspaper Endorsements in 2012

It was a close race in newspaper endorsements, too. According to *Editor & Publisher* magazine, in 2012, 191 newspapers endorsed Barack Obama compared to 212 opting for Mitt Romney. By comparison, in 2008, Obama had 287 endorsements to John McCain's 159 and in 2004, John Kerry received 213 endorsements compared to 205 for George W. Bush. Obama, however, won the circulation war. The reported circulation of the newspapers endorsing him was 17,824,339 compared to 12,683,375 for papers favoring Romney.

Among the largest circulation papers endorsing Obama in 2012 were the *New York Times, Washington Post, Los Angeles Times, Chicago Tribune, Boston Globe, Seattle Times, San Jose Mercury News, Minneapolis Star Tribune, Saint Louis Post Dispatch, Denver Post, Pittsburgh Post Gazette, San Francisco Chronicle, Hartford Courant, Philadelphia Inquirer, Miami Herald, Detroit Free Press*, and *Cleveland Plain Dealer*.

Among the leading circulation papers endorsing Romney were the *New York Daily News, Houston Chronicle, Fort Worth Star-Telegram, New York Post, Boston Herald, Des Moines Register, Dallas Morning News, Columbus Dispatch, Washington Times, Arkansas Democrat Gazette, Arizona Republic, Oklahoman, Omaha World-Herald, Albuquerque Journal*, and *Las Vegas Review Journal*.

Source: *Editor & Publisher*, "2012 Presidential Endorsements," http://www.editorandpublisher.com/election/.
Editor & Publisher, "Tally of Newspaper Endorsements—Obama in a Landslide, at 287 to 159." http://www.editorandpublisher.com/eandp/search/article_display.jsp?vnu_content_id=1003875230.

Television

Since the 1960s, television has eclipsed newspapers as the most important and influential news medium in the United States. A 2012 survey by the Pew Research Center found that 69 percent of respondents named television as a primary source for news about political campaigns, compared to 34 percent for the Internet, 22 percent for newspapers, and 16 percent for radio.[76] The influence of television on presidential elections extends well beyond the coverage of campaigns by journalists. Expenditures for television advertising dependably constitute the largest single budget item of any serious presidential campaign.

Many observers consider the "television age" in American politics to have begun in 1960, when presidential candidates John F. Kennedy and Richard Nixon participated in a series of televised debates—inaugurating what has now become a quadrennial tradition. Almost uniformly, accounts of the 1960 campaign treat the debates as decisive events that gave Kennedy a crucial advantage in what turned out to be a very close election. The handsome, poised Kennedy came across very well on television, especially in comparison to Nixon's shifty eyes and five-o'clock shadow. In fact, the belief that Americans who listened to the debates on the radio (and thus judged the candidates purely on the basis of their words, not their looks) considered Nixon the winner, while television viewers favored Kennedy, has become a staple of American campaign lore, although little evidence actually exists to substantiate it.[77]

To candidates, strategists, pundits, and media critics alike, the lesson of the 1960 debates is clear: television coverage can significantly influence the outcome of elections, and the medium tends to reward superficiality over substance. The truth is probably more complex. Television's moving pictures and sound give it an immediacy that print journalism lacks. The medium is also better suited to covering politics as a battle of personalities than of ideas; in-depth discussions of policy tend to lack the necessary visual images to make compelling television. At the same time, the same factors that limit the influence of newspapers on the course of electoral campaigns often similarly constrain the effects of electronic media as well. Television coverage of politics is often intentionally bland in order to minimize controversy, many viewers adhere to their preexisting political beliefs and evaluations even in the face of the contradictory opinions of TV talking heads, and most Americans won't receive even strong, compelling political messages in the first place. Ratings for current affairs programming routinely pale in comparison to those for prime-time entertainment, talk shows, sporting events, and other staples of the medium; even "news" broadcasts are devoting more and more attention to human interest stories, celebrity gossip, and other, more popular, topics at the expense of political issues or events. More highly flavored cable news programs tend to attract small audiences of like-minded viewers.

As with newspapers, the influence of television appears to peak during the presidential primary season. Contenders for party nominations are usually much less well-known to the national electorate than incumbent presidents or major-party nominees, allowing media coverage to color the public's perceptions of the candidates. Since primary elections are contested by multiple candidates within the same party, substantive differences among them on salient public policy issues tend to be relatively minor, further encouraging television coverage to focus on the contenders' differing personal lives, styles, personalities, and strategies. And the idiosyncrasies of the primary process itself—beginning with the Iowa caucus and New Hampshire primary in January or February of a presidential election year and continuing through months of sequential primary elections and caucuses in all fifty states—allow for television coverage to exert significant influence on the outcome, as news media interpretations of the results in the early states have proven to have an immense effect on the behavior of voters in subsequent primaries.

For one thing, candidates for the nomination do not automatically receive equal attention from reporters. Candidates must be "taken seriously" by the media in order to earn sufficient, respectful coverage. In 2008, for example, eight Democratic candidates sought their party's nomination for the presidency. Three of them—Representative Dennis Kucinich of Ohio, Senator Chris Dodd of Connecticut, and former senator Mike Gravel of Alaska—were, by media consensus, relegated to a second tier of candidates presumed to have no plausible chance to win the nomination. While they campaigned actively, making personal appearances, raising money, and participating in candidate debates, they were largely ignored by the news media, reducing their slim electoral chances still further.

In 2004, former governor Howard Dean of Vermont was also initially considered a decided underdog in comparison to Senator John Kerry of Massachusetts, Senator John Edwards of North Carolina, Senator Joseph Lieberman of Connecticut, and

Representative Richard Gephardt of Missouri. Dean compensated by attacking his rivals by name for their support of the U.S. invasion of Iraq in early 2003. Since journalists love to cover personal conflict between candidates, Dean's criticisms generated a great deal of publicity for his campaign. While Dean portrayed himself as motivated by principle, he was not reluctant to comment on the political advantages to be had in adopting such an approach. "It's made me into a candidate who's not a long shot anymore," he told reporters. "It's put me into a position where there are now five significant candidates, not four."[78]

But Dean ultimately suffered as much as he benefited from the ways of modern television journalism. Reporters and pundits obsessed with the state of the horse race anointed Dean not only the front-runner but, in many accounts, the presumptive Democratic nominee by early 2004—even though a single primary vote had yet to be cast. Media expectations for Dean's performance in the first-in-the-nation Iowa caucus were therefore extraordinarily high. When he placed a distant third on caucus night, well behind Kerry and Edwards, journalists and pundits on the lookout for surprising results that make a good story gleefully piled on.

Dean's energetic concession speech in Iowa included an improvised exhortation to his followers to take their fight to subsequent primaries and caucuses. After naming a number of states, seemingly at random, Dean raised his fist with an enthusiastic shriek. Footage of the "Dean scream" was replayed endlessly on television over the following days, as political analysts who had just weeks before been soberly predicting a certain Dean nomination now eagerly branded him a loser and perhaps something of a nut. For many Americans who had not been following the race closely until the Iowa caucus, their first televised exposure to Dean was therefore decidedly negative. Unsurprisingly, Dean was never able to work his way back into serious contention, withdrawing from the race several weeks later without winning a single state primary.

The large field of contenders seeking the 2012 Republican presidential nomination similarly discovered the potential power of a single moment on live television to reshape the race and profoundly affect the electoral fortunes of candidates. During an appearance on Fox News Channel on June 12, 2011, former Minnesota governor Tim Pawlenty attacked his absent Republican rival Mitt Romney for enacting universal health care legislation while Romney was governor of Massachusetts, charging that the federal Affordable Care Act signed into law by Barack Obama in 2010 (and which most Republicans strongly opposed) was modeled on Romney's plan. "You don't have to take my word for it," Pawlenty told Fox News host Chris Wallace. "You can take President Obama's word for it. President Obama said that he designed Obamacare after Romneycare and basically made it 'Obamneycare.'"[79] Yet when Pawlenty was invited to repeat his accusations the next day in Romney's presence at a New Hampshire debate attended by both candidates, he declined to confront Romney directly, saying only that Obama had made a connection between the two health care plans without associating himself with the comparison or repeating the "Obamneycare" charge. As *Time* magazine noted, Pawlenty's "wimp out . . . reinforced impressions that the Minnesotan was too mild-mannered for the raucous presidential race," and Pawlenty soon abandoned his campaign after a disappointing performance in a straw poll in Iowa.[80]

With Pawlenty out of the running, Governor Rick Perry of Texas loomed as Romney's most formidable potential challenger for the nomination. Perry could boast a more consistently conservative record in office than the ex-Massachusetts governor, hailed from a large state with an extensive network of deep-pocketed Republican donors, and seemingly held the potential to mobilize the electoral support of evangelical Christians in key primary states. Yet Perry, too, was unmade by poor showings in televised debates. In a November 9, 2011, event broadcast on the CNBC cable network, Perry, who was running on a platform that called for the elimination of three existing federal cabinet departments, could only recall two of them when discussing the issue (Commerce and Education), frantically searching his mind for the third (Energy) before admitting, "I can't. Sorry. Oops!" The incident was sufficiently awkward that even Perry's rivals, visibly uncomfortable as he fumbled to complete his response, tried to jog his memory by suggesting possible answers; Representative Michele Bachmann of Minnesota told a reporter afterward that "we all felt very bad for him."[81] The "oops moment" damaged Perry's standing in the eyes of the news media, and his campaign never recovered.

The rise and fall of these and other candidates reveals much about the role of media attention, particularly television coverage, in shaping the outcome of presidential nominations. Television tends to emphasize candidate personalities and the horse race over qualifications or policy prescriptions. It treats politics as entertainment, hoping that keeping the level of excitement high will keep viewers tuning in. So, according to the study by C. Anthony Broh, reporters do what they can to hype up the contest. They

(1) avoid predictions if they are definitive; (2) avoid reporting percentages if they are not close; (3) report the attitudes and preferences of subgroups that cast doubt on the outcome; (4) compare polls to a time period that can demonstrate a narrowing or constantly close gap between the candidates; (5) report voter reaction to spectacles of the campaign; (6) distort results that do not generate excitement; and (7) question the validity of polls that show a wide gap. Furthermore, they interpret methodological ambiguities involving undecided voters and sampling error in ways that maximize shifts in campaign support.[82]

Candidate choices continuously interact with media interpretations. Hillary Clinton faced a barrage of negative attention after her third-place finish in the Democratic caucus in Iowa and never received coverage as favorable as Barack Obama during the remainder of the 2008 nomination season. In contrast, John McCain's victory in the New Hampshire primary the following week generated a great deal of positive publicity that helped him in subsequent Republican primaries. Knowing that dramaturgical stereotypes (who the good guys are, who the leaders are, who's out in left field, and so on) tend to persist and that the front-runner of today may be carried along only by early exposure, journalists may seek to resist the obvious.[83] This, however, is hard to do, because it must be done within certain rules of the news-gathering business. Newspapers and television news programs require headlines and leads. Ignoring an act can be as dangerous as attending to it, since candidate under- and overexposure may be evident only in retrospect. Since they need news, members of the media are swept along by the tide of events to which they contribute and in which they swim, very much like the rest of us.

For the first thirty years or so of the television age, political coverage was mainly limited to the nightly evening news broadcasts of the three major broadcast networks (NBC, CBS, and ABC), along with various public affairs programs like *Meet the Press*.

The rise of all-news cable channels, beginning with CNN in the 1980s, greatly increased the volume of coverage available. CNN, which once stood alone as a news-only network, spun off several sister channels such as Headline News, and attracted competition from Fox News Channel and MSNBC. Media consultants now speak of a "24-hour news cycle," in which the demand for fresh content for news stories is a round-the-clock constant. Campaigns face a phalanx of journalists and pundits who are perpetually desperate for new things to talk about; as a result, small developments often inspire at least temporary media frenzies. Candidates must be "on" at all times; remarks meant to be private can be picked up by open microphones—such as George W. Bush's vulgar description of a *New York Times* reporter in 2000 or Barack Obama's 2008 characterization of rural Pennsylvania voters as "bitter" and tending to "cling to guns or religion or antipathy to people who aren't like them or anti-immigrant sentiment or anti-trade sentiment as a way to explain their frustrations"—and replayed *ad infinitum* on cable news. These episodes tend to pass without major long-term effects, but candidates concerned about their portrayal in the news media seek to avoid them whenever possible.

Much of the programming aired on cable news channels does not constitute "news" at all. These media outlets often devote less time to original political reporting than to analysis and opinion. Political analysts tend to be primarily interested in describing and elaborating campaign strategy, discussing the results of public opinion polls and other measures of the candidate horse race, and making predictions about the outcome of elections and other major political events (such as the selection of running mates). Commentators often represent a particular ideological perspective that largely determines their interpretation of the candidates and campaigns. Political junkies may tune in to satisfy their particular interest in the details of the campaign or to hear reinforcement of their political views, but most Americans tend to be less interested, limiting the potential influence of such pronouncements on public opinion or voting behavior in the mass electorate.

The Internet and Other New Media

A growing number of Americans get most of their news about candidates and campaigns from the Internet via computers and cell phones. Young people, in particular, are especially likely to look online for political information. This trend will only continue to increase over time, making political content on the World Wide Web an important segment of news media coverage in future elections.

Many of the most widely visited websites for information about current affairs are maintained by established news organizations such as CNN and the *New York Times*.[84] The content on these sites generally mirrors that of the organizations' print or television coverage, although special online-only features are becoming more common. While the increasing popularity of the Internet as a source for news has further reinforced the growing demand for political content originally prompted by the rise of cable television's twenty-four-hour news cycle, placing a great deal of pressure on organizations to be the first to report breaking news in order to scoop the competition, many Web users rely on the sites of prestigious newspapers and television channels to supply them with information about political events. Heavily trafficked portal sites such as Yahoo, MSN, and America Online also feature top news stories on their front pages, mostly courtesy of wire services that supply stories to newspapers. To many people, therefore, the Internet serves as a convenient vehicle for information transmission, but the content that they consume online is not unique to the Web; it largely mimics the coverage available elsewhere in newspapers or on television.

For users who maintain a particular interest in politics, however, the Internet offers an unmatched array of sources that generate a constant stream of information. Some online enterprises, such as Politico, focus specifically on the political world; others, such as Slate or Buzzfeed, combine political coverage with other forms of news and entertainment content. Many websites cater to audiences with particular ideological or partisan leanings. The Huffington Post, Salon, ThinkProgress, and Talking Points Memo are popular sites among liberal Democrats, while conservative Republicans prefer the Daily Caller, Breitbart, Newsmax, and the Blaze. In the early years of the Internet, online-only ventures were mostly devoted to supplying opinion and commentary on current events, or to aggregating and promoting news stories that were first broken by other, more traditional journalistic outlets. Today, however, many of these sites engage in original reporting as well, and it is now quite common for hints of new political developments to surface first online. With social media platforms such as Facebook and Twitter allowing journalists, campaign professionals, and attentive voters to keep tabs on political events on a minute-by-minute basis over the course of the day (and night), contemporary presidential campaigns occur in a state of permanent media frenzy.

The Internet also provides the opportunity for like-minded citizens to interact with each other and engage in various forms of political activism. A number of websites, most notably Daily Kos (for Democrats) and RedState (for Republicans), allow readers to comment on stories, post their own original content, and engage in political discussions. Users of these sites also coordinate volunteer efforts and hold online fund-raising drives on behalf of favored candidates.

The advent of the Internet age has fundamentally changed the behavior of candidates and campaigns. Its unparalleled capacity for transmitting information—not just text, but audio and video clips as well—around the world means that any political development can be instantly disseminated to the entire nation. Campaigns locked in electoral combat now race to counter any attack from the other side immediately after it emerges; after the rise of social media, one campaign staffer noted, "Rapid response became more rapid. It became almost instantaneous."[85] Tactics have also evolved in response to technological change. Campaign managers now routinely send workers called "trackers" to follow opposing candidates at all public events with a video camera in tow, hoping to capture hard evidence of any misstatement or gaffe that might "go viral" on the Internet—a practice that has been known to ensnare politicians in controversy from time to time.[86]

On September 17, 2012, the website of the liberal opinion magazine *Mother Jones* released excerpts from a surreptitiously filmed video recording of Republican presidential nominee Mitt Romney speaking to a small group of donors at a private fund-raising event in Florida earlier in the year. In the footage, Romney stated that "there are 47 percent of the people who will vote for [Obama] no matter what . . . who are dependent upon government, who believe that they are victims, who believe that government has a responsibility to care for them. . . . These are people who pay no income tax. . . . And so my job is not to worry about these people. I'll never convince them that they should take personal responsibility and care for their lives."[87]

The release of what soon became known as the "47 percent" video immediately roiled the presidential race. At a hastily organized press conference hours after the first excerpts surfaced, Romney acknowledged that his remarks were "not elegantly stated," but stood behind the substance of his argument.[88] But Romney found it difficult to put the story behind him. After *Mother Jones* uploaded the footage to the video hosting site YouTube, it attracted over 3 million views in a single week, and the remarks became easy fodder for pundits, talk show hosts, and late-night comedians, as well as the Obama campaign.[89] Several weeks later, after perceiving that he had been damaged politically by the release of the video, Romney reversed course, telling Sean Hannity of Fox News Channel that "I said something that's just completely wrong. . . . My life has shown that I care about 100 percent [of Americans], and that's been demonstrated throughout my life. And this campaign is about the 100 percent."[90]

The 2008 and 2012 Obama campaigns set new standards for creative use of electronic technologies that were central to their candidate's success. Five aspects of Obama's use of the Internet and new media amounted to an approach that future campaigns are sure to emulate. First, candidate speeches and staff video statements were deployed regularly on the campaign site, the candidate's Facebook site and on YouTube, giving viewers a sense of membership in the campaign. Second, the campaign created ads that only appeared on these Internet sites. Third, the campaign site provided a variety of means for volunteers to contact voters through information on the website. Fourth, the campaign website, following the 2004 innovations of the Dean campaign, facilitated meet-ups among Obama supporters, a sort of Internet-driven social networking. Fifth, the campaign website provided a wide range of contribution options for supporters, inviting even very small contributions.

The exploding popularity of social media, especially Facebook and Twitter, prior to 2012 also prompted the candidates to raise their investment and engagement in these new channels of personal communication. Obama adviser Stephanie Cutter explained how these networks were used by her campaign:

> Given our challenges in dealing with the traditional news media, we saw an opportunity to go around that filter and directly to our supporters and those that we needed to persuade, which was a much more valuable communication to them than reading something in a newspaper. We had 33 million people on Facebook following Barack Obama. Those 33 million were friends with 90 percent of Facebook users in the United States. . . . So we could communicate with 90 percent of Facebook users in this country, which in sum total is more than the people that voted for us. So we did that very diligently. It was largely a positive conversation online. Because when you're communicating with people on Facebook . . . it's about getting them to share something with their friends. They're more likely to share something if they're proud of it. . . . People trust their information when it's coming from a Facebook friend much more than if it's me on TV saying something.[91]

In addition, the Obama campaign employed its Internet operation to facilitate grassroots campaign training. Reflecting the candidate's background as a community organizer, the campaign devoted great resources to training of volunteers at "Camp Obama," where attendees went through "a vigorous two to four day program" including "training on setting up and running phone banks, planning and organizing a door knocking program." The goal, according the campaign website, was to create "self sufficient, independent teams that take responsibility for all aspects of a campaign within their congressional district" and who would be in daily cybercontact with campaign headquarters.[92]

The Internet and grassroots efforts, combined with polling, gave the Obama campaign impressive amounts of "real-time" data that allowed them to be tactically quite agile throughout the primary and general election campaign. Obama's campaign manager, David Plouffe, described how these various approaches produced tactical prowess:

> We'd say ok, if the election were held this week based on all our data, put it all in a blender, where are we? And obviously, with technology today, we could measure this very carefully. . . . It makes you enormously agile. You've got real-time data, and that makes you make scheduling decisions and resource-allocation decisions and where to send surrogates and you're adjusting those by the end multiple times a day. Not just down to the media market, but down to chunks of voters in those media markets.[93]

Future presidential campaigns will build on these innovations.

INCUMBENCY AS A RESOURCE: THE PRESIDENCY

The presidency is one resource that, in any given election year, must of necessity be monopolized by one party or the other. A president seeking reelection enjoys many special advantages by virtue of incumbency. To begin with, a president is much better known than any challenger can hope to be. Everything the president does is news and is widely reported in the media. The issues to which presidents devote attention are likely to constitute the national agenda because of presidents' unique visibility and capacity to center attention on matters that they deem important. To this extent, presidents are in a position to focus public debate on issues they think are most advantageous. Presidents can act and thereby gain credit. If they cannot act, they can accuse Congress of inaction, as Harry Truman did in 1948 and Gerald Ford did in 1976. Since Truman won and Ford lost, this strategy, like all strategies in an uncertain world, evidently has mixed effects.

Faced with a crisis in foreign affairs, and there are many, a president can gain politically by handling it well or by calling on the patriotism of the citizenry to support its chief executive when the nation is in danger. But if the problem lingers, it soon becomes a nagging liability. A significant example of a foreign crisis took place during the early stages of the 1980 campaign, when Iranian revolutionaries seized the American embassy in Teheran on November 4, 1979, taking American diplomats hostage just as Senator Edward Kennedy of Massachusetts announced that he would run for the Democratic nomination against the incumbent president, Jimmy Carter. Before the hostage crisis began, Kennedy was outdistancing Carter in a poll of potential Democratic primary voters by 54 percent to 31 percent (with 15 percent undecided). When the crisis occurred, voters, including Democrats, rallied around the flag, and Carter's support shot up to 48 percent, with 40 percent for Kennedy and 12 percent undecided. Carter announced that he would suspend active campaigning, and he used his crisis responsibilities as a reason to refuse to meet his rival in debates. He continued to campaign from the White House, however, with great success.[94] Unfortunately for President Carter, the crisis dragged on too long, and after he had disposed of the Kennedy primary challenge, Carter's popularity suffered a serious decline, reverting to its pre-crisis level and resulting in his defeat in the general election.

As Carter discovered in 1980, incumbent presidents benefit from international crises on their watch only as long as the American people have confidence in their ability to handle the problem. A successful resolution of the issue may be rewarded with an impressive surge in popularity, but high approval ratings fade over time as the electorate turns its attention to other issues. George H. W. Bush lost his bid for reelection in 1992 despite reaching a job approval rating of 90 percent after the United States successfully drove the Iraqi Army out of the adjacent nation of Kuwait the year before. By the time of the election, Americans' gratitude for Bush's handling of the Persian Gulf crisis had been superseded by widespread disapproval of the performance of the national economy during his tenure in office.

And if the crisis remains unresolved, impatience sets in. American invasions of Korea in the 1950s, Vietnam in the 1960s, and Iraq in 2003 all initially received broad support from the mass public, but as military operations dragged on for several years without clear evidence of resolution or troop withdrawals, Americans increasingly voiced their disapproval of the wars—and of the presidents who started them. Harry Truman (1952) and Lyndon Johnson (1968) both chose not to seek reelection due to their severely weakened public standing as a result of the events in Korea and Vietnam, respectively, while Democratic victories in the 2006 and 2008 elections reflected voters' growing frustration with the performance of George W. Bush in managing the war in Iraq years after U.S. forces first occupied the country.

As the symbol of the nation, presidents can travel and make "nonpolitical" speeches to advance their candidacy subtly while appearing to remain above the partisan fray, in contrast to challengers who can be accused of exploiting troubled times for their own political advantage. Presidents can also use the power of their office to pursue specific policies that may appeal to specific electoral groups. In the midst of his reelection campaign in June 2012, Barack Obama signed an executive order loosening the enforcement of immigration laws on individuals who had entered the United States without authorization as children. This policy change was designed to enhance the president's popularity among Latinos, a key voting bloc in the upcoming presidential election. Stuart Stevens of the opposition Romney campaign observed in retrospect that Obama's action "raised the profile of the issue, and that was the sort of thing you can do as president. I felt it was very smartly played. That is an example of the advantage that . . . incumbents have."[95]

The life of the sitting president is not necessarily one of undiluted joy, however. If the national economy worsens, if a natural disaster strikes, or if a battle is lost to hostile forces, the incumbent is likely at least over the long run to be blamed. Whether actually responsible or not, presidents are held accountable for bad times and have to take the consequences.[96] Herbert Hoover felt deeply the sting of this phenomenon when the people punished him as incumbent president for the Great Depression, turning him out of office in a landslide in the election of 1932.[97] The defeat of incumbent presidents Gerald Ford (1976), Jimmy Carter (1980), and George H. W. Bush (1992) were also primarily due to perceptions of weak national economic performance. Incumbents Ronald Reagan, Bill Clinton, and Barack Obama were also blamed for hard economic times in the first two years of their administrations; voters expressed their disapproval with the status quo in the 1982, 1994, and 2010 midterm elections, respectively, by voting out large numbers of the president's partisan allies in Congress. Fortunately for all three presidents, the national economy in each case soon began to recover. By the time each incumbent stood for reelection two years later, voters had become more positive about the direction of the country, and responded by awarding him a second term in the White House.

Incumbents have a record; they have or have not done things, and they may be held accountable for their sins of omission or commission. Not so the candidates out of office, who can criticize freely without always presenting realistic alternatives or necessarily taking their own advice once elected. Barack Obama opposed the Iraq war and strongly criticized the George W. Bush administration's handling of the ensuing occupation, but once in office adopted policies quite similar to those in place at the time of his inauguration. The incumbent is naturally cast as the defender of the current administration and the challenger as the attacker who promises better things to come. We cannot expect to hear the person in office say that the opposition could probably perform as well or to hear the challenger declare that he or she really could not do any better than the incumbent, although in a political system that encourages compromise and has enormous built-in inertia, both statements may be close to the truth.

Barring catastrophic events—depression, war, scandal—the political power of modern presidents is strong enough to assure renomination by their own party within the two-term limit imposed by the 22nd Amendment to the Constitution. This is not merely because the presidency is the greatest, most visible office in the land, with claims on the loyalty of many, if not all, potential rivals. The president's party can hardly hope to win by repudiating the president. To refuse the incumbent the nomination would, most politicians feel, be tantamount to confessing political bankruptcy or ineptitude.

This rule was bent but not broken in 1980 by Senator Edward Kennedy's prenomination opposition to Jimmy Carter and in 1976 by former governor Ronald Reagan's challenge to Gerald Ford. Nor was it broken in 1968. The challenges of Eugene McCarthy and Robert Kennedy to Lyndon Johnson in that year demonstrated that the costs of party insurgency are high: not only do insurgents rarely win their party's nomination, but when internal party divisions are strong, their party usually loses the general election. It was not only the fact that Edward Kennedy sought to take the Democratic nomination away from Carter in 1980, but also that he persisted right up through the convention, refusing to give Carter his wholehearted endorsement, that hurt the Democrats. Consequently candidate Carter was unable to focus on his Republican opponent as early as he would have liked. No subsequent president has faced a primary challenger with a serious chance of winning the nomination; Ronald Reagan (1984), Bill Clinton (1996), George W. Bush (2004), and Barack Obama (2012) all ran unopposed for renomination, while George H. W. Bush (1992) faced a protest candidate in challenger Pat Buchanan, a former White House aide and conservative columnist who ran an initially energetic campaign but never posed a serious electoral threat.

INCUMBENCY AS A LIABILITY: THE VICE PRESIDENCY

The advantages of incumbency do not necessarily extend to a sitting vice president seeking to succeed a president of the same party, as Richard Nixon discovered in 1960, Hubert Humphrey in 1968, and Al Gore in 2000. A vice president suffers from the disadvantages of having to defend an existing record without necessarily benefiting from it. He or she cannot differ too much with the current administration without alienating the president and causing an internal rift in the party. At the same time, a vice president cannot claim experience in the presidential office. Even voters who approve of the performance of the incumbent administration may not give the vice president any credit for it. This is the most difficult strategic problem of all for candidates.[98]

George H. W. Bush in 1988 was the first sitting vice president to be elected in succession to a retiring president since Martin Van Buren succeeded Andrew Jackson in 1836. Why, despite the historical rarity of the event, did Bush win? He obtained the nomination of his party largely, it appears, because primary voters in the Republican Party considered him the logical successor to Ronald Reagan, and Reagan was extremely popular at the end of his second term. This may help also to explain why Bush won the general election. George H. W. Bush was of course not an incumbent president, but as the sitting vice president he was as close to an incumbent president as it is possible to be without actually being one. In the 1988 election, most incumbents, whether they were Democrats or Republicans, did extraordinarily well for all offices, as they usually do in conditions of peace and prosperity. Scholars who use sophisticated models to attempt to forecast presidential elections have, on the whole, employed assumptions stressing such variables as the condition of the economy somewhat in advance of the election, and they all produced numbers suggesting a Bush victory.[99] Indeed, some of them did so even during the spring and summer months when Democratic nominee Michael Dukakis was leading Bush in public opinion polls.

Vice President Bush also may have run a more effective campaign than his Democratic rival. There is unusually strong agreement among campaign professionals that Dukakis campaigned badly in the general election. This overlooks the fact that he did well enough in the primary season, winning the Democratic nomination in a crowded field of candidates, in handling the demands of rival candidate Jesse Jackson thereafter, and in his vice presidential pick of the magisterial Senator Lloyd Bentsen of Texas. There is, likewise, strong agreement that the Bush campaign was well tailored to make the best of the vice president's chances, conveniently overlooking Bush's ill-advised selection of Senator Dan Quayle of Indiana as his running mate. So if we accept the professional assessment of the effects of the campaign—as on the whole we do—we must do so in the face of the fact that every winning campaign looks better in retrospect and every losing campaign looks worse than it probably was.

In the presidential election of 2000, Vice President Al Gore faced the strategic difficulty of claiming credit for the Clinton-Gore administration's popular economic policies while simultaneously distancing himself personally from Bill Clinton in the wake of the Monica Lewinsky affair. Gore was disadvantaged by his proximity to Clinton and the lack of an independent grant of authority by which he could demonstrate that he was his own man. His difficulties ultimately resided in the weak constitutional powers and perceived junior partnership of the vice presidency. Americans often view vice presidents as something of a comic sidekick to the president, which can make it difficult for them to be taken seriously in their own right as strong and capable leaders. Yet the vice president's status as the successor to the presidency on the occasion of the incumbent's death or resignation requires that the position be filled by an experienced and accomplished figure. From this dilemma flow the problems characteristic of the vice presidency.

For much of American history, vice presidents were routinely shut out of the presidential decision-making process. Before Harry Truman assumed the presidency upon the death of Franklin D. Roosevelt in April 1945, for example, he had met with Roosevelt only briefly and infrequently and was largely unaware of the president's declining health. "Boys, if you ever pray, pray for me now," remarked a shaken Truman to a gathering of newspaper reporters one day after becoming president. "I don't know whether you fellows ever had a load of hay fall on you, but when they told me yesterday what had happened, I felt like the moon, the stars, and all the planets had fallen on me." Since the 1970s, however, the vice president has become more likely to serve as a key member of the presidential administration, working closely with the president as a trusted political adviser, liaison to influential interest groups or members of Congress, emissary to foreign leaders, or (in the case of Dick Cheney, vice president under George W. Bush) manager of the federal bureaucracy.

In return for continuous exposure to the entire range of problems confronting the government, vastly improved access to the president, and a closer view of the burdens of the presidency, the modern vice president must also carry some of these burdens. Which burdens are carried, how many, and how far are up to the president. Withholding cooperation would impair the vice president's relationship with the president. This would be bound to affect his or her capacity to fulfill the constitutional obligation of the vice presidency, which is to be genuinely prepared in case of dire need.

Vice presidents can hardly fulfill their constitutional responsibilities by resigning, nor, in midterm, can they be dismissed. Thus modern vice presidents must discipline themselves to loyalty to the president. This sometimes has painful consequences for vice presidents, especially when they attempt to emerge from the shadow of the president and run for the presidency on their own. The worst modern case was probably Vice President Hubert Humphrey's difficulty in 1968 in persuading opponents of the Vietnam War that he had deeply disagreed with President Johnson's policies, as he had privately done, while publicly defending them. Even after four years out of office, Walter Mondale found himself criticized for President Carter's perceived failures during the 1984 campaign. In 1988, Vice President George H. W. Bush was alternatively attacked as servile and insufficiently loyal.[100] Like Humphrey and Nixon before him, Bush found it difficult to run independently on his own record. Al Gore in 2000 found the legacy of Bill Clinton's personal behavior in office so burdensome that he was unable to capitalize on the Clinton administration's public record of peace and prosperity.

There seems to be no way for vice presidents to avoid the dilemmas built into the office. Unless scrupulously loyal, they cannot get the access to the president that they need to discharge their constitutional function; when loyal to the president, they are saddled, at least in the short run, with whatever characteristics of the president or the administration's program that the president's enemies or their own care to fasten on them. A vice president sits there in the limelight, visible, vulnerable, and for the most part, powerless.

From 1836 until 1960, when Richard Nixon was nominated, no incumbent vice president was put forward for the presidency. Since 1960, several vice presidents—Johnson, Humphrey, Ford, Mondale, Bush, Quayle, Gore—have run for president in subsequent elections; all but Quayle succeeded in capturing their party's nomination. Johnson and Ford became presidents before seeking election as their party's presidential nominee, but the others did it on their own. Now even defeated vice presidential candidates, from Henry Cabot Lodge to Edmund Muskie to Sargent Shriver to Bob Dole to Joseph Lieberman to John Edwards, often launch their own presidential campaigns four years later.

As long as vice presidents have some chance to eventually run for the presidency, as they do at present, and are not arbitrarily excluded from further consideration as independent political leaders in their own right, there will be plenty of takers for the vice presidential nomination. This contributes to the strength of political parties. Vice presidential nominees can balance tickets, help to unite their party, and campaign effectively with party workers and before the public (as described further in chapter 4). Thus, vice presidential nominees can help elect a president. It is after the campaign is over that the vice president's problems begin.

THE BALANCE OF RESOURCES

Clearly, the social framework within which presidential election strategies must be pursued distributes advantages and disadvantages rather importantly between candidates and parties. We have attempted to explain why the unequal distribution of key resources such as money and control over information do not necessarily or automatically lead to election victories for the parties and candidates who possess and use most of these resources. Might there not, however, be a cumulative effect that would greatly assist those who possessed both more money and more control over information? This effect might develop, but it is not with us at present. The two major parties have enjoyed a relatively close balance regarding money and control of information in recent years. In 2000, the Republican Party and its candidate spent more but the Democrats organized a superior get-out-the-vote effort. In 2004, the spending balance was close to even, with the Republican victory arguably deriving from better strategy, more centralized command of resources, and George W. Bush's status as an incumbent president during wartime. The solid Democratic victory in 2008 came from a clear edge in fund-raising, strategic superiority due to an innovative combination of grassroots tactics supplemented by creative use of new campaign technologies, and, perhaps most importantly, a favorable national political environment due to the unpopularity of the sitting Republican president. The narrower Democratic triumph in 2012 reflected a more even financial playing field and a modest edge due to the incumbency of Obama. It is hard to see a clear pattern of partisan advantage in these recent contests, suggesting that the fundamental factors shaping presidential outcomes do not strongly and consistently favor either side.

PART II

Sequences

THE NEXT two chapters follow the chronology of the election year, first describing the procedures governing the nominations of the major candidates, then discussing the course of the campaign leading up to election night. The behavior of candidates, delegates, journalists, and voters can best be understood in the strategic context of the institutional rules structuring the electoral process.

CHAPTER 4

The Nomination Process

IN ORDER to be nominated by a major party for president of the United States, a candidate must win the votes of a simple majority of delegates to the party's national convention, held every summer of a presidential election year. Before the 1970s, most of these delegates were chosen by state party organizations under the control of governors, senators, and other party elites; ambitious politicians seeking a presidential nomination thus spent the years before an election courting the support of these leaders. Now, candidates win nominations by accumulating delegates pledged to their candidacy via a months-long sequence of primary elections and caucuses held in all fifty states, the District of Columbia, and every U.S. territory—a time-consuming, complicated, and costly process.[1]

When the field of potential nominees includes only one major candidate, such as an incumbent president seeking renomination for a second term in office without significant opposition within the party, the rules governing presidential nominations do not matter much. But if two or more serious contenders emerge, the procedural mechanics of the nomination system direct the process by which the field of candidates is narrowed to a single party choice. Some rules apply equally to both sides, while others are unique to the Democrats or the Republicans. Some are consistent and long-standing, while others are the subject of frequent revision. Here are the most important rules in their current form:

1. Both national parties require all pledged delegates (i.e., delegates who are chosen to attend the national party convention as formally committed supporters of a particular presidential candidate) to be selected within a roughly three-month window from early March to early June of a presidential election year (except for those delegates representing states that have received special permission to vote earlier, as noted below).[2] In both parties, the vast majority of convention delegates are chosen either in state primaries, in which party-affiliated voters cast a ballot at a traditional polling place for their favored candidate, or in caucuses, which consist of a number of meetings around the state in which party members discuss and measure support for each of the candidates. As a practical matter, candidates must contest the vast

majority of primaries and caucuses on the nomination calendar in order to collect enough delegates to win.[3]

2. Both parties grant special dispensation to a few states to hold early primaries and caucuses before the rest of the nation is allowed to begin the delegate selection process. The first event on the nomination calendar is always the Iowa caucus, held in January or February of a presidential election year, followed closely by the New Hampshire primary. In recent years, the Nevada caucus and South Carolina primary have then followed. Other states have chosen from time to time to schedule primaries and caucuses prior to the normal selection window to compete with the authorized early states, though they risk incurring penalties from the national party organizations (such as a severe reduction or outright elimination of their delegate seats at the national convention) by doing so.

3. For both Democrats and Republicans, the number of delegates allocated to each state is based on formulas that take into account both the state's number of electoral votes and the extent to which it has supported the party's candidates in recent elections. Thus, candidates for the nomination have a particular incentive to win primaries and caucuses in populous states that usually vote for their party. Democrats also award bonus delegates to states holding their primaries and caucuses in April or later in order to discourage excessive front-loading of the nomination calendar.

4. In the Democratic Party, a candidate in a state primary or caucus who receives more than 15 percent of the vote in any congressional district within the state is entitled by national party rules to gain a proportionate share of the delegates chosen in that district. Democrats also require state delegations to be evenly divided between men and women. The Republican Party, by contrast, allows states to choose proportional representation, winner-take-all allocation, or a combination thereof for awarding delegates to candidates based on the results of primary elections or caucuses. However, states holding Republican primaries or caucuses before March 15 are not permitted to employ pure winner-take-all rules (with the exception of the four designated early states).

5. Democratic elected officials and members of the Democratic National Committee hold automatic seats as voting delegates to the national convention and are not required to pledge their support to any candidate as a condition of delegate status. These "superdelegates" constituted 19 percent of the Democratic delegates in 2008 and 13 percent in 2012. On the Republican side, a smaller group of party officials similarly receives automatic voting rights at the convention regardless of favored candidate.

These rules are central to the presidential nomination system; they shape the strategies adopted by candidates. Since the party reforms of the early 1970s, the most important attribute of the nomination process is that candidates compete in state contests—primaries and caucuses—in which delegates are selected by large popular electorates. The rules of delegate selection and fund-raising require candidates to obtain a broad base of popular support both within states (for delegates) and across states (for money). These considerations encourage candidates to act as early as possible to form campaign organizations and solicit support from party leaders, financial donors, and activists. While the Iowa caucus and New Hampshire primary ostensibly mark the beginning of the electoral calendar, serious competition among candidates actually starts many months before the voters begin to select pledged delegates to the national conventions.

BEFORE THE PRIMARIES

One dependable rule of thumb under the current system is that the more people you have to convince, the more time it takes. The nomination process has become very long, giving early starters an advantage. Candidates must also raise a great deal of money from private donors in order to purchase television airtime and construct strong campaign organizations. This, too, dictates an earlier start to the campaign. Anybody who is already familiar to the American public—whether an incumbent of high office or a well-known celebrity—enjoys an initial advantage due to widespread name recognition, but most candidates must rely on heavy advertising and news media coverage in order to introduce themselves to voters beyond their home states who may not have previously heard of them. In December 2006, shortly before Senator Barack Obama of Illinois announced that he would seek the presidency in 2008, only 53 percent of Americans surveyed by Gallup knew enough about Obama to express an opinion of him; this figure had increased to 87 percent by the end of 2007, reflecting the publicity received by Obama's presidential campaign over the intervening year.[4]

Among the axioms of existing conventional wisdom to bite the dust in 1972, the first post-reform election, was the notion that an early declaration of candidacy was a sign of weakness and that it therefore behooved potential contenders to postpone jumping into the race, with all the inconvenience and running around that active campaigning entails, as long as they possibly could. Such coyness ultimately destroyed the chances of the initial Democratic front-runner in 1972, Senator Edmund Muskie of Maine, who took too long to organize an effective campaign. In 1976 this lesson was greatly reinforced when former governor Jimmy Carter of Georgia, a virtually unknown outsider before the primaries began, parlayed early, narrow wins in Iowa, New Hampshire, and Florida into the Democratic nomination. Candidates now recognize that there is an advantage to forming their campaigns as soon as possible in order to hire capable staff, build an organizational infrastructure, raise money, and attract attention from journalists and support from other politicians and party activists; as a result, unofficial signals of likely candidacies in the next election now routinely emerge during the first year of a new presidential term, with formal entries into the race usually occurring in the first six months of the year before the election.

As the most recent presidential election to produce highly competitive nomination contests in both parties, 2008 serves as an illustrative example of the extent to which the active campaign begins in earnest long before the voting starts. Multiple potential candidates started to lay the groundwork for a possible 2008 campaign by the spring of 2006—nearly two full years before the first presidential primaries. By April 2007, the Republican field officially included Senators John McCain of Arizona and Sam Brownback of Kansas, former governors Mitt Romney of Massachusetts, Mike Huckabee of Arkansas, Tommy Thompson of Wisconsin, and Jim Gilmore of Virginia, former mayor of New York Rudy Giuliani, and Representatives Duncan Hunter of California, Tom Tancredo of Colorado, and Ron Paul of Texas. Among the Democrats, Senators Hillary Clinton of New York, Barack Obama of Illinois, Chris Dodd of Connecticut, and Joe Biden of Delaware had announced presidential bids, as had former senators John

Edwards of North Carolina and Mike Gravel of Alaska, Governor Bill Richardson of New Mexico, and Representative Dennis Kucinich of Ohio.

As some contenders began to formally organize their campaigns, hiring experienced consultants and fundraisers while building support among political leaders in key states, others, after testing the waters, decided not to jump in. Senators Bill Frist of Tennessee and George Allen of Virginia declined to enter the race for the Republican nomination after initially signaling interest, as did Senator Evan Bayh of Indiana and former governor Mark Warner of Virginia on the Democratic side. Though Brownback, Tancredo, Thompson, and Gilmore all briefly pursued active campaigns, they withdrew before the primaries began in the face of scant public support. The large sums of money that several candidates in both parties had raised by midsummer of 2007, six full months before the first primary elections, demonstrated that the presidential race was already well underway at that point (see table 4.1).

The importance of an early start in contemporary nomination contests was confirmed by the plight of former senator Fred Thompson of Tennessee (no relation to Tommy Thompson), who deliberated for months before finally announcing his candidacy for the 2008 Republican nomination in September 2007—long after most of his rivals. Not only did Fred Thompson's tardiness cost him potential supporters who had in the meantime endorsed one of his opponents, but his late start and relaxed campaign schedule also suggested less than total commitment to a pursuit of the presidency. He finished a distant third in the Iowa caucuses and received only 1 percent of the vote in the New Hampshire primary, folding his campaign soon thereafter.

In 2012, Barack Obama's incumbency ensured that only the Republican Party would have a competitive nomination contest. Eventual nominee Mitt Romney formally declared his bid for the nomination on June 2, 2011, although the announcement was rendered somewhat anticlimactic by the fact that Romney had been behaving like a presidential candidate in all but name—traveling to Iowa and New Hampshire, campaigning and raising money for Republican congressional and gubernatorial candidates, and releasing a book entitled *No Apology* that was highly critical of Obama's

TABLE 4.1. Early Money in the 2008 Election

Democrats		Republicans	
Hillary Clinton	62.2	Mitt Romney	44.4
Barack Obama	58.9	Rudy Giuliani	34.2
John Edwards	23.2	John McCain	24.7
Bill Richardson	13.3	Sam Brownback	3.3
Chris Dodd	12.1	Ron Paul	3.0
Joe Biden	6.5	Tom Tancredo	2.8
Dennis Kucinich	1.1	Duncan Hunter	1.4
Mike Gravel	0.2	Mike Huckabee	1.3
		Tommy Thompson	0.9
		Jim Gilmore	0.4
TOTAL	177.5	*TOTAL*	116.4

Source: Federal Election Commission quarterly reports, http://query.nictusa.com/pres/.
Note: Figures represent funds raised between January 1 and June 30, 2007, in millions of dollars.

performance as president—for more than a year by the time he officially launched his 2012 campaign. In fact, it was only a slight exaggeration to characterize Romney as having barely left the campaign trail since his withdrawal from the previous nomination contest in 2008.

At the time of his official entry, Romney joined former House speaker Newt Gingrich of Georgia, Representative Ron Paul of Texas, former governors Tim Pawlenty of Minnesota and Gary Johnson of New Mexico, and Georgia businessman Herman Cain as declared candidates for the 2012 Republican nomination. Within a few weeks, the field expanded further to include former senator Rick Santorum of Pennsylvania, former governor Jon Huntsman of Utah, and Representative Michele Bachmann of Minnesota. Governor Rick Perry of Texas was a late entrant into the race, formally announcing his candidacy on August 13, 2011; like Fred Thompson four years before, Perry's comparative delay in building a presidential campaign may have contributed to his ultimate lack of success in debating his rivals, constructing a strong field organization, and winning support from voters in early states. As Perry chief strategist Dave Carney admitted in retrospect, "I think there are hundreds of things that we could have done differently that would [have made Perry] better prepared to run. When you have never talked to legislators and county chairmen and political activists in the early states, when you are doing that days before getting in the race, and raising money and getting up to speed on issues, clearly that's not ideal. . . . We should have, if he was going to do this, started years ago."[5]

During the long pre-primary phase, the candidates are not just raising money and hiring campaign staff. They also take the ideological temperature of their party, attempting to shape a message that will appeal to the loyal partisans who turn out to vote in state primaries and caucuses. Knowing that most of the voters in Republican primaries are philosophically right of center, Mitt Romney, Rick Santorum, Newt Gingrich, and their rivals spent a lot of time in 2011 and 2012 aiming their remarks on issues such as taxes, health care, and immigration toward this part of the political spectrum. Similarly, the fact that the dominant faction of the Democratic Party is left of center has not been lost among Democratic contenders. When former governor Howard Dean of Vermont unexpectedly gained momentum in early 2003 by criticizing his Democratic opponents for supporting the U.S. invasion of Iraq ordered by George W. Bush, he sent them scrambling to emphasize the ways in which they disagreed with Bush's Iraq policies, lest they be punished by Democratic primary voters for insufficient ideological loyalty. This issue emerged again in 2008; Barack Obama's consistent opposition to the Iraq War put fellow candidates Hillary Clinton, John Edwards, Chris Dodd, and Joe Biden, who had also all voted to authorize the operation as senators in 2002, on the defensive during their battle for the Democratic nomination.

Another candidate objective during the pre-primary phase is to achieve the status of being appraised by the news media as a "serious contender." This ordinarily requires that a candidate should have previously won at least one major election for public office and raised a competitive amount of campaign cash. In addition, journalists pay attention to signs that candidates are hiring experienced, competent staff—campaign managers, strategists and spokespeople, fundraisers, pollsters, media consultants, speechwriters, policy analysts—and are establishing organized field campaigns in early primary states, maintaining a high level of public activity, and doing respectably in straw polls conducted at various party meetings around the country and in public opinion surveys of potential primary voters—polls that everyone says "don't count," although of course they do. All this activity is monitored by members of the increasingly watchful news media, who in turn pronounce candidates to be "serious" or "not serious," with attendant consequences for the candidate's credibility with potential donors of campaign funds.

Although objective measures of the relative standing of the candidates are scarce during the pre-primary period, the political press is constantly preoccupied with the status of the horse race—who's ahead, who's behind, who's gaining or losing support. One yardstick, increasingly relied upon by media analysts, is provided by the federal requirement that presidential candidates regularly report their fund-raising and spending totals. Howard Dean's rise from near-obscurity to status as a leading candidate for the 2004 Democratic nomination in the eyes of journalists was due in large part to his success at attracting financial contributions in the summer and fall of 2003, which prompted a great deal of positive media coverage. Similarly, Barack Obama's capacity to represent a significant challenge to Hillary Clinton for the 2008 Democratic nomination was first revealed in April 2007 with the public release of the candidates' quarterly fund-raising figures. Despite being a relative newcomer to national politics with only a little more than two years of experience in the U.S. Senate, Obama raised $25 million in contributions during the first quarter of 2007, nearly as much as Clinton, and proceeded to outraise her over the next three months, much of it from small donations via the Internet. According to media commentators, Obama's unexpected financial success soon established him as Clinton's chief rival within the party, while other candidates who were less adept at attracting donations became relegated to second-tier status. Not since Jimmy Carter in 1976 had a candidate emerged so suddenly to become a serious contender for the presidency.

Public endorsements by prominent party leaders such as state governors, members of Congress, and other well-known officials can also serve as an indicator of the health of a presidential campaign. In 1999, George W. Bush, then the governor of Texas, succeeded in winning the support of all of his fellow Republican governors before the voting in Iowa even began—a formidable achievement that undoubtedly dissuaded other potential candidates from jumping in the race. Both John Kerry in 2004 and Barack Obama in 2008 benefited from the personal backing of Senator Edward Kennedy of Massachusetts, a figure who commanded considerable respect and affection among Democratic Party activists. In some cases, a lack of endorsements may be an equally telling measure of a candidate's standing among his or her political peers. John Edwards trailed far behind both Obama and Hillary Clinton in winning endorsements for his 2008 presidential candidacy; even Kerry, who had selected Edwards as his own vice presidential running mate in 2004, opted to endorse Obama instead. This pronounced lack of enthusiasm among Democratic leaders was fully vindicated when Edwards became publicly entangled in a major scandal later in the year that brought his political career to an ignominious end.

Televised debates are another means by which candidates can distinguish themselves in the months before the primaries and caucuses begin. The near-ubiquity of cable news channels and Internet video outlets ensures that journalists, party activists, and engaged citizens who are interested in evaluating the candidates' debate performances firsthand now have ample opportunity to do so. The Republican presidential candidates participated in an extensive series of more than twenty debates in 2011 and 2012, several of which produced key turning points in the race. In particular, poor debate performances by Tim Pawlenty and Rick Perry severely damaged their presidential candidacies (as described further in chapter 3), while other candidates with limited financial resources, such as Newt Gingrich and Herman Cain, took advantage of the national stage provided by these events to attract free positive publicity. Attention-grabbing unscripted moments, whether to the benefit or detriment of the candidate, frequently became fodder for cable news replays and viral video clips on the Internet for days and weeks afterward. Mitt Romney's campaign manager Matt Rhoades later remarked that "it was just shocking how [the debates] shook up the race week after week and how many people were watching these things."[6]

However, Republican leaders concluded in retrospect that the debates had encouraged candidates to compete for the support of an ideologically motivated audience by taking sharply conservative policy positions that later proved to be political liabilities in the general election (such as Romney's explanation at a January 2012 debate that his plan to address illegal immigration in the United States amounted to "self-deportation"); they also harbored suspicions that some debate sponsors, such as the left-leaning cable channel MSNBC, intentionally chose unsympathetic moderators or questions in order to portray Republicans in a negative light. After the 2012 election, the Republican National Committee adopted rules requiring televised debates in future Republican nomination contests to be held under the auspices of the RNC itself in partnership with news organizations selected by the national party. Candidates who participate in any other debates will, under the rules, be prohibited from taking part in the officially authorized events.[7]

The lessons of the pre-primary stage in the contemporary nomination process have become clear: long before the voting begins, candidates must work to achieve personal visibility, raise money, and assemble strong campaign organizations. Visibility is important because the news media introduces candidates to the voters and shapes popular perceptions of the various contenders. Money is important because it can buy television advertising and campaign infrastructure that communicates the candidate's message to the public. Organization is important because that is what it takes to turn out supporters in elections. A large field of candidates normally begins the election season with presidential ambitions, making the nomination system a winnowing process in which the successive hurdles of primaries and caucuses knock off more and more contenders until only one survivor remains in each party. In advance of these events, the candidates' tasks are to build financial war chests, hire staff, command as much positive media coverage as they can, and give personal attention to states voting early in the nomination calendar.

Pre-primary activities thus take up more and more time and absorb more and more resources in preparation for the primaries and caucuses that select delegates to the national conventions. The nomination campaign is in full swing long before the first state elections, as candidates battle each other for positive coverage from journalists and support from party officials, interest groups, and financial contributors. This period has been dubbed the "invisible primary" in recognition of the fact that fierce competition among candidates begins well before the voting starts, profoundly shaping the choices made by voters once they enter the process.[8]

IOWA AND NEW HAMPSHIRE:
FIRST IN THE NATION

Due to various accidents of history, the states of Iowa and New Hampshire have achieved what appears to be a perpetual right to hold the first two electoral events of the presidential nomination season every four years. Iowa, which selects its delegates through a series of broadly participatory local, county, and state caucuses and conventions, always votes first, early in the calendar year of a presidential election. And New Hampshire, site of the first primary election, comes next—usually about a week after the Iowa vote.[9]

The Iowa caucus is only the first stage of a delegate selection process that culminates at state party conventions several months later. Although it is the precinct meetings, the early events, that attract media attention, frequently candidates who do not win the caucus end up with delegates from Iowa to the national convention, as John McCain did in 2008 and Mitt Romney did in 2012, because the field of active candidates has usually narrowed considerably by the time of the state-level conventions. Given the complicated relationship between the caucus results and the ultimate composition of Iowa's national convention delegations, it is a wonder that there is so much attention paid to the caucus. The news coverage is heavy because the voting in Iowa and New Hampshire is, in effect, the gateway to a long and complex nomination process, and participants and observers very much want whatever information they can glean from the results in the first two states, if only to position themselves for the next round of events. The media need to know to whom to give special attention. Financial supporters of various candidates want to know whether it is worthwhile to continue to give or steer money to their first choices, or whether it is time to jump to other alternatives. Voters want to know which candidacies are viable, which futile.[10]

Thus the outcomes in Iowa and New Hampshire exert a massive influence on the election results in subsequent primaries and caucuses. Over and over, these two small and not entirely representative states have demonstrated the power to set some candidates on a path to the White House while forcing others to permanently surrender their presidential ambitions. The following historical examples, drawn from the past five decades of post-reform nomination politics, illustrate the repeated capacity of voters in Iowa and New Hampshire to shape the electoral choices of the entire nation.

1972

In 1972 the Republican incumbent, Richard Nixon, faced only token opposition. The Democratic caucus in Iowa, in contrast, was quite important. Operating under obsolete strategic premises, presumed front-runner Senator Edmund Muskie of Maine officially entered the race just three weeks before the Iowa vote. Neither Muskie nor Senator George McGovern of South Dakota invested much effort in Iowa. Muskie defeated McGovern in the caucus by a margin of 36 percent to 23 percent, with another 36 percent of Iowa Democrats remaining uncommitted to any candidate.

The surprising closeness of this result pushed Muskie into overwork and an unaccustomed public display of emotional behavior in front of the offices of the *Union Leader* newspaper in Manchester, New Hampshire.[11] When the news media analysts were finished interpreting the results of the New Hampshire primary, prior expectations that the U.S. senator from a neighboring state should win an overwhelming victory of over 50 percent completely obscured the fact that Muskie had in fact placed first once again (46 percent to 37 percent). Because his win was 4 or 5 points less impressive than expected, thereby supposedly revealing his weakness as a candidate, Muskie's support, especially financial support, began to dry up, and he withdrew from the race altogether by April 27, effectively conceding the nomination to McGovern. The front-running Muskie campaign was nibbled to death by ducks before it began, demonstrating the power of the Iowa and New Hampshire results to determine presidential nominations in the post-reform era.

1976

In 1976, incumbent president Gerald Ford, who had succeeded to the office upon the resignation of Richard Nixon in 1974, faced a serious challenge for the Republican nomination from former California governor Ronald Reagan. Ford won the official Iowa straw poll on the night of the caucus, but by only a small margin (45 percent to 43 percent); both candidates ended up with eighteen delegates to the national convention. Ford's subsequent victory in New Hampshire made him the front-runner for the nomination, although Reagan rallied later in the year.[12]

On the Democratic side, the candidate who focused hardest on Iowa was former governor Jimmy Carter of Georgia. Hamilton Jordan, Carter's campaign manager, put together a strategy that was exactly three events deep, requiring strong showings in Iowa and New Hampshire, followed by a careful positioning as the anti-George Wallace (i.e., racially liberal) southern candidate in the Florida primary.[13] Though he was initially a virtual unknown outside Georgia, Carter's strategy dovetailed nicely with those of his main competitors, Senator Henry (Scoop) Jackson of Washington, who suffered from a late start, and Representative Mo Udall of Arizona, who ran a disorganized campaign. Although he finished as high as second in seven primaries in 1976, Udall came in fifth in Iowa with 6 percent of the vote, behind "uncommitted" with 37 percent of the caucus vote and Carter with 28 percent.

The next day, *New York Times* reporter R. W. Apple minimized the strong uncommitted sentiment and created the first major instance in which the Iowa caucus combined importantly with news media spin to launch a presidential candidacy, writing that Carter "scored an impressive victory in yesterday's Iowa Democratic precinct caucuses, demonstrating strength among rural, blue-collar, black, and suburban voters."[14] Apple's front-page article, with its strong and coherent story line, cast a long shadow. It contained many elements that in later years would cause concern, notably the use of such a word as "impressive" (to whom?) in the lead paragraph of what was ostensibly a news story and the belittling of the uncommitted vote because of the disappointed "forecasts" or expectations of anonymous politicians.

This friendly publicity set the stage for New Hampshire, where Carter, positioning himself as an ideological moderate in relation to his Democratic opponents, received 28 percent of the vote, good enough for a first-place finish in a large field of contenders. Despite starting the 1976 campaign with little support (or even name recognition), and despite receiving less than 30 percent of the vote in both states, Carter's victories in Iowa and New Hampshire made him the instant front-runner in the Democratic race, thanks in large part to positive coverage by the press, and he was able to ride this electoral momentum through the primary season to successfully capture the nomination.

1984

The Republican nomination contest was quiet in 1984, owing to the unopposed candidacy of incumbent president Ronald Reagan. On the Democratic side, former vice president Walter Mondale overwhelmed everybody in the Iowa caucus, collecting 49 percent of the vote in a large field of contenders. Colorado Senator Gary Hart came in a distant second with 16 percent of the vote.

This was apparently enough to identify Hart as Mondale's chief competitor for the nomination, rather than Senator John Glenn of Ohio, who finished in sixth place with 4 percent. The news media constructed a horse race out of the unpromising material of the Hart candidacy, gave him a great deal of positive coverage during the ensuing week, and boosted him into a surprisingly decisive win in the New Hampshire primary.[15] Hart received 41 percent of the New Hampshire vote, with Mondale placing second at 29 percent and Glenn a distant third with 13 percent.[16]

It seems clear enough why the news media need a horse race, given their extraordinary investment in delegate-selection coverage and the logic of their competition for business. The Iowa caucus helps the media sort out the story: it was the Iowa results in 1984 that decreed that Gary Hart and not John Glenn should be the chief threat to Mondale's campaign, and it was the media that made the horse race.

1992

A senator from Iowa, Tom Harkin, ran for president in 1992, and the other Democratic candidates quickly declared the Iowa caucus irrelevant due to the expectation that Harkin would win overwhelmingly in his home state—a judgment reporters accepted. The focus of press coverage leading up to the February 18 New Hampshire primary, then, was not the events in Iowa, but instead the problems of the presumed Democratic front-runner, Governor Bill Clinton of Arkansas. Clinton and his wife Hillary had appeared on the CBS news program *60 Minutes* immediately following the Super Bowl in January to respond to rumors of his marital infidelity, and in early February questions regarding the governor's exemption from military service during the Vietnam War made newspaper headlines around the nation. Once the leader in polls of likely New Hampshire voters, Clinton lost his advantage to former Massachusetts senator Paul Tsongas by the week before the primary, and many journalists, mindful of the adultery scandal that befell Gary Hart in 1987, began to suggest that Clinton's candidacy might be doomed.[17]

The news media's death watch over the Clinton campaign was suspended when Clinton finished a strong second to Tsongas in New Hampshire, receiving a better-than-expected 26 percent of the vote. Though he didn't actually win the election, an unabashed Clinton delivered what was, in effect, a victory speech on the night of the New Hampshire primary, proclaiming himself "the comeback kid"—a clever strategy that succeeded in convincing the media of his continued viability (the *New York Times* account published the following day described Clinton's "resilient candidacy").[18] Because journalists had their own doubts about Tsongas's credibility as a national candidate, and because the rest of the Democratic field (Harkin, Senator Bob Kerrey of Nebraska, and former California governor Jerry Brown) had failed to catch on with New Hampshire voters, Clinton was still treated as a serious contender despite his loss in the primary, and he ultimately won both the Democratic nomination and the presidency later in the year.[19]

On the Republican side, early expectations of a non-contest were jarred when former White House aide and conservative commentator Pat Buchanan received 37 percent of the New Hampshire vote against incumbent president George H. W. Bush, who was held to 53 percent. Just as Minnesota senator Eugene McCarthy's surprisingly close loss to incumbent president Lyndon Johnson persuaded the press that Johnson was unpopular in 1968, Buchanan's loss to Bush focused media attention on the nation's economic recession rather than Bush's successes in foreign policy. Though Buchanan's showing in New Hampshire was interpreted by journalists as a sign of Bush's electoral weakness, his ability to win renomination was never in doubt; Bush won every primary and took the bulk of delegates from each caucus state.

The aftermath of the 1992 New Hampshire primary once again demonstrated the news media's capacity to affect election outcomes in the primary season by interpreting results in early contests against a backdrop of consensus expectations which candidates are deemed to have exceeded or failed to meet. Had Bill Clinton continued to lead in the polls during the week of the election, journalists would have considered his nine-point loss to Paul Tsongas a devastating defeat; the resulting bad publicity might have jeopardized Clinton's candidacy.[20] The political damage sustained by Clinton shortly before the vote lowered media expectations for his performance enough that observers largely adopted the campaign's proffered story line of a Clinton "comeback" on election night. Just as the press treated Clinton like a winner in New Hampshire despite his loss in the actual vote, Bush endured a great deal of negative attention even after placing first in the Republican contest, because the willingness of more than a third of New Hampshire Republicans to vote against an incumbent president of their party supposedly demonstrated Bush's political vulnerability.

2004

The incumbency of George W. Bush precluded a contest on the Republican side in 2004. The Democrats, however, had a lively race. It produced a definitive result in Iowa that held up all the way to the nomination.

By early 2003, many political insiders saw Senator John Kerry of Massachusetts, a decorated Vietnam War veteran, as the initial Democratic front-runner.[21] However, former Vermont governor Howard Dean began to win significant support among Democratic voters during the summer and fall of 2003, thanks to his sharp attacks on the Bush administration and his status as an "outsider," not connected with the congressional Democrats in Washington who had, according to some liberals, failed to provide effective opposition to Bush's policies. Dean's popular campaign website brought in large numbers of financial donations from citizens across the country, and he began to attract serious attention from journalists, many of whom had initially dismissed him as a second-tier candidate. By mid-January 2004, Dean was leading in polls of Democratic voters in Iowa, New Hampshire, and across the country; had secured the endorsements of the Democrats' previous standard-bearer, Al Gore, Gore's 2000 primary opponent

Bill Bradley, Iowa senator Tom Harkin, and several major labor unions; and was bringing in over $1 million a week in online campaign contributions. Kerry, meanwhile, had fired his first campaign manager in November 2003 and was forced to loan his campaign over $6 million from his own very deep pocket to keep it operational after several months of unsuccessful fund-raising. Conventional wisdom in Washington said that Dean was the man to beat.[22]

Under these circumstances, Kerry's victory in the Iowa caucus on January 19 shocked most political observers. Two weeks earlier, Adam Nagourney of the *New York Times* had written from Iowa that "not even the biggest boosters of . . . Mr. Kerry are saying [he has] much of a chance of winning the caucuses here."[23] But Kerry finished first with 38 percent of the vote; almost as unexpectedly, Senator John Edwards of North Carolina came in a strong second with 32 percent.[24]

Dean, whose third-place Iowa finish (with only 18 percent) fell far short of expectations, suffered an instant transformation from the presumptive favorite in the race to a widespread target of derision and mockery.[25] Members of the news media—who may have felt considerable embarrassment after having enormously overstated Dean's appeal—seized on an exuberant whoop that had punctuated the candidate's unscripted concession speech on the night of the caucus, endlessly replaying clips of the "Dean scream" on cable television news programs and late-night comedy shows over the following week (more than six hundred times, by one count) in order to portray him as exhibiting an overly emotional, unhinged persona.[26] Referring to its much-touted (and unprecedented) Internet support, a wisecrack also made the rounds that the Dean campaign was the latest overhyped dot-com bust.[27]

Kerry's surprise win in Iowa had a profound effect on his fortunes in the New Hampshire primary the following week. A poll conducted just before the Iowa caucus showed him running a distant third in New Hampshire, winning just 12 percent (compared to 32 percent for Dean and 23 percent for retired General Wesley Clark).[28] But the massive media publicity generated by the events in Iowa boosted Kerry (from neighboring Massachusetts) into first place while dealing Dean (from neighboring Vermont) a damaging blow. Kerry won the January 27 New Hampshire primary by capturing 39 percent of the vote, with 26 percent for Dean, 13 percent for Clark, and 12 percent for Edwards, solidifying his position as the Democrats' leading candidate. By the end of February, Kerry had virtually wrapped up the nomination, while erstwhile front-runner Dean failed to win a single primary outside of his home state.

2008

For the first time since 1952, 2008 featured nomination contests without an incumbent president or vice president running in either party. That left both races wide open, and a large field of candidates emerged on each side.

New York senator Hillary Clinton began the campaign as the widely acknowledged favorite for the Democratic nomination. Due to her eight years as First Lady before entering the Senate, Clinton was well known to Democratic voters and enjoyed support from many veteran party leaders.[29] Clinton advisers initially viewed John Edwards, the Democrats' vice presidential nominee in 2004 who was making a second run for the presidency, as her most serious potential challenger.[30] But Senator Barack Obama of Illinois demonstrated a surprising ability to keep pace with Clinton in fund-raising during 2007, though he continued to trail her throughout the year in public opinion polls and endorsements of elected officials.

Strategists for Obama calculated that their candidate's chances of winning the nomination almost certainly required placing first in the Iowa caucus. A Clinton victory, they predicted, would most likely allow her to sweep the states that followed and quickly force him from the race. As a result, recalled Obama campaign manager David Plouffe, "front and center for all our considerations on spending money and time was: Would it help us win Iowa?"[31] While Edwards also devoted a great deal of attention to Iowa, campaigning energetically across the state for months before the caucuses, Obama boasted both a financial advantage and a far superior campaign organization, spending $9 million on advertising (compared to Clinton's $7 million and Edwards's $3 million) and opening thirty-seven Iowa field offices.[32] Assuming that most party regulars would favor Clinton, Obama's campaign combined innovative technology with traditional grassroots organizing to mobilize Iowans who did not normally participate in the caucus, such as many independents and young people, an approach that the Clinton team initially viewed with a skeptical smirk. "Our people look like caucus-goers," said one Clinton adviser while surveying candidate supporters at the Iowa Democratic Party's annual dinner in November 2007, "and his people look like they are 18 [and on] Facebook," the social networking website used by the Obama campaign as a tool to target the youth vote.[33]

Polls conducted just before the caucus showed a tight three-way race, but Obama ultimately triumphed with 38 percent of the delegate vote, outdistancing Edwards at 30 percent and Clinton a whisker behind at 29 percent. Obama's strategy was vindicated by the record turnout: about 240,000 voters participated on the Democratic side, nearly double the 2004 figure and far exceeding the predictions of the campaigns and the press.[34] His better-than-expected showing dominated news media coverage of the caucus—the *New York Times* declared that Obama had "rolled to victory" producing a "significant setback" to Clinton—and vaulted him into strong leads in several opinion surveys conducted in New Hampshire over subsequent days, suggesting a likely repeat performance there the following week.[35]

But Hillary Clinton defied the polls to claim a narrow victory in the New Hampshire primary, winning 39 percent of the vote to 37 percent for Obama and 17 percent for Edwards. On the day before the election, Clinton had uncharacteristically displayed open emotion at a campaign appearance in a Portsmouth coffee shop; with an audible catch in her voice, she told a voter that "this is very personal for me. . . . Some of us put ourselves out there and [campaign] against some difficult odds." Footage of the incident had led the nightly news broadcasts of all three major television networks on the eve of the primary, and advisers to both Clinton and Obama believed in retrospect that the sympathy it inspired among the electorate contributed to her surprise victory (in contrast to Muskie in 1972 and Dean in 2004, whose exhibitions of passion were seen as damaging gaffes).[36] The split decision between Iowa and New Hampshire set the stage for a protracted battle for delegates between Obama and Clinton that did not conclude until early June, representing the longest contested race for the Democratic nomination since 1972.

The Republican nomination race ran truer to the usual pattern, with a clear front-runner emerging in New Hampshire and virtually locking up the nomination by the following month. Senator John McCain of Arizona, the eventual nominee, began the pre-primary phase as one of the strongest potential contenders in the eyes of the news media (due to his second-place finish in the last contested Republican nomination race eight years before) but soon suffered from lackluster fund-raising efforts and a debilitating series of shakeups among top campaign staff; as one adviser later recalled, "in July 2007 the McCain campaign was dead as dead can be . . . the press kept [asking], 'When's he going to quit?'"[37] However, McCain's opponents had problems of their own. Former New York mayor Rudy Giuliani, though he initially led in most national polls due to high name recognition, took liberal positions on social issues that limited his appeal among Republican primary voters. Mitt Romney, former governor of Massachusetts, had abundant funds but faced skepticism from conservative Protestants over his Mormon faith and previous support for legalized abortion. Mike Huckabee, former governor of Arkansas and a Baptist minister, proved to be an impressive speaker and debater but found difficulty in expanding his appeal beyond his evangelical base in the South and rural Midwest. Former Tennessee senator and Hollywood actor Fred Thompson entered the race in the fall of 2007 to some fanfare but failed to ignite much voter interest in his campaign.

As he had done in 2000, McCain gave limited attention to the Iowa caucus in order to focus on the more favorable terrain of New Hampshire. After some active campaigning in Iowa, Giuliani followed suit, ultimately pulling out of New Hampshire as well in order to make a last stand in the Florida primary later in the month. This left Romney with an opportunity to place first in Iowa and coast on the resulting publicity to a second victory the following week in New Hampshire, where he was well-positioned as the former governor of a neighboring state.

Unfortunately for Romney's strategy, Huckabee upended him in the caucus straw poll by a solid nine-point margin (34 percent to 25 percent). Huckabee had little ability to capitalize on this success—his base of support among born-again Christians was not well-represented in the New Hampshire electorate—but Romney's loss in Iowa proved sufficiently damaging to his candidacy that New Hampshire was left open to capture by McCain, who received 37 percent of the vote there to 32 percent for Romney and 11 percent for Huckabee. Despite a smaller campaign war chest than those of Romney and Giuliani, McCain placed first by narrow margins in the crucial ensuing primaries in South Carolina (defeating Huckabee by 33 to 30 percent) and Florida (besting Romney by 36 to 31 percent), setting the stage for victories on February 5 in the large states of California, New York, Illinois, New Jersey, Missouri, and his home state of Arizona that gave him a near-insurmountable lead in the pledged delegate count.

2012

With no contest in the Democratic Party in 2012 as Barack Obama ran unopposed for renomination, public attention focused instead on the field of potential Republican challengers to the sitting president. Mitt Romney's second-place finish in the 2008 primaries had provided him with valuable name recognition and campaign experience; though some Republicans were not enthusiastically committed to another Romney candidacy, opposition to the former Massachusetts governor failed to coalesce behind a single rival. Governor Rick Perry of Texas, former House speaker Newt Gingrich, former senator Rick Santorum of Pennsylvania, and even ex-Godfather's Pizza CEO Herman Cain each experienced brief periods of forward momentum in national polls during the months before the Iowa caucus, but none of these alternatives succeeded in achieving a sustained surge in popular support among Republican leaders, activists, or voters. (Cain did not even last long enough to compete in Iowa, withdrawing from the race due to scandal before the end of 2011.)

Despite his sizable fund-raising advantage and organizational strength, Romney faced a tough battle in Iowa. The large share of evangelical Christians within the population of Republican caucus-goers rendered the state challenging terrain for his candidacy, as had been demonstrated by his loss there to the underfunded Mike Huckabee four years before. In the end, Romney finished in a dead heat with Santorum atop the Iowa vote with 25 percent apiece (a protracted recount ultimately found that Santorum had edged Romney by a margin of just thirty-four votes statewide). Representative Ron Paul of Texas placed third with 21 percent, followed by Gingrich at 13 percent, Perry at 10 percent, Representative Michele Bachmann of Minnesota at 5 percent, and former governor Jon Huntsman of Utah at 1 percent.

While Romney may have been temporarily humbled by narrowly losing to a rival whom he had heavily outspent (by a roughly 7-to-1 margin in Iowa, counting super PAC expenditures on both sides), the results were not particularly unfavorable in a political sense for the former Massachusetts governor.[38] Like Huckabee before him, Santorum derived most of his popular support from strong social conservatives, who constitute a much smaller proportion of the Republican vote in New Hampshire than they do in Iowa. By denying a positive outcome to Gingrich and by severely damaging Perry's candidacy, the Iowa results failed to dislodge Romney from his position as the clear favorite in the race. He scored an easy win in the New Hampshire primary the following week (taking 39 percent of the total vote, as compared to 23 percent for Paul, 17 percent for Huntsman, 9 percent each for Santorum and Gingrich, and 1 percent for Perry), placing him firmly in the lead for the Republican nomination. Though Gingrich's subsequent victory in the South Carolina primary and Santorum's success in several later state elections kept the race unresolved until March, Romney retained his front-runner status throughout the rest of the primaries and ultimately captured the nomination with relative ease.

WHAT DO THESE HISTORICAL VIGNETTES TEACH?

1. Candidates ignore Iowa and New Hampshire at their peril. This does not mean that losing Iowa and New Hampshire is sufficient to lose the nomination or that doing well is sufficient to win. It does mean that the results in both states can be a tremendous help or a significant hindrance to every campaign.

2. This is so not because of their size or number of delegates but because of their temporal primacy: Iowa results, plus media spin, influence the results of the New Hampshire primary. These two events together, plus more media spin, shape the race as it proceeds to the remaining states.

3. While winning either Iowa or New Hampshire does not ensure nomination, losing badly in both states effectively extinguishes the viability of a candidacy. Since the modern nomination system was implemented in 1972, only one eventual nominee has ever finished below third place in either Iowa or New Hampshire (John McCain in 2008, who did not campaign extensively in Iowa—in order to focus

on New Hampshire—and finished fourth by less than five hundred votes).[39] Over the same period, every nominee in both parties has won at least one of the first two states except for George McGovern in 1972 and Bill Clinton in 1992, whose second-place finishes were both treated as victories by the news media. With few exceptions, candidates have learned these lessons and responded by focusing intensively on Iowa and New Hampshire for months before the voting begins, knowing that they need at least one strong performance to remain plausible contenders for the nomination.

4. Political pundits tend to identify a single candidate in each party as the front-runner prior to the elections in Iowa and New Hampshire, based principally on candidates' relative fund-raising totals, positions in national polls of potential primary voters, and public support from party leaders and elected officials. Status as the widely acknowledged leading contender, however, raises expectations for that candidate's performance in the early states; as a result, receiving a significant yet lower-than-predicted share of the vote can produce substantial negative publicity. While the "invisible primary" period plays a critical role in structuring the nomination contest before the voting begins, the victories of John Kerry (on the Democratic side in 2004), Barack Obama (on the Democratic side in 2008), and John McCain (on the Republican side in 2008) over rivals who were more heavily favored going into the primary season illustrate the capacity of voters in Iowa and New Hampshire to fundamentally reorder the existing race once they make their preferences known.

STATE PRIMARIES

Candidates for presidential nominations now routinely hit the campaign trail nearly a full year before the first votes are cast. Once the events in Iowa and New Hampshire have passed, however, elections in other states follow quickly in subsequent weeks, soon narrowing the field to a single remaining candidate in each party. Only in rare cases, such as the Democratic nomination contest in 2008, does the race remain undecided for long. Each state and U.S. territory holds a primary or caucus during the winter or spring of a presidential election year in order to select that state's delegates to the national party conventions.

The national parties impose rules on this process, specifying the number of delegates allotted to each state, the time frame within which the delegates must be selected, the formulas by which candidates may be awarded delegates pledged to support them at the convention based on their relative standing with the voters, and so on. However, individual states maintain some flexibility, such as the decision whether to hold a presidential primary administered by the state government or opt for a caucus organized by the state parties. More than two-thirds of the states, selecting the bulk of the delegates in both parties, currently hold primary elections.

A more important decision than the choice between primaries and caucuses, however, is the date on which a state's elections occur. As reliably keen observers of the dynamics of presidential nominations, state politicians and party officials across the nation have largely—and correctly—concluded that states voting early in the primary season exert far more influence over the outcome than those scheduled near the end of the process, when one candidate has usually wrapped up the nomination. Over time, states have moved their presidential primaries further ahead in the calendar, hoping to have a greater say in the determination of the party nominees and therefore receive more attention from candidates—a phenomenon known as "front-loading."

In 1976, Democratic presidential primaries were spread out over a relatively long period: after New Hampshire on February 24, only five states held primaries in March, and only two held primaries in April. Twelve primaries were held more than three months after the New Hampshire primary, including contests on June 8 in the populous states of California, New Jersey, and Ohio.[40] This schedule certainly granted greater importance to early primaries because winning in February and March helped candidates receive attention and raise money for the later events. This meant that early and vigorous participation in primaries was already the only strategy available to serious presidential aspirants. Nevertheless, many of the actual delegates were selected late in the process.

As state leaders began to understand the importance of the early contests, more states moved their primaries or caucuses earlier and earlier in the spring, hoping to gain additional influence over the nominations. The 1988 election introduced the phenomenon of "Super Tuesday," when a number of states scheduled primaries on the same day near the beginning of the nomination calendar. While Super Tuesday in 1988 was principally the result of coordinated efforts among Democratic leaders in the South to increase their region's voice in the presidential nomination contest, in subsequent elections it has simply represented the collective consequence of individual states' attempts to maximize attention and clout by holding primaries or caucuses on the first date permitted by the national parties (not including the special recognition given to early states such as Iowa and New Hampshire). As table 4.2 reveals, by 1992 state contests in both parties, but especially on the Democratic side, had become particularly concentrated in the first two weeks of March. Even so, nearly half of all pledged Democratic delegates in 1992—and 55 percent of Republican delegates—were still chosen in April, May, or June.

The rate of front-loading accelerated in subsequent elections. After 1992, the large delegate prizes of California, New York, and Ohio, along with several smaller states, moved from their long-standing places near the end of the primary calendar to the increasingly popular first Tuesday in March. By 2000, fully half of the total number of Republican pledged delegates and nearly two-thirds of the Democratic delegates were selected during the first two weeks in March alone. Winning the first round of primaries was now important not merely to signal a candidate's viability or to raise money for future contests but because most of the delegates were actually chosen early in the calendar.

In 2004, the Democratic Party followed the Republicans' lead in 2000 and moved the start of the national delegate selection window forward by one month. A number of states immediately responded by rescheduling their primaries and caucuses to take advantage of the new timeline, predictably converging on the first Tuesday in February, the earliest allowable date under the revised party rules. For some observers, the traditional moniker "Super Tuesday" seemed insufficient by 2008 to convey the potential importance of this event, now including primaries or caucuses in twenty-four states; many in the seldom hype-averse press corps began referring instead to "Super Duper Tuesday" or "Tsunami Tuesday." Seeking to maintain their jealously guarded first-in-the-nation status, Iowa and New Hampshire responded by scheduling their elections in early January. The 2008 Iowa caucus was held only two days after the New Year, with the New Hampshire primary following on January 8.

TABLE 4.2. The Front-Loading of the Presidential Primary Calendar, 1992–2012

	Jan.	Feb. 1–15	Feb. 16–29	March 1–15	March 16–31	April	May	June/July
DEMOCRATS								
1992								
States	0	1	3	22	5	6	8	6
Pct Delegates	0.0	1.4	1.6	37.0	10.9	18.0	10.6	20.3
Cumul. Pct Delegates	0.0	1.4	3.0	40.1	51.0	69.0	79.7	100.0
2000								
States	1	1	0	28	3	4	9	5
Pct Delegates	1.4	0.6	0.0	65.3	5.4	9.5	11.5	6.3
Cumul. Pct Delegates	1.4	2.0	2.0	67.3	72.7	82.2	93.7	100.0
2008								
States	6	29	2	6	0	1	5	2
Pct Delegates	8.8	60.8	2.8	12.4	0.0	4.7	9.5	0.9
Cumul. Pct Delegates	8.8	69.6	72.4	84.8	84.8	89.5	99.1	100.0
2012								
States	4	2	1	12	3	14	9	6
Pct Delegates	3.6	3.8	0.7	18.2	6.7	29.3	21.0	16.8
Cumul. Pct Delegates	3.6	7.4	8.0	26.2	33.0	62.2	83.2	100.0
REPUBLICANS								
1992								
States	0	1	4	15	4	8	13	6
Pct Delegates	0.0	1.1	3.9	30.4	9.7	17.4	18.1	19.6
Cumul. Pct Delegates	0.0	1.1	4.9	35.3	45.0	62.3	80.4	100.0
2000								
States	2	3	6	21	3	2	9	5
Pct Delegates	2.4	2.1	11.6	50.0	6.0	5.6	14.3	8.0
Cumul. Pct Delegates	2.4	4.5	16.1	66.1	72.1	77.7	92.0	100.0
2008								
States	7	28	1	5	0	1	6	3
Pct Delegates	9.4	57.4	1.7	13.2	0	3.3	11.2	3.8
Cumul. Pct Delegates	9.4	66.8	68.5	81.7	81.7	85.0	96.2	100.0
2012								
States	4	3	2	18	2	8	7	7
Pct Delegates	5.0	3.8	2.7	33.5	5.3	14.7	18.2	17.0
Cumul. Pct Delegates	5.0	8.8	11.4	44.9	50.1	64.8	83.0	100.0

Source: Compiled by authors.

Note: This table includes the District of Columbia but excludes all territories of the United States not represented in the electoral college.

In order to avoid future occurrences of primaries and caucuses within mere days of the holiday season, the Democratic and Republican national committees engaged in an unprecedented cooperative initiative after 2008 to standardize an election schedule for both parties. The plans enacted by the national parties for 2012 called for early states such as Iowa and New Hampshire to vote during the month of February, with the rest of the nation holding primaries and caucuses between March and June—in effect, a return to the calendar as it existed in the 1980s and 1990s. Republicans also modified their rules to ban the use of pure winner-take-all delegation allocation before April 1, increasing the incentive for states to hold their elections later in the year. (This rule was slightly relaxed after 2012 to permit pure winner-take-all primaries and caucuses beginning on March 15.)

As table 4.2 illustrates, these party rules reforms succeeded in partially reversing the trend toward a severely front-loaded calendar. A number of states that had voted in February during the 2004 and 2008 elections moved their primaries later in the spring for 2012 in order to remain compliant with the stricter national party requirements. Predictably, most chose a March date instead, though New York decided to wait until April to vote and California returned to its pre-1996 tradition of holding an early June primary. In addition, a federal court ruling unrelated to the presidential nomination process forced the delegate-rich Texas primary to be delayed from its statutory March date until May 29. While the first day of the delegate selection window—now the first Tuesday in March—remained the most popular single date for states to schedule their primaries and caucuses (preserving the Super Tuesday phenomenon), it no longer resembled a quasi-national primary with nearly half the states in the nation voting simultaneously, as had occurred in 2008. However, a few rogue states still insisted on holding January or February primaries despite a lack of authorization by the national parties, prompting Iowa and New Hampshire to schedule their events during the first ten days of the year once again in order to preserve their traditional place at the front of the electoral line.

Both national party committees embarked on a renewed effort in 2016 to enforce a primary and caucus window beginning in March for all but the specially designated early states of Iowa, New Hampshire, Nevada, and South Carolina, with the Republican Party approving a new internal rule that would sharply reduce the number of delegate seats at the national convention allocated to states that scheduled their primaries or caucuses prior to that date without authorization. Only time will tell, however, whether the parties will find more success on this front in the future than they did in 2012.[41] A few states have regularly demonstrated a willingness to flout party rules (and to withstand any penalties imposed on them for doing so) in order to hold early primaries that they hope will prove influential in the nomination process.

For example, Michigan and Florida scheduled their 2008 primaries for January 15 and 29, respectively, in a brazen challenge to the delegate selection window approved by the national parties. State politicians, eager for national attention and sway over the nomination outcomes, predicted that candidates would not risk alienating the voters of two large, politically competitive states by ignoring their presidential primaries, and that the national parties, for similar reasons, would back down from threats to penalize Michigan and Florida by denying them delegate seats at the nominating conventions. On the Republican side, the states' gamble was largely successful. Though the

Republican National Committee responded by reducing the size of each state's convention delegation by one-half as punishment for holding unauthorized early primaries, this was not a particularly effective sanction in practice, since a state's influence on presidential nominations is based mostly on when it votes, not how many delegates it has.[42] The major Republican candidates competed seriously in Michigan and Florida, and both states had a significant impact on the nomination contest. Mitt Romney's victory over John McCain in Michigan kept his campaign alive, at least temporarily, while McCain's first-place finish in Florida two weeks later ended the candidacy of Rudy Giuliani and dealt Romney a serious setback that foreshadowed his poor Super Tuesday performance and subsequent withdrawal the following week.

The national Democratic Party penalized Michigan and Florida much more severely than did the Republicans, passing resolutions denying both states any representation at the national convention. The Democratic candidates then signed an agreement not to campaign in either state. Hillary Clinton won both primaries more or less by default, though she claimed victory after the fact; in Michigan, she was the only major candidate to place her name on the ballot. (Even so, 40 percent of Michigan Democrats voted for an uncommitted slate of delegates as a way to express support for Barack Obama.)

As the Democratic nomination contest dragged on into the spring with Obama holding a slender but steady lead over Clinton in the overall pledged delegate count, Clinton campaign officials began to call for the Democratic National Committee to reconsider the sanctions imposed on Michigan and Florida. Some observers floated the possibility of holding new primary elections in the two states, though this was soon dismissed as infeasible. On May 31, the party's Rules and Bylaws Committee met in Washington to resolve the issue. The committee rejected the Clinton campaign's proposal that the Michigan and Florida delegations be restored at full strength and divided between the candidates on the basis of the January primary results, opting instead to grant each state's delegates half votes at the convention and to award 59 of the 128 pledged delegates from Michigan to Obama even though he had not appeared on the ballot—a decision that effectively ended Clinton's already slim chances of winning the nomination.[43] Despite much speculation at the time that the voters of Michigan and Florida might resent the penalty enforced on the states by the national Democratic Party (rather than holding their own state leaders responsible for scheduling primaries in violation of the rules), the entire debacle was long forgotten by the fall, and Obama ultimately carried both states against McCain in the general election.

The saga of Michigan and Florida in 2008 was but one pitched battle in an ongoing war between state officials and national party leaders for control of the presidential nomination process. While the self-interested actions of state governments seeking power and attention by intentionally violating the scheduling requirements imposed by the national parties may inspire little sympathy from residents of more cooperative states elsewhere in the nation, these actions also raise the legitimate question of whether Iowa and New Hampshire should continue to receive special dispensation under the rules of both major parties to hold the first caucus and first primary in every presidential nomination season. This issue has emerged regularly in recent years. Within the Democratic Party, representatives of labor unions and racial minorities, two key components of the party's electoral coalition, have often complained that their constituents are significantly underrepresented in the electorates of Iowa and New Hampshire, and therefore exert less influence on the outcome of presidential nominations than they believe that they deserve based on their share of the national population.

Responding to these and similar arguments, the Democratic National Committee appointed an internal commission after the 2004 election to study the nomination sequence. The commission, cochaired by former U.S. secretary of labor Alexis Herman and Representative David Price of North Carolina, recommended that the party continue to recognize the traditional right of Iowa to hold the first presidential caucus and New Hampshire the first primary, but that it should also allow two additional states to schedule early events before the bulk of other primaries and caucuses takes place. The DNC voted to authorize Nevada, a state with a significant union presence and Latino population, to hold a caucus after Iowa. South Carolina, a state in which a large proportion of the Democratic electorate is African American, received approval to hold the second primary of the election calendar.[44] After 2012, the Republican Party adopted a similar carve-out provision formally recognizing Nevada and South Carolina as additional early states with the right to schedule elections prior to the March opening of the national delegate selection window.

These changes to the primary sequence increased the influence of those two states on the Democratic nomination in 2008 but did not shorten the unusually long and evenly contested nomination battle. Clinton's narrow victory in Nevada and Obama's landslide win in South Carolina replicated the divided outcomes of Iowa and New Hampshire, keeping both candidacies viable heading into Super Tuesday. Given the awkward tendency of reforms to work in ways not originally envisioned by their proponents, only further experience can determine whether they will have the intended effect—or any effect at all—on the outcome of presidential nominations.

How have changes in the primary calendar over time influenced the outcome of presidential nominations? In practice, front-loading has mostly worked to reduce the amount of time between the beginning of the primary season and the point at which a presumptive nominee emerges. Once the voting starts, pressure quickly builds for unsuccessful candidates to drop out of the race. Most presidential contenders only contest a handful of states before they are forced to withdraw, usually due to financial hardship and encouragement from party leaders to rally around the front-runner. A front-loaded primary schedule simply accelerates this process, usually producing a nominee in a matter of weeks instead of months.

Consider the effects of front-loading on the 2008 Republican primary season. Rudy Giuliani, leader in many national polls for most of 2007, ultimately decided not to contest either Iowa or New Hampshire because of his lack of appeal in either state. Giuliani attempted an unorthodox strategy of waiting until the seventh GOP contest, the Florida primary on January 29, to begin his run for the nomination. By that time, his string of distant finishes in all the previous states had fatally damaged his candidacy, and he quickly ended his campaign after winning just 15 percent of the Florida vote. Mitt Romney, the best-funded of the candidates, staked his strategy on early successes in Iowa and New Hampshire. He won neither. Winning only the Nevada and Wyoming caucuses and the primary in Michigan (where his father had been governor) in January, his campaign was finished by John McCain's multiple victories on Super Tuesday, February 5. Mike Huckabee won the Iowa caucus, defeating the better-funded Romney in an upset, but finished far behind in New Hampshire and, crucially, lost South Carolina to McCain on January 26 despite its large population of evangelical Protestants.

McCain, for his part, emerged, as front-runners usually do, by winning the New Hampshire primary. Despite declining to compete fully in Iowa and finishing fourth there, he prevailed in New Hampshire by five points over Romney and, after a Michigan primary setback, won the crucial South Carolina and Florida primaries in late January. On Super Tuesday, just a month after the Iowa caucus, McCain won primaries in nine states, driving Romney from the race and becoming the near-certain Republican nominee. Only Huckabee remained as an active opponent for a few more weeks, and by early March, McCain's victory was assured, even though the primary season nominally continued through the first week of June.

Why did most candidates campaign actively for months before the primaries, only to drop out of the race so soon after the voting began? An explanation lies in the common interpretation of electoral outcomes in early states by political elites, journalists, and voters. Romney discovered that the more resources expended in early states, the higher the media expectations become, and he couldn't meet them. Early success in Iowa must be replicated quickly in other states or, as Huckabee found out, momentum quickly disappears. Unfortunately for the former Arkansas governor, his sparsely funded campaign and limited national appeal could not translate his victory in Iowa into broader success. McCain met traditional media expectations by winning New Hampshire and then triumphing in the key contests in which all of his rivals were also seriously engaged, South Carolina and Florida. Echoing a common interpretation of the results, the *New York Times* termed McCain's Florida victory "a decisive turning point in the Republican race" that redounded greatly to the Arizonan's benefit.[45]

The 2008 Democratic race, exceptional in that it featured two leading candidates who actively competed until June, did produce a traditional winnowing effect on the rest of the Democratic field. The failure of John Edwards to win the caucus in Iowa, where he had devoted more time and spent a larger share of his campaign's money than any other candidate, served as a death knell for his campaign; subsequent distant third-place finishes in New Hampshire, Nevada, and South Carolina led to his withdrawal from the race before Super Tuesday. Several other candidates who fared poorly in the first two contests—Bill Richardson, Joe Biden, and Chris Dodd—also folded their campaigns shortly afterward. Only Hillary Clinton and Barack Obama, both unusually well funded and each popular with a large fraction of Democrats nationally and in most states, were able to survive into the second month of voting. Both exceeded media expectations in the early contests, Obama by winning Iowa and Clinton by prevailing in New Hampshire, which enabled their campaigns to continue. The atypically inconclusive results of Super Tuesday (Obama won 13 states and 847 delegates, compared to 9 states and 834 delegates for Clinton) ensured that the bruising competition between them would persist. Even after Obama won nine consecutive state contests in mid-February, amassing a virtually insurmountable lead in the pledged delegate count, Clinton rebounded in March and April with primary victories in Ohio, Texas, and Pennsylvania that kept her candidacy afloat.

In 2012, seven Republican candidates began the primary season by competing in the Iowa caucus on January 3. One candidate, Michele Bachmann, ended her campaign immediately after finishing sixth in Iowa; two more, Rick Perry and Jon Huntsman, dropped out after the New Hampshire primary the following week. Front-runner and New Hampshire victor Mitt Romney scored another key win in the Florida primary on January 31 and took a commanding lead in the pledged delegate count with victories in multiple states on Super Tuesday, March 6. After another first-place finish in the March 20 primary in Illinois, Romney became the presumptive nominee of the party with more than ten weeks remaining in the primary calendar.

Victorious candidates in the first events, or those who exceed media expectations for their performance, can ride the resulting "momentum" to further success in states holding primaries in the following days. At the same time, candidates who stumble early on have little opportunity in a front-loaded primary process to right their campaigns in time to prevent additional defeats that only compound their problems. The central limitation facing the advocates of front-loading is the dependable tendency of party leaders, journalists, and voters to interpret the very first events of the primary season as important evidence of the relative standing of the candidates. As long as political elites consider the results in Iowa and New Hampshire worthy of extensive attention, hyping winners and disparaging losers, the outcomes in those states will exert a strong effect on the results of subsequent primaries and caucuses, even—perhaps especially—if those elections follow closely behind. As long as voters, confronted with a field of multiple contenders within the same party who are mostly not well known to them, look to the decisions of their counterparts in other states for guidance about which candidate to support, the very first states in the electoral sequence will continue to have the loudest voice in the process.

Over the years, states have attempted to gain influence over nominations in ways other than front-loading. One common strategy employed to attract candidate and press attention is the organization of regional primaries. Perhaps if several contiguous states with presumably similar interests coordinate their delegate selection events on a single date, they can compel candidates to show interest in whatever issues are of particular interest to that region. Such primaries have not, for the most part, been particularly successful, in part because states are unable to monopolize a date on the primary calendar. Should other states share the day, candidates may choose to campaign extensively only in the largest states within the region (say, Massachusetts in a New England regional primary) and give less attention to the smaller states.

At least one other strategy is common. States that are home to a prospective candidate may manipulate the delegate selection process in order to help the "favorite son." If the candidate is expected to win the state, the victory presumably provides extra publicity. If the candidate is worried about losing the state or failing to meet news media expectations, however, he or she may not benefit from an early home-state primary; even hinting at this may generate negative press coverage. This happened to John McCain in 1999. Arizona Republicans had moved their primary to mid-February in 1996, following New Hampshire by only a week. McCain was reported to be in favor of moving the primary back in the schedule, after the key New York and California primaries, in order to avoid the possibility of an embarrassing loss—or narrow victory—in his home state affecting results elsewhere. In this case, however, Arizona Republicans failed to respect McCain's wishes and left the date of the primary early, on February 22, 2000. McCain's fears ultimately went unrealized; he won the state easily.[46]

Thus the design of the presidential nomination process continues to be in constant flux from one election to the next. Most states, as well as both national parties, have demonstrated a great deal of willingness over the past several decades to manipulate the primary calendar for various purposes. At the root of this incessant tinkering is the unfortunate truth that most political actors, as well as many observers, perceive the current nomination system to be significantly flawed and therefore in need of further reform, a topic to which we return in chapter 6.

Despite a significant degree of change over the past several decades, especially in the timing of state contests, there have been some consistent patterns across elections. "Regardless of the different nominating rules . . . there is a dynamic affecting both parties that makes early defeats devastating," observes Rhodes Cook. "No candidate in either party in recent years has mounted a successful comeback during the mop-up period."[47] What helps a candidate overcome a poor early performance? "One of the problems of being a dark horse," notes Dotty Lynch, Gary Hart's pollster in 1984, "is that you need some true believers with you. Without an issue like George McGovern had in 1972 or a [devoted, ethnically based] constituency like Jesse Jackson has, a lot of people give up on you and you may give up on yourself."[48] Candidates also benefit from raising enough money up front to outlast disappointing outcomes in the early going. Barack Obama and Hillary Clinton both did that in 2008, allowing her to overcome an initial Iowa setback and him a surprising loss in New Hampshire. The two factors—a loyal activist following and the capacity to raise money early—may be but do not have to be connected.

Because primaries are the battlegrounds of the nomination process, the news media play a crucial role in how nominees are chosen. Since primary voters lack the guidance that differing party labels provide during general elections, and since primary events are often full of uncertainty, media reporting about who is ahead or behind or how seriously candidates should be taken assumes considerable importance. Therefore, a significant part of running for president includes trying to manipulate how media analysts interpret primary elections both before and after they take place. This is known as "spin control."[49] The contestant who loses but does better than expected may reap greater advantage from a primary than the one who wins but falls below expectations. It is therefore manifestly to the advantage of candidates to make modest pre-election predictions and to then tout results as more favorable than anticipated once the votes are counted.

A good example of spin control was the effort of Bill Clinton's 1992 campaign to declare a victory in New Hampshire as the "comeback kid," even though he had lost the primary to Paul Tsongas.[50] The press accepted the idea of a resurgent Clinton, ignored the other candidates, and gave Tsongas little of the positive coverage a winning candidate might ordinarily receive.[51] In contrast, Bob Kerrey's decisive victory (with 40 percent of the vote) in South Dakota one week later netted him much less favorable publicity than Clinton's second-place showing in New Hampshire. Kerrey succeeded with the voters, but failed in the crucial job of spin control.

Substantial evidence exists that voters absorb opinion poll results and gather other impressions of viability which then exert considerable influence over their choice of candidates. But information on policies, character, and leadership ability is comparatively scarce and is assimilated slowly.[52] "It appears safe to conclude," John G. Geer writes, "that most primary voters do not compare the issue positions of candidates when voting."[53] One reason that primary voters do not perceive much issue distance between the candidates, is, perhaps, because, being members of the same party, there is in fact not that much difference. Another reason may be that candidates are purposely unclear. Since it may well be advantageous for candidates to appeal differently to various audiences, they may, like Barack Obama or Mitt Romney, appear moderate to some people and firmly liberal or conservative to others.

There are bandwagon effects in primaries. Gary Hart rose from 2 percent of national support early in February 1984 to 33 percent in three weeks. Jimmy Carter went from near obscurity, 1 percent in January 1976, to 29 percent by mid-March. John Kerry was the favored candidate of 9 percent of Democrats nationwide in a *Time/CNN* poll conducted in mid-January 2004, before the Iowa caucus. After his victories in Iowa and New Hampshire, Kerry surged to 43 percent in the same poll by February 6.[54] Newt Gingrich led Mitt Romney in an aggregation of national polls by 11 percentage points (32 percent to 21 percent) on December 5, 2011; six weeks later, after Romney had achieved a virtual tie in Iowa and an easy victory in New Hampshire, he had pulled ahead of Gingrich in the national vote by a comparable margin of 30 percent to 20 percent.[55] As Collat, Kelley, and Rogowski define the term, "a bandwagon effect may be said to exist if a given decision-maker supports, from among some set of contenders, not the contender he most prefers, but the contender who seems most likely to win."[56]

If voters can be swept along by the sheer momentum of events, the strength of their issue preferences or of their assessments of leadership ability must be very low. On what basis, then, do citizens choose? As the nominating campaign moves along, voters do develop feelings about the personalities of the candidates. In a study of primary voters in Los Angeles, California, and Erie, Pennsylvania, John Geer demonstrates that comments centered on the candidates' personalities predominate in the reasons given for voting in primaries.[57] Since much of the debate in the primary is about who among members of the same party can provide the best leadership, Geer thinks voter concentration on candidates' personal qualities is reasonable. Others disagree. Henry E. Brady and Michael G. Hagen argue "primaries seem to be seriously flawed by forcing voters to commit to candidates before they can learn about . . . policy positions, electability and leadership ability of those standing for the nomination. . . . American primaries force people to choose before they are ready."[58]

Since the effects of primaries are cumulative, it is especially important to study how earlier events affect later ones. Larry M. Bartels argues that the nomination victories of Republican Gerald Ford and Democrat Jimmy Carter in 1976 were due to the accumulation of momentum, with over half of Carter's support in primaries coming from his early successes.[59] Perhaps the most interesting finding comes from a study by Lawrence S. Rothenberg and Richard A. Brody showing that voter turnout declines toward the end of the primary season.[60] This makes sense; if the early primaries dominate the process and sharply constrain alternatives available later on, then it would follow that people would see less purpose in turning out for later ones. In 2008, turnout declined in the Republican primaries after Super Tuesday, as McCain had become the presumptive nominee, but not in the Democratic contests, which featured a still-unresolved battle between Obama and Clinton. A close competition hyped by the news media always draws voters.

It is also important to examine the rules governing the process by which the votes of citizens are transformed into the distribution of delegates among candidates. No one pretends that primaries are perfect representations of the electorate that either identifies with a particular political party or is likely to support the party's leading vote-getter. For one thing, voters are not allowed to rank their preferences, so a candidate's popularity with voters who gave their first-choice votes to others is unknown. Voter turnout in primaries is also usually much lower than in the November election and is likely to contain a larger proportion of dyed-in-the-wool party supporters. Even in 2008, with highly competitive nomination races in both parties and a prolonged contest on the Democratic side that lasted until the final day of primaries in June, just 29 percent of the eligible voting-age population participated (as compared to 62 percent in the November general election).[61] It is not so much low turnout, however, as the combination of low turnout with first-choice election rules that can bias the results.

There are two basic ways of converting votes into pledged delegates. One is winner-take-all: whichever candidate places first receives all the delegates. The other is proportional: all candidates who reach a certain threshold—15 percent, for example—divide the delegates among themselves in accordance with their relative shares of the vote. States may use either system to allocate delegates based on the vote across the entire state, within individual congressional districts, or both. Because the national Republican Party mostly leaves these decisions up to the states, allocation methods in Republican primaries can vary dramatically. In 2012, Florida Republicans used a winner-take-all system at the state level; because Romney placed first in the state, he gained all of Florida's pledged delegates even though he received less than half (46 percent) of the popular vote. In California, most Republican delegates were apportioned by the winner-take-all system at the level of individual congressional districts; candidates gained three delegates for each district that they carried. In New Hampshire, Republican delegates were divided proportionally among candidates based on their shares of the statewide vote, while Texas awarded delegates proportionally by congressional district.

Historically, proportional allocation has not been widely used in Republican primaries; most states have apportioned delegates in a winner-take-all fashion either at the state or district level, or both in combination.[62] However, the national Republican Party now requires that all states (other than the four designated early states) holding primaries or caucuses before March 15 must use proportional allocation—although these states are still permitted the option of allowing a candidate who receives more than 50 percent of the total statewide vote to collect all the delegates from the state, a rule sometimes known as "conditional winner-take-all." Party leaders adopted this reform to discourage extreme front-loading; it can also work to prolong the nomination process by making it more difficult for a single candidate to quickly amass a commanding lead in the delegate count.

The national Democratic Party does not permit winner-take-all delegate allocation under any circumstances. Instead, it requires states to apportion most of their delegates proportionally by congressional district. The remaining share of the state's pledged delegates must be allocated proportionally based on the statewide popular vote. Candidates who win at least 15 percent of the vote in a district or state are entitled to receive delegates under national party rules.

The prevalence of winner-take-all delegate allocation in their party gives Republican candidates a strategic opportunity not available to Democrats. A Republican late bloomer, by winning later primaries, conceivably could hope to overcome a front-runner's early delegate lead. Though Ronald Reagan won no primaries until late March, for example, he almost took the 1976 nomination away from Gerald Ford by receiving all the delegates from such late-voting large states as California and Texas. In contrast, Democratic rules requiring proportional representation make it difficult for lagging Democratic candidates to catch up in the delegate count. Even if front-runners falter, proportional representation slows their momentum only a little in the later primaries. Once Hillary Clinton fell behind Barack Obama among pledged delegates in mid-February 2008 due to Obama's success in a series of primaries and caucuses, proportional representation rules blunted her progress in making up lost ground in March and April despite primary victories in several populous states.

In fact, had winner-take-all apportionment been in place for Democrats in the largest state primaries in 2008, Clinton would have received the nomination on the strength of her victories in California, New York, New Jersey, Texas, Ohio, and Pennsylvania. Obama ultimately collected more pledged delegates than Clinton under the proportional rules that were actually in effect by doing well enough in large states to reap a significant share of their delegates while winning lopsided victories in several medium-sized primary states (such as Maryland, Virginia, and Wisconsin) and a number of small states holding caucuses where Clinton failed to compete. At the same time, the widespread use of proportional allocation in Republican primaries would have worked to the advantage of Mitt Romney's first, ultimately unsuccessful bid for the Republican nomination in 2008. Romney finished a close second or third in the populous states of Florida, Georgia, and Missouri but did not receive a single pledged delegate from any of them due to winner-take-all apportionment, while his 35 percent share of the statewide vote in California netted him only 15 of 170 delegates.

Of course, these hypothetical outcomes fail to account for the alternate strategies that the candidates would surely have pursued under different institutional rules. Because the Democratic Party currently requires all states to use proportional allocation, Democratic presidential candidates face a particularly strong incentive to build active campaign organizations virtually everywhere, since they can win delegates even if they fail to place first. Successful campaigns devote a great deal of attention to the details of party procedure, identifying particular states and even congressional districts within states where resources should be directed to maximize the number of delegates gained. The Obama campaign was considered particularly adept on this score in 2008, especially in comparison with the less savvy Hillary Clinton operation. Clinton aide Harold Ickes later claimed that chief strategist Mark Penn—a bitter rival of his within the campaign—mistakenly thought the February 5 California primary was winner-take-all and that Clinton's likely victory there would virtually clinch the race. "How can it possibly be," Ickes asked sarcastically, "that the much vaunted chief strategist doesn't understand [Democratic Party rules requiring] proportional allocation?"[63] Assuming that the Democratic race would be effectively decided on Super Tuesday due to their candidate's strength in most of the populous states holding primaries that day, Clinton campaign officials failed to build strong organizations in caucus states or states holding elections in subsequent weeks, to her great disadvantage.

Highly competitive nomination contests, like the Democratic race in 2008, are particularly valuable in illustrating the tremendous procedural complexity of the contemporary presidential primary system and the need for candidates to employ sophisticated strategic and tactical approaches in order to navigate it successfully. The process is a complicated and ever-evolving network of institutions, actors, and rules in which national party organizations, state legislatures and governors, candidates, interest groups, journalists, and voters all interact to produce a presidential nominee. For citizens, their degree of influence over the process mostly reflects the position of their state in the sequential series of elections occurring over the course of the primary season. Residents of states at the front of the calendar will usually have a choice of multiple candidates actively seeking their support; those who must wait until May or June to participate almost always find that the nomination has already been effectively decided by their fellow party members elsewhere in the nation.

STATE CAUCUSES

The majority of delegates to the national party conventions are selected by means of state primary elections. In 2012, for example, 60 percent of the delegates to the Democratic convention were chosen in primaries, 13 percent were unelected superdelegates (discussed further below), and 27 percent were selected via state caucuses or conventions. This represents an unusually high proportion of delegates chosen via caucuses, however, since several states opted to spare the expense of holding their usual primaries in 2012 due to the lack of a contested Democratic nomination. In 2008, only 12 percent of Democratic delegates were chosen in caucuses—yet they ultimately proved decisive to the outcome in what turned out to be a hard-fought nomination race that year. It is therefore important to examine how caucuses differ from primary elections, and how these differences matter for candidate strategies and electoral outcomes.

The party caucus is a legacy of the pre-reform presidential nomination process. Caucuses or state conventions were commonly used before 1972 to select delegates who would attend the national convention as representatives of the state party. As a result, these delegates' votes would often be influenced, and were commonly controlled outright, by party leaders and elected officials from their home states. Attempts by candidates to court their support were usually made after these delegates were selected by state parties. The first strategic requirement for the candidate seeking to influence these delegates was an intelligence service—a network of informants who could report on which delegates were firmly committed, which were wavering, and which might be persuaded to provide second- or third-choice support. Advance reports on the opportunities offered by internal division in the state parties, the type of appeal likely to be effective in each state, and the kinds of bargains to which leaders were most amenable were also helpful. The costs of this information were high in time, money, and effort, but it was worthwhile to the serious candidate, who needed to know how to maneuver to increase support and block opponents.

After the disastrous 1968 national convention in Chicago, the Democratic Party created an internal committee, the McGovern-Fraser Commission, to propose changes to the party rules governing presidential nomination procedures. The commission recommended, and the Democratic National Committee agreed, that states be required to select delegates via a process in which all registered voters who identify as members of the party may participate. Republicans soon adopted a similar provision. Although most states have opted to satisfy these mandates by holding primary elections, several states—most notably Iowa—have retained the caucus system of delegate selection, merely opening them to all eligible party voters. The use of caucuses is most widespread among lightly populated states in the Midwest and West and within territories of the United States such as Guam and American Samoa. Today, however, the delegates selected in caucuses can no longer be said to represent the state party or its leaders. As in primaries, these delegates are pledged to support a specific candidate at the national convention, and are chosen by caucus participants to reflect their own preferences.

In general, caucuses differ from primaries in two key respects: there are often many fewer voting sites within the state—perhaps only one per county—and participation requires attending a (possibly lengthy) party meeting at a specific time, usually on a weekday evening. As a result, turnout rates for caucuses are consistently quite low, since the sacrifice in time and energy required of voters far exceeds that of a simple primary election. Iowa, site of the first and most prominent caucus, is a partial exception to this generalization due to the extraordinary amount of candidate activity (and media coverage) that descends on the state every four years and stimulates levels of voter participation that approach those of some primaries.

Caucus procedures vary from state to state. Some caucuses resemble simple straw polls, while others take the form of extended sessions at which a great deal of other party business is transacted. Iowa Democrats employ a unique two-stage process in which each candidate's supporters openly declare their preferences by congregating in a group to be counted by party officials. If a candidate fails to receive enough support in the first round of voting to gain at least one delegate from the precinct to the county party convention, that candidate's supporters are free to distribute themselves among other candidates for the second count, which determines the final allocation of delegates. The results reported to the news media on caucus night are not, in fact, the actual votes of individual Iowans, but instead represent the share of county convention delegates won by each candidate through this system, which particularly benefits candidates who are popular second-choice alternatives for voters whose preferred candidate was eliminated in the first round of their precinct caucus. Later on, these county conventions choose representatives to the state party convention, which in turn selects Iowa's national convention delegation.

The nature of caucuses tends to reward candidates who have extensive campaign organizations in the state able to mobilize voters to attend the caucus meetings and navigate their procedural complexity. Candidates with particularly devoted followings often finish higher in caucuses than in primaries, since their supporters are more willing to make the required effort to participate. In 2008, for example, Representative Ron Paul of Texas, running as an outspoken libertarian candidate for the Republican presidential nomination, consistently performed much better in caucuses than in primaries. Of the ten states in which Paul received at least 15 percent of the vote, six held party caucuses. His strongest showing was in the February 5 caucus in Montana, where he took 25 percent, placing second to Mitt Romney. Paul's appeal was quite limited even within the Republican electorate, but the low-turnout caucus system allowed his small faction of fervent supporters to cast a greater share of the vote than they did in primaries dominated by more casual, more moderate voters.

On the Democratic side in 2008, Obama strategists placed special emphasis on competing in caucuses, which they believed would favor their strong grassroots organization and high level of supporter enthusiasm. "[T]he first six [Super Tuesday] states we staffed were caucus states," recalled Obama adviser Steve Hildebrand. "That was a strategic decision."[64] The Clinton campaign, in contrast, was wary of caucuses, especially after Clinton's disappointing performance in Iowa, and believed that the time commitments they require prevented the participation of working-class voters who preferred their candidate. According to one campaign aide who spoke to her on the subject, "Hillary . . . hated caucuses [because] her supporters had jobs to go to, they were waitresses and day care workers. . . . 'The caucus system skews to the wealthy!' she said."[65]

As a result, Clinton made little effort in most caucus states, openly conceding them to Obama. This decision allowed the Obama campaign to rack up overwhelming margins among caucus delegates that effectively counteracted much of Clinton's success in larger primary states. On February 5, for example, Obama received nearly 80 percent of the vote in the Idaho caucus, winning fifteen of the state's eighteen pledged delegates. This net gain of twelve delegates for Obama from Idaho more than negated the fifty-nine-to-forty-eight delegate advantage won by Clinton courtesy of her ten-point primary victory on the same day in New Jersey, where more than fifty times as many Democrats had turned out to vote. The Texas Democratic Party holds a simultaneous primary and caucus dubbed the "Texas two-step," with each event selecting a share of the state's delegates to the national convention. True to form, while Clinton won the Texas primary vote in 2008, Obama prevailed in the caucus—and ultimately won more delegates from the state.

SUPERDELEGATES

The reforms instituted in 1972 were designed to eliminate the direct power of party officials to control the outcomes of presidential nominations. The Hunt Commission of the early 1980s, one of a succession of internal Democratic Party committees charged with proposing further reform measures, recommended that party leaders be brought back into the nomination process by granting them automatic seats as delegates at the national convention that did not require them to be pledged beforehand to support a particular candidate. The Democratic National Committee agreed, creating delegate positions known formally under party rules as unpledged Party Leaders and Elected Officials (PLEO) delegates, but popularly referred to as "superdelegates."[66]

Who are the superdelegates? All sitting Democratic senators, representatives, and governors receive automatic delegate status, as do all members of the Democratic National Committee (including all state party chairs and vice chairs) and all current and former Democratic presidents, vice presidents, congressional leaders, and national party chairs. About eighty "add-on" superdelegate positions are also distributed among the state parties to fill however they wish; these seats are often given to state legislative leaders or mayors of large cities. Superdelegates usually number about eight hundred, constituting less than 20 percent of all Democratic convention delegates. Typically, slightly more than half of the superdelegates are members of the DNC.

In most elections, as we have seen, a presumptive nominee emerges fairly early in the process and soon collects a majority of delegates by winning a succession of primaries and caucuses, making the preferences of superdelegates irrelevant to the outcome. In 1984, superdelegates overwhelmingly supported Walter Mondale, and did so not late in the convention but relatively early in the primary season. Whether Mondale could have won without them, or, as is more likely, they helped sustain his strength during his bid, the superdelegates did matter.

But only in 2008 did superdelegates play a central and highly visible role in determining the Democratic nominee. Hillary Clinton began the year claiming an edge in public support among superdelegates, but at no point did she have a majority—perhaps an indication of the limit of her candidacy's appeal. As Barack Obama gained a slowly growing lead in pledged delegates during the primary season, his superdelegate support steadily increased as well, including some defections from Clinton. By mid-February, it became clear that the margin between Clinton and Obama in the pledged delegate count would be sufficiently close to allow the superdelegates, in principle, to decide the contest. Both campaigns devoted a great deal of energy to courting unpledged delegates, announcing each new endorsement with much fanfare as the news media—and even the general public—focused with intensifying interest on what had previously been a procedural obscurity. Many DNC members accustomed to relative anonymity were suddenly swamped with attention from journalists, campaign operatives, and voters hoping to divine or influence their choice of candidate. The nation's youngest superdelegate, a twenty-one-year-old college student from Wisconsin named Jason Rae, was taken to breakfast by Hillary Clinton's daughter Chelsea and received telephone calls from Bill Clinton and former secretary of state Madeleine Albright on behalf of the Clinton campaign, while the Obama team dispatched Senator John Kerry, the 2004 Democratic presidential nominee, to discuss party strategy with him.[67] Rae's status as an overnight political celebrity among his peers was cemented when he was interviewed in his dormitory room by a correspondent from *The Daily Show* on Comedy Central.

Once it became clear that Obama would outdistance Clinton in the pledged delegate count but remain short of an overall majority, requiring superdelegate votes to put him over the top, the Obama campaign gained a powerful argument with which to sway undecided superdelegates: how could the party rightfully deny the nomination to the candidate who had won the most support among the Democratic electorate? Clinton advisers countered with a two-part response. First, they argued that Clinton had actually received more total votes than Obama, but this was only true if the results of the disqualified Michigan primary were counted—an election in which Obama had not appeared on the ballot. Second, Clinton made the case to superdelegates that she would be a far stronger candidate for the party in the general election, telling several of them privately that she considered Obama to be unelectable.[68]

Obama ended the primary season on June 3 with a 124-vote lead over Clinton in pledged delegates (1,748 to 1,624). Though members of the news media had previously speculated that the nomination fight might continue into the summer, perhaps even to the national convention, enough previously neutral superdelegates endorsed Obama on the final day of the primaries to provide the necessary 2,142 delegates for the nomination, allowing him to claim victory in his remarks that evening. Clinton conceded the race several days later. In this case, the superdelegates technically determined the outcome of the nomination process, but in fact merely ratified the results of the pledged delegate selection contests.

Much was made in 2008 of the potential power of unpledged delegates not chosen by primary or caucus electorates to select the party nominee when the pledged delegates turn out to be closely divided. For this very reason, however, it is difficult to envision a scenario in which superdelegates would collectively deny the nomination to a candidate finishing first in the pledged delegate count. Presumably, only under unusual circumstances would party officials risk a certain firestorm that would divide the party and raise questions about the legitimacy of its nominee just as the general election campaign began. As the events of 2008 made clear, superdelegates are hardly a unified cabal of party insiders conspiring to exert control over the nomination process. Like any large group of political figures, they face differing personal incentives and disagree among themselves as to the best course of action. Many declined in 2008 to make public endorsements before the end of the campaign, wishing, perhaps prudently, to avoid angering nearly half the party (and, possibly, the eventual nominee) by openly favoring one candidate over the other. Of course, if superdelegates are nearly certain to endorse the preferences of party voters as expressed through the pledged delegate selection events, it raises the question of whether their existence provides any additional substantive value to the party or the nomination process.

The Republican Party also seats unpledged delegates, though they are less numerous and have received little public attention. All Republican National Committee members and state party chairs, but not elected officials, enjoy *ex officio* status as automatic delegates to the national convention. This group constitutes less than 10 percent of the total number of Republican delegates.

At one time, party leaders might have been expected to represent a moderating influence on the more ideologically extreme issue activists who served as pledged delegates. For party officials to play a moderating role, however, they must be moderate themselves. The ideological polarization of the major parties over the past half-century makes this increasingly unlikely. While party leaders might have other grounds upon which to differ with the preferences of activists—for example, they might place more value on the perceived electability of a presidential nominee in a general election—the experience of 2008 suggests that there is little prospect of superdelegates exercising a collective veto over the party membership's choice of candidate even if they have the mathematical power to do so.

THE NATIONAL PARTY CONVENTIONS

The national party conventions are four-day events held by both major parties in the summer of a presidential election year to formally nominate candidates for president and vice president, to approve an official platform, and to resolve other internal party matters. Each party's national committee usually selects a site and date for the convention between eighteen months and two years in advance of the event itself. Political considerations are often important in tipping the balance between competing potential host cities. Democrats chose Denver in 2008 partly because the party was seeking to increase its strength in the West and because the state of Colorado, long a Republican bastion in presidential politics, had been recently trending Democratic. Republicans chose Saint Paul, Minnesota, in 2008 in part because the Twin Cities media market encompasses large areas of the presidential swing states of Minnesota, Iowa, and Wisconsin. In 2012, the Democrats met in Charlotte, North Carolina, to recognize that state's growing electoral competitiveness, while Republicans chose Tampa in the perennial battleground state of Florida. The parties opted for populous swing states once again in 2016, with the Republicans meeting in Cleveland, Ohio, and the Democrats assembling in Philadelphia, Pennsylvania.

Other considerations include the quality of the facilities, the suitability of the convention hall to television coverage, sufficient hotel and entertainment accommodations, and (for Democrats) the availability of places to meet and stay with acceptable records on the treatment of labor unions.[69] The parties prefer to bring their publicity and their business to cities and states where the mayor and the governor are friendly members of the party, since this may give added access to (and control of) public facilities. In 2008, Colorado's Democratic governor Bill Ritter and Minnesota's Republican governor Tim Pawlenty both satisfied that objective, as did Democratic governor Bev Perdue of North Carolina and Republican governor Rick Scott of Florida in 2012—and Democratic governor Tom Wolf of Pennsylvania and Republican governor John Kasich of

Ohio in 2016. In 2004, the Republicans selected New York, thanks in part to the presence of a Republican mayor, Michael Bloomberg, and governor, George Pataki. Aides to George W. Bush also wished to use the convention to emphasize the president's record on fighting terrorism by holding it in the same city as the World Trade Center attacks of September 11, 2001. Democrats, meanwhile, chose Boston as the site of their 2004 convention, which turned out to be the hometown of their nominee that year, John Kerry.

The timing of conventions varies between mid-July and early September. Since the four-year periodicity of presidential elections always coincides with the Summer Olympics, parties are careful not to schedule their conventions during the weeks when Americans are especially distracted from politics by the spectacle of international athletic competition. By tradition, the party of the sitting president holds its convention after the party of the opposition, whether or not the incumbent is seeking another term in office. It was once common for the two national conventions to be separated by a month or more, but in 2008, 2012, and 2016 the parties opted to schedule them in consecutive weeks.

PARTY DELEGATES AT THE CONVENTIONS

In bygone days, presidential nominations were actually decided at the conventions, rather than months in advance by the results of primaries and caucuses. Today's conventions can therefore seem anticlimactic in comparison, with the participants holding more symbolic than substantive importance. It is still valuable, however, to know something of the delegates themselves, since they represent the more engaged and committed sector of the party to which they belong. Who are they? Who do they represent? What do they believe? Repeated studies of convention delegates allow us a perspective on the changing nature of party activists. While delegates today no longer have independent influence over the choice of the presidential nominee, they still play a role in platform debates and in establishing the image the party projects on television. If we should ever have a deadlocked convention, in which no single candidate enters with a majority of delegate votes, delegate attitudes and behavior will take on even more importance.

Each of the major parties has its own distinctive style and norms. "Republicans," Jo Freeman observes, "perceive themselves as insiders even when they are out of power, and Democrats perceive themselves as outsiders even when they are in power."[70] This difference can be elaborated: Republicans in convention are ideologically oriented, while Democrats think of themselves as members of subgroups. As the more hierarchical party, Republicans stress loyalty to the chosen leader and the organization. The more varied and egalitarian Democratic Party, in Freeman's words, "has multiple power centers that compete for membership support in order to make demands on, as well as determine, the leaders."[71] For Democratic delegates, therefore, subgroup caucuses are significant reference groups. The component parts of the Republican Party, states and geographic regions and ideological factions, do not maintain robust lives outside the party structure, as do the Democratic caucuses of African Americans, union members, feminists, gay rights activists, or environmentalists, nor on the Republican side do they make decisions and proposals as much as serve as conduits of information downward to delegates. Democrats go to caucuses, as Freeman says, while Republicans go to receptions. Republicans "network" with the candidate organizations, while Democrats make demands. Democrats expect their nominee to pay attention to their problems, while Republicans are more likely to think that the winner ought to get his or her way until the next time.[72]

The Democratic rules governing delegate selection have succeeded in increasing the proportion of racial minorities and women in attendance over the decades. But even if delegates differ somewhat by income and education, political activists are still a rather elite group. Table 4.3 reveals the differences in income between delegates and party voters for both parties in 2008, the last year for which data are available.

Educational differences between delegates and the broader universe of party identifiers were even more striking. About seven in ten delegates from both parties had college degrees, compared to one in five among rank-and-file Democrats and one in three of rank-and-file Republicans. Little had changed from 1975, when Jeane Kirkpatrick concluded, "The delegates to both conventions were an overwhelmingly middle to upper class group."[73] Summarizing the demographic composition of delegates from 1944 to 2008, table 4.4 reveals a gradual rise in the education level of delegates. But the big change evident over the same period is the four-and-a-half-fold increase in the participation of women (with the conspicuous exception of the 2008 Republican convention, which also had a particularly old group of delegates).[74] From 1972 to 1976, half of female Democratic delegates were employed in the public sector, either in government itself or in public education. This was also true of a little over a third of Democratic male delegates. Among Republicans, somewhat more than a third of female and just under a fifth of male delegates were government employees. Over a quarter of all delegates were union members, most of them from teachers' and other public-sector unions. For women in particular, then, M. Kent Jennings concludes, "public employment is a key route to the avenues of party power."[75]

As the party traditionally favoring government, it is to be expected that Democratic delegates would come more frequently from the public sector. This may also explain why they seek higher spending on domestic programs. But there is nothing inherent in government employment that would necessarily lead to a preference for lower spending on defense or against military intervention in the Middle East or for liberal positions on social issues. For that we must look to an ideological explanation.

TABLE 4.3. Income of Delegates and Party Voters in 2008 (in Percentages)

	Voters	Delegates
Democrat's Income		
Less than $50,000	43	10
$50,000 to $75,000	21	17
Over $75,000	26	70
Republicans' Income		
Voters, 2008		
Less than $50,000	31	5
$50,000 to $75,000	22	22
Over $75,000	39	66

Source: "*The New York Times*/CBS News Poll 2008 Republican National Delegate Survey," http://graphics8 .nytimes.com/packages/pdf/politics/20080901-poll.pdf.

TABLE 4.4. Selected Delegate Surveys, 1944–2008 (in Percentages)

	1944 Dem.	1944 Rep.	1968 Dem.	1968 Rep.	1976 Dem.	1976 Rep.	1984 Dem.	1984 Rep.	2004 Dem.	2004 Rep.	2008 Dem.	2008 Rep.
By sex												
Men	89	91	87	83	67	69	49	54	50	57	51	68
Women	11	9	13	17	33	31	51	46	50	43	49	32
By education												
High school or less	24	23	N.A.	N.A.	N.A.	N.A.	11	12	5	6	4	3
Some college	18	18	N.A.	N.A.	N.A.	N.A.	18	25	18	20	12	15
College graduate	12	16	10	–	21	27	20	28	24	29	26	31
More than college degree	46	41	44	34	43	38	51	35	53	44	55	50
By age												
Average age (in years)	52	54	49	49	43	48	44	51	51	53	52	56
Convention attendance												
Never attended convention before	63	63	67	66	80	78	74	69	57	55	57	58
By ideology												
Liberal	–	–	–	–	40	3	50	1	41	1	43	–
Moderate	–	–	–	–	47	45	42	35	52	33	50	26
Conservative	–	–	–	–	8	48	5	60	3	63	3	72

Sources: Barbara G. Farah, "Delegate Polls: 1944 to 1984," *Public Opinion* (August/September 1984): 44. Reprinted with permission of American Enterprise Institute for Public Policy Research; "*The New York Times*/CBS News Poll National Delegate Surveys," 2004 and 2008 http://www.nytimes.com/packages/html/politics/20040829_gop_poll/2004_gop_poll_results.pdf; http://www.nytimes.com/packages/html/politics/20040724poll/20040724_delegates_poll_results.pdf; http://graphics8.nytimes.com/packages/pdf/politics/20080901-poll.pdf; http://graphics8.nytimes.com/packages/pdf/politics/demdel20080824.pdf

Notes: 1984 figures are a combination of the CBS News poll, the *New York Times* poll, and the *Los Angeles Times* poll; the 1968 and 1976 figures come from the CBS News poll.

Delegates are more likely to represent the ideological left or right, while the bulk of the voters out in the country remain closer to the center. This pattern has occasionally resulted in the nomination of a presidential candidate who is also ideologically extreme. The classic examples were the Republicans in 1964 and the Democrats in 1972. The former selected the very conservative Senator Barry Goldwater of Arizona, while the latter chose the very liberal Senator George McGovern of South Dakota. In each case, studies found that convention delegates held political beliefs that were not shared by ordinary members of their party. In each case, the nominee lost badly in November partially because of defections from his own party to the opposition candidate. At the 1972 Democratic convention, McGovern supporters shared the same attitudes whether they were male or female, white or black, young or old. Perhaps what happened is that activists in both parties, enjoying high social and economic status but without professional commitment to party unity or party organization, grew at once farther apart from one another and from the voters. The participant sectors of the parties were far more polarized in 1972 than they had been in the 1940s and 1950s in two directions—one party from the other at the elite level, and elites in both parties from their followers.[76]

Evidence from representative governments throughout the world demonstrates that voters have more ideologically moderate views than elected officials, who in turn are more moderate than party activists.[77] While the general public prefers smaller government and restrictions on abortion far more than Democratic elites do, it also likes environmental regulation and deficit reduction a lot more than Republican elites do. Tables 4.5 and 4.6 compare the views of delegates to the Democratic and Republican national conventions in 2008 to the positions of Democratic and Republican identifiers, and to all voters. On nearly every issue, convention delegates were significantly more extreme than the rank-and-file members of their own party, and were far more so than the less ideologically oriented American electorate.

Trends in the ideological dispositions of party activists in the two parties are reflected in changes in the composition of the two delegate populations over time. Democratic delegates have become somewhat more liberal, and Republicans more conservative, reflecting the growing polarization of American political elites also seen in congressional voting behavior in recent decades.[78] The view that the major parties were essentially alike, which was never true, is even less true today. The consequences of ideological polarization, which is what we have been describing, are well known: heightened conflict and the risk of political instability. According to the venerable theory of cross-cutting cleavages, when people agree on some issues and disagree on others, the need to call on each other for support sometimes moderates the severity of conflict at other times. Polarization, recently on the rise, by putting the same people in opposition on issue after issue, increases antagonism.

THE CONVENTION AS ADVERTISING

Party conventions were probably always seen, in part, as a means of advertisement. At the least, listening to convention speeches and talking to peers might furnish delegates with rhetoric to use in local campaigns back home. But until the age of modern electronic media, conventions were primarily concerned with nominating candidates and other internal party activity.

TABLE 4.5. Democratic Delegates to the Left of Rank-and-File Party Members and Public, 2008 (Percentages in Agreement with Statements)

	All Voters	Democratic Voters	Democratic Delegates
2001 tax cuts should be made permanent	47	34	7
The U.S. was right to invade Iraq in 2003	37	14	2
Abortion should be permitted in all cases	26	33	58
Gay couples should be allowed to marry	34	49	55
Protecting the environment is more important than developing new energy sources	21	30	25

Source: "*New York Times*/CBS News Poll 2008 Republican National Convention Delegate Survey," http://graphics8.nytimes.com/packages/pdf/politics/demdel20080824.pdf.

Television arrived at the conventions in 1952 and transformed their role, with the help of party reforms that ended the old system of selecting nominees via deliberation and compromise. Now, conventions are for selling candidates.[79] The proceedings are planned in order to promote the presidential nominee, running mate, and party to a national audience. The substantive business of conventions, such as putting the names of candidates before the assembled delegates and approving the party platform, is scheduled for afternoon or early evening sessions before the broadcast networks' live coverage goes on the air. Prime time is filled with speeches meant to appeal to voters, along with documentary films prepared beforehand to keep viewers interested.[80] Indeed, conventions are now judged by pundits on how well they are organized as advertisements. Any intrusion of substantive debate (such as platform disagreements) into the convention is considered a breach of unity and therefore a sign of weakness in the party. More serious still is poor entertainment. Woe to any convention such as the one in New York that renominated Jimmy Carter in 1980, in which the mechanism for releasing brightly colored balloons from the roof of Madison Square Garden malfunctioned, thus providing commentators with a handy metaphor for the incumbent president's stalled reelection bid.[81] Carter's misfortune contrasts strikingly with Barack Obama's 2008 acceptance speech spectacle, featuring a well-delivered address before a cheering crowd of 80,000 people in a football stadium followed by outdoor fireworks.

The advertising content of the conventions is influenced by the decisions of television news producers; the parties try to provide programming that they believe the networks will allow people to see, now that the parties cannot count on extensive coverage. Currently, the broadcast networks cover the conventions through their nightly news reports, their morning shows, and one- or two-hour wrap-up programs from the conventions during prime time, while cable news channels cover them live throughout the day and evening, albeit with frequent cutaways from the proceedings for analysis

TABLE 4.6. Republican Delegates to the Right of Rank-and-File Party Members and Public, 2008 (Percentages in Agreement with Statements)

	All Voters	Republican Voters	Republican Delegates
2001 tax cuts should be made permanent	47	62	91
The U.S. was right to invade Iraq in 2003	37	70	80
Abortion should be permitted in all cases	26	13	5
Gay couples should be allowed to marry	34	11	6
Protecting the environment is more important than developing new energy sources	21	9	3

Source: "*New York Times*/CBS News Poll 2008 Republican National Convention Delegate Survey," http://graphics8.nytimes.com/packages/pdf/politics/20080901-poll.pdf.

and punditry.[82] Uninterrupted gavel-to-gavel coverage of convention business can now be found only on the C-SPAN cable network or via online streaming.

By using the convention as advertising, the parties hope to receive a "bounce" in the support their candidates get in the polls. Since the advent of modern public opinion research, only Lyndon Johnson in 1964 (who was already winning by a landslide) and George McGovern in 1972 (who had a disastrous convention) failed to improve in voter surveys taken immediately after their conventions. One might think that this effect would dissipate as broadcast networks reduced the amount of convention coverage and as viewers had more options than network television. But the public still appears to respond positively to the conventions, at least temporarily. In 1996, both Bill Clinton and Bob Dole received healthy bounces of several percentage points in the polls, as did George W. Bush and (especially) Al Gore in 2000.[83] The nominees in 2004, George W. Bush and John Kerry, each received a more modest convention bounce, pegged at 4 percentage points apiece by the *Washington Post*/ABC News poll.[84] Assessing the 2008 bounces is complicated by the back-to-back scheduling of the conventions, but both Barack Obama and John McCain did seem to receive small poll boosts from the party conclaves.[85] In 2012, Obama received a noticeable bounce of several points from his convention, though polls disagreed about whether Mitt Romney did the same.[86]

How do the parties turn what once was a business meeting into advertising?

1. The layout of the convention hall itself is designed with television, not the comfort of the delegates, as the first priority. As the late Bob Squier, a leading Democratic media consultant in the 1980s, said, "To be blunt, the room is designed to be a television set." Another Democratic media expert, Frank Greer, said in praise of the 1988 convention: "It has become clear that, as it should be, this is a convention designed and presented for TV viewers more so than for delegates on the floor. It's a chance to talk to people in their living rooms and not the delegates on the floor."[87]

2. The delegates, far from having an important role in deciding party business, have been reduced to serving primarily as extras. "Homemade" handwritten signs are actually constructed by the party to reinforce campaign themes; neither party normally allows delegates to bring in their own banners. Not even crowd noises are left to chance: at its 1992 convention in Houston, the Republican Party "arranged that, at key moments, troops of rehearsed young people flooded onto the floor and filled the first fifty feet in front of the podium and in the aisles. They knew what to chant when, and they were standing in front of most of the delegates so they couldn't be missed by the cameras."[88]

3. Both parties try to script as much as possible of the convention, carefully orchestrating the words and images delivered from the podium and providing suggested responses to likely interview targets. Speeches are preapproved by campaign advisers, fed into teleprompters, and timed so that signs and chants from the floor can be properly coordinated with them. Convention organizers try to present an appealing public image by attempting to contradict unfavorable stereotypes about the kinds of people who belong to their party. For example, observers at the 2004 Republican convention noted that there was a far higher proportion of members of minority groups at the speaker's podium, or providing the musical entertainment, than in the hall as delegates.[89] Similarly, the Democrats that year emphasized the Navy service of their nominee, John Kerry, in order to counter perceptions during a time of war that the party was antimilitary. Kerry began his acceptance speech by giving a salute to the assembled delegates and telling them that he was "reporting for duty."[90]

Very little is left to chance. The parties treat their conventions as extended commercials for the presidential ticket and for the party as a whole.[91] This is not necessarily a bad thing: many commentators have urged the networks to make available free airtime for the parties to present their messages directly to the voters during the fall campaign, not realizing that the conventions already serve that purpose (though broadcast networks have devoted progressively less time to convention coverage over the last several elections). First and foremost, the candidate wants a united party.[92] Rival candidates or disgruntled party leaders who are in a position to disrupt this unity may extort small advantages from the nominee, a significant strategic resource for Jesse Jackson's candidacies in the 1980s. By threatening messy floor fights over several issues, Jackson won changes to Democratic Party rules, cutting the number of superdelegates and requiring that all delegates be awarded to candidates on a proportional rather than a winner-take-all basis.

The unusually close Democratic primary contest in 2008 meant that nearly half of the delegates attending the party's national convention to nominate Barack Obama had been strong supporters of Hillary Clinton's unsuccessful presidential campaign. After the long battle of the nomination season, Obama's campaign advisers were somewhat mistrustful of both Hillary and Bill Clinton and worried about their behavior at the convention. *Newsweek* later reported "nervousness that the Clintons, with an eye on [another presidential run in] 2012, might try to steal the show, perhaps by demanding a noisy floor vote that would show how close Hillary had come to the nomination. The Obamaites figured that the Clintons could be counted on to do just enough to say that they tried to help Obama—but maybe not so much that he won in November."[93] Ultimately, both Clinton spouses delivered well-received convention speeches that endorsed Obama without equivocation, to the great relief of both the Obama team and Democratic leaders worried about a divided party heading into the fall campaign. Nor did the Clinton faction cause Obama any procedural difficulties; during the traditional roll call of state delegations, Hillary Clinton introduced a "surprise" motion from the floor that Obama be nominated by acclamation—a stunt that was choreographed by convention planners to occur during the networks' evening news broadcasts, thus maximizing public attention.[94] With the assistance of both Clintons, Obama succeeded in convincing the news media and, by extension, the voters that the party had united around his candidacy.

The rare moments when true spontaneity is injected into the proceedings of a modern convention usually turn out to be bad news for both the nominee and the party. In the midst of a speech in support of Mitt Romney at the 2012 Republican convention in Tampa, Academy Award-winning actor and director Clint Eastwood launched into an impromptu routine in which he improvised an antagonistic conversation with an absent Barack Obama, represented by Eastwood's placement of an empty chair on the stage next to him. Romney campaign staff insisted afterward that they were unaware in advance of Eastwood's plans to ad lib at great length. Reviews in the news media were decidedly unkind—the *New York Times* described the speech as "the most bizarre, head-scratching 12 minutes in recent political convention history," CNN called it "rambling" and "vaudevillian-like schtick," and the *Washington Post* characterized it as "like your crabby uncle doing dinner-table comedy"—while the unexpected oddness of Eastwood's behavior made his remarks an instant viral sensation on social media, leaving Republicans deeply frustrated that the performance diverted popular attention from Romney's own acceptance address later in the evening.[95] The response to Eastwood's "empty chair" speech will no doubt lead to an even tighter degree of control over speakers at future national conventions, as campaigns seek to minimize any potential sources of distraction or embarrassment during their week in the public spotlight.

THE VICE PRESIDENTIAL NOMINEE

After the national convention finally nominates a presidential standard-bearer, it turns to the routine task of ratifying the nominee's choice for vice president. Party nominees for president and vice president always appear on the ballot together and are elected together; since 1804 a vote for one has always been a vote for the other. Presidential contenders therefore select their running mates in order to help them achieve the presidency. They look for a vice presidential candidate who is politically and personally compatible with themselves, who promises to inspire respect and enthusiasm among the electorate, who will be judged as sufficiently qualified to assume the presidential office if the need arises, and who possesses some desirable qualities that the presidential nominee lacks (in American political parlance, the running mate must "balance the ticket").

The vice president's constitutional role as the presiding officer of the Senate is mostly honorific, while the office's specific powers and responsibilities in the executive branch are subject to the will of the president and are not necessarily extensive.[96] Yet the vice presidency is the position from which presidents of the United States are most frequently drawn. One-third of our forty-four presidents, and four of the last nine, previously served as vice presidents. Five were later elected president in their own right; eight took office upon the death of their predecessors; and Gerald Ford succeeded because of President Nixon's resignation. American history has given us fourteen good reasons—one for each vice president who ascended to the presidency—for inquiring into the qualifications of vice presidents and for examining the criteria by which they are chosen.

Historically, geographic considerations often played a large role in the selection of a vice presidential candidate. A running mate from a different region of the country was thought to broaden the appeal of the presidential nominee, while a resident of a populous, politically competitive state could potentially deliver the state to the party, thus offering an advantage in the electoral college. The classic example of this approach is Senator John F. Kennedy's selection of Senate Majority Leader Lyndon Johnson to join him on the Democratic ticket in 1960. A liberal Catholic from Massachusetts, Kennedy needed to carry a number of southern states in order to win the election and chose Johnson, an energetic, folksy Texan, to be his ambassador to the region. Johnson spent much of his time campaigning in the South during the final weeks of the race, concentrating especially on his home state, ultimately won by the Democrats by less than fifty thousand votes.[97]

This geography-based approach to vice presidential selection still seems to influence the thinking of many political pundits, who inevitably consider governors, senators, and other officials from key swing states to be likely potential candidates when speculation turns—as it inevitably does in the summer of a presidential election year—to the identity of the vice presidential nominees. Since Kennedy chose Johnson in 1960, however, most presidential candidates have not selected running mates from large or competitive states. In fact, the home states of the last two vice presidents, Dick Cheney of Wyoming and Joe Biden of Delaware, cast just three electoral votes apiece and were both already considered safe territory for their party (as was Alaska, home to 2008 Republican vice presidential nominee Sarah Palin), suggesting that contemporary presidential candidates tend to pick running mates whom they believe will help them win votes everywhere, not just within a single state or region. Though Representative Paul Ryan of Wisconsin, chosen as Mitt Romney's running mate in 2012, did hail from a battleground state, there is little indication that geography played a major role in Romney's decision (campaign aide Beth Myers later remarked that Romney "didn't pick Paul Ryan to put Wisconsin in play")[98]; in any event, Ryan had never run statewide in Wisconsin and his congressional constituency covered only one-eighth of the state.

If the party is split by ideological differences, the selection of a running mate from a rival faction can encourage unity. In 1964, Lyndon Johnson chose a prominent liberal, Senator Hubert Humphrey of Minnesota, as his vice presidential nominee. Johnson's own credentials as a liberal Democrat had weakened from his early days as a New Deal congressman; when Kennedy picked him as vice president, he had been opposed on these grounds by labor leaders and by party officials from several of the most important urban Democratic strongholds. Gerald Ford, with his midwestern and congressional background, may have had the same thing in mind when he chose a more moderate, eastern establishment figure, Governor Nelson Rockefeller of New York, to be vice president on his elevation to the presidency. Later, threats from the right wing of the Republican Party to his own nomination chances caused Ford to dump Rockefeller and replace him for the 1976 election with the more conservative Senator Bob Dole of Kansas. Ronald Reagan, more securely tied to the Republican right wing than Ford, leaned toward the moderate side of his own party in picking George H. W. Bush in 1980. Bush, in turn, looked to the right when selecting a running mate in 1988, settling on Senator Dan Quayle of Indiana, who not only offered solid conservative credentials but also, Bush hoped, would appeal to young people and women, two groups of voters the Republicans were targeting.[99] One measure of how the Republican Party had changed in twenty years was that Bob Dole, placed on the 1976 ticket by Ford to please party conservatives, selected former representative Jack Kemp of New York as his own running mate in 1996 in part to placate Republican activists not convinced of Dole's zeal for cutting taxes.[100]

Though presidential candidates have some freedom to select running mates who differ from themselves ideologically, the issue positions of the vice presidential candidate must still be acceptable to party activists. According to later press reports, John McCain initially favored Senator Joseph Lieberman of Connecticut, the 2000 Democratic vice presidential nominee who had subsequently become an independent and endorsed McCain for president, as his running mate in 2008 in order to reinforce his campaign message of bipartisanship and to bolster his appeal to independent voters and wavering Democrats. But McCain campaign aides argued that Lieberman's liberal views on social issues—as well as the fact that he was not even a Republican—would anger the party faithful, possibly leading to an open revolt on the floor of the convention. Looking back after the election, McCain's chief campaign strategist Steve Schmidt claimed that Lieberman's selection "would have been an exciting and dynamic pick . . . that would have been electrifying to the broader electorate," but that McCain "would not have been able to get him nominated through the convention . . . we would have blown up the Republican Party."[101] Similar concerns eliminated Tom Ridge, a former Republican governor of Pennsylvania and secretary of homeland security who favored legalized abortion, from consideration as well.[102] (The fact that many on the right were already suspicious of McCain's own devotion to conservative principles merely strengthened the perceived need for his running mate to be an ideologically orthodox Republican.) McCain ultimately selected Palin, who proved to be popular with party loyalists. Likewise, influential Democratic congressman Barney Frank of Massachusetts responded to rumors that Barack Obama might consider former senator Sam Nunn of Georgia as his vice presidential nominee by publicly warning Obama in June 2008 that he viewed a long-standing record of opposition to gay rights as disqualifying Nunn for a position on the Democratic ticket.[103]

Factional divisions may not necessarily be based on ideology. The long, hard-fought primary campaign between Obama and Hillary Clinton in 2008 inspired widespread speculation that the winning candidate might feel compelled to choose the loser as his or her running mate in order to heal the rift in the party. As it became increasingly clear that Obama would prevail, Clinton supporters were most vocal in calling for a "unity ticket." It appears that the Obama campaign never seriously considered Clinton as a potential vice presidential nominee, concluding that such a move was not necessary in order to win the backing of her followers in the general election. Instead, Obama cemented his reconciliation with Clinton after his victory over McCain by selecting her to be the first secretary of state in his presidential administration.

Another way to balance the ticket is to focus on experience. Presidential nominees who have served little or no time in Washington will typically select a veteran of Congress or the executive branch to reassure voters and the news media that their administration will be competent—and to help them govern successfully once in office.

Jimmy Carter, a one-term former governor of Georgia, chose a popular senator, Walter Mondale of Minnesota, in 1976 to compensate for his own lack of federal experience. Similar considerations drove four other state governors to choose prominent Washingtonians as their running mates—Ronald Reagan's selection of former representative, CIA director, ambassador to China, and Republican National Committee chair George H. W. Bush in 1980, Michael Dukakis's pick of Texas senator Lloyd Bentsen in 1988, Bill Clinton's choice of Tennessee senator Al Gore in 1992, and George W. Bush's selection in 2000 of former House Republican whip, presidential chief of staff, and secretary of defense Dick Cheney all fit this model. Barack Obama, less than four years into his first term in the Senate when nominated for the presidency in 2008, selected six-term fellow senator Joe Biden as his vice presidential candidate in part to address concerns about his own qualifications.

Presidential nominees with long careers in Washington, on the other hand, tend to prefer running mates who are notably younger or who are political "outsiders" in order to provide a fresh-faced contrast to themselves. Examples of this pattern include Richard Nixon choosing Governor Spiro Agnew of Maryland in 1968, George H. W. Bush selecting Dan Quayle in 1988, John Kerry picking first-term senator John Edwards of North Carolina in 2004, and McCain's selection of Palin in 2008. Mitt Romney's choice of Paul Ryan in 2012 represented a new spin on this approach; Ryan, though he was more than twenty years younger in age, had served seven terms in Congress and chaired the House Budget Committee, thus bringing to the ticket extensive federal government experience that Romney lacked.

Personal characteristics or reputations of potential running mates also matter. In the 2000 election, both presidential candidates had perceived deficiencies that they sought to address with their vice presidential selection. Al Gore picked the upright and conspicuously pious Joseph Lieberman to offset the charge that Democrats were morally lax, while George W. Bush picked the veteran administrator Dick Cheney to address the perception that he was incurious about the workings of government. The well-born and detached John Kerry chose John Edwards in 2004 in part to benefit from Edwards's blue-collar roots and telegenic style. Barack Obama's advisers hoped in 2008 that the selection of Joe Biden would help them appeal to working-class white voters who had mostly supported Hillary Clinton over Obama in the Democratic primaries and who were being courted heavily by the McCain campaign. McCain, meanwhile, calculated that choosing Palin might attract female voters disappointed by Clinton's absence from the Democratic ticket.

Recent vice presidential candidates have sometimes been distinguished politicians who had a great deal to recommend them as holders of high office. But the assistance that they could offer their parties in winning the election was undoubtedly an important consideration in their selection. If it is impossible to find one person who combines within his or her heritage, personality, and experience all the virtues allegedly cherished by American voters, the parties console themselves by attempting to confect out of two running mates a composite image of traditional-modern, rural-urban, principled-pragmatic, experienced-outsider, energetic-wise leadership that evokes geographic, ethnic, and partisan loyalties among a maximum number of voters. That, at least, is the theory behind the balanced ticket.

Because the choice of a vice presidential candidate is designed to help the presidential nominee get elected, it is invariably shaped by the strategic environment at the time of the decision. A candidate who is leading in the polls may pick an unexciting but dependable running mate, while an underdog might prefer the option that offers higher risk but a potentially greater reward in the hope of changing the dynamics of the campaign. This last strategy has twice led to the selection of female nominees for the vice presidency by trailing candidates who hoped that an unorthodox running mate would transform the race. Walter Mondale's selection of Representative Geraldine Ferraro of New York in 1984 did not fit traditional patterns of ticket balancing; her views were quite similar to his own, and Mondale had served longer than Ferraro in federal office. Far behind in the polls, Mondale was hoping instead that choosing a woman would mobilize female support and invigorate his candidacy. Richard Brookhiser argues that "the best justification for Mondale's audacity, though, was that it was audacious. . . . Prudent losers remain losers. The first woman on a major party ticket might shake things up."[104] Ferraro's problems with family finances, however, proved to be an unwelcome distraction during the fall campaign, and Mondale lost the election by a wide margin.

In 2008, John McCain took a similar gamble by choosing Sarah Palin, a first-term governor of Alaska who was virtually unknown outside her home state. Palin's selection, announced on the morning after Obama's well-received acceptance speech at the Democratic convention, achieved McCain's goal of catching the Obama campaign, the news media, and the American electorate by complete surprise. McCain advisers were aware of the risk inherent in opting for a running mate with no previous experience in the national political arena, but, like Mondale, concluded that a bold vice-presidential choice offered them the best hope of victory; as one campaign official explained after the election, "We were down nine [percentage points in the polls]. We needed a game changer."[105]

Palin proved to be a charismatic campaigner, but her limited familiarity with national politics, revealed in a series of media interviews, soon became a liability. Political scientist Gerald Pomper concluded that her "ultimate effect on the election is uncertain, but it was probably harmful to McCain" because many in the public came to view her as unqualified for high office.[106] One academic study estimated that Palin's presence on the ticket cost McCain two percentage points in the popular vote, serving as an exception to the usual pattern that running mates seldom substantially affect electoral outcomes.[107] McCain's previous bouts with skin cancer and potential status as the oldest first-term president in American history made the issue of succession to the presidency more salient than usual, to Palin's further disadvantage.

If good results require noble intentions, then the criteria for choosing vice presidents leave much to be desired. Especially able politicians may become vice president because of the political advantages that they promise to bring to the campaign trail, rather than their ideal fitness for the position itself. Yet all successful vice presidential candidates must reassure the public that, regardless of whatever other qualities they may possess, they are not only capable of serving ably in the (not inherently powerful) office for which they have been nominated but are also prepared to lead the nation should circumstances require them to assume the presidency at a moment's notice. There is little sensible reason for a presidential candidate to select a running mate who inspires significant doubt on this point, though it has occasionally happened due to other considerations weighing more heavily in the mind of the nominee. However, history suggests that a risk-averse approach to vice presidential selection is nearly always preferable. A well-received yet unexciting choice may not win millions of votes that the presidential candidate would not have otherwise received, but an attention-grabbing yet controversial pick can, at the least, introduce unwelcome distractions in the midst of a hard-fought campaign, and perhaps even cost the ticket a degree of popular support.

Though prospective running mates are now routinely subjected to extensive vetting by campaign staff, no presidential candidate has the time or resources to research every aspect of a potential vice president's background. Instead, nominees have increasingly turned in recent years to the pool of potential running mates who not only have been thoroughly investigated but also have extensive experience dealing with the national news media: former presidential candidates. George H. W. Bush in 1980, Lloyd Bentsen in 1988, Al Gore in 1992, Jack Kemp in 1996, John Edwards in 2004, and Joe Biden in 2008 had all been scrutinized and tested in previous presidential primaries before their selection as vice presidential running mates. None of them encountered scandal or significant bad press during the fall campaigns. Three vice presidential nominees over that period who had not been previously exposed to national journalists, Geraldine Ferraro in 1984, Dan Quayle in 1988, and Sarah Palin in 2008, ultimately brought far more than their share of turmoil with them, as did George McGovern's original running mate in 1972, Senator Tom Eagleton of Missouri, who left the ticket during the campaign after it was revealed that he had been medically treated for depression. If future presidential nominees want to play it safe in their choice of running mates, they will give special attention to this small group of prescreened possibilities.

THE FUTURE OF NATIONAL CONVENTIONS

If contemporary conventions are really only for advertisement, why do they matter at all? A comparison with the electoral college is instructive. Ever since the early days of the republic, electors virtually always vote as they have been instructed by their states. The majority wins. Should no candidate receive a majority, electors still have no decisive say in the outcome, because under the Constitution the selection is made by Congress from among the top three finishers.[108]

Delegates to nominating conventions, even under the current rules, are in a somewhat different position. While their votes on the nomination are (in normal years) simply a matter of registering the preferences of the voters who chose them, even then they have to vote on platforms and rules. These votes may be important, and the delegates are free to make their own decisions. Even hand-picked delegates have the option of opposing their candidate's preferences, should they so choose.

Far more important, however, is that in the event of deadlock—if no single candidate controlled a majority of delegates going into the convention—the delegates would have the responsibility of selecting the nominee. If the contest is merely close, we would expect few delegate defections, since they have been in most cases selected by candidates mainly on grounds of potential loyalty. A good test of that was the Democratic convention in 1980, when Senator Edward Kennedy hoped to use favorable preconvention publicity to sway the convention. The hope turned out to be unrealistic. In the key test vote, delegates pledged to incumbent president Jimmy Carter stayed loyal to their candidate.

Should no single contender enter the convention with a majority, however, loyalty might matter less. Pundits often mull over this hypothetical scenario early on in the primaries, when no candidate has yet built a sizable majority in the delegate count.

Yet even the lengthy 2008 Democratic nomination battle between Hillary Clinton and Barack Obama resulted in a peaceful, exuberant coronation of Obama at the national convention. As we have seen, a deadlocked convention is not particularly likely. Such a result would almost certainly require at least three candidates to reach the convention with large numbers of delegates; if the convention is divided between only two candidates, one or the other will hold a majority of delegates, no matter how slender. Since the normal operations of primaries and caucuses, along with the media interpretations of victory and defeat, typically reduce the field of presidential aspirants substantially in the first few weeks of the nomination race, a deadlocked convention with three or more candidates is an improbable result. This is particularly true on the Republican side, where the presence of winner-take-all primaries reduces the capacity of also-ran candidates to accumulate delegates. The last convention requiring more than one delegate roll call vote to choose a presidential nominee occurred in 1952, well before the modern system of delegate selection was established. Still, deadlock is theoretically possible, and if it happens, it will be the delegates who will have to choose the party nominee.

How would a modern, post-reform convention handle such a decision? The same rules that have made conventions rubber stamps for voters in primaries also would make bargaining difficult once there. In order to reach the convention, candidates would need intense factional support; delegates selected for those traits would, presumably, be ill-equipped to negotiate away their vote for the candidate to whom they were loyal. The candidates themselves, then, might be the only ones able to negotiate—and candidates fresh off the campaign trail, having endured negative ads and other attacks from each other, might not be eager to cut a deal, or even able to bring along their supporters if they did make a deal.

If the candidates did not resolve their differences, how else would the delegates reach a decision? Some, no doubt, would turn to factional leaders. State delegations might work together, even across candidate lines. Still others might remain unconnected, waiting until someone found a resolution. Given the enormous size of modern conventions (the Democrats seated over five thousand five hundred delegates in 2012, compared to the one thousand one hundred delegates who nominated Franklin D. Roosevelt in 1932), it would be impossible for serious, one-on-one deliberation to take place without some sort of organization emerging. If not, we might expect the media to dominate the proceedings, with delegates swayed by the latest reported rumors and speculations.

Given the modern convention's lack of resemblance to a true deliberative body, it is all but certain that national party leaders would attempt to broker an agreement of some kind—for example, by uniting two contenders on a single presidential ticket—in the period between the end of the primary season and the start of the convention. A convention that assembles with the presidential nomination still unresolved would risk spinning into chaos that would jeopardize the chances of the party in the general election; at the least, it would substantially impede the ability of the eventual nominee to prepare for electoral battle with the opposition. The prospect of convention deadlock, while improbable, increases the incentives of party elites to attempt to nudge secondary candidates out of the race as soon as it becomes clear that they cannot win the nomination on their own but can only act as spoilers by denying the front-runner an overall majority of delegates.

Just as the news media have interacted with political forces to produce the ratifying rather than the deciding convention, so the two have combined to give the conventions their electoral meaning. Deprived of their substantive importance beyond officially confirming the choice of party voters in primaries and caucuses, the conventions become an opportunity for campaign publicity with the party united behind a single candidate and touting his or her plethora of virtues. Without the need to worry about winning the nomination at the convention, candidates can more carefully consider how they want to manage the presentation of their party to the public. Thus national conventions serve dual roles. In a strictly formal sense, they represent the culmination of the nomination process. In terms of their political importance, however, they are best seen as notable milestones in a general election campaign that is, by mid-summer, already well underway.

CHAPTER 5

The Campaign

AFTER THE END of the national party conventions, it was once a tradition for the two presidential candidates to "relax" for a few weeks until Labor Day, when they were supposed to start their official campaigning. Nowadays, the general election campaign begins once both parties have in effect chosen their nominees, usually well in advance of the national conventions in the spring prior to the November election. Once the conventions ratify their selection, the two candidates confront the voters directly, each carrying the banner of a major political party. How do the candidates behave? Why do they act the way they do? What kind of impact do their activities have on the electorate?

For the small minority of Americans who are party activists, campaigns serve as a signal to get to work. How hard they work depends in part on whether the candidates' political opinions, slogans, personalities, and visits spark their enthusiasm. The workers may sit on their hands, or they may pursue their generally unrewarding jobs—checking voting lists, mailing campaign flyers, phone-banking, ringing doorbells—with something approaching fervor.

For the majority of the population, most of whom normally keep their distance from politics, campaigns call attention to the advent of an election. Some excitement may be generated and some diversion (as well as annoyance) provided for those who turn on the television to find that their favorite program has been preempted by political talk or who answer the telephone only to hear a prerecorded message exhorting them to vote. The campaign is a great spectacle. Conversation about politics increases, and some citizens become intensely involved as they get caught up by campaign advertising and mobilization.

Campaigns usually do not function so much to change the minds of citizens as to activate or reinforce previous convictions. As the campaign wears on, the underlying party identification of most people rises ever more powerfully to the surface. Republican and Democratic identifiers are split further apart—polarized—as their increased awareness of party competition emphasizes the things that divide them.[1]

The substance of campaigns depends on the political context. The swiftly changing nature of the electoral environment makes it unwise for candidates to lay down all-embracing rules for campaigning that cannot meet special situations as they arise.

Candidates may prepare for battle on one front and discover that unexpected developments force them to fight on another. Yet political actors must rely on some sort of theory about the probable behavior of large groups of citizens under a few likely conditions. There are too many millions of voters and too many thousands of possible events to deal with each one individually. The candidates must simplify their pictures of the political world or its full complexity will paralyze them; the only question is whether or not their theories, both explicit and implicit, will prove helpful to them.

What kind of organization should they construct? Where should they campaign? What kinds of appeals should they make to which voting groups? How specific should they be in their policy proposals? What kind of personal impression should they seek to create or reinforce? How far should they go in attacking the opposition? How should they behave in debates with their rivals? These are the kinds of strategic questions for which presidential candidates need answers—answers that vary depending on their party affiliations, their personal attributes, whether they are in or out of office, and on targets of opportunity that come up in the course of current events.

THE WELL-TRAVELED CANDIDATES

The central goals of a presidential candidate's campaign are to persuade undecided voters to back the candidate while simultaneously mobilizing existing supporters to vote and work on behalf of the campaign in large numbers. To this end, candidates seek to maintain a high level of visibility throughout the duration of the election season by making public appearances all over the country in order to attract positive attention from voters and the news media.

Long ago, when publicly campaigning on one's own behalf was considered undignified, presidential nominees faced the serious choice of whether to conduct a "front porch" campaign or to get out and meet the people. The first president to make a campaign speech, William Henry Harrison at Columbus, Ohio, in June 1840, was scolded for his pains: "When," the *Cleveland Adviser* asked, "was there ever before such a spectacle as a candidate for the Presidency, traversing the country advocating his own claims for that high and responsible station?" Now, each candidate rents an airplane and hires speechwriters, maps out an itinerary, and flies off in all directions. Veteran campaign reporter David Maraniss of the *Washington Post* describes the campaign bubble that includes the candidates, their advisers and accompanying reporters:

> "The bubble" is what surrounds the traveling road show of any presidential campaign. It includes the candidate, the staff, the press, the plane, the bus and all the electronic gear of the hustle—after all, even in the television era, someone's still got to get out there and do the job—yet it is not so much a tangible phenomenon as a metaphysical one, a way of looking at things, at once cynical and cozy, but mostly just weird. It is where you find both the real story and yet an utterly false one, a speed-blurred picture of a very large country. The bubble is addictive yet debilitating.[2]

There is method in the ceaseless coast-to-coast travel of the presidential candidates over the course of a campaign. Specifically, their behavior is dictated by the strategic implications of the electoral college. Candidates know that electoral votes, allocated on a state-by-state basis, determine the outcome of the election, not the national popular vote. States award their entire allocation of electoral votes under the unit rule to the candidate who places first in the statewide popular vote, even if by a small margin or with less than a majority.

As a result, candidates have no incentive to spend precious time and campaign resources contesting states in which the outcome is not in doubt. Instead, they concentrate on the swing states that are considered winnable by either side. These politically competitive states are also commonly referred to as "battleground" states, reflecting their status as the centers of campaign activity by both candidates.[3] Populous swing states are especially targeted by campaigns, since their large caches of electoral votes are particularly valuable prizes.

Candidates identify potential swing states by whether they have delivered victories to both parties within recent memory, and according to the results of public opinion polls conducted during the campaign. Since the 1990s, most states in the deep South and interior West have voted for Republican candidates by large margins, while the Northeast—New England, New York, New Jersey, Maryland—and the Pacific Coast (especially California) have constituted a similarly reliable geographic base for Democrats.[4] As a result, candidates of both parties tend to ignore these sections of the country, preferring to focus their attention on states expected to be highly competitive. Over the final month before the 2012 election, neither presidential candidate or running mate made a public campaign appearance in the safely Republican states of Alabama, Alaska, Arizona, Arkansas, Georgia, Idaho, Indiana, Kansas, Kentucky, Louisiana, Mississippi, Missouri, Montana, Nebraska, North Dakota, Oklahoma, South Carolina, South Dakota, Tennessee, Texas, Utah, West Virginia, and Wyoming, or the securely Democratic states of California, Connecticut, Delaware, Hawaii, Illinois, Maine, Maryland, Massachusetts, Minnesota, New Jersey, New Mexico, New York, Oregon, Rhode Island, Vermont, and Washington.[5]

Instead, both Barack Obama and Mitt Romney spent the final weeks of the 2012 campaign fighting over the minority of states deemed to hold the balance of power in the electoral college, focusing in particular on swing states with large numbers of electoral votes such as Florida, Ohio, Virginia, and Colorado. Every four years, voters in politically competitive states receive frequent visits from the two candidates, their spouses and running mates, and other top political figures, and are bombarded with advertising and mobilization efforts from both sides attempting to win their support. As Obama adviser Anita Dunn recalled, "Everything in our campaign was driven by battleground states."[6] The candidates' single-minded focus on courting the residents of politically competitive states is a perennial characteristic of presidential contests; on August 4, 2004, George W. Bush and John Kerry found themselves campaigning for votes at the same time within a half-mile of each other in Davenport, Iowa.[7] This attention was vindicated by the results of the 2004 election in Iowa, won by Bush with a margin of only about 10,000 votes out of more than 1.5 million cast.

As the campaign wears on, the candidates take repeated soundings from opinion polls and are likely to redouble their efforts in states where they believe frequent personal visits might turn the tide. The actual itinerary is made by a campaign scheduling team—a phalanx of up to two hundred fifty employees, approximately thirty to forty to plot the schedule and the rest to handle the press and advance work. Schedulers start the process rolling as they determine where the candidate will appear. They adopt two rules for this task: "Go where the polls say an appearance by the candidate can make a difference. Make it look good on television."[8] The scheduler manages this operation so that nominees and running mates get the most value from their appearances. Thus schedulers not only arrange more candidate visits to big competitive states than to smaller, more secure states, but identify particular cities or media markets within the state where a personal appearance might be expected to pay the greatest electoral dividends.

Schedulers try to make plans in advance if possible, but arrangements can change quickly as survey results suggest increasing margins of safety in a given state or reveal new states in need of attention. The McCain campaign, running behind in the polls in the fall of 2008, made scheduling decisions "on the fly" as strategists looked for states where McCain could possibly overcome Barack Obama's lead. The Obama campaign, for its part, capitalized on its financial advantage and favorable position during the final weeks of the campaign by targeting normally Republican-leaning states like Indiana and North Carolina as polls indicated increasing electoral opportunities in such places; this approach paid off when both states voted Democratic for president for the first time in over thirty years.

Schedulers also decide on the type of event to put onto the candidate's itinerary. Early in a campaign, a candidate will attend many fundraisers: some large dinners, some intimate gatherings of significant contributors. As the campaign gains momentum, fund-raising is increasingly transferred to a full-time staff and the candidate's time is devoted to public events, usually with a theme to attract television news coverage. The most common type of event in the weeks before a general election is the large outdoor rally. Entertainers (usually country music stars for Republicans, rock-and-rollers or hip-hop artists for Democrats) and prominent political figures are often enlisted to warm up the audience before a candidate's speech. Some campaigns organize multiday excursions, with candidates traveling between appearances in key states by train, boat, or bus, in order to court additional media attention.

Candidates hold other types of events as well, visiting factories, schools, and diners, delivering addresses to prominent interest groups such as the NAACP and the Veterans of Foreign Wars, and hosting "town hall meetings" in which they respond to questions from voters. As ever, their use is dictated by campaign strategy, with positive coverage on television the most important objective. In 2008, Obama advisers became concerned that their frequent use of outdoor rallies attended by large, adoring crowds confirmed the McCain campaign's criticism of Obama as possessing more glamour than substance. They quickly organized alternative events designed to show their candidate's policy-minded side.[9] But other formats have potential pitfalls of their own. A questioner at a Minnesota town hall meeting held by McCain in October 2008 told the candidate that she couldn't trust Obama because he was "an Arab," prompting McCain to quickly grab the microphone to contradict her and express his belief that his opponent was "a decent family man."[10]

Once the schedulers have booked an appearance for the candidate, the campaign's advance team moves in. Its responsibility is to ensure that the event happens without a hitch and that the candidate's message is presented to an adequately prepared press corps, ready to include the day's sound bite in their story or on the evening news. The advance team's responsibilities include ensuring security for the candidates, arranging transportation (candidates can change vehicles a dozen times or more in one day) and housing, overseeing site setup, and providing campaign signs, buttons, and banners for the crowd. Campaign staff must make certain that the press has audio and visual access to the candidate and facilities from which to file stories, that equipment feeds are working properly, and that the promotional materials on the spot evoke the campaign's theme. For example, Obama's events in 2008 featured signs and rhetorical references reflecting his primary campaign theme of "change," while McCain highlighted his reputation as a political maverick with a message of "reform."

It is beside the point that no one knows whether this frenetic campaign activity does much good. Richard Nixon learned from his enervating experience in 1960, when he pledged to visit all fifty states and then had to follow through on his promise despite a severe illness; in his subsequent campaigns for president in 1968 and 1972, Nixon relied less on in-person campaigning and more on radio and television appearances. Nowadays, most candidates follow a regional strategy geared to earning coverage on local news broadcasts in key competitive states, but they benefit from the existence of national media as well. No matter where the candidates are, the network news programs are likely to report on their activities, extending the reach of a candidate's message far beyond his or her immediate audience.[11]

It is the candidate's job, in this environment, to stay "on message"—that is, if the campaign theme is trust, to emphasize words such as "honesty" or "reliable" in prepared speeches and to work themes of trust into impromptu remarks to the press and public. It is also the candidate's job to deliver a speech with great enthusiasm, no matter how many times he or she has had to reuse the same lines; to avoid doing or saying anything that could be considered embarrassing; and, generally, to be "on" at all times. Presidential candidates must expect to appear before the voters live and on television throughout the campaign, knowing that a small mistake can have devastating consequences.

Sheer physical endurance is required. Bob Dole, running behind in the polls in the final stages of the 1996 contest, embarked on a "96 Hours to Victory Tour," the idea being that he would not stop campaigning (except for quick naps) during the four days before the election:

> Dole caught a cold, and by Monday he could barely speak. But he was buoyant and cheerful, drinking a tea called Throat Coat and gaining strength from surprisingly large and lively crowds that showed up at diners and bowling alleys, high-school gyms and airport hangars, in small towns across the country. . . . Dole's plane got a flat tire on Monday afternoon, so Dole moved into [the press plane], where he dozed up front while his aides tried to hush the serenades by reporters.[12]

John McCain endured a similar final push in 2008, visiting seven states from Florida to Nevada over a twenty-hour trip that ended after midnight on Election Day. Such grueling campaign schedules are potentially risky—an exhausted candidate is more likely to lose his or her temper or commit a damaging gaffe in front of the press or public—but nervous staffers often convince candidates to hold as many events as possible, fearful of the "what if" second-guessing that would inevitably follow a narrow defeat.

Journalists, not voters, are the immediate audience for much of what candidates do while running for the presidency. John Buckley, press secretary to Representative Jack Kemp of New York in 1988, estimated that "if you discount travel time, I'd say that the media take a third of a candidate's entire day. It's not just the news conferences, but one-on-one interviews, hotel room press briefings, radio and television shows, editorial board discussions, back-of-the-car interviews and conversations." Nicolle Wallace, senior adviser to John McCain's 2008 campaign, recalled that McCain "did two to three hours of battleground [state] media [interviews] every day from the middle of August to Election Day . . . with three or four network affiliate reporters in a market and the print reporters . . . plus a satellite tour, and if we were hitting two states, he'd do that twice."[13]

The effect of all this planning and the demands on the candidates' time mean that candidates can seem to be puppets with the campaign staff pulling the strings, ushering them from one performance to another. Indeed, candidates often complain of stress, fatigue, and sometimes confusion as they are whirled from place to place. But this view underestimates the importance of the candidate, who is ultimately responsible for communicating his or her vision to the voters and, if victorious, is also responsible for implementing it.

PERSUADING VOTERS

Political campaigns have two objectives: to persuade voters open to either candidate ("the swing vote") to support their side (or, at the very least, not to support the opposition), and to inspire their own loyalists (the "base vote") to turn out in large numbers and to work hard at persuading and mobilizing others. Sometimes these goals can conflict, as when an ideological appeal designed to motivate the party base risks alienating independent-minded swing voters. But nearly every campaign activity is designed to further one or both aims, with successful campaigns managing to find an appropriate balance between them.

As we discussed in chapter 1, most voters are not particularly open to persuasion; they align with one of the two major parties and nearly always vote for their party's nominee. The ability of a political campaign to affect whether an individual votes or not is similarly constrained. Citizens who have strong political beliefs, who follow current events closely, and who consider political participation to be an important civic duty will tend to turn out on Election Day regardless of campaign mobilization efforts, while those who don't know much and don't care much about politics will generally remain beyond the reach of even the most ambitious get-out-the-vote operations. In addition, most states require voters to have been registered for at least thirty days in order to participate in an election, further complicating the task of bringing new voters into the electoral process. Yet the success of a campaign at persuading and mobilizing key sectors of the electorate can be critical to the outcome of the election, with small marginal differences often representing the difference between victory and defeat.

Historically, the outstanding strategic problem for Democratic politicians has been to get their adherents to turn out to vote for Democratic candidates. Democrats therefore stress appeals to the faithful. One of the major problems for the party, as we saw in chapter 1, is that while the Democratic Party has usually enjoyed a numerical advantage over Republicans among the adult population as a whole, most citizens who identify as Democrats are found at the lower end of the socioeconomic scale and are usually less likely to turn out to vote than those with Republican leanings. So the Democrats put on voter registration drives and seek in every way to get as large a turnout as possible. If they are well organized, they scour the lower-income areas for voters, provide babysitters, and arrange for cars to get the elderly and infirm to the polls, or make sure they have absentee ballots. In states with provisions for early voting, these mobilization efforts can stretch over a week or more.

While the Republican Party is disadvantaged by the overall preponderance of Democratic identifiers in the potential electorate, this gap has diminished over time. The Democrats held a twenty-point edge in the 1960s (54 percent Democratic to 34 percent Republican); by 2000, 39 percent of voters identified as Democrats, 35 percent as Republicans. In 2004, the Republicans had drawn even among actual voters (37 percent each), according to national exit polls.[14] The traditional Democratic advantage reappeared in 2008 and 2012, due in large part to an overwhelming Democratic edge among voters under the age of thirty.[15]

The fact that Republican candidates won seven of the ten presidential elections between 1968 and 2004 even as more Americans considered themselves Democrats demonstrates that party identification, though a powerful indicator of individual voting habits, cannot by itself account for aggregate electoral outcomes. Other factors besides party have been shown to influence the decisions of voters, and are thus of intense interest to campaigns and political analysts alike. Chief among these are the role played by policy issues and by personal evaluations of the candidates in determining the choices made in the voting booth.

Economic Issues

On the broad range of economic affairs and "pocketbook" issues, the Democrats are usually favored as the party most voters believe will best meet their needs. Table 5.1 illustrates the persistence of this view over the decades; more often than not Democrats have received credit as the party most likely to bring prosperity. Democrats are also usually perceived as more in touch with the interests of everyday Americans. One familiar image for many voters is that the Democrats are more concerned "about people like me." Surveys by the Pew Research Center for the People and the Press, for example, found that from 2004 to 2007, 50 to 55 percent of Americans held this view of Democrats, but only 25 to 30 percent perceived Republicans this way.[16] A campaign in which the salient issues are economic, therefore, is more likely to aid the Democrats than the Republicans.

The Democratic Party's modern tendency has been to be "liberal" in several senses of that word. It promises something for everyone. Democrats support extensions of social welfare programs financed by the federal government, an increased minimum wage for the underpaid, health care coverage for the uninsured, job training for the unemployed, better prices for the farmer, additional federal funding for education, programs to protect the environment, and so on. No one is left out, not even business people, who are promised prosperity and given tax benefits, although they usually remain opposed to the additional government regulation of private industry supported by most Democratic candidates.

As a result, opinion surveys usually show that most voters tend to consider themselves closer to the Democratic than the Republican position on economic matters, and to trust the Democratic Party more than the GOP to handle the economy and domestic policy issues such as health care, education, and Social Security. Democratic candidates therefore seek to exploit this advantage by focusing on these topics while on

TABLE 5.1. Which Party Is Better for Prosperity? (in Percentages)

	Republican	Democratic	No Opinion
1952 January	31	35	34
1956 October	39	39	22
1960 October	31	46	23
1964 October	21	53	26
1968 October	34	37	29
1972 September	38	35	27
1976 August	23	47	30
1980 September	35	36	29
1984 August	48	36	24
1988 September	52	34	14
1990 October	37	35	28
1992 October	37	45	18
1996 July	41	42	17
2000 October	40	47	13
2002 September	42	42	16
2005 September	41	46	11
2007 September	34	54	12
2012 September	42	51	7

Source: Data from "Party Images," Gallup.com, http://www.gallup.com/poll/24655/party-images.aspx.

the campaign trail. Yet there are limitations to this strategy. While voters say they are in favor of social programs, they do not like the spending totals that emerge from them—hence Democratic vulnerability to being tagged as serving "special interests." When voters become concerned that excessive government spending has led to inflation, large budget deficits, or high taxes, Democrats are at a disadvantage.

In order to blunt the Democratic advantage on economic matters, Republicans often seek to frame elections as a choice between big government and individual liberty. But because most expensive federal programs, such as Social Security and Medicare, are quite popular with voters, candidates are well advised to be vague concerning the exact types of excessive spending that they oppose. George W. Bush assured his audiences during the 2000 campaign that, due to the federal budget surplus which existed at the time, his ambitious tax cut would not require reductions in entitlement programs that benefit the middle class. In 2012, Mitt Romney found a safer political target in the Affordable Care Act, Barack Obama's controversial health care legislation, promising to repeal it if elected.

Another potentially fruitful tactic for Republican candidates is co-optation. In 2000, then-candidate Bush proposed an initiative, later titled No Child Left Behind (NCLB), that would significantly increase federal spending on public education in exchange for implementing standardized national evaluations of student and school performance. Bush successfully positioned himself as the "education candidate" in the race despite the traditional Democratic edge on the issue, and the enactment of NCLB was one of the major achievements of his first term in office. Bush also succeeded in passing legislation that added a prescription drug benefit to the federal Medicare program—another attempt to challenge Democratic supremacy on domestic policy matters.

When the nation's economy is booming, the incumbent president tends to claim (and receive) credit from the electorate, while tough economic times lead voters to favor a change in party control—even though the connection between economic performance and the policies of a presidential administration is complex at best. The historic Democratic advantage in the realm of economic policy stems in part from the fact that Republican presidents were in office when the Great Depression began in 1929 and during four sizable but shorter recessions more recently (1970–1971, 1982–1983, 1991–1992, and 2008–2009). But Democratic presidents have also suffered blame for poor economic conditions on their watch. After the advent of "stagflation" during the presidency of Jimmy Carter (1977–1981), the Republican Party was for some time deemed the party of prosperity.

In 2008, the faltering national economy worked to the electoral benefit of Barack Obama and his fellow Democrats. Though John McCain was not the incumbent president, Obama succeeded in associating his opponent with Bush's unpopular economic policies in the minds of many voters while positioning himself as the candidate of change. The onset of a serious crisis threatening the financial sector in late September ensured that the nation's economic woes would dominate news coverage in the weeks before the election; McCain's chief campaign strategist admitted afterward that he realized then that McCain's chances of victory were negligible.[17]

By 2012, the American economy had returned to positive but sluggish economic growth, with the national unemployment rate declining from a peak of 10.0 percent in October 2009 to 7.8 percent three years later. The Obama reelection campaign argued that the nation was moving in the right direction thanks to the policies of the incumbent presidential administration—though Obama and his advisers, mindful of the electorate's still-considerable dissatisfaction with the state of the economy, were careful not to appear out-of-touch by seeming to overstate the extent of the recovery (especially after Obama made an off-the-cuff remark in a June 2012 press conference that "the private sector is doing fine," which earned him widespread criticism for appearing far too sanguine about the economic condition of the nation). For opponent Mitt Romney, the continued weakness of the economy after four years of Obama's presidency represented a convincing reason to adopt a new approach—and Romney, a former management consultant and head of a private equity firm, argued that his experience in the business world gave him valuable expertise in creating a positive economic environment. Voters ultimately sided with Obama once again, though his margin of victory in 2012 (3.9 percentage points in the national popular vote) was substantially smaller than it had been in his first election in 2008 (7.3 points).

Foreign Issues

The fact that the Democrats occupied the presidency during World Wars I and II, the Korean War, and the initial stages of heavy American involvement in Vietnam once convinced most voters that Democrats tended to lead the country into war. Republicans were then known as the party of peace, a position underscored by Senator Bob Dole (a decorated hero of World War II) in the 1976 vice presidential debate when he said: "I figured up the other day, if we added up the killed and wounded in Democrat wars in this century, it would be about 1.6 million Americans, enough to fill the city of Detroit."[18] The GOP was known as the party of isolationism, arguing that the United

States should refrain from joining international organizations or alliances, while Democrats often favored heavier engagement in world affairs.

After 1964, when Senator Barry Goldwater of Arizona, the Republican nominee, convinced people that he would use the American military to intervene in a great many places around the world, the Democrats became the party of peace, a feeling reinforced by George McGovern's anti–Vietnam War candidacy in 1972, by President Jimmy Carter's concern with international human rights and peace agreements, by President Ronald Reagan's belligerent rhetoric against the Soviet Union and other American enemies in the 1980s, and the two wars against Iraq fought by George H. W. Bush and his son George W. Bush in the 1990s and 2000s. Thus, in recent years, the Democrats have enjoyed the advantage of being considered the peaceful party. While neither party remains "isolationist" in the historical sense, Republicans tend to be more protective of American sovereignty in international affairs, and are therefore more skeptical of the United Nations and other international organizations, as well as American ratification of multilateral treaties.

The Republicans hold other advantages in the realm of foreign policy. They are usually considered better able to handle military affairs, or to conduct a war should the need arise.[19] Table 5.2 reveals that the GOP has consistently appeared to the public over the past several decades as the party best able to handle issues of war, peace, and national security. George W. Bush won reelection in 2004 in part because most Americans believed that he would better lead the "war on terrorism" than Democratic nominee John Kerry.[20] But this perception abruptly disappeared during Bush's second

TABLE 5.2. Democrats versus Republicans on Foreign Policy (in Percentages)

	Republican	Democratic	No Opinion
1952 January	36	15	49
1956 October	46	16	38
1960 October	40	25	35
1964 October	22	45	33
1968 October	37	24	39
1972 September	32	28	40
1976 August	29	32	39
1980 September	25	42	33
1984 August	30	42	28
1988 September	43	33	24
1990 October	34	36	30
1992 February	39	39	22
2002 September	50	31	19
2005 September	48	37	15
2007 September	42	47	11
2012 September	45	45	10

Sources: "Party Best for Peace," *Gallup Poll Monthly*, February 1992. After 1992: Data from "Party Images," Gallup.com, http://www.gallup.com/poll/24655/party-images.aspx. 1992 question: "Which party is the best for peace?" Prior to 1992: "Which party will keep the country out of World War III?" After 1992: "Which political party will do a better job of protecting the country from international terrorism and military threats?"

term due to his administration's unpopular and (for a considerable time) unsuccessful military occupation of Iraq.

The distinction between domestic and foreign policy has always been a bit artificial. It has been maintained because of the ability of the United States to insulate its domestic economy from international forces. Today, in the age of globalization, that ability is diminishing. The Reagan, George H. W. Bush, and Clinton administrations wanted to reduce international trade barriers to serve their foreign policy and business allies, but each had a hard time beating back protectionist forces worried about domestic unemployment. During the Cold War, it was possible to see American relationships with European or Asian nations mainly in the context of containing the Soviet Union; since then, it has become increasingly clear that American workers and consumers have foreign policy interests. Barack Obama and John McCain differed sharply on trade policy during the 2008 election, with Obama expressing more skepticism toward unfettered global trade than McCain, but the trade policy of his presidential administration did not represent a dramatic break from that of his free-trading predecessors.

Social Issues

What about the third great cluster of problems, the "social issues"—variously labeled (and understood) as crime, race relations, gay rights, abortion, school prayer, and gun control—that involve lifestyles as well as distributions of benefits?[21] Although it is difficult to tell whether this policy domain works consistently for or against a particular political party, conventional wisdom during the 1980s and 1990s held that the increasing political importance of these issues benefited the more culturally conservative Republicans.[22] That appeared to be the case in the 2000 and 2004 elections, in which socially conservative voters contributed importantly to Republican electoral victories.

Recently, however, Democratic leaders have become more aggressive in raising social and cultural issues that they believe mobilize their own popular base in presidential elections. During the Obama presidency, for example, Democrats adopted campaign rhetoric that characterized socially conservative Republican policies (such as restricting legal abortion and allowing private employers to refrain from providing contraception to employees as part of their health insurance coverage) as constituting a "war on women." In addition, the increasing support for gay rights within the American public has transformed a subject once used by Republicans to put Democrats on the defensive—as in the 2004 presidential election, when Republican leaders sponsored a number of state ballot referendums instituting same-sex marriage bans in order to increase the turnout of socially conservative voters, while George W. Bush endorsed a constitutional amendment prohibiting same-sex marriage nationwide—into an issue that Democrats increasingly perceive as politically advantageous. After opposing same-sex marriage during his first presidential campaign in 2008, Barack Obama announced in the spring of 2012 that he was changing his position on the issue, reflecting both increasing public support of same-sex marriage and growing pressure on Obama from Democratic activists and interest groups to support their favored view.

Social issues affect the parties in different ways. The Republican Party may be thought of as a coalition of social conservatives and free-market libertarians. As long as the party concentrates on economic issues, both factions can usually agree on limited government. But on social issues the libertarians favor individual choice and are against government intervention even to protect traditional values. Social conservatives, however, oppose abortion and support school prayer, both of which entail a more intrusive government.

Within the Democratic Party, tensions have historically existed between social liberals, who tended to be white-collar northern WASPs, Jews, and African Americans attracted to the party's progressive positions on civil rights and women's issues since the 1960s, and the more culturally traditional working-class Catholics and white southerners who identified as Democrats primarily due to their economic interests. These divisions inspired consistent efforts by Republican candidates over the years to emphasize issues that were thought to divide the Democrats substantially more than the Republicans, with the hope that Democratic voters who disagreed with their party's nominee would defect to the GOP in presidential elections. These "wedge issues" were often social issues such as crime and affirmative action (prominent campaign topics in the 1970s and 1980s) and, more recently, gun control, same-sex marriage, and partial-birth abortion.

Ideological divisions within Democratic ranks do remain. In a 2005 study by the Pew Research Center for the People and the Press, two of the largest blocs of Democratic voters were "liberals" and "conservative Democrats," while all three major Republican groups were various types of ideological conservatives.[23] However, the party has become more unified over time, due in large part to the migration of conservative southern whites from the Democrats to the Republicans beginning in the 1960s. Moreover, although social issues are becoming more important in American politics over time, most academic studies conclude that economic preferences still weigh more heavily in determining the party identification and candidate choice of American voters.[24]

Presentation of Self

In addition to party affiliation, positions on policy issues, and performance in office, some voters also base their choice of candidates on their personal impressions of the nominees. A candidate benefits from appearing trustworthy, reliable, knowledgeable, mature, empathetic, pious, even-tempered, kind but firm, devoted to family and country, and in every way normal and presentable. To this end, a great deal of campaign activity is devoted to the portrayal of the candidate as a likable person and typical American. Candidates deliver speeches in front of backdrops draped with flags, grill hot dogs and toss footballs for the benefit of television cameras, and relate charming personal anecdotes about themselves and their families to journalists and voters. No amount of expostulation about the irrelevance of all this ordinariness as qualification for an extraordinary office wipes out the fact that candidates must try to conform to the public stereotype of goodness, a standard that is typically far more demanding of politicians than of ordinary mortals.

To be sure, the prevailing standards of normality have evolved considerably over time. Until the mid-twentieth century, all presidents—and nearly all serious contenders for the office—were white male mainline Protestants who traced their ancestry to the British Isles or northern Europe. The landslide defeat of Al Smith, the first Roman Catholic nominee for the presidency, in the 1928 election convinced many political observers that the United States would not elect a Catholic president—an assumption finally refuted by John F. Kennedy's narrow victory in 1960. (Enough anti-Catholic sentiment still existed at the time for Kennedy to find it necessary to deliver a major public address during the campaign denying that he would take orders from the pope if elected.) Other obstacles fell in subsequent elections: Jimmy Carter became the first evangelical Christian president in 1976; Michael Dukakis, the son of Greek immigrants, became the first descendant of southern or eastern Europeans to win a major-party nomination in 1988; Joseph Lieberman in 2000 was the first non-Christian on a national ticket; and Mitt Romney became the first-ever Mormon presidential nominee in 2012. Though two women have unsuccessfully sought the vice presidency (Democrat Geraldine Ferraro in 1984 and Republican Sarah Palin in 2008), the gender barrier to national office has remained intact. However, Hillary Clinton's near-miss campaign for the Democratic presidential nomination in 2008 suggests that many Americans no longer reject the prospect of a female chief executive.

The historic candidacy of Barack Obama that same year challenged the widespread belief that a significant fraction of white voters would not support a black candidate for president. Many African Americans initially shared this view, backing Obama by large margins for the 2008 Democratic nomination only after his victory in the Iowa caucuses demonstrated that he could also attract votes from whites and thus compete seriously for the presidency.[25] While Obama and his campaign staff expressed great confidence in public that his race (and foreign-sounding name) would not cost him the election, in candid moments they were far less certain. This concern intensified in March 2008 when video footage of inflammatory remarks by the pastor of Obama's church in Chicago, Reverend Jeremiah Wright, surfaced in the news media. Against the recommendations of some of his top advisers who worried that dwelling on the subject of race would be politically unwise, Obama decided to respond to the issue by delivering a televised address in Philadelphia on March 18 in which he distanced himself from his pastor's views while refusing to condemn Wright personally, calling for greater understanding and reconciliation among both black and white Americans. The speech was generally well received in the news media, largely—though not completely—defusing the Wright controversy.

The personal lives and private behavior of candidates may also become fodder for the news media and thereby influence voters' perceptions. Back in John F. Kennedy's time, reporters were aware of his extramarital affairs but evidently thought it wrong to reveal them to the public. But in 1987, a major contender for the 1988 Democratic presidential nomination, former senator Gary Hart of Colorado, withdrew from the race after the press corps uncovered evidence of adultery. Bill Clinton faced similar accusations in 1992 but was able to overcome them—in part, we assume, because the experience of Hart had removed some of the shock factor from the revelations. In what seemed at the time to be an important story, Clinton also admitted to having smoked marijuana while a graduate student in England in the 1960s. Though Clinton's defensive claim that he "didn't inhale" was widely mocked, his disclosure failed to scandalize voters, and several candidates in subsequent elections have acknowledged previous illegal drug use without much being made of the matter. Similarly, while Adlai Stevenson's status as the first major-party nominee to have been divorced inspired some comment when he ran in 1952 and 1956, the multiple marriages of more recent presidential contenders did not attract much notice from the press or public. The pregnancy of 2008 Republican vice presidential candidate Sarah Palin's unmarried teenage daughter caused somewhat more of a stir in the news media, though it seems to have had little effect on the decisions of voters.

It would be a painful process for candidates to remodel their entire personalities in order to comport with what they—or their campaign advisers—believe appeals best to the electorate. And, to be fair, most of the people who run for the presidency are not so far from the mark as to make this drastic expedient necessary. What the candidates actually try to do is to smooth off the rough edges, to counter what they believe are the most unfavorable impressions of specific aspects of their public image. John F. Kennedy, who in 1960 was accused of being young and immature, hardly cracked a smile in his televised debates with Richard Nixon, whereas the latter, who was said to be stiff and frightening, beamed with friendliness. Michael Dukakis, suspected of excessively pacific leanings, allowed himself to be driven around in an army tank.[26] George H. W. Bush was told to lower his voice so as to subdue the impression that he was a "wimp."[27] Clinton was told to "talk straight" and avoid smiling too much, for his previous persona had come across as too slick and insincere.[28] Kennedy restyled his youthful shock of hair, and Nixon thinned his eyebrows to look less threatening. Jimmy Carter made intimate revelations to show he was not cold and calculating but serious and introspective. Gerald Ford was photographed a lot around the White House to show he was in command. Ronald Reagan smiled and ducked when Jimmy Carter tried to portray him as dangerous. George W. Bush counteracted his blue-blooded, Ivy League background by purchasing a ranch in Crawford, Texas, where he was frequently filmed performing physical labor and wearing a cowboy hat.

The little things that some people do not like may be interpreted favorably by others. Hubert Humphrey, the Democratic nominee in 1968, was alleged to be a man who could not stop talking. His garrulousness, however, was just another side of his encyclopedic and detailed knowledge of the widest variety of public policies. He might have talked too much to suit his detractors, but the fact that he knew a lot pleased his supporters. Was Ronald Reagan amiable and charming or was that a vacant expression on his face? Was Barack Obama idealistic and inspirational or insincere and dangerously inexperienced? Was John McCain admirably independent or recklessly impulsive? Was Mitt Romney knowledgeable and steady or robotic and out-of-touch? Voters may also change their opinions of political figures over time, re-interpreting strengths as weaknesses or vice versa. During his successful 2000 and 2004 campaigns and first term as president, George W. Bush was widely praised for being decisive, folksy, plain-spoken, and comfortable in his own skin, in contrast to his Democratic opponents Al Gore and John Kerry, who were often characterized as phony, awkward, and pedantic. As Bush's popularity began to decline markedly during his second term in office, however, his decisiveness came to be seen by many as stubbornness, and his folksiness as demonstrating a lack of gravity and engagement.

In modern elections, candidates who come across well on television hold an obvious advantage. John F. Kennedy, Ronald Reagan, Bill Clinton, and Barack Obama all owed their political success in part to their telegenic skills. Candidates now hire professional specialists who advise them on optimal communications strategy. Most commonly, consultants recommend that candidates develop a simple theme for their campaign and stick to it in prepared and unscripted remarks, debates, and advertisements—a practice known in the political world as "message discipline." As a result, candidates will typically deliver a standard stump speech many times over the course of the campaign. Journalists complain quite a lot about the repetitiveness of presidential candidates, as if campaigns should be designed mostly to keep the news media entertained.

As Obama campaign manager David Plouffe recalled after the 2008 election, "The consistency of our message [of 'change'] drove the press crazy. [They thought it] was boring [and] were annoyed by it."[29] But political consultants note that most citizens do not follow the campaign closely from one day to the next; in order for a candidate's message to take root in the minds of the public, they argue, it must be repeated over and over again. This dilemma ranks high on the list of unsolved (and no doubt unsolvable) problems of American democracy: how to reach the relatively inattentive mass electorate without completely alienating the super-attentive mandarins of the news media through whom a candidate ordinarily communicates with the rank-and-file voter.

Equally important, perhaps, is the desirability of appearing comfortable in delivery. Televised speeches are the major opportunities for a candidate to be seen and evaluated by large numbers of people. Obama benefited greatly in 2008 from his frequent smile, calm demeanor and glowing oratory—the candidate as cool cat. His opponent John McCain was consistently less polished when delivering prepared remarks, often struggling to read his speeches off teleprompter machines, and tended to resist coaching from his handlers and image consultants. McCain aides felt that their candidate fared better in spontaneous interactions with reporters and voters, which more effectively displayed his passion, humor, and penchant for "straight talk."

Both 2008 campaigns placed great emphasis on establishing a positive public persona for their candidate. Obama was considered by his own advisers to personify his message's core message that a fresh approach was needed in the White House during a period when most citizens expressed both frustration with partisan warfare and concern that the nation was moving in the wrong direction. At the same time, he needed to display sufficient poise and fluency with the issues of the day to convince skeptical voters that he was prepared to assume the presidency despite less than four years of experience in the Senate.

John McCain faced his own set of strategic challenges in 2008. Running to succeed an increasingly unpopular fellow Republican incumbent at a time when most voters preferred the Democratic Party's positions on both foreign and domestic policy, McCain sought to redirect the campaign onto more favorable ground by emphasizing two key components of his personal biography: his five years as a prisoner of war in Vietnam (which contrasted with Obama's lack of military service) and his reputation as an independent-minded senator who took on other Republicans over causes such as campaign finance reform and restrictions on pork-barrel spending. "I don't work for a party," McCain told his audience in his acceptance speech at the Republican national convention. "I don't work for a special interest. . . . I work for you."

Mitt Romney's unsuccessful 2012 campaign offers a particularly revealing example of the dilemmas that candidates may face in deciding how to present themselves to the public. Romney operatives placed little emphasis on revealing the candidate's personal side compared to a typical presidential campaign; Romney's television advertising and stump speeches notably lacked extensive biographical content, and he rarely appeared on popular talk shows and other venues that might provide an opportunity to show his personality to voters. After the election, Romney strategist Stuart Stevens defended the decision to eschew a campaign message that focused on Romney's personal qualities, noting that "to capture the totality of him is very difficult. Whenever we would test this [in focus groups], which we did extensively, it never tested well. Voters . . . thought that at a certain point it was sort of like looking at someone's [family photo] album." Romney adviser Kevin Madden similarly recalled that the campaign "tried to make an argument that this [election] is not about . . . 'Who do you like?' But instead it was about, 'Who is going to be most competent? Who is it that can do the job? Who has the better plan for the future?'"[30] Viewing the middling state of the national economy as Obama's chief vulnerability, the Romney campaign wished to define the choice between the candidates on grounds that favored their side, concluding that a debate over which candidate had the most appealing personality would be a distraction from this objective.

After Obama's victory, however, many Romney supporters, including friends and family of the candidate himself, expressed frustration that the election had left voters without a more positive impression of Romney as a person—in part due to a well-funded series of negative advertisements from the Obama campaign and allied super PACs portraying Romney as a ruthless corporate raider who lacked compassion for regular Americans. Kerry Healey, who had served as lieutenant governor of Massachusetts under Romney, lamented that "even at the end of the campaign, I never felt that the American people understood Mitt Romney's genuine character and that is a terrible shame." Even David Axelrod of the opposition Obama camp was surprised by the strategy, later telling the *Boston Globe*, "I questioned why they didn't spend more time and energy early defining Romney in a fuller way so people could identify with him. . . . My feeling is you have to build a candidacy on the foundation of biography. That is what authenticates your message. I was always waiting for that [to] happen."[31]

It is impossible to know for sure whether a more personality-based campaign would in fact have worked out better for Romney. Even if the campaign's strategists and advisers had made a concerted effort to sell their candidate in such a fashion, voters' impressions of political figures are also influenced by other factors such as the opposing campaign and the news media; in Romney's case, press coverage often portrayed him as a clumsy and mistake-prone campaigner, to his undoubted further disadvantage. There is also a limitation to campaigns' ability to construct a public persona for a candidate that is inconsistent with his or her true nature, especially over a long election season that produces a great deal of public scrutiny. Regardless of their source, however, Romney clearly suffered from significant image problems over the course of the 2012 campaign that hindered his attempt to present himself as a preferable alternative to Obama. Future candidates will likely conclude from Romney's defeat that if a candidate does not strongly define himself or herself in the eyes of the voters, others will take the opportunity to do so instead.

Negative Campaigning

Candidates not only cultivate positive personal images of themselves among the electorate, but also work to create unfavorable perceptions of their opponents. At various points in a campaign, there may be a temptation for the candidates or parties to let loose a stream of negative material about the other side. This may have its greatest effect very early, before the opposition can establish its own image with voters. As *The New Republic* explained in response to an outbreak of negative advertising in the 1980s:

> [T]he proliferation of negative ads is simply a result of the consultants' discovery that attacks make a more lasting impression on voters than positive commercials.

More candidates are making the attacks personally, rather than working through stand-ins, because research shows that the ads work better that way. The surge in negative advertising has even given rise to the countertactic known as "inoculation": ads designed to answer potential negative ads even before the attacks air.[32]

Of course, the nominees of the two major parties will always differ quite substantially on public policy questions, or over the performance of an incumbent administration. Negative advertising that simply criticizes the opposition for its issue positions or record in office is a constant part of every presidential campaign. Somewhat more controversial, but often effective, is a more personal attack by a candidate or campaign on a rival—one that claims or implies that the opponent is weak, incompetent, corrupt, mentally unbalanced, dishonest, untrustworthy, morally lax, or even unpatriotic.

Negative campaigning is hardly new to American politics, or even new to television advertising. In 1964, Tony Schwartz produced the most famous political advertisement of its era, the "daisy spot" for the Lyndon Johnson campaign. It shows a little girl standing in an open field, plucking petals from a daisy as she miscounts "four, five, seven, six, six . . . " When she reaches "nine," an ominous voiceover begins a countdown of its own: "ten, nine, eight . . . "At zero, an explosion is heard and a mushroom cloud appears. President Johnson's voice is heard saying, "These are the stakes: to make a world in which all of God's children can live, or to go into the dark. We must love each other or we must die." Like many effective attack ads, the "daisy spot" capitalized on a fear that already existed. Voters saw Barry Goldwater, Johnson's Republican opponent, as a man who might start a nuclear war, and the ad, although it aired only once and never mentioned Goldwater, gained sufficient notoriety to reinforce this perception.[33]

Johnson's campaign also attacked Goldwater for his views on the United Nations, the Social Security Administration, and Medicare. Goldwater responded with his own negative ads, linking the Johnson administration to the "moral decay" of America as the screen filled with pictures of race riots, drug use, alcoholism, and crime. Another spot accused Johnson of corruption and voting fraud.[34]

In the commercial world, this is known as "comparative advertising." The campaign consultants' trade journal *Campaigns and Elections* regularly counsels candidates, in the words of one article title, to "Nail the Opposition."[35] This can be a risky strategy. Research has shown that voters prefer positive, informational advertising that appears to be fair.[36] "Going negative," as it is known, is not therefore the consultants' panacea, but it is a tool to achieve several common campaign objectives: to stigmatize or "characterize" a relatively unknown opponent, to focus the agenda of the campaign on the weaknesses of the other side, or to call attention to an embarrassing blunder on the part of the opposition.[37] Media consultants pay especially close attention to polling results when devising negative ads because they are risky and can backfire.

In August 2004, an organization calling itself the Swift Boat Veterans for Truth funded a small advertising campaign claiming that Democratic nominee John Kerry did not deserve the Bronze Star and Purple Heart awards he received for his service as a navy lieutenant in the Vietnam War. Though the initial ads cost less than $500,000 and ran in only a few television markets, they were quickly noticed by the national political media, which publicized the unconfirmed charges more widely. While the Swift Boat organization was not officially connected to the George W. Bush campaign (which would have been illegal under campaign finance law), its attacks effectively dovetailed with Bush's own strategy of labeling Kerry a "flip-flopper" who could not be trusted, and Bush refused to condemn the ads.[38] Believing that a response would only give the charges more publicity, the Kerry campaign initially ignored them, counterattacking several weeks later only when polling showed that the allegations were hurting Kerry's standing among voters.[39]

The 2008 McCain campaign faced a delicate problem: how to go negative against Barack Obama, the first African American major-party presidential nominee, without encountering charges of racism. McCain's advisers decided to avoid any attacks that might be construed as racial, ruling out any mention of Obama's twenty-year membership in the church of the controversial Reverend Jeremiah Wright. The campaign did repeatedly attempt in October 2008 to tie Obama to (white) former 1960s radical William Ayers, with running mate Sarah Palin accusing Obama of "palling around with terrorists." However, Obama had dealt with both associations during the primary season, making such criticisms seem to be old news. In another line of attack, McCain sought support among fiscally conservative independents and Democrats by suggesting that Obama's economic views were out of the mainstream.[40] Finally, echoing Hillary Clinton's attacks during the Democratic primaries, McCain questioned whether Obama possessed sufficient knowledge, experience, and toughness to assume the presidency. "I know how the world works," declared McCain in his convention address, implying that his opponent might not.

Obama's negative strategy, in contrast, was straightforward, easy to execute, and low in risk. In speeches and ads, Obama's campaign tightly linked McCain's policies to those of the unpopular incumbent, George W. Bush. Obama frequently asserted that McCain represented a "third term" for Bush, a criticism that appeared to resonate, according to surveys revealing that many voters saw McCain and Bush as holding similar views. However, the Obama campaign was not above making personal attacks as well. As McCain's handling of the fall financial crisis became an issue (McCain announced that he was suspending his campaign to deal with the situation but played little role in crafting the congressional response), Obama's ads accused him of "erratic" behavior in what was seen by the press as an insinuation that McCain lacked the appropriate temperament for the presidency and perhaps even as a reference to McCain's age.[41] By Election Day, many voters in key states agreed with Obama's characterization of McCain as an impulsive version of George W. Bush, an image that did not bode well for his electoral fate.[42]

In the late spring and early summer of 2012, the Obama reelection campaign sought to exploit a temporary financial advantage over Mitt Romney, who had just spent most of his available funds winning the Republican nomination, by sponsoring a series of negative ads designed to create an initially unfavorable impression of Romney among undecided voters who knew little about him at the beginning stages of the campaign. This line of attack centered on Romney's previous career as the head of the Bain Capital private equity firm. Obama's ads characterized Romney's business dealings as leading to bankruptcies, plant closures, outsourcing, and layoffs for workers at companies acquired by Bain Capital; in one Obama-produced ad, a former employee of a shuttered company said of Romney that "he doesn't care anything about the middle-class or the lower-class people."[43]

Romney's attacks on Obama in 2012 tended to be less personal than Obama's attacks on Romney; perhaps mindful of the fact that victory required appealing to swing voters who had supported Obama in his first presidential run in 2008, the Romney campaign mostly avoided negative campaigning that questioned Obama's character. Instead, Romney made Obama's performance in office the centerpiece of his case against the incumbent, suggesting that the previous four years had confirmed that Obama was not a capable president. Romney's ads also accused Obama of hostility to private-sector entrepreneurship, of cutting Medicare benefits for senior citizens, and, perhaps most controversially, of "gutting" the work requirements in federal welfare programs—a charge hotly disputed by Democrats.

Campaign professionals maintain that there is a clear line between legitimate attacks on the record, or even the personal background, of opposing candidates, and illegitimate smears. They even argue that "comparative" ads are beneficial, because they give voters important information they otherwise might not learn. There is some justification for this view. But the line between fair and unfair is easily blurred.

In the United States we seem to be in a middle position in regard to mudslinging. It is not everyday practice, but neither is it a rarity. It works best, as one might guess, when it is not answered; when it is effectively countered, it can backfire. A glance at the history of presidential campaigns suggests that vituperation is usually irrelevant to the outcomes of elections and that it may have the problematic effect of reducing political participation by turning off potential voters.[44] John G. Geer argues, on the other hand, that negative advertising in presidential elections actually focuses more on issues and less on personal characteristics than positive advertising does, thus providing voters with more and better information about their electoral choices.[45] Either way, we expect candidates in the future to turn to negative campaigning when they believe the potential benefits outweigh the risks to their own reputations for fair play and serious attention to the issues of the day.

GETTING GOOD PRESS

Although we have seen that it is highly questionable whether news media coverage, on television, in newspapers, or on the Internet, markedly influences voter opinion when the strong cue of party is present, it is still considered important for a candidate to get the most favorable treatment possible from journalists. At least, the candidates and their organizations behave as though it is important; they can and do assiduously court the reporters assigned to cover their campaign.[46] Not only do candidates and their staff coddle the journalists who travel with them, but they follow their press coverage closely and complain about it if dissatisfied.[47]

Because candidates seldom receive uniformly positive treatment, and because journalists view campaign flacks as obstructing their attempts to dig for the (potentially unflattering) truth, a certain degree of conflict governs the interaction between reporters and their subjects. As veteran Republican spokesman Kevin Madden describes the relationship, "The message discipline required to run an effective campaign oftentimes frustrates the press. They always want more access. Their job is to never be satisfied with the access that we're giving them. My job is to be never satisfied with the message discipline that I'm providing them. I think one of the other natural tensions is that I've never met a reporter who doesn't think they could run a better campaign. And I've never met a press secretary, including myself, who didn't think [he or she] could write a better news story."[48]

The volume and angle of press coverage may depend to some extent on how the reporters regard the campaign. If journalists find it easy or difficult to receive cooperation from campaign staff, or if they find the candidate personally likable or unlikable, their impressions may affect the tone of the stories they file. Al Gore's distant relationship with the press in 2000 contributed to his campaign's problems, while George W. Bush's jocularity earned him more kindness from the news media, captured by *Journeys with George*, a documentary on his campaign antics filmed by Alexandra Pelosi, daughter of future Democratic House Speaker Nancy Pelosi and in 2000 a producer for NBC News.

Getting good press, like the rest of the campaign, has become professionalized, with media and communication staff who know how to make the candidate look good on television, in the newspapers, and on the Internet. Little things, such as timing events and announcements to meet the requirements of both morning newspapers and the evening network news programs, or supplying reporters with interviews and human-interest material, can be helpful to candidates. The personalities of the candidates, their ability to command the respect of the sometimes rather jaded men and women assigned to cover them, may count heavily. Candidates also must make the most of their opportunities in public speeches or appearances on radio and television. If what they say and do "makes news," and their press aides are effective in promoting the stories, they may get space through the desire of the media to attract customers.

Thus far, we have spoken of the news media as if they were a monolithic entity. But there are all sorts of news outlets with differing biases, needs, and audiences. A great deal of a candidate's attention is devoted to generating coverage in local newspapers and television in key electoral battlegrounds. Local reporters, who are not experienced at covering presidents and other national political figures, may ask fewer tough questions and produce more positive stories than the more skeptical and campaign-weary journalists from national publications and broadcast networks, and their coverage may have more of an influence on the impressions of voters in strategically important states. Campaign aides often claim that local news media are also more likely to emphasize substantive policy issues, while national reporters tend to be preoccupied with campaign strategy and the candidate horse race.

Finally, there is the overwhelming importance of staging the daily bit of news for the network television news broadcasts, cable channels, and current-events websites. Candidates know that they will be covered every evening, but doing and saying what? In order to seize control of the situation, they stage little dramas: an announcement in front of the Statue of Liberty or in the midst of a picturesque slum; visits to a series of ethnic shops, delicatessens, farms, factories, and shopping centers. If the backdrop is right, the candidate thinks, the coverage may be too. Sometimes it is. Consultants and speechwriters, aware that only a few seconds of a speech will likely appear in news programs, craft short, memorable statements ("sound bites") reinforcing the campaign's message of the day. The nightly network news broadcasts have become increasingly friendly territory for Democratic candidates since 2000. The Center for Media and Public Affairs' content analysis of 2004 and 2008 fall campaign nightly news shows from CBS, ABC, NBC, and Fox News revealed much more positive coverage for the Democratic than Republican nominees, with Barack Obama getting the most positive treatment of any candidate since CMPA's analysis began in 1988.[49]

A new use of television first emerged during the 1992 campaign: the appearance of a candidate on talk shows such as *Larry King Live* and *Good Morning America*. Bill

Clinton was the first to make use of this tactic in the weeks before the New Hampshire primary. His campaign staged several "Ask Bill" television shows in which candidate Clinton took questions from the audience. Clinton performed consistently well in this format; his handlers felt that it brought out his personality and allowed voters to get to know and connect with the candidate. Another candidate who succeeded on this circuit, albeit with some significantly bad moments, was independent Ross Perot. Perot actually announced his willingness to seek the presidency on a talk show: CNN's Larry King was, with persistent prodding, able to get a "reluctant" Perot to agree to run if volunteers placed his name on all fifty state ballots.[50] With that single interview, King launched a candidate and achieved the status of the premier political interviewer of the 1992 campaign season.

Since Clinton and Perot inaugurated the practice, presidential candidates now routinely make appearances on popular television shows, hoping to reach a wider audience of potential supporters. The appearances are often staged, sometimes awkwardly, to showcase a candidate's personal charm, sense of humor, or status as a "regular person." In 2000, both George W. Bush and Al Gore appeared several times on *The Late Show with David Letterman*, sitting for interviews with the host and participating in the nightly "Top Ten List" comedy routine. Bush and Gore also appeared—separately—to poke fun at themselves on an NBC prime-time special broadcast of *Saturday Night Live* sketch comedy material that aired several days before the election.[51] In 2004, John Kerry sought to shed his stiff public image by riding his Harley-Davidson motorcycle onto the set of the *Tonight Show* clad in a leather jacket.[52] Kerry also appeared on *The Daily Show*, a satirical news program on the Comedy Central cable network that is especially popular among young viewers, as did Barack Obama and John McCain in 2008 and Obama again in 2012. Obama also received a formal endorsement from popular daytime host Oprah Winfrey after visiting her talk show and appeared successfully on several similar programs; McCain was featured with more mixed success on programs such as *The View*, *The Tonight Show*, and *Jimmy Kimmel Live*. After comedian Tina Fey's impersonation of Republican vice presidential candidate Sarah Palin on *Saturday Night Live* became a popular hit, Palin herself appeared on the program two weeks before the election, giving *SNL* its highest audience ratings in fourteen years.[53]

The overall value of these appearances is unclear. Some political commentators have criticized the practice, arguing that the hosts of popular talk shows are pushovers for the candidates and do not ask tough questions or follow up on answers the way "serious" journalists do. Instead, these critics argue, candidates should spend more time on the Sunday morning political programs such as *This Week* and *Meet the Press*, where confrontational interviewers will make sure the candidates meet a certain standard. Proponents argue that pop-culture shows are good for the political system because they allow the candidates to reach viewers who do not regularly watch news programs and give them a chance to display a more informal, personal side of themselves to the public.

Of course, even "entertainment" shows present candidates with potential dangers, as John McCain discovered in 2008. McCain canceled a September booking on David Letterman's late-night show mere hours before taping, claiming that he needed to rush back to Washington to deal with the national financial crisis. When Letterman found out that McCain had instead stayed in New York to film an interview with *CBS Evening News* anchor Katie Couric and deliver a speech the next morning, he "smelled ratings and declared war," in the words of the *Washington Post*, mocking McCain on his program for weeks until McCain finally returned to make an apologetic appearance in mid-October.[54] In 2012, the Romney campaign decided that appearances on talk shows carried more risk than reward for their candidate, perhaps due to suspicion that liberal-leaning hosts or producers would show him in an unsympathetic or un-presidential light; Romney turned down invitations to appear on Letterman's program, *The Daily Show*, *The View*, and *Saturday Night Live*, among others.[55]

Whatever the contribution these shows make to American political life, positive or negative, there is no doubt that most candidates will continue to make appearances as long as show hosts will invite them. The free media and direct access to voters are valuable properties, especially for candidates, like Barack Obama, who shine in such situations.[56]

Candidates also appear regularly on radio talk shows. In 2008, John McCain routinely made himself available to conservative talkers, though his relations with some of them, such as Rush Limbaugh, remained cool throughout the campaign. The relative dearth of liberal radio hosts presented Barack Obama with fewer national radio opportunities than those afforded to McCain, though he appeared frequently on programs popular with African American listeners such as those hosted by Tom Joyner and Steve Harvey.[57] Both candidates often conducted brief radio interviews with stations in key states while traveling between campaign stops.

CAMPAIGN PROFESSIONALS

Presidential candidates have never lacked for willing accomplices in their quest for office. In the first partisan election battle in American history, the election of 1800, the crucial New York campaign was led by Alexander Hamilton (for the Federalists) and Aaron Burr (for the Democratic-Republicans). With the resumption of party competition in the 1830s, campaign managers assumed primary responsibility for the conduct of the battle, a pattern that has continued to the present.

Modern campaigns have evolved into something qualitatively different from the pattern of the previous century. It is not the professionalization of the campaign that is new, for the old-time party managers were extremely interested in monetary rewards for their services, but the fact that consultants today are business professionals, not party professionals. The individuals who directed the first century and a half of presidential elections were closely tied to one or another of the political parties and were often part of the party structure. Moreover, the communications technologies and strategies at the disposal of modern consultants that can help them sell their candidates have transformed the entire process of running for the nation's highest office.

In the nineteenth century, campaigns were often carried out by the party organizations. Nowadays, candidates must form their own campaign organizations. These are typically comprised of paid staff, including a campaign manager, consultants, ad makers, speechwriters, pollsters, and field organizers; volunteers; close advisers, often known as a "kitchen cabinet"; and a formal organization, typically consisting of a campaign committee and a finance committee. The paid staff surrounding a modern candidate is drawn from a population of people for whom electoral politics is a full-time career: they are campaign professionals.[58]

What is the nature of campaign professionals? In some ways, they are very different from the party professionals of earlier eras. The people who ran campaigns through the first half of the twentieth century generally were compensated by the spoils system: victorious candidates hired or appointed their supporters to a variety of government jobs. Those who run campaigns now are mostly compensated in salaries and fees for services, although some may receive positions in the White House or the executive branch if their candidate wins the election. Earlier generations of party professionals were mainly generalists. Now, the business of electioneering requires specialization and therefore diversity.[59] The business of the campaign is carried out by staffers or subcontracted to firms that specialize in a particular aspect of the process: polling, advertising production, direct mail, opposition research, voter mobilization, data analysis, fund-raising, information technology, and so forth.

The professionalization of political campaigns has advanced, by all accounts, considerably further in the United States, with its long drawn-out nomination and election processes, than anywhere else among the world's democracies. What is the cumulative effect of the introduction of modern polls, media campaigns, fund-raising efforts, and the people who run these operations on the conduct of the presidential campaign? Does the new agenda-setting mechanism of the opinion poll change the character and conduct of presidential campaigns? Have the campaign professionals altered the substantive content of politics? Are they in it for the money, or do they have their own ideological axes to grind?

We can get a grasp on the relationship between candidates and paid professionals by looking closely at its initial phases. Although candidates are more typically to be found in the role of the suitor, it is not at all unusual for consultants to go prospecting for a candidate if they are short on contracts in a particular election cycle.[60] Once the initial contact has been made, the two sides bargain over a contract that, if signed, will formalize responsibility, set payment agreements, and establish general ground rules that will guide their interactions over the course of the campaign. Key resources, for both parties, are money and a winning reputation. Candidates are looking for the most successful consultant their money can buy, which generally means a firm with a strong recent win-loss record on their side of the ideological spectrum. Consultants likewise prefer winners over probable losers (so they can protect their record) and fat cats over lean. And neither side wants to end up with a partner who is ideologically or personally incompatible.[61]

Not surprisingly, top-flight consulting firms are besieged with offers from candidates and would-be candidates. Big-name presidential hopefuls are similarly able to pick and choose, while no-name candidates must often wait patiently until relatively late in the game and settle for whoever is left. Sometimes a prominent consultant will take on a long-shot candidate to advance a political agenda or because of a personal friendship. Even if the campaign is not generously bankrolled, the publicity attached to running a presidential campaign may lead to future business opportunities for the firm.

Has the increasingly sophisticated technological component of presidential campaigns altered the essential character of the enterprise of seeking office? No longer limited to the analysis of polling data, computers have colonized every level of the campaign process. Computers keep campaigns constantly plugged into the vast world of the Internet, allowing instantaneous communication with supporters, reporters, and the public at large. Campaigns use computers, the Internet, and cell phones for tracking convention delegates, writing fund-raising letters and thank-you notes, accepting and processing donations, drafting news releases, maintaining electronic news libraries, communicating between field and headquarters, and automatic telephoning. The 2008 and 2012 Obama campaigns, drawing on some innovations of Howard Dean's 2004 primary campaign, pioneered new means of electronic communication, creating computer linkups of supporters, gathering record online campaign contributions, and even announcing Joe Biden's selection as vice presidential nominee in August 2008 via text message. There was a clever rationale for this last initiative: the campaign collected the cell phone numbers of thousands of supporters who signed up to be notified of Obama's choice of running mate and who were later solicited for donations and volunteer work.[62]

The results of this electronic revolution are a uniform computer literacy among campaign staffers, a reduction in envelope stuffing and stamp licking on the part of campaign volunteers, and the greatly enhanced ability of campaigns to raise money and get their message across to specially targeted segments of the electorate. The Obama team was considered particularly skilled at electronic communication in comparison to the McCain and Romney campaigns in 2008 and 2012. However, many of the Obama campaign's most effective technological innovations will no doubt be adopted by other candidates of both parties in the future, potentially diluting this advantage.

How powerful are the professionals within the campaign organization? The candidate-client relationship varies considerably from case to case, depending on the experience and stature of each party and the terms of the original contract. It is the candidate, all agree, who has the last word in approving the general strategy of the campaign.[63] Having done this, however, many candidates apparently prefer to absent themselves from the nitty-gritty choices that follow. One survey found that 44 percent of a population of consultants agreed that candidates generally backed off from making decisions on the priority of different campaign issues. Most "were neither very involved nor influential in the day-to-day tactical operation of the campaign."[64]

Consultants (not a shy and self-effacing group of people) will gladly tell you all about the power they enjoy—and should enjoy—as campaign strategists. The late Bob Squier, for instance, who worked for Democrats, said: "It is very possible to go through an entire campaign with a candidate, and when it is all over, they have no idea what went on. It is not to our advantage to explain to them. It is to our advantage to get them to do what we want—what's best for them—with the least amount of fuss."[65]

In recent years, some political consultants have become celebrities in their own right, often as a result of news media coverage portraying them as the brains behind victorious campaigns—a view that most consultants are happy to encourage. James Carville, a plainspoken Louisiana native who served as Bill Clinton's chief campaign strategist in 1992, parlayed his candidate's success in winning the presidency into a lucrative second career as a writer, speaker, and television personality, becoming sufficiently well known that he appeared in cameo roles as himself in several major Hollywood movies. Karl Rove, chief political adviser to George W. Bush and widely credited as the intellectual force behind Bush's two successful campaigns for the White House, became even more prominent a public figure than Carville. Rove is the subject of two major biographies,[66] a *Frontline* special on PBS television, and even a documentary film titled *Bush's Brain*. The 2008 and 2012 victories of Barack Obama elevated Obama's chief strategist David Axelrod into the role of a celebrated political guru; after Obama's reelection, Axelrod announced his retirement from the electoral battlefield to found a new Institute of Politics at the University of Chicago, his alma mater.

Have consultants made presidential campaigns more ideological? Probably not. With the exception of a few ideologically motivated firms, consultants tend to be party loyalists but not issue advocates. There are exceptions. Fund-raising and direct-mail firms (an overlapping set of categories) can afford to be more purist than other sorts of consultants because they hold the purse strings and because they generally target a narrow range of like-minded, politically motivated donors.[67] Possessing precious lists of the names of co-believers, they are more likely to administer an ideological litmus test before entering into a relationship with a candidate, and more likely to call the candidate on the carpet afterward if his or her behavior does not reflect true belief.

Nevertheless, as Larry Sabato says, "for most consultants ideology is a surprisingly minor criterion in the selection of clients."[68] The business logic of consultancy militates against an approach that would too severely limit a firm's clientele, and the game-playing logic of the campaign itself encourages the use of any strategy that will win, regardless of its ideological fit.

Do campaign professionals help candidates obfuscate and blur the issues? With candidates from both parties being coached to court the swing vote in the middle, perhaps consultants contribute to a "Tweedledum-Tweedledee" effect in presidential elections. Mitch Daniels, who became President George W. Bush's first budget director and later the governor of Indiana, sums up the consultant effect this way: "You tend not to make major gaffes, because somebody will spot them. On the other hand, you may not take very many bold actions, because someone will be very nervous."[69]

Has the professionalization of campaigns lowered standards of conduct in presidential elections? Even though the candidate is ultimately responsible for all campaign decisions, the use of paid staff and consultants may change the range of campaign options available and the types of strategies ultimately chosen. Consider the use of negative campaigning. "I love to do negatives," declared media consultant Bob Squier. "It is one of those opportunities in a campaign where you can take the truth and use it just like a knife to slice right through the opponent. I hate the kind of commercials that are just music and pretty pictures."[70] This bit of refreshing candor raises the possibility that the average campaign professional may in fact be different from the average politician.

Candidates are aware, of course, of most of what goes on in their name, but it is easier to sign on the dotted line and have someone else take care of your dirty business for you than to have to haul the bodies away yourself.[71] Other commentators point out that there are limits to what campaigns can say on television, limits that did not apply to old-fashioned campaigns run by thousands of semi-independent and localized party bosses, newspapers, and partisans. In the Internet age, any effort by a campaign to engage in underhanded tactics or smear the opposition can be publicized instantly across the nation. On the other hand, current campaign finance regulations encourage the growth of nominally independent super PACs and other groups that can spread misleading information for the benefit of their favored candidate while allowing the candidate's own campaign to deny any responsibility.

Do campaign professionals undermine partisanship? There is no doubt that consultants have replaced party leaders as major actors in the campaign process. But the decline of traditional party leaders was not caused by the rise of consultants; it was caused by changes in the rules governing the party nomination and election system, which demand that candidates form their own organizations so that they can appeal to large primary electorates in order to win nomination. Those who are hired by those organizations, with rare exceptions, have strong partisan affiliations and do not work both sides of the street. In fact, many have worked for party organizations, and parties provide training in electioneering skills in order to have reliably partisan professionals.[72] "Party affiliation," according to one study, "is by far the most important factor considered by consultants in selecting their clients, outweighing a candidate's electability, ideology, or financial standing."[73]

A good example of the way this works can be seen by looking at the employment history of Steve Schmidt, Republican presidential nominee John McCain's chief campaign strategist in 2008. Schmidt first ran a campaign in 1995, for a Republican attorney general candidate in Kentucky. After working on two California campaigns, he was communications director for Lamar Alexander's short-lived campaign for the Republican presidential nomination in 2000 and then served as spokesman for the National Republican Congressional Committee. Moving to a position at a Washington lobbying firm, Schmidt later joined the George W. Bush White House as an aide to Vice President Dick Cheney. In 2004 he ran the daily media response operation ("war room") for the Bush-Cheney reelection effort. After shepherding the Supreme Court nominations of John Roberts and Samuel Alito through the Senate for the Bush administration, Schmidt managed California governor Arnold Schwarzenegger's successful reelection campaign in 2006. With no prior experience working for McCain, Schmidt initially joined his presidential campaign as an unpaid adviser, intending to remain in California for the duration of the election. Schmidt finally signed on as a full-time consultant during the summer of 2007 as the result of a staff shake-up within the McCain camp. A year later, after yet another organizational reshuffling, Schmidt was placed in control of campaign strategy, having supplanted other aides, such as campaign manager Rick Davis and former advisers John Weaver and Mike Murphy, who (unlike Schmidt) had long-standing personal relationships with the candidate.[74]

Policy Advisers

Everyone has advice for the would-be president. In the old days, most of the policy advice came after the general election as the victor prepared to assume office. Nowadays the advising process has been incorporated into the process of campaigning. The function of the policy adviser is no longer simply to help the future president govern but to help the candidate define and publicize the campaign's position on the issues. There is still some reluctance on the part of candidates to publish official lists of advisers, but all campaigns develop extensive contacts with academics and policy analysts who draw up position papers on specialized issues of foreign and domestic policy and help set the general ideological tone of the campaign.[75] The experts do this at least in part to position themselves to have influence on national policy if their candidate wins.

The lengthy duration of presidential campaigns means that candidates have to develop issue positions at least two years in advance of the election. It is during this initial period that decisions on national policy issues will be made. "If you're . . . in the policy-advising business," explains Pat Choate, an economist and policy analyst who was Ross Perot's running mate in 1996, "you must move on that time schedule."[76]

BOX 5.1. In the Arena: Campaign Professionals on the 2012 General Election Campaign

On Television Advertising Strategies

Stuart Stevens, chief strategist, Romney campaign:

"We always had limited resource questions, and it was a finite amount of money. . . The consensus [in the campaign] was it was really a 20 to 40 million dollar decision and that we'd rather have 20 to 40 million to spend in October. It was a hard decision, but we enjoyed spending that money in October."

Jim Messina, manager, Obama campaign:

"Well, we had a theory which is different. . . . Our theory was, at the end . . . we just didn't think at that point TV mattered . . . Coming out of the conventions our research showed that 75 to 80 percent of all voters had already made up their minds. We just thought that spending earlier was a very important moment because that number in June was 60, 65, 70, and so we banked basically our entire campaign on spending money in June. We moved $65 million out of October and September and put it into June and July."

On Getting Out the Vote:

Jeremy Bird, field director, Obama campaign:

"We had been on the ground for a year in Ohio. . . . [One day] we knocked on 370,000 doors in Ohio. And we had more time to do it. We had more resources. We had a ton of organizers on the ground who had been out for a long time recruiting these volunteers. We had a big head start and a lot of money while these guys were in the primary. And so we were building and we were executing at that point. There were a very small number of persuadable voters we still needed to talk to multiple times, and then the rest was about get-out-the-vote and early voting. That's what we were focused on."

Neil Newhouse, chief pollster, Romney campaign:

"You look at the real hidden story from our side . . . the number of white men who didn't vote in this election compared to white women and compared to four years ago is extraordinary. I mean, it's something like 286,000 white men who voted in Ohio in '08 didn't vote in '12. And in Florida something like 400,000. And these white men were replaced by white women. We were taking a group where we won by 27 points and replacing them with a group that Obama won by 12 or 14."

Source: Institute of Politics, John F. Kennedy School of Government, Harvard University. *Campaign for President: The Managers Look at 2012*. Lanham, MD: Rowman & Littlefield Publishers, 2013, pp. 192, 193, 194, 228, 231).

Introducing a novel idea later on in the game, during the heat of the campaign, is risky, first because the candidate may gain a reputation as an opportunist or a waffler, and second because there will be no opportunity to test the new idea for technical or political feasibility, to get its rough edges smoothed out.

Since in the course of the campaign the candidate is expected to offer judgments on world events as they break into the news, every campaign will typically rely on a "little black book" with the telephone numbers of advisers in different policy areas who can be contacted during emergencies. A dramatic example of this occurred during the 2008 campaign, when a global financial crisis in September damaged the soundness of American credit markets and the overall health of the American economy. The McCain and Obama campaigns scrambled for a response to the problems as the economy and stock market slumped. Obama's economic advisers urged a cautious message of reassurance and support for a bipartisan solution to the problem, while McCain's response was more experimental. He announced that he was suspending his campaign on September 24 and called for cancellation of the first presidential debate scheduled for two days later, then returned to Washington to address the crisis. His consultations with economists, congressional lawmakers and the Bush administration, however, did not place him at the center of efforts to find a solution, which took several weeks to develop. McCain was forced to reignite his campaign after a few days and at the last minute flew to Mississippi to participate in the debate. McCain's problem was that no amount of advice would quickly solve the problem or make him the author of a solution. Obama's cautious reaction proved to be the politically more beneficial response.

Tensions between policy advisers and campaign staffs complicated McCain's response and vindicated Obama's caution. Such conflicts have been a feature of presidential campaigns for decades. Campaign policy experts come in three flavors, according to Janne E. Nolan, Gary Hart's foreign policy and defense adviser in the 1984 campaign: those who believe in the issues they are pushing, those adrenaline junkies attracted by the chance to participate in the events of a presidential campaign, and those who have attached their ambitions to a particular candidate in the hopes of achieving a position in a new administration.[77]

Policy advisers, even of the third type, are a very different breed from pollsters and media consultants. With the exception of the candidate's most senior policy coordinators, they are usually not paid. Their ties to the day-to-day campaign may be tenuous, and they all have nonpolitical careers to return to. Well-known academics may offer advice in an informal capacity to several campaigns in the same election.

Not surprisingly, there is a certain degree of tension between the "flack masters and [the] idea mongers," as Richard Allen (of the latter camp) puts it. "People in flackery don't know ideas and wouldn't know if one hit them at a great rate of speed," continues Allen, who headed the foreign policy issues team on the Republican side for Ronald Reagan's two campaigns.[78]

There may be some justification for this, in view of the demands of the presidential campaign. "There's a big difference," explains William A. Galston, Walter Mondale's issues director in 1984, "between having a position paper and having a politically salable commodity."[79] "If an idea can't be communicated to the public, then it won't be part of the campaign," concludes John Holum, Gary Hart's issues adviser in 1984 and 1988. Someone, in other words, must administer the "test of political marketability."[80]

Polling

Multimillion-dollar polling is the norm in today's presidential elections. Public opinion polls have been used in politics, in varying ways, since the 1930s,[81] but they have not always been as important in shaping campaigns as they are today. As recently as the 1950s, most candidates still viewed polls with considerable skepticism. Some, like Harry Truman, were downright hostile. "I wonder," he said, "how far Moses would have gone if he'd taken a poll in Egypt? What would Jesus Christ have preached if he'd taken a poll in Israel? Where would the reformation have gone if Martin Luther had taken a poll? It isn't polls or public opinion of the moment that counts. It is right and wrong leadership—men with fortitude, honesty and a belief in the right—that makes epochs in the history of the world."[82] Winston Churchill, inhabiting the same political universe, said: "Nothing is more dangerous than a Gallup poll, always taking one's pulse and taking one's political temperature."[83] Like all long-lived politicians in democracies, these exemplary figures undoubtedly paid attention to their intuitions about public opinion. But intuition has now been largely replaced by more accurate methods, and it is hard to ignore these more thorough soundings of the popular will.

The first significant use of polls within a campaign organization occurred in 1960, when surveys taken by Louis Harris helped guide John F. Kennedy's campaign in key primary states. Pioneers such as Harris and George Gallup were followed in succeeding decades by hundreds of professional firms throughout the country that now make up the polling industry.[84] General nationwide public opinion polls not owned or paid for by particular candidates are now regularly taken by Gallup, Harris, Zogby, Rasmussen, the Pew Research Center, and several national media groups: *The Wall Street Journal*/NBC News, *New York Times*/CBS News, *Washington Post*/ABC News, CNN, *Newsweek*, Fox News, and the *Los Angeles Times*.

Other polling operations work for political campaigns, and among these, a few are involved in all phases of presidential campaigning.[85] Campaigns conduct a constant series of polls over the course of an election season, in order to monitor the horse race in key battleground states and to collect information about the electorate's views of the candidates, issues, and national conditions. The modern pollster's role goes far beyond gathering data and analyzing trends. "There's no question that our role has changed from collector of facts to interpreter and strategist," Richard Wirthlin says.[86] They ask: What should be the major campaign issues and themes, or, at least, which would be most attractive to the electorate? How should the candidate attack an opponent's record? What are the candidate's (and the opposition's) perceived strengths and weaknesses, and what can be done to exploit or minimize them? How should the candidate's issue positions or performance in office be framed in order to maximize their popular appeal? The campaign pollster helps make these and a variety of other crucial decisions, such as which states to visit and which groups within the electorate to court, all subject to the candidate's approval.

The intricacies of campaign strategy often seem to fascinate the news media, if not the electorate at large. Campaign consultants may encourage this preoccupation by attempting to convince journalists of their cleverness in pinpointing particular subgroups of voters deemed critical to the construction of an electoral majority and developing a campaign message aimed at these narrow segments of the population. In 1996, Bill Clinton's campaign advisers identified "soccer moms"—white suburban women with children—as an important constituency whose support they especially courted. Political reporters wrote endless stories about this strategy, finding actual mothers of soccer-playing children to interview in order to find out what they thought about politics.[87] In subsequent elections, soccer moms were joined by other supposed social groups, including "office park dads" and "security moms," as key voting blocs, at least according to consultants and journalists.[88] There are good reasons to be skeptical of such claims. The United States is too large and diverse for any single group to be pivotal in an election, especially such specific categories as these. Individuals who share certain demographic characteristics may not agree politically, and a message crafted to appeal to one group may repel another. Still, the increasing sophistication of polling methods now allows campaigns to focus their attention on classes of undecided or persuadable voters whom they think will influence the outcome of the election.

In 2000, the dilemma facing Al Gore's presidential campaign was underscored by the results of polls indicating that while most Americans approved of President Clinton's performance in office, particularly on economic issues, they held much less positive opinions of Clinton personally after an investigation by independent counsel Kenneth Starr disclosed a relationship between the president and White House intern Monica Lewinsky. Gore took pains to distinguish himself from the incumbent under whom he had served as vice president for eight years, dissuading Clinton from campaigning for him and declaring in his speech accepting the Democratic presidential nomination that "I stand before you tonight as my own man." By emphasizing his independence from Clinton, however, Gore ran the risk of failing to capitalize on his association with the popular policies of the Clinton administration.

George W. Bush's campaign strategy in 2000 was similarly inspired by the results of public opinion polls. The Bush campaign discovered that voters were tired of the constant partisan warfare in Washington that characterized the later Clinton years, particularly during the impeachment proceedings of 1998–1999 that left both the president and the Republican-controlled Congress with significant political damage. As the governor of Texas during that time, Bush could credibly claim no association with the unpopular impeachment effort. He promised to be a "uniter, not a divider," and to seek to "change the tone in Washington," noting his success as governor in working with Democrats in the Texas state legislature. To reassure Americans that he would not pursue a strongly ideological agenda—as former House speaker Newt Gingrich had done in the mid-1990s, to the dismay of many voters—Bush described himself as a "compassionate conservative." His rhetoric was expressly designed to appeal to swing voters and political independents who generally found little fault with Clinton's policies but were more critical of Clinton's personal behavior; Bush's oft-repeated promise to "restore honor and dignity to the White House" represented an indirect but easily identifiable reference to the Lewinsky affair.

The 2004 campaign was conducted under very different circumstances; the terrorist attacks of September 11, 2001, and President Bush's declared "war on terror" placed foreign and military policy at center stage. Polls conducted by both campaigns found Bush's chief strength to lie in Americans' support of his fight against Islamic terrorism. Thus Bush endeavored to maintain a link in voters' minds between terrorism and the American-led invasion of Iraq, while the Kerry campaign attempted to distinguish the two, repeatedly arguing that Saddam Hussein's regime had no proven link to the al-Qaeda organization that perpetrated the 2001 attacks. Bush's strategy of labeling his opponent a "flip-flopper" represented an attempt to convince voters that Kerry was weak and indecisive, and therefore unfit for leadership during wartime. Kerry emphasized his record as a decorated Vietnam War veteran—a record called into question by Bush surrogates during the course of the campaign—who possessed the appropriate skills and experience to face the challenges of the day.

Other issues emerged as well in 2004. Polling by the Kerry campaign revealed that Bush's economic policies were considerably less popular than his attempts to fight terrorism, prompting Kerry to criticize Bush's job creation record repeatedly on the campaign trail. While the Bush campaign courted independent voters, it also pursued a strategy of maximizing electoral turnout among his presumed "base" of self-identified Republicans and conservatives. Bush's campaign rhetoric became more explicitly ideological than it had been in 2000, and his public support for a constitutional amendment prohibiting same-sex marriage represented an attempt to inspire high levels of voter turnout among evangelical Christians and other socially conservative segments of the population.

During the summer of 2008, the Obama campaign conducted extensive polling to determine the strengths and weaknesses of the two parties' nominees, fixing on a strategy of associating McCain as closely as possible with the increasingly unpopular Bush presidency. This message proved effective in attracting independent voters to Obama over the subsequent weeks of the campaign. In articulating Obama's strategy, chief strategist David Axelrod argued that America was looking for "the remedy [for the Bush administration], not the replica."[89] To this end, Obama distanced himself from "Washington insiders," as he had done with great success in his contest with Hillary Clinton during the Democratic primaries. Further, Obama's research revealed that voters did not know much about John McCain, despite McCain's previous run for the Republican presidential nomination in 2000 and subsequent prominence in national politics. Joel Benenson, the campaign's pollster, recalled, "What we knew at the start of the campaign was that the notion of John McCain as a change agent and independent voice didn't exist anywhere outside of the [Washington] Beltway."[90] The adverse environment for the GOP, limited voter knowledge about McCain, and large financial advantage made the execution of a fall campaign straightforward for the Obama high command.

Top McCain aides, in contrast, understood that they began the campaign with serious disadvantages. Chief strategist Steve Schmidt recalled: "This was a campaign that was dealt a very, very tough hand of cards. It was highly unlikely that there will ever be another campaign in our lifetimes that [will feature] a worse environment than the environment that John McCain had to run in."[91] Since no simple message was likely to bring down Obama, the McCain campaign focused instead on a series of tactical disruptions designed to throw their opponent off track and open up new opportunities for them. The main chances to introduce surprises that might shake up the race lay in the central events of the fall campaign: the vice presidential selection, the convention acceptance speeches, and the candidate debates. The McCain campaign began their disruptions with a advertisement soon known as the "celebrity" spot, which mocked Obama's trip overseas in late July by comparing him to Paris Hilton and Britney Spears, two pop culture personalities with reputations for vacuous tawdriness. The celebrity label disturbed the Obama campaign, which viewed it as a negative description that might stick to their candidate. McCain's selection of Sarah Palin as his running mate was a bold move that succeeded, in the short term, at catching both the Obama campaign and the news media by surprise, though the questions raised about her qualifications for national office ultimately caused difficulties for McCain. In the end, McCain's strategy involved high-risk tactics that sometimes backfired, helping Obama to maintain his advantage in the polls.

In 2012, polls conducted by the Romney campaign and Republican-allied super PACs revealed that the subpar performance of the national economy during Obama's first term as president represented the incumbent's biggest political vulnerability. As Carl Forti of the pro-Romney super PAC American Crossroads recalled after the election, "Ninety percent of [undecided voters] voted for Obama last time [in 2008]. They liked him. They just didn't like what he was doing to the country. So anything that was attacking his character or his personality was already decided in their mind. . . . It was a question of, can we prove he was not doing the job and shouldn't be given another four years?"[92] Romney strategist Stuart Stevens noted that "we always said that this [election] would be a referendum on Obama."[93] Negative ads produced by the Romney campaign thus primarily emphasized the unsatisfactory economic condition of the nation during Obama's first term in office.

Romney advisers also used survey research to determine how to present their own candidate to voters. As Stevens recalled after the election, "We polled a lot. We tested a lot. We tested four main approaches. The overall Mitt Romney Story—a combination of personal and business/public service. We tested a focus on the business record—how he created jobs and grew businesses. We tested the Romney Mass[achusetts] record—how he turned around a faltering state. And we tested the Romney Agenda as President—what he would do as President. Overwhelmingly, people wanted to know more about what he would do as President. . . . That drove us to launch our 'Day One' series of ads."[94]

For the Obama reelection campaign, polling likewise supported the strategic decision to counter Romney's attempt to frame the election as a referendum on the economic performance of the previous four years. "Obviously we weren't running in the most optimal of circumstances," acknowledged Obama strategist David Axelrod in retrospect. "But we believed that we would prosper from putting [the election] in the context of a choice."[95] Obama chief pollster Joel Benenson examined reams of survey data to find a rhetorical frame that worked to Obama's advantage: "Who would fight for middle class Americans? . . . People didn't think [Romney] was on their side and they didn't think he would fight for their interest."[96]

Polling also allows campaigns to decide which states to contest fiercely and which to ignore. George W. Bush's 2000 campaign discovered that Bush was competitive in the historically Democratic state of West Virginia and that he also polled strongly in Tennessee, even though the latter was the home state of Bush's opponent, Al Gore. The Bush campaign devoted time and resources to these states, initially considered safe for Gore, and carried them both—two key victories in an extremely close election. Likewise, early assumptions that Florida would not be competitive in 2000 (the state usually voted Republican, and Bush's younger brother Jeb served as its governor) were contradicted by polling results indicating a tight race, especially after Gore's selection of a Jewish running mate, Senator Joseph Lieberman of Connecticut, won him significant support in the Jewish communities of South Florida. Both campaigns invested heavily in Florida in the final weeks before the election; on Election Day, the state was so closely divided between Bush and Gore that it took weeks of recounts and extensive litigation before a winner could be determined.

The electoral battleground map in 2004 closely resembled that from four years before. Once again, top campaign targets on both sides included Florida, Pennsylvania, Michigan, Wisconsin, Iowa, Nevada, and New Mexico. Both sides conducted continuous polling in each state in order to pick up the latest trends and react accordingly. While the Gore campaign had pulled its resources from Ohio in the last weeks before the 2000 election, choosing to focus on winning Pennsylvania and Florida instead, in 2004 the state remained a hard-fought battleground up until Election Day, with multiple public appearances from Bush and Kerry and their running mates, constant television advertising and campaign mobilization efforts, and a frenzy of activity by party organizations and outside groups on both sides. Initially promising polls led the Bush campaign to invest resources in the traditional Democratic strongholds of Minnesota and Oregon, while the Kerry campaign actively contested Colorado, a state Gore had conceded to Bush in 2000. Bush's running mate Dick Cheney even took an all-night airplane trip to Hawaii for a campaign appearance a few days before the election after an opinion poll suggested (falsely, as it turned out) that the state, normally a Democratic bastion, was politically competitive.[97]

In 2008, the results of state-level polling likewise determined candidate strategy, but with an additional complication: the Obama campaign's decision to decline public financing for the general election in order to spend unlimited private funds gave them a critical advantage over the McCain team. Obama capitalized on his financial edge (and overall lead in the polls) to contest several states usually conceded to the Republican candidate in presidential elections, thus forcing McCain to spend precious resources defending territory that he otherwise could have taken for granted. When polls taken in the late spring showed unexpected strength in Indiana, Obama spent money establishing an active campaign organization in the state—the first Democratic presidential nominee to do so in decades—and ultimately carried it by a small margin. North Carolina was not initially a top target (Obama made only one visit to the state between June and mid-September), but as surveys continued to suggest a competitive race, the Obama campaign redoubled its efforts there, sending the candidate to the state five times in the final month of the campaign and forcing McCain to respond with three appearances of his own.

McCain's electoral college strategy similarly evolved in reaction to the findings of his pollsters. The campaign decided in early October to transfer resources from Michigan, normally an electoral battleground but judged by McCain advisers on the basis of survey results to be out of reach for their side, to more promising states elsewhere—a move criticized publicly by running mate Sarah Palin.[98] With Obama pulling ahead in several states that had voted for George W. Bush in 2004, including Colorado, Iowa, Nevada, and New Mexico, the McCain campaign concluded that their only chance for victory in the electoral college required carrying a large state that had been won by John Kerry four years before. Identifying Pennsylvania as their best opportunity for an upset, McCain and Palin campaigned frequently in the state during the weeks before the election, but ultimately fell short—as they did in nearly all the battleground states.[99]

Why are polls and pollsters so important to campaigns? Why have they replaced party bosses and cronies of the candidate as the key decision makers? Plenty of attention has been focused on the mistaken or misleading results of polling. Nevertheless, taken together, polls are reasonably accurate indicators of public sentiment. Thus they are a better tool for shaping campaign strategy and content than anything else now available, and this, in the uncertain universe of the presidential campaign, is all that is really necessary to make polls indispensable to the candidate.

One need only consider the information sources that used to govern campaign strategy to appreciate the significance of the advent of modern polling techniques. Nineteenth- and early-twentieth-century indicators of public opinion consisted of reports from precinct captains and state party leaders, crowd sizes and responses at rallies, newspaper editorials and letters to the editor, the candidate's mail, man-in-the-street interviews, and pure hunches. Most of these measures were unreliable. Editorials may signify the views of only a few newspaper owners; letters to the editor represent a lot of writing by a rather small number of activists; crowd responses can be manipulated, or variously interpreted; party leaders may communicate only what they think the candidate wishes to hear.

While polls themselves may be indispensable, their interpreters frequently play much larger roles in presidential politics than would seem warranted for mere keepers of statistics. George H. W. Bush, to take one example, was persuaded by pollster Bob Teeter (with the aid of strategists Roger Ailes and Lee Atwater) to adopt the get-tough strategy of his 1988 campaign.[100] The modern-day polling consultant, in the words of one practitioner, plays an instrumental role in deciding "which states to hit, where people should go, how much money should be spent where, which groups [to] target, and the kinds of money and messages [to] use."[101]

The explanation for this abdication of authority on the part of the candidates and their personal advisers lies partly in the changing nature of polling. With computer-assisted sample selection processes and polling techniques, it has been possible to increase the number of polls taken in the course of a campaign to allow daily surveys in all key states for both campaigns. Moreover, the information obtained from polls has expanded greatly. Originally, opinion surveys were merely a device to measure candidate support; good pollsters would try to isolate which groups within the electorate were more and less likely to vote for the candidate. Nowadays, polls are constructed to address not just how social groups will vote—and the categories here have become progressively more precise—but why they will do so and what might change their minds. Pollsters, in other words, are now being asked to do more than simply report on the state of public opinion; they are now routinely expected to help influence it.

Focus Groups

Focus groups have been a tool of communication and advertising research for decades; by the 1980s, they had become an integral part of campaign strategy. The ideal group consists of about twelve to fifteen voters chosen from the general population to discuss the election and the candidates. A much smaller number is likely to place too much of a burden on each individual, while more than fifteen or so tends to reduce each member's participation. A moderator guides the discussion, focusing on matters of interest to the campaign. Discussions are lengthy—anywhere from one-and-a-half to three hours—so that participants have a chance to express their feelings. The 1988 George H. W. Bush campaign picked Paramus, New Jersey, for their main focus group site because to them it represented a typical American city. They conducted similar sessions in other middle-America settings across the country.

Unlike opinion polls, which depend for their validity on randomly selecting a representative cross-section of voters, focus groups are usually structured to be socially homogeneous "so that the numerous interacting demographic variables do not confuse the issues; to be most productive, all the participants must be on the same wavelength."[102] For example, focus group organizers may not place married, stay-at-home mothers in the same group as single working women because their lifestyles and goals are deemed too different.[103] "The key to focus groups is homogeneity," Bill Clinton's pollster Stanley Greenberg says. "The more homogeneity, the more revealing."[104]

Focus-group interviewing violates most of the accepted canons of survey research. As William D. Wells of the University of Chicago Graduate School of Business says:

> Samples are invariably small and never selected by probability methods. Questions are not asked the same way each time. Responses are not independent. Some respondents inflict their opinions on others; some contribute little or nothing at all. Results are difficult or impossible to quantify and are not grist for the statistical mill. Conclusions depend on the analyst's interpretive skill. The investigator can easily influence the results.[105]

With so many defects, why have focus groups come to be so widely used in political campaigns? Part of the reason is that they are fast and relatively cheap—a few thousand dollars as opposed to $25,000 or more for sample surveys. Another reason to use focus groups is to test campaign messages, ideas, or ads not yet released to the general public. Participants are asked whether particular information affects their views of the candidates. Like Hollywood movies, which can be changed if preview audiences give them poor reviews, political ads can be altered or discarded if focus groups don't like what they see.

The most important reason focus groups are employed is that they give the campaign an opportunity to probe respondents to a greater depth than in regular polls. Deeper feelings and half-formed thoughts of ordinary voters emerge, and in their own words. It is true that the group's responses cannot easily be quantified, but in the hands of a sensitive analyst, focus groups may reveal important insights. "Focus groups allow you to put flesh on the bones," Democratic pollster Mark Mellman says; they provide "a sense of texture you can't get from a poll."[106] In a June 2008 focus group observed by a reporter from the *Washington Post*, moderator Peter Hart asked a group of Pennsylvania voters a series of questions designed to elicit their personal impressions of the candidates: "What kind of neighbor would McCain or Obama be? With which man would you choose to share an hour-long commute to work? Whom would you select to carry the American flag . . . in the Olympics?"[107]

Adviser David Simas revealed after the 2012 election that focus groups allowed Obama's reelection campaign to identify the two candidates' strengths and weaknesses in the eyes of undecided voters. Simas described the typical view of Obama among this segment of the electorate as "I like the president . . . I think he's trying really hard, I think that he shares my values, but I'm concerned that things [i.e., the performance of the national economy] haven't turned around fast enough or they haven't turned around [at all]." These voters also perceived Romney as having "been successful at different things that he's done" with "technical knowledge about . . . the economy" due to his experience in the business sector. The lesson from these findings, according to

Simas, was that Obama needed to make the case to swing voters that Romney's business expertise was not accompanied by sympathy for the economic plight of the average person. "In the focus groups—group after group after group after group—we would hear these undecided, independent voters say things like, 'Look, I need a guy, a president who, from the beginning to the end, his entire focus is going to be on things that grow the middle class because that's the way you grow the economy.'"[108] On the basis of these results, the Obama campaign initiated a series of television ads portraying Romney as advancing the interests of the wealthy at the expense of middle-class workers.

Focus groups can also be used to generate quantitative data. Using hand-held, dial-equipped boxes, participants watching an ad, speech, or debate are asked to register their reactions, positive or negative, by twisting a knob on a scale of zero to one hundred. Dial groups were used by Bill Clinton's consultants in 1992 to address his weaknesses as a candidate. While trying to figure a way out of Clinton's problems, pollster Stanley Greenberg convened a group of middle-aged white women at a hotel in Dayton, Ohio, and asked them to "dial" their reactions to prepared presentations of the candidate and the campaign. Greenberg found that Clinton scored poorly when he looked and sounded like a politician but did well when he answered questions directly and addressed certain popular issues, such as welfare reform. When presenting the results to the campaign, Greenberg superimposed a tracing of the dial readings on the video the subjects had watched, giving Clinton a blow-by-blow report on the "grades" the dial group had given his various responses.[109]

Obama advisers used dial groups to test their candidate's acceptance speech at the 2012 Democratic national convention. While the address received middling reviews from media commentators, Obama officials responded by claiming that undecided voters were, according to their research, less interested in stirring rhetoric than hearing concrete policy proposals for a second term.[110] Cable news channels now routinely convene dial groups during their coverage of televised debates, revealing the real-time reactions of undecided voters to the candidates' performance.

Television Advertising

Despite the explosion of "new media" in recent years—via the Internet and cell phones—candidates still expend considerable resources on television advertising, and the media consultants who produce the ads play a central role in crafting the message of the campaign. Television commercials remain a highly effective means of reaching persuadable voters and can serve a variety of purposes. They can be used to establish name recognition or to improve a candidate's personal image. They can focus on campaign issues, targeting key subgroups in the population. They can be used to capture the attention of the press. Or they can be used to attack the candidate's opponent. This practice has come to be called negative advertising.

There is no standard formula for a political ad, but there are standard time slots. When introduced in the 1950s, television advertising was generally produced to fill five-minute slots. One-minute spots predominated in the 1960s and 1970s, to be eclipsed in the late 1970s by the thirty-second ad, which is still the most common length today.[111]

After the advertisement is filmed, edited, and approved by the candidate, a schedule is prepared that is supposed to help the ad reach the right people. Every ad campaign is somewhat different and must be crafted to take account of the unique assets and deficiencies of the candidate. But amid the varying styles of each campaign, a relatively small number of tried-and-true themes have established themselves over the past several decades. These constitute the advertising consultant's tool kit, from which virtually every television campaign is built. There is the "man-in-the-street" ad, sometimes scripted and sometimes culled from actual interview footage, showing the average voter (or the average member of a targeted constituency group) endorsing the candidate's accomplishments or general integrity. The "sainthood spot" is "devoted to celebrating the candidate's life story and accomplishments." The "news-look" spot ad attempts to use the legitimacy of experts and television newscasters who relate facts about the candidate's record. The "apology" ad is used, usually out of desperation, when a liability develops that is considered so threatening to the candidate's chances of election that he or she must personally apologize to the electorate. "Cinema-verité" spots offer the audience a view into the life of the candidate as he or she is working, walking, or addressing another audience, while the older "talking head" approach (still a staple of spot ads) places the candidate directly in front of the camera so that he or she can talk personally and directly to the audience. The "issue-position" spot defines the candidate's record on an issue of high salience to the electorate or to a key group of voters.[112]

One measure of the centrality of television advertising in the current campaign process can be found in the recently developed "back-and-forth" ad. This innovative format begins with an excerpt from an opponent's spot ad, which is then "answered" in the second sequence, an ad within an ad. This is possible because technological developments have enabled campaigns to produce television ads more quickly, cheaply, and easily. Campaigns now can respond to the opposition's latest round of advertising in a matter of hours. Evidence shows that technology may be closing this time lag even more.

In 2008, one could follow the almost instantaneous responses of the Obama and McCain campaigns to each other, often in the form of ads appearing only on websites. Those ads, though, routinely received free television airtime via news coverage and became major topics of discussion in the blogosphere and on cable news programs. The underfunded McCain campaign used this approach to get its message across. In the late summer, it lampooned Barack Obama's overseas trip with an advertising spot released first on the Internet in which a narrator, referring to Obama, intoned, "He's the biggest celebrity in the world. But is he ready to lead?" The ad's visual juxtaposition of Obama with tabloid-fodder starlets Britney Spears and Paris Hilton generated a great deal of attention (and free publicity) from news media personalities, as was intended, and its message reportedly caused worry in the Obama campaign.

Media professionals attempt to place political commercials in order to reach a targeted viewing audience. "Dissimilar kinds of people," Larry Sabato notes, "watch and listen to different sorts of programs at various times of the day."[113] A media consultant might court news programs' highly educated, well-informed audiences with information-packed ads or spots discussing issues, for example, while viewers of lighter fare might see commercials that emphasized the candidate's personality. The 2012 Obama campaign bought ads on nonpolitical cable networks that are normally ignored by candidates, such as the Food Network and the Hallmark Channel, because research suggested that they could reach undecided voters and inconsistently engaged Democrats.[114] Because about 90 percent of American households now subscribe to cable or satellite systems, campaigns can exploit the multiplicity of cable channels to tailor messages to a specific audience.[115] The late Richard N. Neustadt, a communications law attorney,

BOX 5.2. In the Arena: Which 2012 Campaign Ads Were Effective?

Below is a summary and text of four 2012 campaign ads—two from the Obama campaign and two from the Romney campaign. Campaign analysts labeled two of the ads as highly effective and two as not very effective. Can you guess which were termed effective and which were not? You can view these and other campaign ads at http://www.youtube.com/ by entering the candidate name and ad title in the YouTube search engine.

SPOILER ALERT: at the bottom of this page we report the analysts' verdict regarding effective and ineffective ads.

"The Romney Plan" Content—Mitt Romney: "My plan is to help the middle class. Trade has to work for America; that means crack down on cheaters like China, it means open up the markets. Next, you gotta balance the budget, you gotta cut the deficit, we got to stop spending more money than we take in. And finally, champion small business and have tax policies, regulations, and health care policies to help small business. We put those in place we'll add twelve million jobs in four years. I'm Mitt Romney and I approve this message."

"Swiss Bank Account" Content—Barack Obama: "I'm Barack Obama and I approve this message." Male Voice: "Over the top, erroneous, out of context: big oil's new attack ad. President Obama's clean energy initiatives have helped create jobs for projects across America, not overseas. What about Mitt Romney? As a corporate CEO he shipped American jobs to places like Mexico and China. As governor, he outsourced eight jobs to a call center in India. He's still pushing tax breaks for companies that ship jobs overseas. It's just what you'd expect from a guy who had a Swiss bank account."

"Who Will Do More?" Content—Male Voice: "Who will do more for the auto industry? Not Barack Obama. Fact checkers confirm his attacks on Mitt Romney are false. The truth: Mitt Romney has a plan to help the auto industry. He is supported by Lee Iacocca and the Detroit News. Obama took GM and Chrysler into bankruptcy and sold Chrysler to Italians who were going to build Jeeps in China. Mitt Romney will fight for every American job." *Mitt Romney*: "I'm Mitt Romney and I approve this message."

"Big Bird" Content—Barack Obama: "I'm Barack Obama and I approve this message." Male Voice: "Bernie Madoff, Ken Lay, Dennis Kozlowski: criminals, gluttons of greed and the evil genius that towered over them? One man has the guts to speak his name." Mitt Romney: "Big bird. Big Bird. Big Bird" Big Bird: "It's me, Big Bird" Male Voice: "Big, yellow, a menace to our economy. Mitt Romney knows it's not Wall Street you have to worry about, it's Sesame Street." Mitt Romney: "I'm going to stop the subsidy to PBS." Male Voice: "Mitt Romney, taking on our enemies no matter where they nest."

RESULTS: Darrell West, Director of Governmental Studies at the Brookings Institution, labeled "The Romney Plan" and "Swiss Bank Account" as two of the best ads of the 2012 campaign. Both ads provide information voters may find useful. Mark Silva of Bloomberg News classified "Big Bird" and "Who Will Do More?" as two of the worst ads of the campaign—"Big Bird" because of its silly associations and "Who Will Do More?" because of factual inaccuracies about Jeep production in China. West's lists of best Obama and Romney ads: http://www.brookings.edu/blogs/up-front/posts

predicted: "When we watch the narrowcasting [approach of cable] networks, we may see campaign ads and news programs showing candidates advocating bilingual education on Spanish channels, defending Social Security on channels aimed at the elderly, or playing football on sports channels."[116]

New Media

The continued evolution of communication technology in the decades since the rise of television in the 1950s has inspired presidential campaigns to employ these tools to seek any possible electoral advantage. As satellite broadcasting became common in the 1980s, candidates used it to make remote appearances and send newly produced television spots instantly to stations across the country. The spread of VCRs (and, later, DVD players) allowed candidates to distribute videos of themselves for purposes of fund-raising and voter persuasion. In the 1992 election, several candidates pioneered the use of toll-free telephone hotlines as a way for supporters to volunteer their time and make financial contributions.

With the advent of the World Wide Web in the 1990s, political campaigns began to view the Internet as a potentially powerful means of persuasion and mobilization. Supporters and interested voters can now access a great deal of information provided online, including biographical sketches, policy positions, lists of endorsements, press releases, and personal appearance schedules for the presidential candidate, running mate, and their families. Internet users can sign up for the candidate's mailing list and receive regular e-mail updates from the campaign; candidates also use their websites to recruit volunteers for campaign activities like voter registration drives and phone-banking.

The Internet is growing quickly as a nexus of political activity. A Pew Internet and American Life Project study found that 74 percent of Internet users, representing 55 percent of America's adult population, went online in 2008 "to get involved in the political process or to get news and information about the election. This marks the first time that a Pew survey has found that more than half of the voting-age population used the Internet to get involved in the political process during an election year."[117] Internet platforms that had been road-tested in previous campaigns, such as websites, blogs, and discussion boards, proliferated and achieved new levels of sophistication in 2008. Video sharing and social networking sites that employ digital technology to enhance information sharing and collaboration were adapted for the campaign context. These Web 2.0 applications represent a second generation of Internet-based services that are designed to develop and manage online communities, enabling more seamless interaction and communication among users.[118] In 2008, Barack Obama regularly sent short video messages to supporters via the Web. His campaign also created means for his supporters to meet and organize locally through Internet communication, placed ads on many high-traffic websites, and also sought support at sites frequented by niche audiences, such as video game aficionados and those seeking softer "celebrity" news. The McCain campaign was less active online, largely because they came to it later in the campaign season and with fewer resources.

In 2012, the presidential campaigns' new media strategies evolved substantially from those of the previous election. In particular, the explosive growth of social media and microblogging platforms, especially Twitter, Facebook, and Tumblr, between 2008 and 2012 prompted significant investment in these increasingly powerful avenues of communication. Both the Obama and Romney campaigns maintained a constant presence on social media over the course of the campaign, providing streams of content to keep voters engaged while targeting specific persuasive messages to particular constituencies. For example, the Obama campaign created a number of Facebook groups such as "Women for Obama," "Latinos for Obama," and "Students for Obama," whose members received regular content emphasizing the candidate's positions on such issues as contraception access, immigration reform, and college loans, respectively. The campaigns viewed social media as valuable not only for maintaining constant contact with their existing supporters, but also for reaching undecided voters via the propensity of social media users to "share" or "retweet" campaign messages, which places them in the news feeds of their friends and followers as well.

TELEVISED DEBATES

Presidential debates are major milestones in the general election season because they directly expose the candidates in verbal competition before millions of Americans. For that reason, they hold the potential to influence the public's evaluations of the candidates and thus affect the outcome of the election. Like every other aspect of presidential campaigns, candidates and their advisers approach the debates with an eye toward using the attention generated by the events to their political advantage.

The now-familiar series of debates in the fall of every election year is itself the product of strategic calculation by candidates. In 1960, Senator John F. Kennedy of Massachusetts, the Democratic nominee, issued a public challenge to his Republican opponent, Vice President Richard Nixon, to debate on television, then still a new medium of communication. By holding his own on the issues with the sitting vice president before a national audience, Kennedy hoped to overcome criticism that he was too young (he was forty-three) and inexperienced to assume the presidency. With the benefit of hindsight, many observers now suggest that Nixon was obviously foolish to participate. But Kennedy had placed Nixon in a difficult position, because refusing to debate would have subjected Nixon to criticism for being afraid to face his opponent. Perhaps a record of success in debates going back to high school was not irrelevant in guiding Nixon to his eventual decision to appear on television with his rival.[119] Surveys taken afterward suggest that Nixon miscalculated—that the 1960 debates helped Kennedy.[120] But if Nixon had won the election instead of losing it by a wafer-thin margin, he would hardly have been reminded of any error on his part, and his willingness to debate his opponent might instead have been portrayed as a key to his victory.

Perhaps due to the result of the debates in 1960, when the more experienced candidate came out the loser, Lyndon Johnson in 1964 and Nixon in 1968 and 1972 refused to debate their opponents. Because inertia had begun to work against the idea of debates, the fact that they occurred again in 1976 was somewhat surprising. Although the Democrats did not do especially well in the debates (which included, for the first time, a debate between the vice presidential nominees as well), the Republicans, who took the bigger risk by participating, undoubtedly lost ground twice. One time was when incumbent president Gerald Ford left the impression that in his opinion Poland and Eastern Europe were not under domination at the time by the Soviet Union, a gaffe requiring a subsequent week's worth of "clarifications." The other was when Senator Bob

Dole of Kansas, Ford's vice presidential running mate, misjudged the audience entirely and bounced partisan one-liners ineffectually off the beatific brow of Senator Walter Mondale of Minnesota, thus spoiling one of the few chances the Republicans had to woo Democratic voters.[121]

In 1980, plans for another series of debates were complicated by the presence in the race of an independent candidate, Representative John Anderson of Illinois. Incumbent president Jimmy Carter refused to participate in any event that included Anderson, whom he believed was damaging his chances for reelection, and so in the end only one debate took place late in the campaign between Carter and his Republican challenger, Ronald Reagan. On balance it seems to have helped Reagan, who may have lost on high-school debate rules but projected a benignity that was helpfully at odds with the picture of a dangerous radical that Carter was trying to paint.[122] So Carter became another incumbent who suffered political damage by submitting to a televised debate.

There were two presidential debates in 1984; after the first, it looked as if the sitting president had again lost ground. Reagan's somewhat scattered performance inspired a series of negative news stories telling the public how badly he had done; a *Wall Street Journal* article suggested that perhaps the incumbent's age (seventy-three at the time of the campaign) was catching up with him.[123] Challenger Walter Mondale moved up slightly in the polls. Perhaps, it was thought, Mondale could come from behind to win. In the second debate, Reagan put in a stronger showing, and the age issue was put to rest. "I will not make age an issue of this campaign," the president joked. "I am not going to exploit, for political purposes, my opponent's youth and inexperience."[124] Reagan regained the large lead he had held throughout the campaign and went on to a landslide victory.[125]

Unlike John Anderson in 1980, independent Ross Perot was allowed to participate in the three 1992 presidential debates, at the insistence of George H. W. Bush's campaign. The decision to invite him appears to have been a major strategic error. Apparently, the thinking in the Bush camp was that Perot was disproportionately hurting their candidate, so Bush needed to take him on and show, as one author put it, that Perot was "too small and too shifty to be president."[126] The tactic failed. After the first debate, the overwhelming judgment from journalists was that Perot had in fact won the contest; his folksy, quick one-liners were popular with viewers. The second debate in 1992 used a new procedure—candidates answered questions from a specially selected studio audience of undecided voters rather than from news media personalities, as was traditional. This format, known as a "town hall" debate, favored Bill Clinton, and he was indeed the winner by media consensus. Perot, being short, refused to sit on the stools provided, as his two opponents did, because his feet would not touch the floor. Instead, he stood awkwardly and his discomfort permeated his performance. Overall, Bush did fairly well, but one major gaffe marred his performance and was all the press would discuss for days afterward. A woman from the audience asked him what effect the "deficit" had had on him personally. She probably meant to say the "recession" but misspoke, and Bush did not understand her meaning. "I'm not sure I get it," Bush said, essentially confirming the message the Clinton campaign had been putting forward throughout the year: Bush was out of touch with voters and didn't even acknowledge that there was economic distress in the country, much less suffer from it himself.[127]

Though Democrat Al Gore was not a sitting president in 2000, he faced the same danger most incumbents do in presidential debates: the burden of high expectations. Gore's reputation as a disciplined, on-message speaker with an impressive command of facts and figures contrasted with Republican nominee George W. Bush's public persona as a man less interested in the details of public policy and prone to the occasional malapropism. As with the results of presidential primaries, journalists tend to designate winners and losers in debates based on which candidates exceed or fall short of expectations—a point grasped by the Bush campaign, which sought to influence these expectations before the first event by referring to their opponent as a "world-class debater" while suggesting that any performance by their own candidate that did not end in embarrassment would be a significant victory.[128] Indeed, Bush performed solidly in the first debate with no major gaffes, while Gore's aggressive style—repeatedly interrupting Bush and moderator Jim Lehrer and sighing into his microphone at many of Bush's responses—prompted critical comments from media observers. The day before the second debate, worried campaign staffers forced Gore to watch a parody of his performance on *Saturday Night Live*, in which comedian Darrell Hammond portrayed the vice president as a condescending know-it-all who obsessively repeated the word "lockbox" (Gore's metaphor for his plan to protect Social Security and Medicare funding), who responded to a question asked of Bush as if it were his turn to speak, and who asked for the chance to deliver two closing statements.[129] In the collective media judgment, Gore overcompensated in the next debate, at times appearing excessively deferential to Bush. In the end, though polls showed that viewers were about evenly split over which candidate won, the debates in 2000 were a disappointment to Gore campaign staff who hoped to use them to demonstrate their candidate's strengths, while the Bush side claimed victory since their man performed better than expected.[130]

The 2004 presidential debates reinforced the historical trend that debates, when they matter at all, usually help the challenging candidate. The first debate, on the topic of foreign policy, was generally judged as a victory for Democrat John Kerry—or, rather, a loss for George W. Bush. Media commentators focused less on the substantive content of the candidates' responses to questions than on their bearing and body language. Bush was captured several times on camera making disapproving faces while Kerry was speaking and seemed generally ill at ease and annoyed by his opponent, fidgeting at his lectern and occasionally speaking in broken sentences.[131] The second and third debates—a town hall debate and an event focusing on domestic policy—proved less eventful, although Kerry caused a stir at the final debate by mentioning Vice President Dick Cheney's daughter Mary in response to a question about same-sex marriage.[132] Overall, the debates seemed to help Kerry slightly more than Bush. Kerry improved his standing in the polls over the period that the events were held, drawing nearly even with his Republican opponent in many surveys by the middle of October.[133]

In 2008, Republican John McCain trailed Democrat Barack Obama in the polls and the money race heading into the debates. The McCain campaign hoped to use the national exposure to gain ground by demonstrating that Obama was not up to the job of president. For its part, the Obama team aimed to convince voters of their candidate's readiness and to tie McCain closely to George W. Bush, the incumbent president, whose popularity had declined markedly since his 2004 reelection.

The first debate was held on September 26 on the topic of foreign policy. McCain's advisers had coached their candidate to question Obama's mastery of the subject, but to do so in a way that was not overly hostile (in order to prevent the backlash suffered by Gore in 2000).[134] McCain proceeded to suggest at seven different points during the debate that Obama "doesn't seem to understand" the issue under discussion, while declining to engage Obama directly—even appearing to avoid looking at his opponent.[135] In particular, McCain characterized Obama's willingness to meet with hostile foreign leaders without preconditions as dangerous, implying that Obama was weak and naive while portraying himself as battle-tested and ready to handle any international crisis. Unfortunately for McCain, this approach was interpreted by many in the news media as reflecting a dismissive contempt for Obama, and the absence of any obvious mistakes on Obama's part failed to bolster McCain's charge that his opponent lacked the knowledge and experience to be president.

The McCain campaign promised more attacks on Obama prior to the second debate on October 7. However, the event featured few dramatic confrontations—perhaps due to the town-hall format, which discouraged direct interaction between the candidates. In the third and final debate, held on October 15 and devoted to domestic policy, McCain raised Obama's past association with 1960s radical William Ayers for the first time. He also mentioned an individual who would figure prominently in the campaign's final weeks: Samuel Joseph Wurzelbacher, or "Joe the Plumber." Wurzelbacher, a plumber's assistant encountered by Obama while campaigning in Ohio, was captured on video footage raising concerns with Obama about his proposal to raise taxes on those making more than $250,000 a year. In response, Obama said: "It's not that I want to punish your success. I just want to make sure that everybody who is behind you, that they've got a chance for success, too. . . . When you spread the wealth around, it's good for everybody." Citing the incident, McCain challenged Obama: "You were going to put him in a higher tax bracket which was going to increase his taxes, which was going to cause him not to be able to employ people, which [sic] Joe was trying to realize the American dream."[136] Wurzelbacher became a mascot of sorts for the McCain campaign in the last days of the race, appearing frequently on television and at public events on behalf of the Republican ticket.

In the end, the 2008 debates failed to produce any developments important enough to significantly affect the trajectory of the campaign. For Obama, a relatively uneventful series of debates merely solidified his position as the front-runner in the election. Although McCain failed to narrow Obama's advantage, in truth he had only a limited ability to influence the outcome. McCain's two main lines of attack—that Obama was unqualified for the presidency and that his views were so radical as to resemble socialism—were effectively counteracted by Obama's relatively smooth, measured performance. Had Obama made an embarrassing error or come across as an ideological extremist, McCain's criticisms might have resonated better with the electorate; instead, he found difficulty in rebutting Obama's own claims that McCain had been a strong supporter of George W. Bush's policies.

As the incumbent president in 2012, Obama faced Republican challenger Mitt Romney in a series of debates that turned out to be significant milestones in a close race between the two nominees. Obama entered the October 3 debate on domestic policy with a narrow lead in national and battleground-state polls, prompting some enthusiastic supporters to suggest that a strong performance by the president might seal an electoral victory. But his manner once on stage immediately struck observers as surprisingly disengaged and lethargic. Over the ninety minutes of the debate, a hesitant and often meandering Obama failed to effectively defend his record in office from a series of sharp attacks by a focused and relentless Romney. Echoing the post-debate media consensus, veteran journalist Joe Klein of *Time* described the debate afterward as "one of the most inept performances I've ever seen by a sitting President."[137] Romney, in contrast, exceeded expectations, presenting himself as a pragmatic, results-oriented leader rather than the out-of-touch right-wing multimillionaire depicted by the Obama campaign's negative advertisements. The debate produced an immediate effect on the candidate horse race; Romney gained about 4 percentage points, on average, in the national polls over the following days, bringing him into a virtual tie in the overall popular vote.[138]

The stakes were thus raised considerably for the second presidential debate, held on October 16 and employing the town-hall format in which the candidates answered questions from an audience of undecided voters. It was evident from the first moments of the evening that Obama had revised his approach. "He interrupted, he scolded, he filibustered, he shook his head," noted Peter Baker of the *New York Times* in a post-debate account, describing the newly aggressive president as "intent on redeeming himself by getting in all the points he failed to get in last time."[139]

Romney performed capably once again, but Obama's much-changed demeanor dominated the post-debate analysis, and the incumbent also benefited from some important help at a key moment. After Romney accused Obama of failing to label the September 11, 2012, lethal attack on the U.S. consulate in Benghazi, Libya, as an act of terrorism for fourteen full days after the incident, Obama replied that he had indeed done so the following day at the White House. The two bickered briefly about the matter before debate moderator Candy Crowley of CNN interjected, telling Romney that Obama "did, in fact, sir . . . call it an act of terror." "Can you say that a little louder, Candy?" responded Obama to laughter from the audience, prompting Crowley to repeat her statement. Democrats reveled in the exchange, viewing it as an attempt by Romney to catch Obama in a "gotcha" moment that ended up backfiring, while Republicans raised the concern that Crowley had inappropriately intervened in the proceedings on Obama's behalf.[140] Polls showed that Romney's rise in the polls was stalled by the second debate, preserving a nearly neck-and-neck national race for the rest of October. A third debate on the subject of foreign policy, held on October 22, proved less electorally consequential; Obama retained his aggressive style from the previous event, accusing Romney of advocating "wrong and reckless" policies, while Romney characterized Obama's record in office as leading to a "rising tide of chaos" around the world.

The strategic imperatives surrounding debates have emerged with some clarity. When they matter at all, debates are more likely to hurt sitting presidents and vice presidents than their electoral opponents. Non-incumbents may gain respect simply by keeping their composure as they stand on an equal footing with an occupant of high public office, since the prior expectations for their performance tend to be more forgiving among both the news media and the general public. "Challengers win . . . debates, in many respects, when they walk on stage," argues Obama adviser Anita Dunn. "For the first time, most of the time, they have the same stature as the President of the United States. Suddenly, they seem more presidential, just because they're there. Challengers also have been campaigning full time [while] presidents . . . tend to have a lot going on besides preparing for the debate."[141] This dynamic seems to have worked to the advantage of John F. Kennedy against Richard Nixon in 1960, Jimmy Carter against Gerald Ford in 1976, Ronald Reagan against Carter in 1980, Bill Clinton against George H. W. Bush in 1992, George W. Bush against Al Gore in 2000, and John Kerry against the younger Bush in 2004. In some cases, an incumbent has managed to rebound from a poor first debate by adopting a new approach in subsequent events, as Reagan did against Walter Mondale in 1984 and Obama did against Mitt Romney in 2012.

Political journalists and the custodians of the flame of disinterested public-spirit-edness appear to agree that debates are wonderful exercises in public enlightenment. This scarcely seems credible to minimally intelligent viewers of the actual debates we have had, in which candidates' facial expressions, tones of voice, recitation of prepared one-liners, and overall deportment have often been judged more important to the outcome than any substantive discussion of public policy. As Dunn puts it, "if you're not on offense, you're on defense [and] you will lose. It's that simple."[142] "Civics teachers won't want to hear this," argues James Fallows, a former chief speechwriter for Jimmy Carter, "but the easiest way to judge 'victory' in many debates is to watch with the sound turned off, so you can assess the candidates' ease, tenseness, humor, and other traits signaled by their body language. . . . Having candidates answer policy questions is just a way to find out what we really want to know: how they look and present them-selves, how they look side by side, how they think and speak on their feet, how we feel about them when they address us in their role as potential leaders."[143] Of course, this perspective assumes both that debates are indeed reliable formats for judging these personal qualities and that such attributes can predict a president's success in office—itself a questionable proposition. Nevertheless, televised debates have become a sufficiently entrenched tradition in American presidential elections that both major-party nomi-nees feel compelled to participate in even if they are more likely to suffer politically than benefit from the experience.

Aware of their inherent risk, candidates prepare extensively for these events, spend-ing precious days away from the campaign trail to organize "debate camps" in which they screen video footage of themselves and their opponents, discuss optimal responses and strategies with their advisers, and engage in mock debates with stand-ins imper-sonating their rivals. With the election potentially hanging in the balance, no effort is spared; some campaigns even build full-scale replicas of the debate venue's stage and lighting configuration on which to hold rehearsals. The Romney campaign in 2012 chose Senator Rob Portman of Ohio to portray Barack Obama in multiple practice sessions with the candidate, while Massachusetts senator and 2004 Democratic presi-dential nominee John Kerry stood in for Romney during Obama's debate preparation.[144]

Televised debates are now effectively institutionalized, occurring under the aus-pices of the Commission on Presidential Debates, an organization jointly founded in 1987 by both major parties. The commission normally selects the sites (usually college campuses), dates, topics, and moderators for the debates. Other decisions are resolved by negotiation between representatives of the candidates, with no detail too small to escape their notice. The length of responses to questions, the right of the opposing candidate to deliver a rebuttal or the moderator to follow up on an answer, whether the candidates stand or sit, the height of the table or podiums, the location of the clocks used to time responses, the angles of the television cameras, the use of pencil and paper for taking notes, whether candidates give opening or closing statements—all of these issues and more are the subject of careful, calculated discussion between the rival camps.[145] In 2012, the first debate featured the two candidates standing at match-ing lecterns. In the town hall debate, Romney and Obama used hand-held wireless microphones as they roamed freely around a stage, surrounded by undecided voters perched on risers. In the third debate, the two candidates sat at a single table along with the moderator, as did vice presidential nominees Joe Biden and Paul Ryan in their lone faceoff on October 11.

Campaign advisers' obsessive need to plan for every contingency illustrates the strategic lens through which they view each component of the campaign. The debates are ostensibly designed to educate the public about the candidates' stands on the issues and reveal the capacity of each party's nominee to govern the nation effectively. Yet political actors know that the news media's interest in them is largely due to the chance that a candidate will commit a major mistake or gaffe on live television in front of a national audience; their primary goal is therefore to minimize the probability that their candidate's electoral fortunes are damaged by the experience.

GETTING OUT THE VOTE

As Election Day draws near, presidential campaigns increasingly concentrate their energy on identifying potential supporters within the electorate and ensuring that these voters show up at the polls. Political professionals commonly refer to these efforts as get-out-the-vote (GOTV) activities, the field campaign, or simply the "ground game" (as a complement to the "air war" of dueling television advertisements).

The personal mobilization of voters has undergone something of a resurgence in recent elections. For several decades, campaigns had increasingly relied on television—via both paid spots and free news coverage—to communicate the candidate's message and encourage voter support, viewing the comparatively complex and labor-intensive task of in-person turnout operations as a less central component of their tactical efforts. Beginning in the late 1990s, however, political parties and interest groups shifted more of their resources into field activity, taking advantage of technological advances that allowed them to target voters more precisely than before. This re-emphasis of the ground game may be partially responsible for the rise in voter turnout in presidential elections after 1996 (see table 1.2 in chapter 1).

Before contacting citizens, campaigns must first identify likely supporters; it is counterproductive, of course, to mobilize voters liable to back the opposition. Targeting efforts begin with voters who are registered members of the candidate's political party (in states permitting partisan voter registration) or who tend to participate in the party's primary elections. Voters' registration status and turnout history are matters of public record. Both parties have assembled national electronic databases of voters compiling this and other information in order to best coordinate mobilization activity; for example, a Democratic field campaign might place particular emphasis on contacting registered Democrats with a record of sporadic electoral participation in order to ensure that those voters are aware of the election date and the location of their polling place. Because the vast majority of voters who consider themselves Democrats or Republicans reliably support their party's presidential nominees, campaigns can be confident that successful mobilization of these individuals will net additional votes for their candidate.

What about voters who are registered independents, or unregistered citizens whom campaigns wish to bring into the electorate? Field organizers must look for other clues to determine the likelihood that these people, if they vote, will support their favored candidate. One approach that has recently proven popular with campaigns is the mining of available data such as demographic characteristics, interest group affiliations, magazine and catalog mailing lists, and consumer preferences, which are available for sale by corporations and marketing firms, to estimate individuals' political beliefs—a practice known as "microtargeting." For example, consultants identify hybrid car owners, subscribers to music or gourmet cooking magazines, married couples with different last names, and Sierra Club members as likely Democratic supporters, while sport-utility vehicle drivers, readers of *Golf Digest* or *Field and Stream*, and bourbon connoisseurs are expected to prefer Republican candidates. Campaigns use this information not only to determine which voters should be contacted by field staff, but also what messages might prove especially persuasive in winning their support.[146]

The most common forms of voter contact are the telephone (whether by live volunteers at campaign phone banks or via automated "robocalls" that play prerecorded messages), direct mail, text messaging, and in-person door-to-door canvassing. Research by political scientists Alan Gerber and Donald Green has demonstrated that the latter approach is by far the most effective at increasing voter turnout, though it is also the most costly.[147] Both the 2004 Bush campaign and the 2008 and 2012 Obama campaigns placed particular emphasis on voter mobilization through preexisting social networks, believing that contact by friends, neighbors, coworkers, and fellow parishioners was more likely to stimulate a wavering voter's electoral participation than a knock at the door by a stranger.[148]

Bush's field operation in 2004 was, at the time, widely considered the most effective in decades, setting standards for data collection, voter targeting, and coordination of staff and volunteer activities. But the Obama campaigns in 2008 and 2012 appear to have built voter contact and turnout networks that were unprecedented in modern American politics. Obama field staff gave volunteers the opportunity to assume additional organizational responsibilities designed to increase their commitment and attachment to the campaign. A reporter who witnessed the building of the Obama campaign's infrastructure in Ohio described how one volunteer was recruited by a paid field organizer to a leadership position in the Obama ground operation:

> After Glenna had proven her reliability and effectiveness, Ryan asked her for another special one-on-one meeting where he invited her to formally agree to become [a "Neighborhood Team Leader"]. He spelled out all of an NTL's responsibilities before allowing her to accept it and even gave her a binder spelling it all out in writing: She would work with him to recruit other team members such as coordinators for canvassing, phone banking and data management. Her team would be responsible for connecting with *all* of the Democratic and undecided voters within their "turf." Other volunteers who stepped forward in her area would not be managed by campaign staff, but by Glenna's team. As team leader, Glenna would report results to Ryan a couple [of] times per week and would be held accountable for meeting specific goals by certain deadlines.[149]

The 2008 Obama campaign also benefited from technological innovations. It merged voter lists with financial donation records, e-mail addresses and cell phone numbers, and information provided by field staff and Internet activists to create an integrated database of supporters and targeted voters. This operation allowed officials at the campaign headquarters in Chicago to access real-time data on mobilization efforts in key states all over the country. On Election Day, Obama volunteers stationed in polling places sent names of voters to the campaign via PDA as they signed in, allowing campaign field offices to target their get-out-the-vote operations in the final hours of the election to those supporters who had yet to appear at the polls.[150]

Obama's reelection campaign in 2012 broke new ground in sophisticated data analysis designed to identify and mobilize Democratic supporters in the mass electorate. The Obama technology team built a massive electronic architecture that "unified what Obama for America [the campaign organization] knew about voters, canvassers, event-goers, and phone-bankers, and it did it in real time," according to a post-election profile by *The Atlantic*.[151] The campaign used this information to send targeted communications to voters with specific demographic or ideological profiles: young, single professional women might receive campaign mailings and online messages emphasizing Obama's support for legalized abortion and contraception access, for example, while Latinos would be notified of the candidate's policies on immigration and public education.[152]

The increasing prevalence of early voting and voting by mail in a number of states over the past several elections (see chapter 1) has had a profound impact on the campaign ground game. In these states, getting voters to the polls is an activity consuming several weeks rather than a single day. Campaigns seek to bank as many votes as possible by encouraging their supporters to vote early or by absentee ballot; this also allows mobilization drives to focus more precisely on those who have yet to vote. The rise of early voting also affects the candidates' strategies; rather than wait until the week before the traditional November election date to make their final pitches to voters, candidates must recognize that voting begins in some states as early as the third week in September. "We start having Election Day right around the corner," noted Obama campaign manager David Plouffe in mid-September 2008. Early voting "fundamentally changes two things: timing and budgets," observed McCain political director Mike DuHaime. "You need to close the deal earlier for some voters, and Election Day can be spread out over weeks. That means your get-out-the-vote costs are more than ever."[153]

Like television ads and candidate appearances, campaigns concentrate their voter mobilization efforts in the politically competitive battleground states where either party has a chance to win. Residents of these states may well receive dozens of telephone calls, regular in-person visits, and a steady stream of mailings from the candidates, parties, and interest groups over the final weeks of the campaign. Voters located in states deemed safe for one side or the other, by contrast, tend to see little direct evidence of a presidential election in their neighborhoods or mailboxes. While some may feel envious of the special attention lavished on the denizens of battleground states, others are undoubtedly just as content to be left in relative peace for the duration of the campaign.

CAMPAIGN BLUNDERS

Once an election is over, the losing side is routinely subjected to endless second-guessing by the news media and by its own putative supporters, with its defeat often blamed on strategic mistakes made over the course of the campaign—especially if the candidate lost by a narrow margin or squandered a previous lead in the polls. For example, the decision of New York Governor Thomas E. Dewey, the Republican nominee in 1948, to mute the issues and campaign on empty platitudes in the final weeks of the race was blamed in retrospect for snatching defeat from the jaws of victory.[154] A more vigorous campaign, it was said, would have taken the steam out of Democratic incumbent Harry

Truman's feisty comeback effort and would thus have ensured Dewey's election. Perhaps. What we know of the 1948 election suggests that it provoked a higher degree of voting on the basis of economic class than any of the elections that succeeded it.[155] A slashing attack by Dewey, therefore, might have polarized the voters even further. This would have increased Truman's margin of victory, since there are many more people with low than with high incomes. Had the election gone the other way—and a handful of votes in a few states would have done it—we would have heard much less in retrospect about Dewey's strategic blunders and much more about Truman's lack of popularity.

Democratic nominee Michael Dukakis declared that the 1988 presidential campaign would be about "competence, not ideology." But he did not campaign competently, failing to answer the barrage of charges George H. W. Bush's campaign made in its attempt to introduce Dukakis, unfavorably, to the mass of American voters who had never heard of him. The list of Dukakis's campaign errors, real and alleged, is a long one, and the should-haves and should-not-haves are legion. When asked in one debate what he would do if his wife were raped and murdered—a question, one must observe, that candidates are not usually asked—Dukakis took it not as a signal to pour out his emotions, an act he viewed with distaste, but as an opportunity to discuss the kinds of governmental policies that might cut down on rapes and murders. This, according to the consensus media interpretation, showed that he lacked emotion and was heartless.

Over and over again, Dukakis told his campaign advisers that he would not engage in mudslinging no matter what the provocation. Presumably this eminently desirable position was seen as a source of weakness.[156] "How many times do I have to tell you?" an aide heard him say. "That's not me." Candidate Dukakis was also governor of Massachusetts and felt he should abide by a pledge to the citizens of that state to spend several days a week doing the job. He might have done better had he put himself into the campaign full-time.[157] There were other faults. Dukakis failed to answer questions about national defense, which is, after all, a major presidential responsibility. He did not intervene to decide how to halt damaging internal squabbles in his campaign team. Almost from the beginning, the organization of the campaign was poor in that phones were not answered, supplies were not provided, and activities were not coordinated.[158] By the following year, Dukakis had learned how to blame himself. "I have reluctantly come to the conclusion," he told students at the University of California, "that if they throw mud at you, you've got to throw it back."[159]

No campaign is without its faults. Consider the 2000 election, ultimately decided by a Supreme Court ruling after several weeks of recounts and lawsuits over the treatment of ballots in the state of Florida. In the view of most observers, including many bitter Democrats, Al Gore gave away the election by failing to emphasize the economic prosperity of the nation under the Clinton administration. Gore's debate performances were roundly criticized, as was his low-key, uninspiring public persona, for costing him the race. Yet Gore finished first in the national popular vote, and probably would have won the electoral vote as well if not for a flawed, confusing ballot design in one Florida county that apparently led many votes intended for Gore to be counted instead for third-party candidate Pat Buchanan. Had Gore prevailed in the Florida recount, he would have been credited for running an effective campaign instead of facing accusations of political incompetence.

George W. Bush, by contrast, was seen in retrospect as a particularly skilled candidate. His chief strategist, Karl Rove, has often been labeled a political "genius." But a different outcome in Florida would have forced Bush and Rove to return to Texas as failures. Rove sent Bush to campaign in California during the weekend before the 2000 election, on the theory that a visit by the candidate to a state considered safe for the Democrats would inspire a flurry of news stories about how confident the Bush campaign was of victory. Late-deciding voters, Rove argued, would interpret this coverage as a sign that Bush was going to prevail in the election, and would eagerly jump on the bandwagon of a likely winner, producing a self-fulfilling prophecy. This was almost certainly a misguided strategy that would have led to endless second-guessing in Republican circles had Bush, not Gore, lost the election by a few hundred votes in Florida.

Criticism of John Kerry's campaign after his own narrow loss to Bush in 2004 seemed to combine the widely identified mistakes of Gore in 2000 (stiff, elitist, overly programmed, unappealing candidate) with those of Dukakis in 1988 (personal weakness, failure to respond to attacks from the opposition). Yet Kerry competed effectively with the allegedly more popular Bush throughout the entire campaign, and came within a single state of winning the presidency. Bush enjoyed not only the usual advantages of incumbency, but had seen his job approval rise to near-record levels after the terrorist attacks of 2001. His strikingly risky strategy—again, primarily masterminded by Rove—of advocating strongly conservative policies in order to mobilize the Republican base ultimately alienated a majority of independent voters and nine out of every ten Democrats, leaving little electoral margin for error. Bush's slim victory also left him without the ability to claim a broad popular mandate for his ambitious policy agenda. The centerpiece of his second-term domestic program, partial privatization of the Social Security system, quickly foundered in Congress, and further deterioration of the conditions in U.S.-occupied Iraq led directly to significant Democratic gains in the 2006 and 2008 elections. A more centrist, conciliatory approach to governing during his first term might well have given Bush a more decisive victory in 2004, and would have better preserved his political standing in the face of subsequent adversity.

John McCain's campaign in 2008 was commonly portrayed in the news media as undisciplined, disorganized, and prone to dramatic, attention-grabbing stunts. While this characterization contained some truth, McCain was also the decided underdog in the race, trailing Barack Obama in most polls from the early summer onward, and had little chance of prevailing if the election became a referendum on the policies or performance of the incumbent Republican administration. Under these circumstances, a strategy of playing it safe would have meant near-certain defeat. Instead, McCain and his advisers favored risky moves that, while they stood a good chance of backfiring, also had the potential to transform the race enough to allow a possibility for victory.

Perhaps the biggest gamble made by McCain was his choice of running mate. The campaign planned to announce the vice presidential candidate on the day after the conclusion of the Democratic national convention, in order to draw media attention away from Obama's acceptance address and minimize the traditional post-convention "bounce" in the polls for the Democrats. McCain's initial favorites for the position, independent Senator Joseph Lieberman of Connecticut and former governor Tom Ridge of Pennsylvania, were opposed by senior campaign aides who warned that both men's liberal social views would be unacceptable to party activists.[160] The day before the choice was to be made public, McCain settled on Governor Sarah Palin of Alaska, concluding that Palin's political history—as a reform candidate, she had successfully challenged an incumbent governor of her own party two years before—complimented his own. In addition, McCain hoped that the selection of a female running mate might draw support from disgruntled women who had backed Senator Hillary Clinton of New York in the Democratic primaries. (With an eye toward courting these voters, the original version of Palin's stump speech contained an explicit tribute to Clinton, which was dropped after Republican audiences routinely booed any mention of the former first lady's name.)

The Palin selection certainly generated a great deal of attention, though not in the way the McCain campaign hoped. Although her introduction to the national stage was mostly positive, including a well-received speech at the Republican national convention, less flattering stories soon emerged. A rocky series of interviews with evening news anchors Charles Gibson of ABC and Katie Couric of CBS suggested that Palin was insufficiently informed about national issues. Reports also surfaced that Palin, a self-styled "hockey mom" with a regular-gal persona, had spent more than $150,000 of Republican party money on a new wardrobe for herself and her family in the weeks after her selection as running mate.[161] By the end of October, the press had picked up on evidence of growing tension between Palin and campaign staff, creating further distractions in the final days before the election.[162] Ultimately, though Palin proved popular with the Republican base, her presence on the ticket failed to improve McCain's position in the race, in part because her selection undercut McCain's argument that Obama was insufficiently prepared to serve as president. According to one national survey conducted shortly before the election, 59 percent of voters considered Palin to be unqualified for the vice presidency.[163]

McCain's penchant for taking chances was also apparent in his response to the financial crisis that erupted in mid-September 2008 as a result of the collapse of the Lehman Brothers investment banking firm. On September 24, McCain agreed, upon Obama's initiative, to sign a joint statement of principles about how to address the situation. Immediately after consenting to this approach in a phone call with Obama, however, McCain announced publicly that he was suspending his campaign in order to fly to Washington to resolve the crisis, and urged that the first presidential debate, scheduled for September 26, be postponed. All of these actions were a surprise to Obama, who responded by urging that the debate go on as scheduled because "it's going to be part of the president's job to be able to deal with more than one thing at once."

McCain's rush back to Washington did not go well for him. At a meeting the next day at the White House attended by both presidential candidates, President George W. Bush, and congressional leaders of both parties, it was clear that bipartisan consensus on a plan to bail out collapsing financial institutions did not exist, with House Republicans the key holdouts. McCain urged that their perspectives be heeded in the bailout negotiations, but the candidate himself never became a major participant in deliberations over the bailout package. Meanwhile, he quickly dropped his objection to the first debate and flew to Jackson, Mississippi, to participate, despite the fact that the crisis was no closer to resolution. On September 29, House Republicans defied both Bush and McCain by voting in large numbers to ensure the failure of the bailout plan on the House floor. This triggered a big decline in stocks worldwide, and inspired more frenzied negotiations over the U.S. government's response to the crisis. A revised plan passed on October 2 with more Republican support and was quickly signed into law. Stock values, however, remained depressed throughout the remainder of the campaign season, and a parade of bad news regarding rising unemployment and negative economic growth dominated the headlines throughout September and October.

The Obama campaign, initially puzzled by McCain's actions, hoped that they would label him as unstable and erratic, and polls indicated that public views of McCain's leadership abilities declined with the financial meltdown. Obama, who was generally constructive during the crisis, urging fellow Democrats to support the rescue plan, saw his leadership scores improve. The greater problem for McCain, however, was the very presence of the economic problems themselves. The crumbling economy had benefited the Democrats all year and the September events made the issue dominant for the remainder of the campaign. Polls indicated considerable public opposition to the bailout plan itself. By suspending his campaign and rushing to Washington, McCain had managed to associate himself strongly with both a serious problem, the financial crisis, and the controversial solution to it. Obama, whose reaction to the October economic events was less impetuous, suffered less from the crisis and now had a powerful economic issue buoying his message promising "change." McCain's tactical gamble did not pay off. One anonymous McCain aide complained: "We completely blew it. The execution of a potentially great move couldn't have been worse."[164]

For John McCain in 2008, the use of bold moves was not necessarily an irrational strategy, given his status as the trailing candidate. The problems for him emerged mostly in their flawed execution, which contradicted one of the central messages of his candidacy: that McCain, not Obama, was experienced and dependable. With a steady lead in the polls throughout most of the fall and superior financial and organizational resources, Obama could afford to take a low-risk approach, making his campaign appear to sail along smoothly while McCain flailed about.

In 2012, Mitt Romney's ultimately unsuccessful campaign attracted more than its share of second-guessing from pundits and frustrated supporters alike, especially since many Republicans expected by Election Day that the former Massachusetts governor would defeat the incumbent Obama. Romney was faulted for a supposedly stiff and awkward public persona, for ineffectively disputing the Obama campaign's portrayal of him as a heartless plutocrat who had shipped American jobs overseas during his previous career in the field of private equity, and for failing to craft an appealing campaign message to attract the votes of key groups such as Latinos and young people. The inopportune surfacing in mid-September 2012 of what became known as the "47 percent" video, in which Romney, speaking at a private fund-raising event, dismissed the "47 percent of the people . . . who are dependent upon government . . . who pay no income tax" because "I'll never convince them that they should take personal responsibility and care for their lives," served as a distraction that reinforced Obama's line of attack on Romney as a candidate whose policies tilted toward the economic interests of the wealthy. Finally, the press viewed Romney's campaign organization as logistically and technologically inferior to the Obama team. While Obama received universal admiration for the sophistication of his data analysis and voter mobilization infrastructures, for example, the Romney campaign maintained a flawed internal polling operation that incorrectly predicted victory in key battleground states heading into the election; in addition, Romney's electronic get-out-the-vote database, code-named ORCA, crashed disastrously on the morning of Election Day, leaving the campaign without key intelligence about the status of their voter turnout effort.[165]

Had Romney managed to defeat Obama by a narrow margin, however, critics would have instead emphasized mistakes made by the incumbent. Most notably,

Obama's strikingly poor performance in the first televised debate, which led to a significant shift in public support from Obama to Romney as measured by published news media surveys and the candidates' own polling, would have been seen in retrospect as the central turning point in the race. By some accounts, Obama (who seemed to hold his opponent in personal contempt) had been overconfident in advance of the debate, dismissing the concerns of his advisers that a well-prepared Romney could easily put him on the defensive and keep him there.[166] After the first debate, Obama aides convinced their candidate to adopt a more effective approach for future events by alerting him that another weak showing could cost him the election.[167]

Even promising candidate strategies can run into roadblocks. Should the candidate arrive at a coherent strategy that fits reasonably well with what is known of the political world, he or she will still find that the party organization has an inertia in favor of its accustomed ways of doing things. The party workers, on whom candidates are dependent to some extent, have their own ways of interpreting the world, and a candidate disregards this point of view at some risk. Should the candidate fail to appear in a particular locality as others have done, the party workers may feel slighted. More important, they may interpret this as a sign that the candidate has written off that area and they may slacken their own efforts.

Suppose the candidate decides to divert funds from campaign buttons and stickers to polls and television or transportation, as during the years before soft money, campaigns were more or less required to do given expenditure limitations under the federal subsidy? The candidate may be right in believing that the campaign methods he or she prefers will bring more return from the funds that are spent. But let the party faithful interpret this as a sign that the candidate is losing—where are those familiar indications of popularity?—and their low morale may encourage a result that bears out this dire prophecy. An innovation in policy may shock the loyal followers of the party. It may seem to go against time-honored precepts that are not easily unlearned. Could a Republican convince the party that a balanced budget is not sacred? Or a Democrat that it is? Both parties adopted these views, innovative for them, in 1984. But it left each of them unhappy. The Democrats were left without the rationale for deficit spending in behalf of good causes that had kept them going since the 1930s. The Republicans, who were in office when Reagan built up deficits of unprecedented size in peacetime, had more to worry about. Any adverse economic results—a too-high or too-low dollar on world markets, inflation, lack of industrial competitiveness, unemployment, a cloud of dust keeping food from growing—would surely be attributed to the deficit.

Anthropologists tell us that everyone in the tribe knows what happens when a taboo is violated: bad things happen. If Republicans are not more frugal than Democrats, what are they good for? A selling job may have to be done on the rank and file; otherwise they may sit on their hands during the campaign. It may make better political sense (if less intellectual sense) to phrase the new in old terms and make the departure seem less extreme than it might actually be. The value of the issue in the campaign may thus be blunted. The forces of inertia and tradition may be overcome by strong and persuasive candidates; the parties are greatly dependent on their candidates and have little choice but to follow them, even if haltingly. But in the absence of a special effort, in the presence of enormous uncertainties and the inevitable insecurities, the forces of tradition may do as much to shape a campaign as the overt decisions of the candidates.

FORECASTING THE OUTCOME

As an election draws closer, popular interest increasingly focuses on attempts to predict the outcome. This process of forecasting elections is not at all mysterious; it depends on well-settled findings about the behavior of American electorates, many of which have already been discussed. But it may be useful for citizens to understand how the "experts" go about picking the winner.

There are several ways to do it. One way, popularized over a half-century ago by journalists Joseph Alsop and Samuel Lubell, is to interview the residents of locations that in the past have voted with great stability in one pattern or another. Some neighborhoods, for example, always vote for the Republicans by a margin of 80 percent or better. Let us say that the interviewer finds that only 50 percent of the people questioned in such a neighborhood say that they are going to vote for the Republicans this time, but respondents in traditionally Democratic areas continue to support the Democratic nominee heavily. A finding such as this permits the reporter to make a forecast, even though it is based on only a very small number of interviews that may not represent the opinions of most voters.

Reporters who use this technique very rarely make firm predictions about election outcomes. Instead, they concentrate on telling stories about the clues they have picked up: what they learned in heavily black neighborhoods, what the people in Catholic areas report, what midwestern farmers think, which way people from localities that usually vote for the winning party are leaning, and so on.[168] This technique is impressive because it digs into some of the dynamic properties of what goes into voting decisions. Like a focus group out on the doorstep, it reports which issues seem to be on people's minds. It examines the ways in which members of different social groups view the candidates and the campaign. It is also a technique that can be executed at relatively low cost. But it is unsystematic, because the people interviewed are not selected randomly. Thus the results of this technique would be regarded as unreliable in a scientific sense, even though they may enhance an observer's intuitive grasp of what is going on. The results are also unreliable in the sense that two different journalists using this method may come to drastically different conclusions, perhaps because they seek out interview subjects who confirm their preexisting expectations of what they will find. There is no certain way of resolving the disagreement; nor is there any prescribed method for choosing between their conflicting interpretations.

The strength of forecasting on the basis of historical voting patterns arose out of the general stability of American voting habits from one election to the next. But the weakness of such a technique is also apparent. Sometimes significant changes in the population of an area due to migration or variations in the appeals of parties to different voting groups will throw the historical two-party vote ratios in the sample area out of joint. When a forecast made with this technique is wrong, it is usually quite difficult to tell immediately whether transitory or lasting causes are at the root of it. This limits the usefulness of the forecast greatly because, in the end, it rests on assumptions that have only partial validity in any one election, and nobody can say precisely how or where or to what extent they may be valid.

For these reasons, journalists and other observers have largely turned to public opinion polls conducted during the campaign as more reliable indicators of the standing of the candidates and the likely electoral outcome. Thanks to the modern news media's constant fascination with the candidate horse race, these polls are plentiful during the months before an election. Television pundits also devote attention to the results of opinion surveys, speculating in great detail about the meaning of any apparent trends in the levels of support for each candidate.

Most widely reported polls, such as those conducted by Gallup, Harris, Zogby, Rasmussen, and the major newspapers and television networks, consist of a national sample of roughly one thousand respondents selected by dialing telephone numbers at random. Pollsters screen respondents for their likelihood to vote, asking them if they are registered, if they are paying attention to the campaign, and if they have voted in past elections. They then ask which candidate the respondent would support if the election were held that day. Researchers often collect other information, such as age, race, sex, and party identification, in order to draw conclusions about the standing of candidates among various social groups in the electorate.

Many people are distrustful of poll results because of the relatively small sample size of most surveys. They wonder how the opinions of the thousand or so potential voters interviewed in any particular poll can accurately represent the views of the more than 100 million Americans who vote in a presidential election. This, by and large, is a false issue. The laws of statistics confirm that a sample of this size chosen at random will almost always be broadly representative of the larger population from which it is drawn. Pollsters commonly report "margins of error" along with their results, which represent the interval within which ninety-five of every one hundred samples could be expected to fall due to chance if the population were sampled repeatedly—usually about four or five percentage points for a standard media poll. In other words, if Candidate A is "really" ahead of Candidate B by ten percentage points in the total American voting population, a poll of one thousand randomly sampled voters might easily find a nine- or twelve-point gap. But it would be extremely unlikely for the poll to report incorrectly that Candidate B is in the lead simply due to random error in the sampling of respondents.[169]

When polls turn out to be wrong, the cause is much more likely to be systematic bias in either the means by which interview subjects are sampled or in their likelihood to respond to the survey than chance error under random selection. The two most famous mistakes in the history of presidential election polling illustrate the dangers of poor methodology. In 1936, the *Literary Digest* magazine mail survey predicted a victory for the Republican presidential nominee, Kansas governor Alf Landon.[170] When Democratic incumbent Franklin D. Roosevelt was overwhelmingly reelected, carrying every state except Maine and Vermont, the *Digest* became a laughingstock and soon thereafter went out of business. The magazine had sent out millions of postcards to people who had telephones asking them how they intended to vote; only 2.3 million people returned their postcards out of 10 million recipients, and those who responded disproportionately tended to be economically well-off. So the *Digest* drew its responses from a group in the population more likely to vote Republican and completely missed the larger number of poorer people who were going to vote Democratic.[171]

In 1948, the Gallup, Roper, and Crossley polls all predicted that the Republican nominee, Governor Thomas E. Dewey of New York, would unseat President Harry Truman. Truman's victory on Election Day was so unexpected that the early edition of the *Chicago Tribune* the following morning famously featured the headline "Dewey Defeats Truman." A committee of social scientists convened after the election to determine what went wrong found that the pollsters had stopped taking surveys too early in the campaign (missing what may have been a late surge for Truman), that they sometimes "corrected" pro-Truman results due to disbelief in their initial findings, and that the quota system then used to sample respondents introduced serious systematic biases into the data that could only be corrected by moving to a method of random selection.[172]

Modern pollsters remain vigilant against possible sources of bias in their surveys. If nobody answers the telephone when they first call, they try again the next day if possible. (Pollsters usually prefer to conduct surveys during weekday evenings, when respondents are most likely to be available to answer their questions.) Researchers polling in an area with a significant Latino population will attempt to hire bilingual interviewers, lest they fail to take the preferences of Spanish-speaking voters into account. Many people—often the vast majority of those contacted—refuse to answer altogether, and this proportion is increasing over time. As long as Republicans and Democrats are equally reticent about sharing their political opinions with telephone interviewers, this tendency will not skew the results, although low response rates make it more difficult for pollsters to achieve their target sample size.

Different pollsters employ different methods, occasionally producing inconsistent results. For example, most survey organizations employ a screen for likely voters, excluding from their reported results the preferences of poll respondents who they believe are unlikely to vote. These screens vary in composition and degree of strictness. Some voters will claim to be undecided between the candidates, especially well in advance of the election. Pollsters differ in their eagerness to push these respondents into declaring a preference. Particular surveys may or may not ask about third-party candidates, who usually perform better in pre-election polls than they do in the election itself.

While the findings of competing survey organizations often diverge slightly at any given point in the election season, and while the events of the campaign—conventions, debates, advertisements, gaffes—cause candidates to rise and fall over time even in the surveys conducted by a single pollster, contemporary survey research has an impressive track record on the whole in forecasting the outcome of recent elections. Most of the final pre-election surveys in 2008 measured a six to nine percent lead for Barack Obama in the national popular vote over John McCain; Obama ultimately won by 7.3 percentage points. George W. Bush's 2.5 percent margin in 2004 was similarly close to the 1–2 percent margin predicted in the final polls.[173] The 2000 election, closer still, was predicted to be such by numerous opinion polls finding a virtual dead heat between Bush and Al Gore, while the more comfortable leads enjoyed by Bill Clinton in 1992 and 1996, George H. W. Bush in 1988, and Ronald Reagan in 1984 in surveys conducted during the final weeks of previous campaigns allowed observers to foresee their decisive victories with ease.

In 2008, Barack Obama's status as the first-ever African American presidential nominee introduced an additional level of uncertainty to polling results. Some observers hypothesized that a certain number of whites who opposed Obama, perhaps on racial grounds, would be reluctant to admit as much to telephone interviewers and would instead falsely report that they supported him, a phenomenon dubbed the "Bradley effect" (after Tom Bradley, a black former mayor of Los Angeles who led in pre-election polls in the 1982 California governor's race but ultimately lost the election by a small margin). Several analysts suggested that the Bradley effect might have been responsible for Obama's surprising loss in the January 2008 New Hampshire primary after leading handily in pre-election surveys, though Obama did not consistently underperform opinion polls in subsequent state primaries. Ultimately, Obama's solid victory on Election Day, in line with most pre-election polls, effectively dispelled such questions.[174]

The accuracy of the polls became a subject of some public debate in the weeks before the 2012 election. Attention to this subject in part reflected a persistent degree of divergence among surveys that, in a close race, were more than sufficient to generate conflicting predicted winners. In particular, the two tracking polls conducted by Gallup and Rasmussen and published daily on the Internet consistently produced results that were more favorable to Mitt Romney than most of the other national pollsters. On October 28, for example, Romney held a four-point national lead over Obama according to Gallup and a three-point advantage according to Rasmussen; in contrast, polls released the following day by CBS News/*New York Times* and YouGov/*Economist* both placed Obama ahead by one point nationwide, while ABC News/*Washington Post* found the candidates tied in the national vote. These varying results gave partisans on both sides ample reason for optimism heading into Election Day.

Some critics also became convinced over the course of the 2012 campaign that most national media polls had become systematically skewed, perhaps intentionally so, in Obama's favor. In particular, many Romney supporters distrusted public poll results, suggesting that the seven-point national Democratic edge in aggregate party identification measured by the 2008 exit polls would be replicated, or nearly replicated, in 2012. A number of professional pollsters employed by Romney and other Republican candidates shared this view; as one later admitted, "I had no expectation that Democratic advantage in party ID would be the same as it was in 2008."[175] Romney awoke on Election Day expecting to defeat Obama due in part to optimistic predictions made by his own campaign's polling team; he was sufficiently confident of the outcome to prepare a victory address in advance, but did not draft a concession speech until after learning late in the evening that he had indeed lost the election.[176] Strategist Eric Fehrnstrom later acknowledged that the Romney camp "genuinely believed that we were on the march . . . and this was going to be a plus-300 electoral [vote] victory for Mitt Romney. That was not spin. Our opinions were informed by the polling that was done."[177] If anything, the pre-election polls understated Obama's actual victory margin (which equaled 3.9 percentage points in the national popular vote, as compared to a margin of 0.7 points in the final RealClearPolitics polling average, 1.5 points in the *Huffington Post* Pollster aggregation, and 2.7 points in the FiveThirtyEight forecast); contradicting Republican expectations, the national exit poll found a six-point Democratic advantage in party identification nationwide—only one point lower than in 2008.

Of course, presidential elections in the United States are not decided by direct popular vote, as demonstrated by the election of 2000 when George W. Bush received an electoral vote majority while placing second in the national popular tally. Election analysts are also therefore intensely interested in the relative standing of the candidates in key battleground states. While the number of publicly released statewide polls has increased substantially over the last few elections, they are still less common—and, sometimes, less reliable—than the traditional national surveys. When the election is not close, state results are less important; a candidate who is ahead by five or ten percentage points in the national popular vote can be confident of a victory in the electoral college as well. In the 2000 and 2004 elections, two of the closest presidential contests in American history, the differences between the popular and electoral vote proved much more consequential.

In 2000, uncertainty over the election outcome extended far beyond the pre-election telephone surveys of potential voters to encompass the exit polls used by television networks to forecast the state-by-state results on the night of the election. Exit polls are surveys of actual voters in key precincts who are asked about their vote choice as they leave their polling place. These polls are not based on random samples of the entire voting population, and are subject to both sampling bias (since voters at some precincts are more likely to be sampled than others, and those who vote early or via absentee ballot will not be sampled at all) and response bias (since some voters may be more willing to respond to a news media survey at their polling place than others). But the news media find exit polls useful, both for projecting state results on election night before all the votes are actually counted, and for drawing preliminary conclusions about the demographic and ideological composition of the electorate in a given year.

Exit polls had occasionally caused problems before 2000. In 1980, NBC declared a landslide Reagan victory on the basis of decisive survey results nearly three hours before polling places closed on the West Coast. Many believed that this announcement depressed turnout, as westerners who hadn't already voted decided not to bother, and thus affected the outcome of more competitive local races in those states.[178] In 1996, several television networks incorrectly projected a Democratic victory in a U.S. Senate race in New Hampshire based on exit polls showing a five-point margin between the candidates; the declared "winner" ultimately lost by three percentage points.[179]

The events of election night in 2000 turned out to be utterly disastrous. Television networks pronounced Democrat Al Gore the winner in Florida on the basis of erroneous exit polls shortly after voting ended in most (though not all) of the state. Several hours later, as Republican George W. Bush pulled ahead in the reported vote returns, the networks retracted their Florida projections. As Bush clung to a small lead in the early hours of the morning, networks then called the state—and therefore the election as a whole—for the Texas governor, though within hours Gore had drawn even on the strength of late-reporting South Florida precincts, requiring yet another retraction as it became clear that the winner could not be determined at least until all absentee votes were tallied. Thus began a weeks-long battle over the counting of Florida ballots that ended only when the U.S. Supreme Court halted all recounts in mid-December by a 5–4 vote, effectively handing the presidency to Bush.

The embarrassing performance of the television networks in 2000 prompted some post-election soul-searching among journalists. Joan Konner, former dean of Columbia University's Graduate School of Journalism, was a member of an independent commission formed by CNN after the 2000 election debacle to determine what went wrong. She found that "among the obvious failings were an emphasis on speed over accuracy in reporting; excessive competition [among networks] and the pressure to come in first; outdated technology; human error; a flawed polling and projection system; and, finally, overconfidence in the system and in the polls themselves."[180] It is troubling in retrospect that the networks did not exercise more caution when reporting results based on exit polls with known sampling and response biases. Surely few viewers would remember afterward which network was the first to project the outcome in any given state; the damaged credibility resulting from an incorrect prediction far outweighs any "credit" gained from the aggressive declaration of winners and losers.

The television networks' newfound election-night patience was immediately put to the test in 2004. Exit polls conducted on Election Day for a consortium of news media clients initially indicated an electoral college victory for John Kerry. By mid-afternoon, the poll results had leaked onto the Internet, even affecting the performance of the stock market.[181] Displaying a relative abundance of caution, however, the networks declined to make projections in close states based purely on the exit polls. As Democrats who had been reveling in the leaked poll numbers looked on in horror, the polls were proven wrong again as the actual vote returns came in. By the end of the evening, enough actual votes in key states had been counted to declare Bush the winner once again.

Predicting presidential elections is largely a matter of satisfying curiosity. It is a great game among political experts and other interested parties to guess who will win, and we look to the polls for indications of the signs of the times. But this kind of forecasting is ultimately of limited importance. After all, we get to know who has won very soon after the polls close (except in the unique circumstance of 2000) with much greater detail and accuracy than surveys can supply. The bare prediction of the outcome, even if it is reasonably correct state by state, tells us little about how the result came to occur. More may be learned if it is possible to analyze survey data in order to determine what kinds of groups—ethnic, racial, economic, regional—voted to what degree for which candidates. Yet our enlightenment at this point is still not great. Suppose we know that in one election 60 percent of Catholics voted Democratic and in another election this percentage was reduced to 45. Surely this is interesting, but unless we have some good idea about why Catholics have switched their allegiance, our knowledge has hardly advanced. The polls often tell us "what" but seldom "why." The more comprehensive post-election surveys by academic researchers—such as the University of Michigan's National Election Studies, conducted for every presidential election and most midterm elections since 1948—can provide additional evidence addressing the "why" questions.[182]

The usual polling technique consists of interviewing cross-sectional samples of the American public at various points in time. The samples may each be perfectly representative of the population at large, but different individuals constitute each successive sample. This method makes it difficult to determine with any reliability why particular individuals or classes of people are changing their minds because pollsters do not interview the same people more than once. To overcome this limitation, a researcher can conduct a panel survey, in which a single sample of the voting population is interviewed at various intervals before Election Day and perhaps afterward.[183] This technique makes it possible to identify the people who make up their minds early and those who decide late. These groups can be reinterviewed and examined for other distinguishing characteristics. More important, perhaps, voters who change their minds during the campaign can be studied. If a panel of respondents can be reinterviewed over a number of years and a series of elections, it may become possible to discover directly why some people change their voting habits from election to election. Or focus groups can be used to frame survey questions more sensitively. On the other hand, the added attention given to panel respondents may completely contaminate their responses and make them wholly atypical of the general population.[184]

Consumers of polling data should be attentive to factors that may cause apparent discrepancies in the results of different surveys. One explanation might be that the populations sampled by the polls are different. Some polls report results only for registered voters or those who say they are likely to vote, which is different from sampling a cross-section of the total adult population. The closer the population polled is to the actual electorate, the more accurate the survey in predicting the outcome.

Contradictory results might also emerge from differences in question wording. For example, an item measuring party identification produces one set of results if it asks respondents about their party allegiance "in general," and another set if it asks about their party affiliation "as of today." The first measure tends to be more stable over time, while the latter is more sensitive to respondents' evaluations of the current president or candidates.[185]

Understanding what is being measured, when, and how, is indispensable in interpreting the results of polls. In general, observers should treat the findings of any single poll with a certain dose of skepticism, especially if they are counterintuitive or out of line with other surveys. When multiple polls are in agreement, consumers can be much more confident in the results.

The statistical aggregation of poll results can also produce greater accuracy; when individual polls differ, the truth is often somewhere in the middle. In the spring of 2008, a thirty-year-old professional baseball statistician named Nate Silver attracted a great deal of notice on the Internet for creating quantitative models that produced impressively accurate predictions of presidential primary outcomes. For the general election, Silver built a website, FiveThirtyEight, on which he posted daily computer simulations of the election outcome in each state based on demographic data, previous election results, and the latest public statewide and national polls, using a weighted formula that took into account the sample size and date of each poll and the relative credibility of the pollster. Silver's site, the name of which refers to the total number of votes in the electoral college, became one of the most popular destinations on the Web for political junkies during the 2008 campaign, and his final projection, released on the afternoon of Election Day, correctly predicted the outcome in forty-nine of fifty states—demonstrating both the power of sophisticated data analysis and the potential of the Internet to allow individuals with specialized expertise to find a wide audience of interested readers outside the channels of the traditional news media.[186] By the 2012 election, Silver had moved his forecasting operation to the *New York Times* website, where he confirmed his predictive power by accurately projecting the electoral outcome in all fifty states (in 2014, Silver brought FiveThirtyEight with him as he left the *Times* to join the ESPN sports network).

COUNTING THE VOTE

How votes are counted—how efficiently and how accurately—becomes important mostly when elections are very close. This issue therefore became significant in the aftermath of the 2000 election. On election night it appeared that the Democratic candidate, Al Gore, led the Republican candidate, George W. Bush, very narrowly in popular votes nationwide, and that the candidates were virtually tied in the electoral college. The outcome of the entire election depended on the popular vote in Florida, a state in which serious problems immediately emerged in the administration and mechanics of voting and vote counting.

Each Florida county had its own ballot type and format, and in at least one populous county the ballot was designed in a way that caused voters to be confused about how to indicate their preferences, probably to Gore's disadvantage.[187] In numerous locations, ballots were cast that could not be counted by the machinery available to produce an automatic count and disagreements therefore arose about whether, and how, these ballots could be counted by hand. The Bush and Gore campaigns appealed to the Florida judiciary to resolve these issues, but the Florida Supreme Court's ruling was preempted by a 5–4 decision of the U.S. Supreme Court along ideological lines to take jurisdiction and to halt the ongoing manual recount of ballots, effectively awarding the official popular vote in the state to Bush by a 537-vote margin (2,912,790 to 2,912,253). As a result, Bush received Florida's twenty-five electors and won the election with 271 total electoral votes, one more than a majority.[188]

The legal issues raised by the conduct of the 2000 election and the *Bush v. Gore* court decision have continued to resonate in subsequent years, judging from the volume of commentary generated in law journals and elsewhere.[189] The relevant political issues are somewhat easier to identify:

1. The winner in the electoral college actually lost the national popular vote in 2000 for the first time since 1888, but constitutional rules governing the outcome are evidently so well settled that there was no serious claim that Bush's entitlement to the presidency was in any way impaired by the fact that Gore had received more total votes. Indeed, Bush not only assumed office without difficulty but was free to interpret his mandate to govern without much concern for the circumstances of his victory. The 2000 election renewed calls from some quarters for the reform or abolition of the electoral college, but these proposals received, as usual, only limited support among the members of Congress and state legislators who would need to initiate any change in the present system of presidential selection (see chapter 6 for further discussion of this issue).

2. The entire topic of election administration continues to require thorough ventilation. In fact, insufficient information is widely available on this subject. We know that different states administer elections differently, that there are several kinds of machinery used for recording and counting ballots, each with technical imperfections, that standards for uniformity in how ballots are judged to be valid are themselves not uniform, and that ballots in different localities differ in their contents and design.[190] There may be systematic flaws that deprive different subgroups in the population of equal access to the ballot or equal treatment in the counting of their votes.[191] Ballot design and electoral administration have, as the result of the 2000 election, become matters for intensive further study.

3. There had previously been a widespread tacit assumption that votes in presidential elections were counted more or less as cast, with electoral results reliably reflecting voter intent. The slovenly performance of the state of Florida in 2000 in accurately and efficiently determining the voting preferences of its citizens suggested that this assumption was wrong, and not only in Florida. As a matter of political strategy, one presidential candidate, Governor Bush, strenuously worked to prevent Florida ballots that did not register a preference on the automatic machinery from being counted at all. Impartial studies after the fact by news organizations established that he needn't have worried; if they had been counted he would have won

anyway.[192] The spectacle of a candidate for public office going to court to attempt to deprive voters of their vote is nonetheless worth contemplating.

The voting equipment at issue in the Florida recount was the Votomatic punch-card ballot, then in widespread use (about 30 percent of the national electorate voted via punch-card technology in 2000). The Votomatic system required voters to use a stylus to detach perforated squares from a cardboard ballot corresponding to their preferred candidates. Punch-card ballots were popular with county and state election administrators because they were inexpensive to use and could be counted quickly by machine. However, many voters found the perforations, called chads, difficult to remove completely, leaving partially dislodged chads that left voter intent unclear even under human inspection. "Hanging" chads remained attached to the ballot by only one of four corners, "swinging" chads by two corners, and "dimpled" chads were not detached at all but appeared to have been unsuccessfully pierced by the voter. The varying standards adopted by different Florida counties for how completely the chad needed to be removed in order to constitute a valid vote provided the evidentiary basis for the Supreme Court majority's finding that the manual recounts underway in December 2000 violated the Equal Protection Clause of the 14th Amendment.

Subsequent research demonstrated that punch-card systems produced unusually large rates of undervotes, or ballots that failed to register a vote for any candidate, and that the proportion of undervotes was disproportionately high in precincts with large populations of racial minorities and low-education voters, though the specific mechanism for this is not fully understood. In places where punch-card systems were replaced by other types of voting equipment, the proportion of undervotes declined regardless of the racial or educational profile of the voting population.[193] Punch-card ballots also produced non-trivial rates of overvotes, which occur when a voter—whether by accident or confusion—selects more than one candidate for a single-member office, thus voiding his or her vote.

In the wake of the controversy surrounding the 2000 election, Congress enacted the Help America Vote Act (HAVA), which married Democratic concerns about uncounted votes with Republican concerns about voter fraud. In addition to providing almost $4 billion in federal funding for the purchase and implementation of modern voting systems by state election administrators, HAVA required the creation of statewide voter registration lists and that persons registering to vote supply a driver's license number or social security number, set requirements for disabled access to voting equipment, and established a voter's right to cast a provisional ballot in the event that his or her name does not appear on the registration rolls. The legislation also required states to establish uniform standards for counting valid votes.[194]

The combination of the debacle in Florida and the funding provided by HAVA virtually eliminated punch-card ballots from American elections; by 2008, only a few counties in Idaho were still employing the technology.[195] A number of states replaced them with electronic voting systems, which use computer touch screens to register voter preferences; the results are saved on memory cards that are processed once the polls close. While the touchscreen machines are user-friendly and can eliminate overvotes by preventing voters from choosing more than one candidate for each office, some voters and watchdog groups remain suspicious that they are vulnerable to fraud via surreptitious reprogramming. Even if electronic systems simply malfunction, a recount is impossible unless the machines also provide paper backup. This issue arose in the 2006 midterm election, when a large number of touchscreen machines in Sarasota County, Florida, mysteriously failed to register the selections of thousands of voters in a hard-fought congressional race.[196] For this reason, a growing number of states and localities require electronic systems to provide a "paper trail" of voter preferences, while other jurisdictions, after adopting touchscreen machines in the wake of the 2000 election, subsequently abandoned them in favor of optical scan equipment. The proportion of the American electorate using electronic voting systems rose from 12 percent in 2000 to 38 percent by 2006, but then decreased to 32 percent in 2008 as concerns spread over their potential risks.[197] As of the 2012 election, 33 percent of registered voters lived in jurisdictions with touchscreen machines.[198]

Optical scan systems require voters to fill in an oval or connect a line corresponding to their favored candidate on a machine-readable paper ballot. They have become the most prevalent form of voting technology in the United States, used by states and counties representing more than 60 percent of the national electorate in 2012. Optical scan equipment is popular because votes can be counted automatically by machine, yet a physical ballot remains that can be examined manually if the scanner malfunctions. They can also prevent overvotes; an optical scanner at a Los Angeles polling place rejected the ballot of California governor Arnold Schwarzenegger in 2010 because he had mistakenly voted for two different U.S. Senate candidates, requiring him to fill out a fresh ballot in order to have his vote count.[199]

Yet optical scan systems have their limitations. Some voters fail to follow instructions—placing a checkmark in the oval beside a candidate's name or circling it instead of coloring it in, for example, which may render their preference unreadable by the scanning machine—or make ambiguous marks that leave their intent unclear. In the 2008 election for U.S. Senator from Minnesota, Republican incumbent Norm Coleman and Democratic challenger Al Franken were separated by a sufficiently small margin in the initial tally to trigger a manual recount of every optical scan ballot in the state, with a special panel of judges authorized to resolve disputes. This procedure, carried out in a series of public hearings attended by the press and representatives of the candidates, revealed the capacity of some voters to cast ballots that defied easy interpretation:

> Some ballots presented little difficulty; in one instance, a voter had clearly filled in the bubble beside Coleman's name but had accidentally, or in a moment of indecision, touched his pencil tip in Franken's bubble, leaving a small dot. The judges gave the vote to Coleman. Other ballots provoked long, absurdist exchanges. One ballot—from Beltrami County—became locally famous. The voter had filled in the bubble for Franken but had printed "Lizard People" in the write-in area. After a few minutes of discussion, Marc Elias, a lawyer for Franken, spoke up. "My argument would be this 'Lizard People' is not a genuine write-in," Elias said. "In other words, is not a person."
>
> "Do we know that for sure?" one of the judges asked. . . .
> The judges voted to have the ballot tossed out.[200]

Facing another close presidential election in 2004, both the Republican and Democratic parties mobilized large teams of poll watchers and lawyers to monitor election procedures in several states where the vote margins were expected to be narrow.

Though the presidential contest transpired without major problems, irregularities in a state-level election in North Carolina and an extremely close and disputed result in the Washington governor's race showed that voting in the United States did not yet meet high standards for accuracy or reliability. Since 2004, electronic voting machines— once widely considered the best remedy for the problems associated with punch-card ballots—have themselves become the targets of criticism by computer scientists and other skeptics worried about the possibility of hackers reprogramming the machines to register incorrect results, or the more likely chance that improper handling by inadequately-trained poll workers could unintentionally jeopardize the vote count. As Americans increasingly engage in early voting, an individual machine is sometimes used to record several thousand votes over a period of days or weeks. Erasure of these votes could throw a close contest into question.

It should be recalled that despite intense division over the 2000 presidential result, at no point did a crisis develop. Armies did not mobilize. Tanks did not rumble in the streets. There was never a moment when the politicians responsible for the flow of events could not refer to valid laws stipulating what they were supposed to do. Though the problematic punch-card equipment primarily responsible for the Florida contro-versy has almost completely disappeared from American voting booths, no system can completely eliminate inaccuracy or the possibility of a contested election outcome. For the foreseeable future, close elections will no doubt stimulate careful attention to elec-tion procedures from experts and others with legal training, as was the case in 2004. Greater oversight of election administration and the adoption of better voting technol-ogy may reduce the likelihood that another presidential election will be decided by the courts on the basis of disputed results.

PART III

Issues

IN THE CONCLUDING chapters we discuss issues of public policy raised by the way in which Americans conduct their presidential elections. There are always complaints about election processes, as there are about nearly every aspect of American politics. Our discussion attempts to deal with some of the more long-lasting and widely held criticisms. We attempt also to place presidential elections into the broader context of the American political system, asking whether and how these elections serve the purposes of democracy.

CHAPTER 6

Appraisals

REFORM UPON REFORM

IN 1968 the Democratic Party endured a season of turmoil: its incumbent president, Lyndon Johnson, withdrew his candidacy for another term; a leading candidate to succeed him, Senator Robert Kennedy of New York, was assassinated; and its national convention in Chicago was conducted amid extraordinary uproar. Delegates to the convention chose Vice President Hubert Humphrey, who had not competed in a single primary election, to be the Democratic nominee for the presidency. In the aftermath of the 1968 election, an internal party committee charged with studying potential reforms to the presidential nomination process—known as the McGovern-Fraser commission after its two chairs, Senator George McGovern of South Dakota and Representative Donald Fraser of Minnesota—was constituted and a year later unveiled proposals for changing nomination procedures. The most important reform measure instituted by the Democratic Party upon the recommendation of the McGovern-Fraser commission was a new requirement forcing states to choose delegates to the national convention via primary elections or caucuses in which all party voters are eligible to participate.

While the presidential nomination system created by the McGovern-Fraser reforms is, in a broad sense, still in place more than four decades later, a series of successor commissions designed to address remaining—or, in some cases, newly emerging—perceived flaws in the process has continued to make frequent further changes to Democratic nomination procedures. The Hunt commission, formed after the 1980 election, created the position of superdelegates in order to allow Democratic party leaders a vote at the national convention. The Fowler commission, created in 1985, lowered the popular vote threshold required for a candidate to receive pledged delegates in a state primary or caucus from 20 percent to 15 percent. The Herman-Price commission of 2005 responded to concerns that the electorates of Iowa and New Hampshire were insufficiently diverse by authorizing the states of Nevada and South Carolina to hold additional early elections before the opening of the national delegate selection window. Sometimes, these commissions have opted to reverse or modify the reforms instituted by their predecessors—such as the Democratic "Change Commission" of 2009–2010, which responded to concerns over the potentially decisive role of superdelegates in the 2008 primaries by reducing their relative proportions at future conventions.[1]

Republicans, too, have undergone significant reforms. The widespread adoption of presidential primaries as a means of selecting state convention delegates to comply with McGovern-Fraser requirements after 1968 brought fundamental change to the Republican nomination process as well. More recently, the national Republican Party has instituted its own internal reforms gaining additional control over nomination procedures, despite its traditional reluctance to intrude on the autonomy of its state parties. At its 1996 national convention, it created a Task Force on Primaries and Caucuses that recommended allocating "bonus delegates" to state parties to schedule their contests later in the nomination process in order to avoid the "front loading" of too many contests at the outset which would produce a hasty outcome. Though the national party approved this reform (which has since been repealed), the nomination process was even more extended in 2000 than in 1996.[2]

After the GOP presidential defeat in 2008, the national party for the first time mandated that states follow national delegate selection rules. The Republican National Committee attempted to coordinate their nomination contest calendar with that of the Democrats and to penalize state delegations that failed to adhere to its new calendar and delegate selection procedures. The state parties in Florida, Michigan, and Arizona failed to comply and instead moved their contests to January. The Republican National Committee inflicted the punishment only on Florida, but still allowed its winner-take-all procedure, which also violated the new rules, to determine the state's delegate allocation.

The Republican National Committee revised its national rules after the failure of previous efforts in 2012. Penalties for state noncompliance were stiffened: states would lose at least two-thirds of their delegates if they ignored the 2016 rules. The RNC reaffirmed its 2012 schedule guidelines, allowing four early states—Iowa, Nevada, South Carolina, and New Hampshire—but imposing the two-thirds delegate reduction penalty for states that moved their contests before March 1. To further shorten the primary calendar, states had to complete their delegate selection forty-five days before the 2016 national convention, which would be moved from around Labor Day to mid-summer. The RNC also moved to restrict the number of debates during the primaries, which had grown to an unwieldy twenty-six in the 2012 contest. A national party committee would select debate venues and moderators. Candidates who failed to comply with the national party's schedule would be barred from all party-authorized debates.[3] Both national parties have enacted elaborate rules to "improve" their presidential nomination processes for the 2016 election. It is fair to say that for much of the past fifty years, change has been in the air.

Previous chapters have incorporated the results of many of these reforms into the description we have given so far, concentrating on features of the presidential nomination process as it exists at present and on the political consequences that flow from the system as it is now organized. Some of these features have been part of the landscape of American politics for a generation or more; others are newer, and the changes they may bring about lie mostly in the future. Nevertheless, if there is one certainty about presidential elections, it is that the system of party nominations is subject to continuous pressure for change.

In this chapter we appraise some of these changes and proposals for future change of the American party system and its nomination and election processes. Because of the rapid reforms of the past few years, some of the impetus behind certain suggestions for further reform has slackened, while other ideas seem likely to be pursued with renewed vigor. As past solutions lead to future problems, new proposals enter the agenda and old ones depart. As times change, moreover, old concerns become outdated and new ones take their place. Under the party system of the 1950s and 1960s, for instance, with conservative Democrats and liberal Republicans limiting policy agreement within their respective parties, the cry went out for greater cohesion within the parties. Too little ideological unity within the parties was widely blamed for the lack of consistent party policy positions across a wide range of issues. How, it was then argued, could voters make a sensible choice if the parties did not offer internally consistent and externally clashing policy views? This is not so great a problem today, as evidence of ideological consistency within each party grows. Recent studies document record levels of partisan polarization in Congressional floor voting and a growing ideological distance between partisans in the electorate.[4] We now often hear concern about the negative consequences of excessive polarization between the parties. In the same way, reforms stressing mass participation have in due course been succeeded by measures emphasizing the benefits of elite experience, such as the creation of superdelegates—which in turn prompted a backlash among many Democrats in 2008 when it appeared that party elites might consider contravening the mass public's preferences, leading to the proposed reimposition of limitations on superdelegate influence. Thus the preoccupations of one era give way to those of its successors.

New proposals for change stem on the whole from two camps, which for purposes of discussion we wish to treat as distinct entities. The first movement we call *policy government*; the second we refer to as *participatory democracy*. Advocates of policy government urge strengthened parties, not as the focus of organizational loyalties so much as vehicles for the promulgation of policy. For them parties polarized by sharply contrasting issue positions is a desirable end. Participatory democrats urge "openness" and "participation" in the political process and advocate weakening party organizations and strengthening candidates, factions, and their ideological concerns. While the two sets of reformers appear to disagree about whether they want parties to be strong or weak, this comes down to a difference in predictions about the outcome of the application of the same remedy, for both in the end prescribe the same thing: more ideology as the tie that binds voters to elected officials and less loyalty to political parties as organizations.

THE POLITICAL THEORY OF POLICY GOVERNMENT

Policy government reform had its antecedents at the turn of the twentieth century in the writings of Woodrow Wilson, James Bryce, and other passionate constitutional tinkerers who founded and breathed life into the academic study of political science. The descendants of these thinkers have through the years elaborated a series of proposals that are embodied in a coherent general political theory. This theory contains a conception of the proper function of the political party, evaluates the legitimacy and the roles of Congress and the president, and enshrines a particular definition of the public interest.[5] Over time we seem to be achieving an approximation of the party cohesion that these reformers of yesteryear wanted, and so it is worthwhile to attend to the pros and cons of the debate their proposals brought about.

This group of party reformers suggested that democratic government requires political parties that (1) make policy commitments to the electorate, (2) are willing and able to carry them out when in office, (3) develop alternatives to government policies when out of office, and (4) differ sufficiently to "provide the electorate with a proper range of choice between alternatives of action."[6] They thus come to define a political party as "an association of broadly like-minded voters seeking to carry out common objectives through their elected representatives."[7] In a word, party should be grounded in policy.

Virtually all significant party relationships are, for these reformers, mediated by policy considerations. The electorate at large—not merely political activists—is assumed to be motivated by policy positions and officeholders conscious of mandates. Policy discussion among party members is expected to create widespread agreements upon which party discipline will then be based. Special interest groups are to be resisted and accommodated only as the overall policy commitments of party permit. The weaknesses of parties and the disabilities of governments are seen as stemming from failure to develop and support satisfactory programs of public policy. Hence we refer to this theory of party reform as a theory of policy government. This theory holds "that the choices provided by the two-party system are valuable to the American people in proportion to their definition in terms of public policy."[8] It differs from the participatory brand of party reform (which we address later) in that policy reformers believe they are revitalizing party organizations, whereas participatory democrats are likely to be indifferent to party organization.

Opponents of policy reform believe that democratic government in the United States requires that parties first and foremost undertake the minimization of conflict between contending interests and social forces.[9] We call them supporters of *consensus government*. For consensus government advocates, the ideal political party is a mechanism for accomplishing and reinforcing adjustment and compromise among the various interests in society to prevent severe social conflict. Whereas policy government reformers desire parties that operate "not as mere brokers between different groups and interests but as agencies of the electorate," supporters of consensus government see the party as an "agency for compromise" and view the current polarization of American politics as deeply inimical to the project. Opponents of party reform through policy government hold that "the general welfare is achieved by harmonizing and adjusting group interest."[10] In fact, they sometimes go so far as to suggest that "the contribution that parties make to policy is inconsequential so long as they maintain conditions for adjustment."[11] Thus, the theory of the political party upheld by critics of the policy reform position is rooted in a notion of consensus government. Advocates of policy government behave as if problems of consensus, of gaining sufficient agreement to govern, have already been solved or do not need to be solved. Believing that there is no problem of stability, they concentrate on change. Their critics downplay policy not because they think it unimportant but because they think maintaining the capacity to govern is more important than any particular policy. Distrusting the consequences of polarization and fearing instability, they are less concerned with enhancing the system's impulses to change.

A basic cleavage between advocates of policy government and advocates of consensus government may be observed in their radically opposed conceptions of the public interest. For advocates of consensus government, the public interest is defined as whatever combination of measures emerges from the negotiations, adjustments, and compromises made in fair fights or bargains among conflicting interest groups. They feel the need for no external criteria by which policies can be measured in order to determine whether or not they are in the public interest. As long as the process by which decisions are made consists of intergroup bargaining, within certain specified democratic, constitutional "rules of the game," they regard the outcomes as being in the public interest.

For advocates of policy government, the public interest is a discoverable set of policies that represents "something more than the mathematical result of the claims of all the pressure groups."[12] Some overarching notion of the public interest, they argue, is necessary if we are to resist the unwarranted claims of "special interest" groups. While this suggests that there are in principle criteria for judging whether a policy is in the public interest, apart from the procedural test applied by supporters of consensus government, these criteria are never clearly identified. This would not present great difficulties if policy government advocates did not demand that an authoritative determination of party policy be made and that party members be held to it. But information about the policy preferences of members is supposed to flow upward, and orders establishing and enforcing final policy decisions are supposed to flow downward in a greatly strengthened pyramid of party authority. Without criteria of the public interest established in advance, however, party leaders or commentators can define the public interest in any terms they may find convenient.

If we were to have parties that resembled the ideal of this first set of party reformers, what would they be like? They would be coherent in their policies, reliable in carrying them out, accountable to the people, disciplined and hierarchical internally, sharply differentiated from and in conflict with partisan opponents. Supporters of this ideal believe this will lead to a salutary and clarifying polarization of politics. What would it take to create a party system organized by the principles of policy government?

For the parties to carry out the promises they make, the people responsible for making promises would have to be the same as or in control of the people responsible for carrying them out. This means, logically, one of two alternatives. Either the people who controlled party performance all year round would have to write the party platforms every four years at the national conventions, or the people who wrote the platforms would have to be put in charge of party performance. In the first case, the party platforms would have to be written by leaders such as the members of Congress who at present refrain from enacting laws favored by both national conventions. State and local political leaders would write their respective platforms. Under such an arrangement, which reflects the procedural complications introduced by the separation of powers and the federal structure embedded in the U.S. Constitution, very little formal, overall coordination or policy coherence seems likely to emerge. Since the main point of policy government is to create logically coherent, unified policy that makes possible rational choices by voters, we observe that this first alternative as a way to fulfill the demands of party reformers will not work.

In fact, the alternative most often recommended by advocates of policy government is that the ideas animating the platforms at the national party conventions should be in charge. These platforms must make policy that will be enforced on national, state, and local levels by means of party discipline—that is, getting rid of party officeholders who disagree. This arrangement also has a fatal defect: it ignores the power of the

people who do not write the convention platforms—all those party activists not
selected to represent the candidate-centered forces at the national convention. How
are independently elected members of Congress to be bypassed? Will present-day
local and state party leaders acquiesce in this rearrangement of power and subject
themselves to discipline from a newly constituted outside source? It is hard to see
what the enforcement mechanism would be. Party reform has already gone some
distance toward reducing the influence of elected officials in the presidential nomination process. Will they give up their independent capacity as public officials to make
policy in their own arenas—Congress, the state legislatures—as well? Generally, we
assume they will not.

One reformer says: "As for the clash of personal political ambitions in the United
States, they are being completely submerged by the international and domestic concerns of the American public. War and peace, inflation and depression are both personal and universal issues; tariff, taxes, foreign aid, military spending, federal reserve
policies, and hosts of other national policies affect local economic activities across the
land. Politicians who wish to become statesmen must be able to talk intelligently about
issues that concern people in all constituencies."[13]

But the increasing importance of national issues will not necessarily lead to greater
power in the hands of party leaders with national (that is to say, presidential) constituencies. There is no necessary connection between political power in the national arena
and the emergence of issues having national scope. National issues undoubtedly have
great importance, especially among the ideologically more cohesive Republicans.[14] But
delivery on national promises is frequently thwarted by the power of local interests able
to influence national institutions, for example, the people in the congressional districts
that elect influential members of the House of Representatives. So far, the increasing
nationalization of policy has been most conspicuously accompanied not by the rise of
nationally cohesive groups but by increases in the strength of single-issue groups. Our
parties present contrasting constellations of such group agendas.

The people who have the most to lose from policy government are the leaders of
Congress. The major electoral risks facing national legislators are local. This does not
mean that legislators will necessarily be parochial in their attitudes and policy commitments. But it does mean that they cannot be bound to support the president or
national party leaders on issues of high local salience on which their constituents hold
a differing view. In order to impose discipline successfully, the national parties must be
able either to control sanctions at present important to legislators, such as nomination
to office, or to impose still more severe ones upon them. At the moment, however, our
system provides for control of congressional, state, and local nominations and elections
by geographically localized candidates, electorates, and (to a lesser extent) party leaders.
Presidents are not totally helpless in affecting the outcomes of these local decisions, but
their influence, especially considering the power of incumbent members of Congress
to maintain themselves in office, is in most cases quite marginal.[15]

In the light of this, one obvious electoral precondition of disciplined parties would
have to be that local voters were so strongly tied to national party issues that they would
reward their local representatives for supporting national policy pronouncements, even
at the expense of local advantage. To a certain extent, by virtue of the influence of
national news media and the rising educational level of the electorate, as well as some
increase in the general propensity of the most active citizens to think ideologically,

this condition can be met. The issues on which the national party makes its appeal must either unify a large number of constituencies in favor of the party or appeal at least to some substantial segment of opinion everywhere. But even if this could be accomplished with regularity, it would be strategically unwise for parties to attempt to discipline members who lived in areas that were strongly against national party policy. This would mean reading the offending area out of the party and weakening the party's overall appeal in federal elections. Therefore, reformers must show how they intend to contribute to the national character of political parties by enforcing national policies on members of Congress in those areas where local constituencies are drastically opposed to national party policy or whose constituents do not pay attention to issues but care more for the personality or the constituent services of their representatives in Congress.[16] Insofar as leeway exists, let us say, for liberal northeastern Republicans, a diminishing breed, to support liberal programs and for conservative Democrats, who are much scarcer in the South than they once were, to oppose them, the parties will, in fact, have retained their old, "undisciplined," "irresponsible" shapes. Insofar as this leeway does not exist, splinter groups of various kinds are encouraged to split off from the established parties. Party changing among office holders, once unheard of, becomes more common.

Another way of achieving disciplined parties may be more promising. We have seen that party activists and, to a lesser but meaningful extent, legislators have become ideologically more coherent. This has not occurred by command but by evolution: northern liberal Republicans have moved into the Democratic Party and conservative southern Democrats into the Republican Party.[17] As the parties have become more ideologically distinctive across a wider range of issues—social, environmental, and foreign policy, as well as economic—some activists who feel most uncomfortable have been changing allegiances.[18] For proponents of party cohesion, this is the good news. The bad news is that a strong party line breeds splits. Among Republicans, this means the prospect of future conflict between free-market libertarians and social conservatives. Among Democrats, internal party divisions tend to center on social and cultural issues. Party leaders increasingly seek to activate "wedge issues" that divide their opponents. Democrats raise environmental and education issues, which split Republicans; Republicans talk about partial-birth abortion and same-sex marriage, which divide Democrats.

Conflict within and between parties may be good for them and for the nation. Conflict can invigorate discussion and enlighten the public about the bases of party differences. Much depends on the extent to which discussion quickly polarizes groups that have strong interests in definitions of the situation that are already so well formed and structured as to inhibit the search for creative solutions.

A second method for reducing the independent power over policy of independently elected congressional leaders has begun to have an effect in national politics. This method addresses not the prospects for nomination and election of congressional leaders but rather their opportunities to lead in Congress. Adherence to the conservatism of the majority of Republicans in Congress has in general always been a prerequisite of leadership within the Republican Party. What internal conflict there has been among Republicans has been based not on ideology but style. The emergence of Newt Gingrich in the 1990s as Republican leader meant not a shift to the right but the adoption of a confrontational approach to House business by Republicans. Gingrich's successors have, like him, been mainstream conservatives, as are the leaders of the Senate Republicans.[19]

Among congressional Democrats, in the past more room existed for congressional leaders—at any rate for committee chairs, who were selected by seniority—to take whatever policy positions they pleased. Since the late 1950s, sentiment grew in Congress that conservative Democratic committee chairs should be more responsive to the policy preferences of the majority of the majority party, and in the 1970s the Democratic caucus of the House of Representatives acted to remove committee chairs they regarded as unresponsive. Despite the unlimbering of a new weapon—the House Democratic caucus—that could encourage party cohesion in Congress, it was not used consistently quite in this way, and concerns related to the management of Congress itself turned out to be more significant than the shaping or enforcement of party policy in the activities of the reactivated Democratic caucus when the Democrats were in the majority. The Republicans, during the Gingrich speakership (1995 to 1998), violated seniority regularly as part of an effort to centralize control of policy. The revolt that deposed Gingrich in 1998 was at least in part an effort to return greater powers to the committees. But Republican leaders still retained significant influence over committee chairs.

This series of reforms since the early 1970s has resulted in congressional parties in which a strongly ideological leadership retains a great deal of power over committee chairs and rank-and-file members. By any measure, both Republicans and Democrats are currently more internally unified and more dissimilar from each other than at any time in living memory. During the presidential administration of George W. Bush, this new model of policy government extended still further to an increased degree of authority enjoyed by the executive over the legislature. Republican party leaders in Congress acted as if their primary duty was to carry out a programmatically coherent agenda set by the president. Disputes between the White House and Capitol Hill were few (Bush did not veto a single bill during the first five years of his presidency), and independent congressional oversight of executive branch activity nearly disappeared. Under unified Democratic control early in Barack Obama's presidency, Congress demonstrated somewhat more independence from the executive branch, although Obama succeeded in enacting most of his first-term legislative goals over near-unanimous Republican opposition. Congress remained severely divided along party lines, with few examples of substantive bipartisan cooperation.

We might expect advocates of policy government to be cheered by such developments. After all, Bush and the Republican majorities in Congress came closest during the 2000–2006 period to instituting their vision of a clear, ideological policy agenda implemented via strong party discipline. Voters were presented with a stark choice between the parties at election time, allowing Republican officeholders to claim that their victories represented a "mandate" on behalf of the party's principles. Recent studies of congressional voting reveal a legislature more polarized by party in floor voting than ever before.[20]

It is not at all clear whether this increasing importance of party ideology has been good for the parties, much less the nation itself. Several policies implemented by the Bush and Obama administrations proved unpopular with voters, demonstrating that narrow election victories do not actually confer broad mandates to execute a comprehensive issue agenda. Bush's popularity ratings dropped as the U.S. war in Iraq suffered significant setbacks. In 2006, voters communicated their disapproval of his performance in office by turning control of both houses of Congress over to the opposition Democrats. Congressional Republicans suffered particularly heavy losses in liberal and moderate districts in the North, where voters registered their strong objections to the policies of the ruling GOP by defeating even centrist Republican incumbents.

Similar results in 2008 ushered in Democratic dominance of Congress and the presidency under Barack Obama. In turn, Obama's pursuit of a liberal policy agenda increased the electoral vulnerability of moderate Democrats from the South and West who, in adopting policy positions, faced an unappetizing choice between satisfying either their party leaders or their constituents. Obama's declining popularity led to heavy losses for these Democrats in the 2010 midterm elections, giving control of the House of Representatives back to the Republican Party while further increasing the extent of ideological polarization and partisan rancor within Congress.

Are parties that take relatively extreme positions more "responsible" or "accountable" to the generally moderate and ideologically inconsistent American electorate than parties that allow for greater flexibility on issues? Reforms that reinforce party polarization risk offering voters a clear choice—but between two equally unpalatable options. To a large extent, advocates of policy government have succeeded in implementing their goals, but the results may have proven less popular—and less conducive to well-functioning government—than they foresaw.

REFORM BY MEANS OF PARTICIPATORY DEMOCRACY

The second type of reform movement we identify as participatory democracy. The efforts of those who advocate participatory democracy and who have attempted to make the Democratic Party the vehicle of this approach to government have met with considerable success over the past fifty years, as the history of presidential nomination reform attests.[21] The recent advent of the Tea Party has subjected the Republican Party to participatory demands as well. Here we wish to contemplate the theory of politics that underlies this position. Ordinarily, participatory democrats criticize the American political system in two respects. First, they argue that elections have insufficient impact on policy outcomes of the government. These critics see too weak a link between public policy and what they believe to be the desires of electoral majorities. Second, there is the critique of the electoral process itself, which argues that policy does not represent what majorities want because undemocratic influences determine election results. These criticisms are simple-minded in one sense and cogent in another. They are simple-minded in that they ignore the immense problems that would have to be overcome if we were truly serious about transforming America or any large, diverse population into a participatory democracy. They are cogent in that responsiveness to majorities on questions of policy is a fundamental value that gives legitimacy to democratic government. The connection between such criticism and the legitimacy of government makes it important to deal at least briefly with some of the issues and problems that should be raised (and usually are not) by judgments of this fundamental nature.

The first and obvious question to ask is whether the criticisms are based on fact. Is the American system unresponsive to the policy desires of a majority of its citizens? Unfortunately, there is no unambiguous way to answer this question. If we focus our attention, for example, on the mechanics of the policy process, we find what appears to be government by minorities. In some policy areas a great number of people and interests, organized and unorganized, may have both a say in the open and some influence on the final product. But fewer individuals may be involved in areas dealing with other problems and policies, some of which will be of a specialized nature, of limited interest, and so on. Even members of Congress do not have equally great influence over every decision: committee jurisdictions, seniority, special knowledge, party, and individual reputation all combine to weigh the influence of each member on a different scale for each issue.

So we must conclude that if we adopt direct participation in and equal influence over the policy decisions of our government (the decisions that "affect our lives") as the single criterion of democracy, then our system surely fails the test. So, we might note, does every contemporary government of any size known to us, possibly excepting two or three rural Swiss cantons.

Another approach might focus on public opinion as an index of majority desires. Using this standard, a quite different picture emerges. Policy decisions made by the government mostly have the support of popular majorities. Where this is not true, the apparent lack of "responsiveness" may have several causes, not all of them curable: (1) conflicts between majority desires and intractable situations in the world (e.g., a hypothetical desire for peace in the Middle East); or (2) public attitudes favoring certain sets of policies that may be mutually incompatible (such as the desire for low taxes, generous benefits, and balanced budgets); or (3) clear, consistent, and feasible majority desires that are ignored by the government because the desires are unconstitutional or antithetical to enduring values of the political system, to which leaders are more sensitive than popular majorities. Surveys, for example, have from time to time revealed majorities in favor of constitutionally questionable repressive measures against dissenters and the press.

Criticisms of the popular responsiveness of presidential elections are more difficult to assess. American electoral politics does respond to the application of resources such as money that are arguably undemocratic and that cause the influence of different actors to be weighed unequally. In a truly democratic system, it could be argued, the system would respond to votes and only votes. All methods of achieving political outcomes other than registering preferences by voting would be deemed illegitimate. As we have indicated, however, money, incumbency, energy and enthusiasm, popularity, name recognition, ability, and experience are all valuable assets within the structure of American politics. Is this avoidable? Should we attempt to eradicate the influence of these resources?

Political resources and the people who possess them are important primarily because campaigns are important. Campaigns are important because the general public needs to be alerted to the fact that an election is near. Partisans must be mobilized, the uncommitted convinced, perhaps even a few minds changed. Resources other than votes are important because—and only because—numerical majorities must be mobilized.

American politics responds to diverse resources because many citizens abstain from voting and are hard to reach by campaigners. Sometimes this is described as political apathy. Why is political apathy widespread? There are several alternative explanations. Perhaps it is because the system presents the citizenry with no real alternatives from which to choose. Yet voting participation in presidential elections seems to rise and fall without much regard for the ideological distance between candidates of the major parties.

Perhaps there is apathy because the public has been imbued with a "false consciousness" that blinds them to their "real" desires and interests. They would participate if they knew better. This explanation is traditionally seized on by the enlightened few to deny value to the preferences of the ignorant many. The people, we are told, are easily fooled; this testifies to their credulity. They do not know what is good for them; this makes them childlike. But when the people cannot trust their own feelings, when their desires are alleged to be unworthy, when their policy preferences should be ignored because they are not "genuine" or "authentic," or there are not enough of them, they are being deprived of their humanity as well. What is left for the people if they are held to have no judgment, wisdom, feeling, desire, and preference? Such an argument would offer little hope for democracy of any sort, for it introduces the most blatant form of inequality as a political "given": a structured, ascribed difference between those who know what is "good" for themselves and those who must be "told." No doubt it is true that much of the time we do not know (without the advantage of perfect foresight) what is best for us. But that is not to say that others know better, that our consciousness is false but theirs is true. Persons who make the "false consciousness" argument do not believe in democracy.

A more hopeful and less self-contradictory explanation of political apathy might note that throughout American history a substantial number of citizens have not wished to concern themselves continually with the problems and actions of government. Many citizens prefer to participate on their own terms, involving themselves when they feel like it with a particular issue area or problem. These citizens' participation is necessarily sporadic and narrower than that of the voter interested in all public problems and actively involved in general political life. Many other citizens (surely a majority) are more interested in their own personal problems than in any issue of public policy.[22] These citizens meet their public obligations by going to the polls at fairly regular intervals, making their selections on the basis of their own criteria, and then supporting the actions and policies of the winners, whether they were their choices or not. In the intervals, unless they themselves are personally affected by some policy proposal, most of these citizens may wish to be left alone. Given the complexity of issues and the uncertainty surrounding the claims of candidates, citizens may arrive at their voting decisions by asking themselves a simple, summary question: are things (the domestic economy, world affairs) better or worse than they were? This is a reasonable way to decide, but it does not offer much future policy guidance to political leaders.[23]

The literature on apathy may say more about the values of the students of the subject than about the ostensible objects of their studies. Those observers who approve of existing institutions are likely to view apathy as relatively benign; they believe people do not participate because they are satisfied and they trust institutions to do well by them. Those who disapprove of existing institutions naturally find the defect in the institutions themselves; they believe people do not participate because they are denied the opportunity or because they rightly feel ineffectual. Observers who view individuals as capable of regulating their own affairs see these individuals as deciding case by case whether it is worth the time and effort to participate. Projecting the investigator's preferences onto citizens does not seem to us a useful way of learning why this or that person chooses to participate in political life. As political scientists and citizens, we think self-government an ideal so valuable that we would not impose our own views on those who decide they have better things to do.

Studies have from time to time shown unfavorable citizen attitudes toward the political system, a phenomenon sometimes called "alienation," which appears to have increased since the 1960s. As we argued earlier in this book, these attitudes do not explain low rates of voting participation; persons who score high in these unfavorable attitudes have been shown to participate at about the same rate as the nonalienated.[24] So we surmise that a great many citizens who do not vote abstain because they are concerned with other things important to them, like earning a living or painting a picture or cultivating a garden, and not because they feel it is so difficult to influence outcomes. In short, for them, politics is peripheral. Given the secondary importance of politics in many people's lives, making it easier to vote does increase turnout. But even lowering barriers to participation does not reduce abstention from voting to zero or anything like zero.

Consider a society in which all citizens were as concerned about public matters as the most active. Such a society would not require mobilization: all who were able to would vote.[25] The hoopla and gimmickry associated with political campaigns would have little effect: this citizenry would know the record of the parties and the candidates and, presumably, would make reasoned choices on this basis. Should such an active society be the goal of those whose political philosophy is democratic? This question should not and cannot be answered without first addressing the problem of how such a society could be achieved.

Without attempting to be comprehensive, a few difficulties merit some specific comment. First and foremost, political participation, as Aristotle made clear several thousand years ago, takes a great deal of time. For this reason (among others) a large population of slaves was felt necessary to assist participatory government: it freed Athenian citizens from the cares of maintaining life and thus provided them the leisure time that made their political activity possible. But having rejected some 150 years ago this particular "solution" to the problems related to relatively large-scale participation, we must deal with the fact that most American citizens work for a living. They lack the disposable time that permits professionals and college students and other privileged people to choose their working hours. Most citizens lack the time, even if they had the temperament and training, to engage continually in politics. To the degree that representative institutions—political parties, legislatures, elected executives—are disregarded in favor of more direct modes of activity, the majority of the people will be without the means through which they can most effectively make their will felt. In short, to impose requirements of direct participation on those desiring a voice in decisions would be to ensure that the incessant few rather than the sporadic many would rule: thus the 1960s slogan "power to the people" really proposed to replace a representative few, who were elected, with an unrepresentative few, who were self-activated.

In well-known work, the philosopher Jürgen Habermas has argued that the only way to make a democracy legitimate, for it to be considered a true democracy worthy of support, is for it to approximate the conditions of what he calls "an ideal speech situation." Every person would be equally interested and active. Each would have equal rights, money, information, and all other resources necessary for effective participation.[26] What could be wrong with such an ideal? Nothing at all, we think. If it were to be realized in practice in a very diverse society, however, it might lead to surprising results. For a diverse society may lead to the expression of diverse values. Individualists, for example, adhere to the ideal of equality of opportunity so that people can be different, and some may consequently end up with more resources than others. This expresses a different equality from that postulated by Habermas. Other people, for example, Christian fundamentalists, may prefer a more patriarchal or hierarchical set of values in which different people occupy different statuses. Thus it is helpful to consider whether democracy is only about equality or whether it may be about enabling people who hold different values to live together peaceably.

Thus there are practical difficulties with a theory that requires high levels of political participation. We raise this issue not because we are opposed in principle to the idea of an active, participatory, democratic society. By persuasion and political education the majority of our citizens might indeed be convinced that the quality of our shared existence could be improved through more continuous devotion to public activity. This is quite different from arguing that the rules of the game should be changed to reduce the influence of those who at present lack the opportunity or desire to be active. Efforts to implement ideal goals when the preconditions and the means of achieving these goals do not exist are self-defeating. Actions that in the name of participatory democracy restrict the ability of most of the people to have their political say are not as democratic as advertised.

SOME SPECIFIC REFORMS

Comprehensive reform of the political system rides in on tides of strong feeling. Until such feelings exist among party activists, rational advocacy looking toward reform is wasted; once such feeling exists, rational advocacy is superfluous. So the type of analysis we undertake here is bound to be uninfluential. We attempt it only because thoughtful citizens may find it instructive to consider the consequences of the best-laid plans. Once these consequences have had an opportunity to manifest themselves, however, a new generation of reform may be in order. After all, practically everything that reformers object to now was once somebody's favorite reform.

We suspect that the achievement of many—not all—of the specific objectives of party reformers would be detrimental to their aims and to those of most thoughtful citizens. Let us consider, for example, three specific reforms of governmental machinery that are commonly advocated to make the parties more responsive to popular will and more democratic. Party reformers often advocate a variety of changes to the nomination process, changes to party convention procedures, and modification or abolition of the electoral college. We address each of these topics in turn.

The Nomination Process

In order to evaluate the strengths and weaknesses of the current presidential nomination process, it would be helpful to suggest a set of goals that most Americans might accept as desirable and important.[27] The following six standards appear to meet this test: any method for nominating presidential candidates should (1) help secure vigorous competition between the parties, (2) maintain some degree of cohesion and agreement within each party, (3) produce nominees who are likely to win voter support, (4) lead to the choice of nominees who are reasonably well-qualified, (5) lead to the acceptance of the nominees as legitimate, and (6) result in officeholders who are capable of generating support for public policies they intend to pursue. We first look at some suggested alternatives to the current nominating system.

The most common nomination reform proposal would replace the sequential series of state primaries and caucuses now in place with a national direct primary election held on a single date in the spring of a presidential election year. Advocates of this reform argue that a national primary would be more equitable than the current system, which gives disproportionate influence to states voting earliest in the calendar. Iowa and New Hampshire, two small and somewhat unrepresentative states, hold particular sway in determining the presidential nominees of both parties every four years, while the frequent emergence of a presumptive nominee soon after the first primaries often renders later elections in more populous states irrelevant to the outcome.

Defenders of the current system counter that there is an advantage in allowing two small states to vote first. Candidates competing in Iowa and New Hampshire must engage in "retail politics," building support by making frequent personal appearances and winning the backing of party activists. As Everett Carll Ladd argues,

> By leading off, manageable little Iowa and New Hampshire enable less well-known and well-heeled candidates to gain attention through presenting their wares to real people in real election settings. If a candidate with moderate resources, and previously lacking a national reputation, manages to impress a fair number of voters in these small states, isn't this laboratory experience of some considerable interest to the country?[28]

This merely points to a more general problem of financing national primary elections. It is quite possible that eight or more candidates might compete in a true, fifty-state, national primary. In a year when there is no incumbent president in the race, it is not hard to imagine a crowd of challengers in both parties hustling all over the United States campaigning in such an election. It would take, of course, enormous amounts of money. The parties could hardly be expected to show favoritism and so could not finance these candidates. The pre-primary campaign, therefore, would assume enormous importance and would be exceedingly expensive. Nationwide challengers would need access to very large campaign war chests. It would help if they were already well known. They would also have to be quite sturdy physically.

We know that voters often find it difficult to distinguish among candidates of the same party, especially when these candidates are not previously familiar to them. Voters in a national primary could be expected to make evaluations by knowing one or two of the candidates' names in favorable or unfavorable contexts, liking or not liking their looks, identifying or not identifying with their ethnic or racial characteristics, attending to their treatment in the press, responding to television advertisements, or relying on some other means of differentiation having nothing whatever to do with ability to do the job, or even with their policy positions. Since patents on policy positions are not available, it is reasonable to suppose that more than one candidate would adopt roughly the same set of positions, virtually eliminating any important substantive differences between them.

A national primary would present another potential complication: in a field of multiple candidates, no single individual would be likely to receive a majority of the votes.

Under current party rules, candidates must win support from a majority of delegates to be nominated; the Democratic Party's insistence on the proportional allocation of delegates virtually ensures that a potential nominee must receive close to a majority of the popular vote. The establishment of a national primary would therefore increase the likelihood of a deadlocked convention—or, at least, a flurry of deal-making by candidates after the primary to provide one contender the necessary number of delegates. It is hard to see how this alternative would better reflect the will of the voters than the current system.

Of course, the parties could amend their rules to grant the presidential nomination to the first-place winner of the national primary, regardless of whether that candidate gained a majority of the total vote. This measure would allow for the possibility that a candidate could win the nomination despite receiving support from just 20 or 30 percent of the party's voters—a much less democratic outcome than we now have, since who knows how the rest of the electorate might have distributed itself if it had known what the rank order of the candidates was going to be? Another possibility would be for the top two finishers to contest a second fifty-state runoff election after the first primary and before the general election. Whatever advantage such a requirement would offer in terms of majoritarian legitimacy would seem to be more than outweighed by the substantial cost in money and energy associated with forcing presidential candidates to contest up to three national elections within a year's time.

Absent a single national primary, some advocates of nomination reform have proposed that the sequential nature of state primaries and caucuses be retained, instead introducing a system of rotation such that different states take turns at the front of the nomination calendar. For example, individual states could be classified into one of four, six, or eight geographic regions. Each regional grouping would hold primaries or caucuses on the same date, with the dates spaced at biweekly or monthly intervals over the spring of an election year, and the regions would rotate every four years such that each set of states received an equal opportunity to vote early (and thus exert the strongest influence over the outcome). As with the national primary, there appears to be substantial popular support for what seems at first glance to be a more "fair" and "equal" process than the status quo.[29]

Such plans, however appealing they may seem in the abstract, would require substantial cooperation from the state governments that actually schedule and administer primary elections. As we have seen, even the current system, which requires only that states hold their primaries and caucuses within a common chronological window, still produces less than total compliance by individual states seeking attention from candidates and influence over the outcome. There is little reason to believe that states would universally respect plans implemented by the national parties that attempted to dictate specific election dates for each state. Iowa and New Hampshire, in particular, aggressively defend their first-in-the-nation status and would likely refuse to respect such regulation. Even if the national parties followed through on threats to strip non-compliant states of most of their delegates, candidates would likely continue to contest early states in order to generate positive media attention and position themselves for later contests.

The presidential nomination process continues to evolve even without the imposition of comprehensive reforms by the federal government or national parties. Front-loading of the nomination calendar as the result of individual states' decisions to schedule their primaries and caucuses earlier in the season has sometimes resulted in a quasi-national primary on the first permissible date for most states to hold elections; in 2012, about half the states had voted by March 10. As long as the national parties allow Iowa, New Hampshire, and a few other states to vote before the rest of the nation, however, these early states will continue to hold a disproportionate influence over nominations, winnowing the field of candidates and structuring the choices faced by voters in subsequent primaries. At the same time, front-loading has increased the need for candidates to raise large amounts of money and build extensive campaign organizations prior to the start of the primaries, in order to have the capacity to capitalize on favorable media coverage as a result of strong performances in Iowa and New Hampshire.

The Decline of the National Convention

High on the list of practices that in the past were regarded as objectionable was the secret gathering of party leaders in the "smoke-filled room" to select a presidential nominee. Some likened this to a political opium den where a few irresponsible party bosses, hidden from public view, stealthily determined the destiny of the nation.[30] Yet it is difficult to see who, other than the party's leaders, should have been entrusted with the delicate task of finding a candidate to meet the majority preference. If head-on clashes of strength on the convention floor could not resolve the question, the only alternatives were continued deadlock, anarchy among scores of leaderless delegates splitting the party into rival factions, or some process of accommodation.

National conventions no longer pick presidential nominees; they merely ratify the work of primaries and caucuses. But let us suppose that some national convention in the future must choose a nominee because no single candidate enters with support from a majority of delegates. Would we require that a smoke-free successor to the smoke-filled room be abolished and with it all behind-the-scenes negotiations? All parleys would then be held in public, before the delegates and millions of television viewers. Could the participants resist spending their time scoring points against each other in order to impress the folks back home? Bargaining would not be taking place because the participants would not really be communicating with one another. No compromises would be possible; if they were attempted, leaders would be accused by their followers of selling out to the other side. Once a stalemate existed, breaking it would be practically impossible, and the party would probably disintegrate into warring factions.

An extensive system of state primaries in which delegates are more or less compelled to vote for the candidate to whom they are pledged has led to the eclipse of negotiation processes without any formal action of a convention. This was the case even in the hotly contested 2008 Democratic nomination contest. Hillary Clinton, trailing narrowly in pledged delegates at the end of the primaries, recognized the impossibility of productive negotiations with delegates pledged to Barack Obama. She conceded the race in June, months before the national convention. Since delegates cannot change their positions except by direction of the candidate to whom they are pledged, there is little point in bringing party leaders together for private conferences. Sharply increasing the number of pledged delegates introduces great rigidity into the convention because under conditions of stalemate no one is in a position to switch his or her support.

Although the Democratic Party provides for hundreds of party leaders and elected officials to attend the national convention with full voting rights as unpledged superdelegates, it is far from obvious whether these individuals could, under any circumstances, effectively exercise independent influence over the identity of the party's presidential nominee. Most of the time, a single candidate wins decisively among pledged delegates chosen in state elections, making the preferences of the relatively small proportion of superdelegates irrelevant to the outcome. But even in 2008, when the pledged delegates were closely divided between Obama and Clinton, the prospect of the superdelegates serving as a collective independent tiebreaker was challenged by a number of figures within the party who saw such an act as illegitimately ignoring the voice of "the people" as measured by the results of state primaries and caucuses. House Speaker Nancy Pelosi, for example, publicly expressed her belief that "it would do great harm to the Democratic Party if superdelegates are perceived to overturn the will of the voters."[31] This was the (self-interested) position of the Obama campaign, the consistent leader in the pledged delegate count throughout the primaries, and it seemed to carry increasing weight with undecided superdelegates as the nomination process continued into the late spring.

Acting to her own strategic advantage, Hillary Clinton argued unsuccessfully that superdelegates retained the power to act according to their own judgment about the best nominee for the party in the general election. Clinton's case was weakened by the lack of conclusive evidence that she was, in fact, a more electable candidate than Obama; public opinion polls at the time showed both Democrats performing about equally well in trial heats with John McCain, the presumptive Republican nominee. But even if most superdelegates had seen Clinton as a hypothetically stronger candidate in the general election, they would have also needed to consider the likelihood that the nomination of a candidate without the largest bloc of pledged delegates would threaten both to ignite fierce dissension within the party and to undermine the nominee's legitimacy as the rightful Democratic standard-bearer. The concept of a "democratic" nomination process has taken hold so completely in the years since the party reforms of the 1970s that an attempt by the party's own popularly elected officials to independently influence the outcome, even in a case in which public sentiment is evenly divided, would be guaranteed to raise widespread charges of tyranny and injustice. Party leaders are likely to calculate that uniting around even a potentially flawed candidate provides a greater chance of winning in November than risking a damaging intraparty battle that could continue to the national convention, or even beyond it.

Normally, party officials view the convention as an opportunity to aid party unity in a variety of ways. It provides a forum in which initially disunited fragments of the national party can come together and find common ground as well as a common nominee. The platform helps in performing this function. In order to gain a majority of electoral votes, a party must appeal in some way to most major population groups. Since these interests do not always want the same thing, it is necessary to compromise and, sometimes, to evade issues that would lead to drastic losses of support.

Reformers' concerns with party platforms stem primarily from two assumptions: first, that there is a significant demand in the electorate for more clear-cut differences on policy; second, that elections are likely to be a significant source of guidance on individual issues to policymakers. Yet both these assumptions are either false or highly dubious. As we have seen, on a wide range of issues leaders in both parties are much further apart than are ordinary citizens, who have been separated by rather small differences.[32] Issue polarization is most pronounced among the politically active. When party platforms spell out clear and important differences between the parties on policy, it usually reflects a desire of party leaders to please themselves rather than demands from the electorate.

Some critics objected to the traditional convention's stress on picking an electable nominee, rather than the "best candidate" regardless of popularity. This objection is not compatible with the democratic notion that voters should decide who is best for them and communicate this decision in an election. Only in dictatorial countries does a set of leaders arrogate unto themselves the right to determine who is best regardless of popular preferences. Unpopular candidates can hardly win free elections. Unpopular presidents can hardly secure the support they need to accomplish their goals. Popularity can be regarded as a necessary element for obtaining consent in democratic politics.

Although popularity is normally a necessary condition for nomination, it should not be the only condition. The guideline for purposes of nomination should be to nominate the best of the popular candidates. But "best" is a slippery word. A great deal of what we mean by "best" in politics is "best for us" or "best represents our policy preferences," and this can hardly be held up as an objective criterion. What is meant by "best" in this context includes such personal qualities as experience, intelligence, and decisiveness. Nevertheless, it is not at all clear that an extremely conservative voter would prefer a highly intelligent liberal candidate to a moderately intelligent conservative. Personal qualities clearly are subject to discount based on the compatibility of interests between voters and candidates.

For some critics, the defect of conventions lies not only in their poor performance in nominating candidates but also in their failure to become a sort of "superlegislature," enforcing the policy views of the platform on party members in the executive branch and Congress. We have previously indicated that such enforcement is most unlikely to be achieved. Let us suppose for the purposes of argument that the conventions could somehow become much more influential on matters of national policy. How could either party retain a semblance of unity if the stakes of convention deliberations were vastly increased by converting the platform into an unbreakable promise of national policy? If one believes that an increase in heated discussion necessarily improves the chances of agreement, then the problem solves itself. Experience warns us, however, that airing sharp differences, particularly when the stakes are high, is likely to decrease agreement.

The fact that platforms are not binding permits a degree of unity necessary for the delegates to stay put long enough to agree on a nominee. By vastly increasing the number of delegates who would bitterly oppose platform decisions and possibly leave the convention, the binding platform would jeopardize the legitimacy of the convention's nominating function. Paradoxically, in such circumstances it would be difficult to resist the temptation to make the platform utterly innocuous in order to give offense to no one at all.

Even so, platforms do have a far from negligible impact on public opinion. Platform planks are enacted as governmental policy slightly more than half the time.[33] Programs favored by the public, according to opinion polls, are twice as likely to be enacted if they also appear in party platforms.[34] When large majorities favor programs, both parties are likely to put them in their platforms; when the public is somewhat more divided and important constituencies object, the parties are capable of going against popular majorities. Thus Republican platform planks on welfare and economic issues and Democratic provisions on labor unions and affirmative action tend to run counter to majority opinion.[35] The question of whom the parties are for, special or general constituencies, is resolved by going for the majority when it is substantial and modifying that position when it conflicts with special party concerns.

It is possible that the traditional, decision-making national conventions were more effective in realizing the six goals that we postulated earlier would commonly be accepted as desirable—party competition, some degree of internal cohesion, candidates attractive to voters, qualified candidates, acceptance of nominees as legitimate, and a connection between winning the nomination and governing later on—than the primary- and caucus-based method as it has existed since the reforms of the 1970s. Absent an unlikely return to the old ways, however, it is unclear whether further fundamental changes to the current system, such as the establishment of national or rotated regional primaries, would sufficiently address contemporary concerns about the fairness or effectiveness of the nomination process without introducing a new set of even more undesirable flaws. The propensity of both national parties to fiddle almost continuously with the procedural rules of the game, often in an inconsistent pattern from one election to the next—by turns raising and lowering the number of superdelegates, for example, or alternately encouraging and discouraging the front-loading of the primary calendar—reflects not only widespread dissatisfaction with the nomination system as it now exists, but also the absence of a clear alternative that would gain consensus support among both party leaders and members of the public.

Some observers have concluded that the post-1968 reforms have effectively been reversed by resourceful party leaders who have been able to regain control over the nomination process. One view, advocated most extensively by the political scientists Marty Cohen, David Karol, Hans Noel, and John Zaller, holds that the highly visible and procedurally complex interaction of primaries, caucuses, media interpretation, and electoral momentum has a much smaller effect on the outcome of nominations than is commonly understood.[36] According to these scholars, elected officials and other powerful figures in both major parties have managed to compensate for the enactment of the 1970s-era reforms (which were intended to deprive party elites of control over nominations) by coordinating among themselves to steer valuable resources—such as financial contributions and positive publicity—to a favored contender prior to the start of the primary calendar, thus giving that candidate a decisive advantage once party voters begin to make their choices. While some recent candidates, such as Barack Obama in 2008, have still managed to win the nomination of their party without beginning the primary season as the anointed front-runner, this perspective draws welcome attention to the importance placed by contemporary candidates on courting public endorsements and institutional support from influential party figures as the race takes shape. In a year in which the vast majority of the leadership within a party mobilizes on behalf of one candidate at the expense of others, voters are likely to weigh such support quite heavily as they make their choices at the ballot box—perhaps rendering the particulars of nomination procedures less central to the outcome under such circumstances.

The Electoral College

In 2000, the candidate who received the most votes failed to become president for the first time in 112 years. But while many Democrats viewed George W. Bush's victory over Al Gore as illegitimate, their objections were based primarily on the controversy over the counting of votes in Florida and the active role of the Supreme Court in halting recounts, not the rare discrepancy between the popular and electoral vote. While advocates of electoral reform renewed their efforts in the wake of the 2000 election, the absence of strong public pressure for modifying or abolishing the electoral college hindered their cause, leaving the institution intact for future elections.

Even so, debate over the merits of the current procedure for selecting presidents continues in some quarters, and from time to time a state or group of states will consider changing its method of allocating electoral votes. In 2004, a Colorado ballot initiative would have repealed the state's winner-take-all apportionment of electors in favor of proportional allocation; the measure was rejected by a two-to-one margin. Three years later, a bill allocating electors by congressional district passed the North Carolina legislature but was quietly killed at the urging of national Democratic officials worried about starting a state-level vote allocation war with the Republican Party. Eleven states—including California, New York, Illinois, New Jersey, and a few others—have joined a national compact of states pledging to cast their electoral votes for the winner of the nationwide popular vote; the compact would take effect once states casting a majority of electoral votes chose to participate. In that case, the current system would effectively be replaced by a simple national popular election without the need for a constitutional amendment. However, the only states voting to join the compact so far have been those in which liberal Democrats control both the state legislature and governorship, leaving the effort far short of a national majority.

The electoral college as it is now constituted, with each state casting as many electoral votes as it has senators and representatives while awarding electors to candidates on a winner-take-all basis, provides an advantage to two groups of states. It yields a modest benefit to very small states, since the Constitution provides that each state elects two senators regardless of population. This means that the ten smallest states, with 3 percent of the total voters in the 2012 presidential election, maintain voting weight in the Senate equal to the ten largest states, home to 50 percent of the voters in 2012. The small states' disproportionate share of senators guarantees them slight overrepresentation in the electoral college as well. After the 2010 census, the seven states casting three electoral votes each had a ratio of 331,472 or fewer residents per electoral vote, while every state with thirteen or more electoral votes had a ratio of 607,972 or more residents per electoral vote.

But the near-universal use of the unit rule method of allocating electoral votes to candidates works to the advantage of large states, especially those that are politically competitive. Candidates who win a narrow majority in California alone receive more electoral votes (55) than they would by carrying all of the fourteen smallest states plus the District of Columbia (54); they can, mathematically, carry California by one vote and not receive any votes in those fourteen states and do a bit better in the electoral college. This encourages presidential candidates to focus their campaign efforts on competitive states with large numbers of electoral votes.[37] In fact, large states are somewhat more likely to be closely divided between the parties, while smaller states are more commonly dominated by one party or the other.

Nearly all electoral reform proposals fall into three basic categories. One would abolish the electoral college outright and weigh individual votes equally everywhere in a simple national popular election. The second option would retain the electoral college but abolish the unit rule in favor of proportional allocation of electoral votes within states. A third possibility also retains the current apportionment of the electoral college but allocates one electoral vote to the plurality vote winner in each congressional district and two electoral votes to the winner in each state.[38]

Allowing a majority (or plurality) of voters to choose a president in a simple national popular election has a great deal to commend it. This is the simplest method of all; it would be most easily understood by the greatest number of people; it is the reform plan favored by the majority of Americans; and it comes closest to reflecting intuitive notions of direct popular sovereignty through majority rule.

How would abolishing the electoral college affect presidential elections? Under the current system, candidates focus their campaign resources on politically competitive states, especially on the populous swing states that cast large numbers of electoral votes. In a national popular election, candidates would concentrate more on mobilizing high voter turnout in states that already supported them, hoping to gain a lopsided popular margin within their party's geographic base. The emphasis would not be on which candidate was going to carry a state but by how many votes he or she was going to win.[39] Small states do not gain influence under this alternative, however, because even those dominated by one party are not populous enough to provide large numbers of votes. Replacing the electoral college with a direct popular election thus mostly benefits medium-sized and large one-party states at the expense of two-party states.

Some advocates of reform criticize the current system for encouraging presidential candidates to focus on courting the residents of swing states while giving less attention to voters elsewhere in the nation. A few critics consider this strategic consequence of the electoral college to be undemocratic because it supposedly sends a message to voters in noncompetitive states that they lack a significant voice in the outcome of presidential elections.[40] However, no clear evidence exists that voters in battleground states exhibit more political efficacy than their counterparts in safe party states. In fact, many Americans are largely unaware of the degree of partisan competitiveness in their home states and show little interest in the details of campaign tactics. Because candidates would still target certain populations or geographic areas more than others even under a system of direct popular election, the abolition of the electoral college would by no means guarantee that voters in each state would receive equal attention from presidential campaigns.[41]

The role of third parties under the direct popular election alternative is also unclear. The current system disadvantages minor parties by requiring candidates to place first in a state in order to receive electoral votes; while the presence of a third-party or independent candidate may deny the first-place finisher a majority of the popular vote, it is much less likely to produce deadlock in the electoral college. For example, no candidate received a national popular majority in 1948, 1960, 1968, 1992, 1996, or 2000, yet in each case one of the major-party contenders gained a majority of electoral votes and thus assumed the presidency. On one hand, instituting a majority requirement in a direct popular election would frequently force the House of Representatives to choose the president; on the other, the prospect of a candidate assuming the presidency with a small plurality of the vote also seems undesirable. Consequently, the electoral college reform amendment that passed the House in 1969 provided for a runoff election between the top two finishers if no candidate secured at least 40 percent of the popular vote in the initial round of voting.[42]

The first effect of this provision would be to increase the influence of splinter parties. If a satisfactory major-party candidate is going to have a second chance to win the office anyway, there is an incentive for any sizable organized minority to contest the first election on its own. That the runoff would likely be used if it were provided for is suggested by 1992, when there was a fairly strong third-party candidate, Ross Perot, in the race. A fourth candidate would have needed only 6 or 7 percent of the national total to keep either major-party candidate from having the required 40 percent (Bill Clinton won with 43 percent, although he received 69 percent of the electoral vote).[43] Once this becomes even a plausible expectation, there is an incentive for various intense minorities to put up their own candidates, and visions of an evangelical Christian party, an African American party, a labor party, a peace party, an environmentalist party, a right-to-life party, a farmers' party, and so on, appear. Whereas one of the strong points of the present system is that it enforces a compromise by penalizing all minorities that will not come to terms, the direct election system could well encourage a continental European situation, in which numerous groups contest the first election and then recombine for the second; at the least, severe changes would be worked on the present system.[44] Should such a result occur in the future, the simplicity, ease of comprehension, and inherent majoritarian rightness of the direct election solution would quickly disappear.

Another proposal is seen by some reformers as an acceptable middle option between the current system and outright abolition of the electoral college.[45] Under this measure, the electoral college is retained but the unit rule is repealed. Instead, the electoral vote in each state is divided among the candidates according to their relative shares of the state's popular vote.

The widespread implementation of proportional allocation would encourage candidates to concentrate their energy on the very biggest states, since only in states with large numbers of electoral votes would campaign activity be likely to influence the popular vote outcome enough to affect the distribution of electors among the candidates. Other states would receive attention to the extent that one or the other candidate was deemed within reach of the numerical threshold necessary to gain an additional elector. The candidates would largely ignore small states because the share of electoral votes allocated to each party in those states would tend to be highly predictable and relatively insensitive to marginal changes in the state's popular vote.[46]

Under the unit rule, candidates who fall short of a popular majority can still win the presidency by gaining sufficiently broad support to place first in states casting at least 270 electoral votes. But proportional allocation would make it very difficult for a plurality winner in the popular vote to gain an electoral majority. As a result, presidential elections would be decided by the House of Representatives with some regularity, as the Constitution provides when no single candidate receives a majority in the electoral college. (Under this provision, the House must choose among the top three finishers in the electoral vote, and each state delegation casts one vote regardless of size.) Even in 1996, when Democratic incumbent Bill Clinton received a near-majority, 49.2 percent of the national popular vote (to 40.7 percent for Republican nominee Bob Dole and 8.4 percent for Reform Party candidate Ross Perot), Clinton would have been denied a victory in the electoral college under proportional allocation, giving the House, then controlled by the opposition Republicans, the opportunity to select the next president. As a result, though the proportional allocation alternative is superficially more "democratic" than the winner-take-all system now in place, elections would be decided by Congress so frequently (requiring only a very close election or a moderately strong third-party candidate) that the presidency would be frequently dependent on the preferences of the legislative branch, not the voters.[47]

A third reform, the congressional district plan, has been proposed as still another "compromise" between the status quo and more radical change. Under this measure, each state allocates two electoral votes to the statewide winner and one electoral vote to the candidate placing first in each House district within the state. Maine and Nebraska, the only states in which the unit rule is not currently in effect, employ this alternative means of apportioning electoral votes to presidential candidates.

Advocates of this proposal argue that its implementation would encourage candidates to contest politically competitive congressional districts within noncompetitive states, thus significantly expanding the electoral battleground. But most House districts are dominated by one of the major parties and are therefore unlikely to be targets for presidential campaigns. One recent study found that only about 10 percent of the national electorate resides within competitive congressional districts inside safe party states and would therefore benefit from the widespread adoption of the district plan.[48]

The most predictable consequence of the district plan would be the introduction of a consistent partisan bias to the electoral college. Under the unit rule, the electoral college does not systematically favor either party; the Republican advantage deriving from the overrepresentation of small, rural states is balanced out by the more efficient distribution of Democratic voters across states. Because the proportion of Republican-leaning House seats perennially outweighs the share of districts favoring Democrats—due to the existence of urban supermajority districts with large numbers of "wasted" Democratic votes—the universal adoption of the district plan would work to the dependable advantage of the GOP. Republican candidates would have prevailed in the electoral college in 1960, 2000, and 2012 under the district plan despite Democratic victories in the national popular vote, while Jimmy Carter would have won a bare electoral majority in 1976 (270 to 268) despite receiving nearly 1.7 million more votes nationwide than his opponent, Gerald Ford.

Since the goals of electoral reform are supposedly to make the system more "fair" and "democratic," it is hard to see the advantage of an alternative that (1) increases the likelihood that the less popular candidate nationwide wins the election, (2) provides no more guarantee against deadlock than the present system (third-party candidate George Wallace in 1968 received 45 electoral votes under the unit rule, but would have received 58 under the district plan), (3) preserves the winner-take-all method, (4) fails to produce a significant expansion of the electoral battleground, and (5) systematically favors one party over the other.

Table 6.1 summarizes electoral outcomes under the unit rule and the three alternative plans for selected presidential elections since 1960. The elections of 1964, 1972, 1976, 1980, 1984, 1988, 2004, and 2008 would have come out the same way under all the plans for counting votes we have been considering. Of those, however, only 1976 and 2004 featured a close margin in the popular vote. Had proportional allocation been in place, the three presidential elections between 1992 and 2000 would all have been decided by the House of Representatives and Barack Obama would have won quite narrowly in 2012. Bill Clinton (in 1992 and 1996) and George W. Bush (in 2000) would

TABLE 6.1. Outcomes under the Unit Rule and Three Alternatives, Selected Elections, 1960–2012

Year	Unit Rule		Popular Vote		Proportional Allocation		District Plan	
2012	*Obama wins*		*Obama wins*		*Obama wins*		*Romney wins*	
	Obama	332	Obama	51.1 %	Obama	272	Obama	264
	Romney	206	Romney	47.2	Romney	265	Romney	274
					Others	1.7	Others	1
2008	*Obama wins*		*Obama wins*		*Obama wins*		*Obama wins*	
	Obama	364	Obama	52.9 %	Obama	289	Obama	301
	McCain	174	McCain	45.6	McCain	248	McCain	237
					Others	1.5	Others	1
2004	*Bush wins*		*Bush wins*		*Bush wins*		*Bush wins*	
	Bush	286	Bush	50.7 %	Bush	280	Bush	317
	Kerry	252	Kerry	48.3	Kerry	258	Kerry	221
2000	*Bush wins*		*Gore wins*		*Winner unclear*		*Bush wins*	
	Bush	271	Bush	47.9 %	Bush	263	Bush	288
	Gore	267	Gore	48.4	Gore	262	Gore	250
			Others	3.7	Others	13		
1996	*Clinton wins*		*Clinton wins*		*Winner unclear*		*Clinton wins*	
	Clinton	379	Clinton	49.2 %	Clinton	267	Clinton	345
	Dole	159	Dole	40.7	Dole	224	Dole	193
	Perot	0	Perot	8.4	Perot/Others	47	Perot	0
1992	*Clinton wins*		*Clinton wins*		*Winner unclear*		*Clinton wins*	
	Clinton	370	Clinton	43.0 %	Clinton	236	Clinton	323
	Bush	168	Bush	37.4	Bush	197	Bush	215
	Perot	0	Perot	18.9	Perot	105	Perot	0
1976	*Carter wins*		*Carter wins*		*Carter wins*		*Carter wins*	
	Carter	297	Carter	50.1 %	Carter	273	Carter	270
	Ford	241	Ford	48.0	Ford	263	Ford	268
					Others	1.9	Others	2
1968	*Nixon wins*		*Nixon wins*		*Winner unclear*		*Nixon wins*	
	Nixon	302	Nixon	43.4 %	Nixon	235	Nixon	290
	Humphrey	191	Humphrey	42.7	Humphrey	225	Humphrey	190
	Wallace	45	Wallace	13.5	Wallace	78	Wallace	58
1960	*Kennedy wins*		*Kennedy wins*		*Kennedy wins*		*Nixon wins*	
	Kennedy	303	Kennedy	49.7 %	Kennedy	270	Kennedy	252
	Nixon	220	Nixon	49.6	Nixon	261	Nixon	280
	Others	14	Others	0.7	Others	6	Others	5

Notes: Results in the unit rule column assume that all electoral votes in a state are allocated to the candidate placing first in the state popular vote. These figures differ from the actual electoral vote in several years due to electors who violated their pledges in 1960, 1968, 1976, 2000, and 2004 (and, in 2008, due to Nebraska's use of the district plan alternative, which allocated one of the state's electoral votes to Obama). "Winner unclear" denotes scenarios in which no candidate receives a majority of electoral votes. The House of Representatives would then select the president from among the three candidates receiving the most electoral votes, with each state casting one vote.

still have won under the district plan, but the format would have crowned Mitt Romney victor in 2012 despite a four-point loss in the national popular vote.

Under the present electoral college system, there has been no time since 1876 when any splinter group has been able to make good on a threat to throw the election into the House of Representatives. Even in 1948, Harry Truman won an electoral college majority despite sizable threats from both a third (Henry Wallace, Progressive) and a fourth (Strom Thurmond, States Rights) party. Only once in the past century—in 2000—has the winner of the popular vote not become president. On the other hand, a direct election plan that required a 40 percent plurality might well have forced a runoff in 1968 and 1992. Proportional allocation would have caused deadlocks in three recent elections, and the district plan would have thrown the election to the popular vote loser three times since 1960, most recently in 2012. In view of their likely effects, it is curious that many reformers have supported such changes to the procedure of electing presidents.

Underlying all these arguments, of course, is the premise that most structural reforms "tend" to shift influences in certain ways. There may well be situations of social polarization that electoral system alternatives by themselves cannot paper over. But while we have argued that there is no better system than the current one, from the standpoint of the professed goals of most reformers, there is one minor change that would aid them. Under the present plan the actual electors who make up the electoral college are in fact free to vote for whomever they wish. These electors are usually party loyalists who are chosen in each state by party leaders. As an almost invariable rule, they vote for the winner in their state, but abuses are possible, and two within memory come to mind. First, the unpledged electors chosen by citizens in Mississippi and Alabama in 1960 decided for whom they would vote only well after the election, treating the preferences of citizens as advisory, not mandatory. This clearly thwarts popular control. Second, this liberty allowed the racial segregationist governor of Alabama, George Wallace, to hope that he could run for president, create an electoral deadlock, and then bargain with one of the other candidates after the election for policy concessions in exchange for the support of the Wallace electors. Wallace did follow through with a third-party run in 1968, but failed to win enough electoral votes to affect the result. An amendment making the casting of electoral votes automatic would dispel both these possibilities.

A final device deserves consideration, the creation of a private commission set up by the Twentieth Century Fund (now the Century Foundation) some years ago. It came up with a proposal for a National Bonus Plan, which would award 102 electoral votes en bloc (two for each state plus the District of Columbia) to the plurality winner of the nationwide popular vote. This plan would make it highly probable that no president could be elected who did not get the most votes. An additional feature is that candidates would be encouraged to get as many votes as they could, even in states where they were sure to lose, because these would add on to the candidate's national popular total.[49] The Bonus Plan would guard against a minority president, preserve the form and the spirit of the constitutional structure, and do all this without encouraging splinter parties.

We have argued that there is no serious reason to quarrel with the major features of the present system, since in our form of government "majority rule" does not operate in a vacuum but within a system of checks and balances. The president, for example, holds a veto power over laws enacted by Congress. If the veto is exercised, a two-thirds vote of each house is required to override it. Treaties must be ratified by two-thirds of the Senate, and amendments to the Constitution must be proposed by two-thirds of Congress or of the state legislatures and ratified by three-fourths of the states. Presidential appointments, in most important cases, must receive senatorial approval. The Supreme Court passes upon the constitutionality of legislative and executive actions. And of course there is impeachment, a political check on the presidency available to Congress. Involved in these political arrangements is the hope that the power of one branch of government will be counterbalanced by certain "checks" from another, the result being an approximate "balance" of forces. In our view, it is not necessarily a loss to have slightly different majorities preponderant in different institutions, but it is definitely a loss to have the same majority preponderant in both political branches while other majorities are frozen out. In the past the electoral college had its place within this system. Originally designed to check popular majorities from choosing presidents unwisely, the electoral college later on provided a check on the overrepresentation of rural states in the legislative branch by giving extra weight to the big-state constituencies of the president.

PARTY PLATFORMS AND PARTY DIFFERENCES

Having reviewed some of the major changes proposed by party reformers, let us return to consider their key argument. Parties, reformers claim, are insufficiently ideological. The voters are not being offered clear choices, and the parties, once in office, are not responsibly carrying out the promises made in their platforms. We argue that American parties do indeed differ—more so now than in the recent past—and that, much of the time, they respond to changes in voter sentiment. Recent surveys of partisan voters and studies of Congressional voting indicate the issue contrast between the parties is now stark. We believe that the solutions offered by reformers are unnecessary and would lead to consequences that even they might not desire.

Party platforms written by the presidential parties should be understood not only as ends in themselves but as means to obtaining and holding public office. It would be strange indeed if a party understood that policies such as Social Security and unemployment compensation were enormously popular and yet refused to incorporate them into its platform.[50] This would have to be a party of ideologues who cared everything about their own ideas and nothing about winning elections. Nor would it profit them much because they would not get elected and would never be in a position to do something about their ideas. Sooner or later, at least in a political system like the United States, ideologues have to make the choice between pleasing themselves and winning elections.

Even when the major political parties are in the hands of moderate leaders, there are clear differences between the doctrines espoused by the two parties, and these are reflected in party platforms. Now, the differences are abundantly clear. The case for the desirability of party reform used to rest on the assumption that American political parties were identical, that this was confusing and frustrating to American voters, and that it was undesirable to have a political system where parties do not disagree sharply. Now we have a chance to find out what happens during a period of relative party polarization.

Imagine for a moment that the two parties were in total and extreme disagreement on every major point of public policy, more so than they are in the United States today. One party would limit American military power to our borders, the other would intervene in every tense situation across the globe. One group would go all-out to improve productivity; the other would put environmental values first. One group would stop Social Security; the other would expand it drastically. One group would raise tariffs; the other would abolish them. Obviously one consequence of having clear-cut parties with strong policy positions would be that the costs of losing an election would skyrocket. If parties were forced to formulate coherent, full-dress programs and were forced to carry them out "responsibly," and in full, then people who did not favor these programs would have little recourse (until the next election). Clearly their confidence in a government whose policies were so little to their liking would suffer, and, indeed, they might feel strongly enough about preventing these policies from being enacted to do something drastic, like leaving the country or not complying with governmental regulations or, in an extreme case, seeking to change the political system by impeachment or by force.

The presidency of Republican Ronald Reagan may give pause to liberal reformers. Though Reagan's campaign rhetoric was too general to alarm voters, in many respects he played the part of the responsible-party president who proposed and attempted to carry out a wide-ranging program designed to modify, if not to undo completely, the efforts of his Democratic predecessors. There was no mistaking his thrust—less domestic government and more money for defense. Reagan tried and to some extent succeeded, at least early in his administration, in carrying out his campaign promises. If the results did not meet with universal approval, citizens cannot say they were not forewarned as to the direction the candidate would take in the event he was elected.

Or consider the performance in office of George W. Bush, who promised to change the climate of partisanship in Washington and to be "a uniter, not a divider" but who in fact wielded his razor-thin majority in Congress in energetic pursuit of right-wing initiatives. Bush was installed in office by a ruling of the Supreme Court that halted the counting of votes in Florida and awarded him the state's electoral votes. Later investigations indicated that had the votes all been counted, Bush would have won, very narrowly, in the electoral college, but owing to the popular votes in other states, Bush became president without winning the popular vote nationwide. The election overall yielded an outcome that was closely split between the major parties. Yet Bush, so long as his party controlled both houses of Congress, made few concessions to the middle ground expressed in the net result.

Barack Obama has followed Bush's example. On election night in 2008, he proclaimed: "We have never been just a collection . . . of red states and blue states. We are, and always will be, the United States of America." But like Bush, Obama governed by his party's agenda and not toward the political middle ground. Obama's presidency resulted in little bipartisan legislation and record levels of partisan polarization in congressional voting and public opinion concerning the performance of the chief executive. Obama, the second Bush, and Reagan have performed in accord with the "responsible government" model, effectively dividing Washington and the public while doing so.

If some citizens prefer more moderation and compromise, they should then consider whether they really want parties and candidates to carry out their programs. Is the argument for party reform that the nation needs more Ronald Reagans, George W. Bushes or Barack Obamas, whether of the right or left? Evidently, given favorable political conditions such as existed in the first two years of the Johnson, Reagan, and Obama presidencies, coherent presidential programs largely enacted by Congress are possible without constitutional reform or further changes, such as we have been discussing, in electoral machinery. It is necessary to have enthusiastic party activists, determined and skillful leaders, and public consent. These are not always available, but they sometimes are. When they are not, perhaps it is wise to make the achievement of large changes not too easy.[51]

CHAPTER 7

American Parties and Democracy

O VER A relatively short period of time (since the 1960s), a new sort of American political system has come into being. Among its features are high degrees of mass participation in formerly elite processes, such as the nomination of presidential candidates, the replacement of political parties with the news media as primary organizers of citizen action and legitimizers of public decisions, the rise in the influence of media-approved and media-sustained interest groups, and the decline of interest groups linked to party organizations. Certain sorts of decision making are easy in a system structured in this way: simple voting, for example, in which alternatives are few and clear-cut. However, complex, deliberative decision making—in which various alternatives are compared one after the other, contingencies are weighed and tested tentatively, second and third choices are probed for hidden consensuses, or special weight is given to intensity of likes and dislikes—is extremely difficult in such a system. Therefore, much influence flows into the hands of those who structure alternatives in the first place—self-starting candidates and the news media.

But the need for organizations to do the job of the parties continues. For presidential elections, we have observed the replacement of the convention with primary elections as the most significant part of the process and the rise of party activists who are more ideological and sometimes more extreme than the rest of the population.[1] Partisanship now correlates increasingly with ideological issue advocacy and polarization is prevalent among partisans in the public and in government.

Because the American political system has moved toward a role for political parties that stresses their activities as policy advocates, it seems to us important to give some attention to the implications of this trend for democratic government. Our argument makes two main points. The first is that it is necessary for parties of advocacy in a democracy to receive mandates on public policy from popular majorities of convinced believers in their programs, but that this condition is not met in America because of the ways in which electorates actually participate in elections and conceive of public policy.

Our second point is that in view of the actual disposition of attitudes toward public policy in the electorate as compared with party elites, the fact that we have entered into an era of parties of advocacy poses some significant and largely unaddressed problems for American democracy. This is because it is not the policy preferences of the bulk of the electorate that are being advocated. Moreover, the implementation of policy through government requires the sort of institutional support that parties can orchestrate only if they have some permanency and are not required to give birth to themselves anew every four years to nominate a candidate, and then wither away.

ELECTIONS AND PUBLIC POLICY

Uncoerced and competitive elections aid in making the political system open and responsive to a great variety of people and groups in the population. But elections do not unerringly transmit the policy preferences of electorates to leaders or confer mandates on leaders with regard to specific policies. The fortunes of the parties rise and fall over time without necessarily reflecting the underlying issue positions of the broader electorate, while the increasing frequency in recent decades of divided government—different parties held the presidency and at least one chamber of Congress for thirty-six of the forty-eight years between 1968 and 2016—makes the interpretation of electoral results as the product of voters' expressed ideological preferences even more difficult.

Consider the series of events between 1992 and 2016. Bill Clinton won the 1992 presidential election by a decisive margin but received only 43 percent of the popular vote. In 1994, Republicans won a landslide election that gave them control of both houses of Congress, yet both Clinton and the Republican congressional majority that opposed him were returned to power in 1996. In 2000, George W. Bush assumed the presidency even though his main opponent, Al Gore, won more popular votes. Bush's narrow popular and electoral vote victory in 2004 was followed by massive Republican losses in 2006 that delivered control of Congress back to the Democrats. In 2008, Democratic nominee Barack Obama won a popular vote majority by a relatively sizeable margin, though 46 percent of voters supported his Republican opponent, John McCain. Obama's successful campaign was built around the popular but vague theme of "change," which capitalized on popular dissatisfaction with the Bush presidency as much as support for any of Obama's own policy proposals. Obama's narrow 2012 reelection victory resulted in great part from his successful negative campaign against Mitt Romney and did not demonstrate widespread public backing for the president's agenda. Obama's Democratic House and Senate were replaced by a Republican House in 2010 and 2012 and a Republican Congress in 2014. Even in a landslide, winners can sensibly claim only a temporary, equivocal mandate. And in any case elections that are clear-cut are rare.

It is easy to be cynical and expect too little from elections or to be euphoric and expect too much from them. A cynical view would hold that the United States was ruled by a power elite—a small group outside the democratic process. Under these circumstances the ballot would be a sham and a delusion. What difference can it make how voting is carried on or who wins if the nation is actually governed by other means? In contrast, a euphoric view, holding that the United States is ruled as a mass democracy with equal control over decisions by all or most citizens, would enormously magnify the importance of the ballot. Through the act of casting a ballot, it could be argued, a majority of citizens would determine major national policies. What happens at the polls would not only decide who occupies public office, it also would determine the content of specific policy decisions. In a way, public office would then be a sham because the power of decision in important matters would be removed from the hands of public officials.

A third type of political system, in which numerous minorities compete for shares in policymaking within broad limits provided by free elections, has more complex implications. It suggests that balloting is important but that it often does not and sometimes should not determine individual policy decisions. The ballot guides and constrains public officials, who are free to act within fairly broad limits subject to their anticipations of the responses of the voters and—this is important in a separation of powers system—to the desires of other active participants.

It is evident that the American political system is of this third type. Public officials do make major policy decisions, but elections matter in that (with very rare exceptions) they determine which of the two main competing parties holds public office. In a competitive two-party situation such as exists in American presidential politics, the lively possibility of change provides an effective incentive for political leaders to remain in touch with followers.

Voters as a whole do not share the clarifying ideological preferences of today's partisan activists. The electorate in presidential elections does not transmit coherent policy preferences to elected officials with a high degree of reliability. There are few clear mandates in our political system because elections are fought on so many issues and in so many incompletely overlapping constituencies. Often the same voters elect candidates to Congress and to the presidency who disagree on public policies. Thus, even if mandates could be identified, they might well be impossible to enact because of inconsistency in the instructions issued to officials who must agree on legislation.[2]

Presidential elections are not single-issue referendums. The relationship between presidential elections and policies is a great deal subtler than the relations between the outcomes of referendums and the policies to which they pertain. In principle, the American political system is designed to work like this: Two teams of politicians, one in office, the other seeking office, both attempt to get enough votes to win elections. In order to win, they go to various groups of voters and, by offering to pursue policies favored by these groups, or by suggesting policies they might come to favor, hope to attract their votes. If there were only one office-seeking team, its incentive to respond to the policy preferences of groups in the population would diminish; if there were many such teams, all on a more or less equal footing, the chances that any one of them could achieve a sufficient number of backers to govern would diminish. Hence a two-party system might be regarded as a kind of compromise between the goals of responsiveness and effectiveness.

The proponents of a different theory, now much in vogue among ideologically driven partisan elites, would say that elections give the winning party a mandate to carry out the policies proposed during the campaign. Only in this way, they maintain, is popular rule through the ballot meaningful. A basic assumption in this argument is that the voters (or at least a majority of them) approve of all or most of the policies advocated by the victorious candidate. No doubt this is plausible, but not in the sense intended because, as we have seen, a vote for a presidential candidate is often an expression of a party habit: particular policy directions are therefore not necessarily meant by the vote. Indeed, citizens may be voting not for a candidate but rather against his or her opponent, or against a past president, saying, in effect, no more of this but not necessarily more of the other party's policies.

Most voters in the United States are not very ideologically oriented. They do not seek to create or to adopt systems of thought in which issues are related to one another in some highly consistent manner. Caring about more than one value, sometimes they prefer a strong government here and a weak one there, or want just not to decide at the present time. Thus voters can hardly be said to transmit strong preferences for a uniform stream of particular policies by electing candidates to public office.

Other basic objections may also be raised to the idea that our elections are designed to confer mandates on specific public policies. First, the issues debated in the campaign may not be the ones in which most voters are interested. Campaign issues may be ones that interest the candidates or that, for tactical reasons, they want to stress, or that interest segments of the press. There is no clear reason to believe that any particular issue is of great concern to voters just because it gets publicity. Time and again, voting studies have demonstrated that what appear to be the major issues of a campaign turn out not to be significant for most of the electorate. Some frequent issues on the stump are simply not the topics of public controversy. In recent elections, in which nobody was for welfare fraud or large budget deficits, everybody was for a strong economy and successful military operation, and nobody favored crime.[3] Other campaign issues, such as 2012's "war on women" argument aimed at the GOP by Democrats or 2004's Republican proposal for a Constitutional amendment preserving traditional marriage, are merely attempts to engage and energize particular segments of the electorate.

A second reason why voting for a candidate does not necessarily signify approval of that candidate's policies is that candidates pursue many policy interests at any one time with widely varying intensity, so that they may collect support from some voters on one issue and from other voters on another. It is possible for a candidate to get 100 percent of the votes and still have every voter opposed to most of the candidate's policies, as well as having every one of those policies opposed by most of the voters.

Assume that there are four major issues in a campaign. Make the further, quite reasonable, assumption that the voting population is distributed in such a way that people who care intensely about one major issue support the victorious candidate for that reason alone, although they differ with that candidate mildly on the other three issues. Thus, voters who are deeply concerned about the problem of defense against terrorism may vote for candidate Jones, who prefers a less militaristic solution, rather than Smith, who espouses a doctrine that requires an aggressive response. This particular group of voters disagrees with Jones's strong support for farm price supports, on the overall size of government, and on national health insurance, but they do not feel strongly about any of these matters. Another group, meanwhile, believes that farmers, the noble yeomanry, are the backbone of the nation, and that if they are prosperous and strong, everything else will turn out all right. So they vote for Jones, too, although they prefer an ambitious anti-terrorism policy and disagree with Jones's other policies. And so on for other groups of voters. Lucky Jones. He ends up with all the votes. Yet each of his policies is preferred by less than a majority of the electorate. Since this is possible in any political system where many issues are debated or otherwise up for grabs at election time, it is hard to argue that our presidential elections give unequivocal mandates on specific policies to the candidates who win.[4]

People vote for many reasons not directly connected with issues. They may vote on the basis of party loyalty alone. Party habits may be accompanied by a general feeling that Democrats are better for the common citizen or that Republicans will keep us safe, or vice versa—feelings too diffuse to tell us much about specific issues. Some people vote on the basis of a candidate's personality, or "image." Others follow a friend's recommendation. Still others may be thinking about policy issues but may be all wrong in their perception of where the candidates stand. It is ordinarily impossible to distinguish the votes of these people from those who know, care, and differentiate accurately among the candidates on the basis of issues. We do know, however, that strongly issue-oriented persons are usually in a minority, while those who cast their ballots with other things in mind are generally more numerous. Voters, if asked, may say they want to move government in a more liberal or conservative direction, but desires of this sort are so general in character, they can be read as approving of nearly anything.

Even if there is good reason to believe that a majority of voters do approve of several policies supported by the victorious candidate, the mandate may be difficult or impossible to carry out. Consider the recent difficulties of achieving and pursuing a presidential mandate. George W. Bush, the popular vote loser in 2000, could hardly claim a mandate then, nor did his narrow victory in 2004 indicate popular approval for his major domestic policy initiative of 2005, the creation of private Social Security accounts, which failed even to receive a vote in Congress that year. Public disapproval of Bush's management of the Iraq War and the federal response to Hurricane Katrina helped Democrats win back Congress in 2006 and take the presidency while increasing their legislative majorities in 2008. Barack Obama encountered similar reversals after his first two years in office that featured Democratic control of national government and ambitious new laws for economic stimulus and health care reform. Rejection of an incumbent administration does not necessarily entail a thorough mandate for the alternative policies of the successor, as Reagan in 1980 and Clinton in 1992 found out, and as Obama discovered as well. All three entered office in the midst of economic problems that ousted the party of their predecessor from the White House; their elections represented an expression of voters' general dissatisfaction with the performance of the previous regime rather than widespread enthusiastic endorsement of their own initiatives.

Leaving aside all the difficulties about the content of a mandate, there is no accepted definition of what size electoral victory gives a president special popular sanction to pursue any particular policy. Would a 60 percent victory be sufficient? What about 51 percent or 52 percent, or cases such as 1992, 1996, and 2000 in which the winner receives less than half the votes cast? And is it right to ignore the multitudes who do not vote and whose preferences are not directly registered? We might ignore the nonvoters for the purpose of this analysis if we were sure they were divided in their preferences between candidates in nearly the same proportions as those who do vote. There is now reason to believe that this is, more or less, true.[5] But we cannot be sure this is always the case. In practice, this problem is easily solved. Whoever wins the presidential election under our current rules—which means winning in the electoral college, not necessarily the popular vote—is allowed to pursue whatever policies he or she pleases, within the very important constraints imposed by the checks and balances of the rest of the policy-making institutions (notably, Congress) in the political system. This, in the end, is all that a "mandate" is in American politics.

Opinion polls and focus groups may help the politician gauge policy preferences, but there are always lingering doubts as to their reliability. It is not certain in any event that they tell the political leader what that leader needs to know. People who really have no opinion but who care only a little may be counted equally with those who are intensely concerned. Many people giving opinions may have no intention of voting for some of the politicians who heed them, no matter what. The result may be that a politician will get no visible support from a majority that agrees with him or her, but instead will get complaints from an intense minority that disagrees. The people who agree with the politician may not vote, while those who differ may attempt retribution at the ballot box—as single-issue interest groups are reported to do. Those voters who are pleased may be the ones who would have voted for the public official in any case. Unless the poll is carefully done, it may leave out important groups of voters, overrepresent some, underrepresent others, and otherwise give a misleading impression. The correlations that are made showing that support comes disproportionately from certain economic or social groups do not explain why some people, often a substantial minority, possessing these self-same characteristics vote the opposite way.

Let us turn the question around for a moment. Suppose a candidate loses an election. What does this signify about the policies he or she should have espoused? If one or two key issues were widely debated and universally understood, the election might tell the candidate a great deal. But this is seldom the case. More likely, there were many issues, and it was difficult to separate out those issues that did from those that did not garner support for the opponent. Perhaps the election was decided on the basis of personal images or some events in the economic cycle or a military engagement—points that were not debated in the campaign and that may not have been within anyone's control. Losing candidates may always feel that if they continue to educate the public to favor the policies they prefer, they will eventually win. Should a candidate lose a series of elections, however, the party would undoubtedly try to change something—policies, candidates, organization, maybe all three—in an effort to improve its fortunes.

How do winning candidates appraise an election? What does this event tell officeholders and their parties about the policies they should pursue when in office? Some policy positions undoubtedly were rather vague, and specific applications of them may turn out quite differently from what the campaign promised. Others may founder on the rock of practicality; they sounded fine, but they simply cannot be carried out. Conditions change and policies that seemed to make sense a few months before turn out to be irrelevant. Democrats may want to spend more on domestic programs and Republicans to cut taxes, but huge deficits endanger both policies. As the time for putting policies into practice draws near, the new officeholders may discover that the policies generate a lot more opposition than when they were merely campaign oratory. And those policies that are pursued to the end may have to be compromised considerably in order to get the support of other participants in the policy-making process. Nevertheless, if they have even a minimal policy orientation, newly elected candidates can try to carry out a few of their campaign proposals, seeking to maintain a general direction consonant with the approach that may—they cannot be entirely certain—have contributed to their election.

The practical impossibility in our political system of ascertaining mandates in some objective sense is one important reason why it is so difficult for parties successfully to fulfill their function as policy advocates. It is, however, entirely possible for parties claiming a mandate to adopt policies that have little or no support in the general population. It is to the exploration of this possibility that we now turn.

PARTIES OF ADVOCACY VERSUS
PARTIES OF INTERMEDIATION

The presidential election process in the United States has undergone a major transformation. As late as 1952, a president of the United States could, and with good reason, dismiss a prospective victory in the New Hampshire primary by the now little-remembered Senator Estes Kefauver of Tennessee as "eye-wash." Now primaries select most convention delegates, and combined with media spin, determine the outcome of the nomination process.[6]

Behind the shift in the role of primary elections lie shifts in the roles of political activists and changes in the powers and the significance of the news media. We believe that these changes and other changes that we have discussed—the shift to the heavy regulation of political money not only in the general election but also in primary elections, the increase in non-candidate-controlled spending in the general election, the vast increase in the number of primaries, and the new rules for converting votes into delegates—add up to a fundamental redefinition of the place of the national political parties in our public life. One way to characterize this redefinition is to say that the conception of parties as agents of consensus government has begun to fade. If we are right, then more and more we can expect candidates and party leaders to raise divisive issues and to emphasize party differences rather than paper them over, in an effort to mobilize adherents to their side of the argument rather than appeal to the masses of people in the uncommitted middle. This was called gratifying the "base" in the George W. Bush administration, and the Obama presidency has followed a similar course.

Ideological activists are now favored by the rules of the game. In the early days of pre-primary activity, the people who become most active are apt to be those who have the most spare time, the most ideological commitment, and the most enthusiasm for one candidate above all others. Since the rules are now written to encourage activity at an earlier and earlier date, in order to raise campaign funds for the primaries and as a necessary condition for being taken seriously by the news media, it follows that activists will have more to say about the eventual outcome of the nomination process.[7] Party officials in the various states, in contrast, who in decades past preferred to wait until they could see a majority forming, under the new rules of the game must ally themselves with one or another active candidate early in the process or forfeit their influence. This applies even to the Democratic high officeholders who get automatic seats at the convention and make up 10 to 20 percent of the total number of delegates. By the time their peculiar skills and interests in majority building might be needed—for instance, at a convention—it is too late for them to steer the process: most of the delegate positions will have been filled by the enthusiasts for particular candidates who won in the various primaries and caucuses.

We can therefore ask how the emerging structure of presidential election politics helps and hinders political parties in performing the tasks customarily allotted to them in the complex scheme of American democracy. In essence, we believe that the parties have been greatly strengthened in their capacities to provide advocacy and weakened in their abilities to provide intermediation or later to facilitate implementation in the political system—that is, governing. Consensus among party activists is now achieved at the expense of increasing dissension within government. Thus party platforms become ever more internally consistent, while government finds it increasingly difficult to relate revenues to expenditures. Budget deficits grew steadily worse during the George W. Bush and early Obama presidencies, as partisan advocacy of tax cuts (for Bush) or spending programs (for Obama) triumphed over the more difficult governance problem of budget management.

Advocacy is strengthened because the rules of the game offer incentives to party leaders and candidates who are able to attract personal followings on an ideological basis. What is lost, in our view, is a capacity to deliberate, weigh competing demands, and compromise so that a variety of differing interests each gain a little. This loss would not be so great if the promise of policy government—to select efficacious programs and implement them successfully—were likely to be fulfilled in performance. But, on the record so far, this is doubly doubtful.

It is doubtful because for many of the problems that form the basis of political campaign discussion—economic growth, crime, poverty, terrorism—there are no known, sure-fire solutions. And second, even if we knew what to do about more of our problems, it is improbable, given the ways in which various forces in our society and responsibilities in our constitution are arranged, that presidents alone could deliver on their promises.

This last dilemma is especially poignant for candidates who speak to a very wide spectrum of issues. Were they elected, then program implementation would require support in Congress, the bureaucracies, state and city governments, and elsewhere. The ability of such policy-oriented candidates to gain the agreement of others depends on many factors that typically are neither discussed nor understood in election campaigns. Yet gaining the agreement of others is part of making policies work. Policy government might enhance the legitimacy of government if it increased the effectiveness of programs, but the insensitivity of its advocates to the needs for consensus makes that unlikely. Under these circumstances, neither policy nor consensus, advocacy nor intermediation, are likely to be served.

Two changes account for the decline in the vital function of intermediation by parties. First, a candidate for the presidency now need no longer build up a mosaic of alliances with interest groups and party leaders. Instead, through the miracle of the mass media (especially television), through mass mailings and Internet messages to appeal for money, presidential candidates can reach every home and touch every heart and claim the allegiance of followers based on ideological or stylistic affinity rather than concrete bargains. The 2008 Obama campaign, touting an attractive "hope and change" pitch, is the preeminent example of successful "affinity politics." This is the first sense in which parties have been diminished in their capacity to mediate between the desires of ordinary citizens and the policies of government: candidates no longer need parties to reach voters.

In a second sense, parties are losing the capacity to mediate between leaders and followers because the formal properties of plebiscitary decision making simply by voting, such as occurs in primary elections, leave little room for a bargaining process to occur. Contingent choices are impossible to express in primary elections straightforwardly through the ballot. Thus a candidate who is acceptable to a sizable majority but is the first choice of only a few systematically loses out under the current primary-driven rules to candidates who might be unacceptable to most voters but secure in their control over a middle-sized fraction (20 to 30 percent, depending on how many candidates play the game) of first-choice votes.

In this sense we can say that "participatory" democracy, as the American party system has begun to practice it, undermines "deliberative" democracy. As more and different people have won the right to participate in the nomination process by voting in primaries, the kinds of communications they have been able to send to one another have not correspondingly been enriched. Participants can vote, but they cannot bargain. They can make and listen to speeches, but they cannot discuss or deliberate.

We have no way of knowing whether the democratic paradox of participation swallowing up deliberation has had the net effect of turning citizens away from political parties. It is in any event true that by a variety of measures—nonvoting, propensity of voters to decline to identify with a political party, direct expressions of disapproval of parties—political parties, like so many other institutions of American society, suffered substantial losses in public confidence after the 1960s. In our view, the most promising way for parties to regain this confidence would be to avoid factional candidates and not only to nominate and elect good candidates but also to help them govern.

What is objectionable about policy government? What could be wrong with so intuitively attractive an idea? Governments must make policies. Surely candidates should be judged, in part at least, on their policy preferences, as well as on indications of their ability to perform when in office. Has there not been, in the recent past, too much obfuscation of issues and too little candor in speaking one's mind? Obviously our society needs more, rather than less, discussion of issues, and greater, rather than less, clarification of alternatives. The problem is that the premises on which policy government is based are false. Most people do not want parties that make extreme appeals by taking issue positions far from the desires of the bulk of the citizenry.[8] Perhaps people feel safer if their parties give them a choice, but they do not want losing to be a catastrophe. This may be why they see no great difficulty in voting for a president of one party and a Congress of another.[9]

It is one thing to say that policy options have been insufficiently articulated and quite another to create conflict and develop disagreements where these did not exist before. Political activists in the United States are more ideological and polarized than at any time since studies were first conducted in the 1930s, and possibly since the 1890s or even the Civil War. Should ordinary citizens be compelled to choose from policy alternatives that appeal to these activists, or are they entitled to select from a menu closer to their tastes? The question is not whether there will be issues, for inevitably there must be, but who will set the agenda for discussion and whether this agenda will primarily reflect differences in the general population or those among elites. Thus one objection to a party of advocacy is that it imposes on the great majority of people preferences to which the majority is largely indifferent or opposed.

The rationale behind parties of advocacy leads to plebiscitary democracy. If it is not only desirable for all citizens to vote in general elections but also for them to choose candidates through preelection primaries, it must be even more desirable for them to select governmental policies directly through referendums. Instead of rule by special interests or cliques of congressmen, the public's interest would supposedly be expressed by the public.

Experience with initiatives and referendums in California and Oregon, where they are thickest on the ground, and elsewhere, however, suggests that this is not quite how things work in practice. Without measures for limiting the number of referendums voters may face at a given election, citizens are swamped by the necessity of voting on dozens of items. Elites, not the people, determine the selection and wording of referendums. And how they are worded is of course extremely important. Money—to arrange for the signatures on petitions to get referendums on the ballot and to sponsor television advertising campaigns for the purposes of swaying voters—becomes more meaningful than ever. The public is faced with a bewildering array of proposals, all sponsored by special interests seeking a way around the state legislature. To learn what is involved in a single seemingly innocuous proposal takes hours of study. To understand twenty or more per election is unduly onerous. Are citizens better off guessing or following the advice of the local newspaper instead of trying to choose a legislator or a party to represent their interests?[10]

To take a famous case, were citizens or legislators better qualified to understand that Proposition 13 in California (passed in 1978) would not only keep property taxes down, which it was advertised to do, but would also, by depriving localities of resources, centralize control at the state level over many areas of public policy, which no one wanted? Were citizens of California, where referendums abound, wise to vote at widely separated intervals for so many mandatory expenditures as to make it difficult for the state legislature to mobilize resources to meet new needs?[11]

A plebiscitary democracy, stressing the direct connection between candidates and voters, could not abide the electoral college. Only direct democracy, mass voting for candidates, would do. Abolishing the electoral college, however, as we have seen, would further decrease the need for forming diverse coalitions. Both the agents of consensus, mediating parties, and the fact of consensus, with political leaders who nurture it, would decline.

After a few decades of severe internal difficulty, when confidence in virtually all national institutions has suffered repeated blows, the need for consensus-building parties seems more clear than ever. Ideological parties might be desirable for a people homogeneous in all ways except the economic; but can a very large multiracial, multiethnic, multireligious, multiregional, multiclass nation such as the United States sustain itself when its main agents of political action—the parties—strive to exclude rather than include, to sharpen rather than dull the edge of controversy?

It is even doubtful that the rise of parties of advocacy leads to a more principled politics. If principles are precepts that must not be violated, when contrary principles are firmly embedded in the programs of opposing parties, one person's principles necessarily become another's fighting words. A few principles, such as those enshrined in the Bill of Rights, may be helpful—indeed essential—in establishing boundaries beyond which governmental action may not go. But too many principles thwart the cooperative government required by the design of the Constitution. As being a Democrat increasingly requires adherence to litmus-tested liberal positions and a Republican to litmus-tested conservative positions, cross-cutting cleavages—organizing people who support one another on some issues while opposing on others—are bound to diminish. With officeholders opposing each other on more issues, and with more issues defined as moral issues, political passions are liable to rise. And so, we suppose, will negative campaigning and popular disapproval of government and of politicians.

Compromise, of course, can also be a curse. If everything were bargainable, including basic liberties, no one would feel safe, and, indeed, no one would be. Similarly, if candidates cared everything about winning and nothing about how they win, if they were not restrained by internal norms or enforceable external expectations, elections would become outrages.

Parties without policies would be empty; parties fixated on only a narrow band of policies are dangerous. Without the desire to win elections, not at any cost but as a leading motive, there is no reason for politicians to pay attention to the people who vote. Winning requires a widespread appeal. Thus the desire to win can lead to moderation, to appeals to diverse groups in the electorate, and to efforts to bring many varied interests together. This is why we prefer parties of intermediation to parties of advocacy. Parties of advocacy do not sustain themselves well in government. They fail to assist political leaders in mobilizing consent for the policies they adopt, and this widens the gap between campaign promises and the performance of government. This, we believe, was the fate of the Republican Party during George W. Bush's time in the White House and the Democratic Party during Barack Obama's presidency.

Because so many of the rules of presidential election politics are changing, we cannot say with a high degree of assurance how parties, candidates, and voters will adapt to the new incentives and disabilities that are continuously enacted into law. We are confident only in asserting that the adaptations they make will be of enormous consequence in determining the ultimate capacity of the American political system to sustain the fascinating and noble experiment in self-government begun on this continent more than two hundred years ago.

Appendixes

Vote by Groups in Presidential Elections, 1976–2012

	1976			1980		
	Carter (D)	Ford (R)	McCarthy (I)	Carter (D)	Reagan (R)	Anderson (I)
National	50 %	48 %	1 %	41 %	51 %	7 %
Sex						
Men	53	45	1	38	53	7
Women	48	51	0	44	49	6
Race						
White	46	52	1	36	56	7
Nonwhite	85	15	0	86	10	2
Education						
Grade school	58	41	1	54	42	3
High school	54	46	0	43	51	5
College	42	55	2	35	53	10
Occupation						
Professional and business	42	56	1	33	55	10
White collar	50	48	2	40	51	9
Manual labor	58	41	1	48	48	5
Labor union household	63	36	1	50	43	5
Age						
Under 30 years	53	45	1	47	41	11
30 to 49 years	48	49	2	38	52	8
50 years and older	52	48	0	41	54	4
Religion						
Protestant	46	53	0	39	54	6
Catholic	57	42	1	46	47	6
Party Identification						
Democratic	82	18	0	69	26	4
Republican	9	91	0	8	86	5
Independent	38	57	4	29	55	14
Region						
East	51	47	1	43	47	9
Midwest	48	50	1	41	51	7
South	54	45	0	44	52	3
West	46	51	1	35	54	9

	1984		1988	
	Mondale (D)	Reagan (R)	Dukakis (D)	Bush (R)
National	40 %	59 %	45 %	53 %
Sex				
Men	37	62	41	57
Women	44	56	49	50
Race				
White	35	64	40	59
Black	90	9	86	12
Latino	62	37	69	30
Education				
Not high school graduate	50	50	56	43
High school graduate only	39	60	49	50
Some college	38	61	42	57
College graduate	41	58	37	62
Postgraduate	–	–	48	50
Income				
Under $15,000	55	45	62	37
$15,000–$29,999	42	57	50	49
$30,000–$49,999	40	59	43	56
$50,000 and over	30	69	37	62
Labor union household	53	46	57	42
Age				
Under 30 years	40	59	47	52
30 to 44 years	42	57	45	54
45 to 59 years	40	60	42	57
60 years and over	39	60	49	50
Religion				
White Protestant	27	72	33	66
Catholic	45	54	47	52
Jewish	67	31	64	35
Marital status				
Married	38	62	42	57
Unmarried	47	52	53	46
Party Identification				
Democratic	74	25	82	17
Republican	7	92	8	91
Independent	36	63	43	55
Region				
East	47	53	49	50
Midwest	41	58	47	52
South	36	64	41	58
West	38	61	46	52

	1992			1996		
	Clinton (D)	Bush (R)	Perot (I)	Clinton (D)	Dole (R)	Perot (I)
National	43 %	38 %	19 %	49 %	41 %	8 %
Sex						
Men	41	38	21	43	44	10
Women	45	37	17	54	38	7
Race						
White	39	40	20	43	46	9
Black	83	10	7	84	12	4
Latino	61	25	14	72	21	8
Education						
Not high school graduate	54	28	18	59	28	11
High school graduate only	43	36	21	51	35	13
Some college	41	37	21	48	40	10
College graduate	39	41	20	44	46	8
Postgraduate	50	36	14	52	40	5
Income						
Under $15,000	58	23	19	59	28	11
$15,000–$29,999	45	35	20	53	36	9
$30,000–$49,999	41	38	21	48	40	10
$50,000 and over	39	44	17	44	48	7
Labor union household	55	24	21	59	30	9
Age						
Under 30 years	43	34	22	53	34	10
30 to 44 years	41	38	21	48	41	9
45 to 59 years	41	40	19	49	41	9
60 years and over	50	38	12	48	44	7
Religion						
White Protestant	33	47	21	36	53	10
Catholic	44	35	20	53	37	9
Jewish	80	11	9	78	16	3
Marital status						
Married	40	41	20	44	46	9
Unmarried	51	30	19	57	31	9
Party Identification						
Democratic	77	10	13	84	10	5
Republican	10	73	17	13	80	6
Independent	38	32	30	43	35	17
Region						
East	47	35	18	55	34	9
Midwest	42	37	21	48	41	10
South	41	43	16	46	46	7
West	43	34	22	48	40	8

	2000			2004	
	Gore (D)	Bush (R)	Nader (G)	Kerry (D)	Bush (R)
National	48 %	48 %	2 %	48 %	51 %
Sex					
Men	42	53	3	44	55
Women	54	43	2	51	48
Race					
White	42	54	3	41	58
Black	90	8	1	88	11
Latino	67	31	2	56	43
Education					
Not high school graduate	59	39	1	50	49
High school graduate only	48	49	1	47	52
Some college	45	51	3	46	54
College graduate	45	51	3	46	52
Postgraduate	52	44	3	55	44
Income					
Under $15,000	57	37	4	63	36
$15,000–$29,999	54	41	3	57	42
$30,000–$49,999	49	48	2	50	49
$50,000 and over	45	52	2	43	56
Labor union household	59	37	3	59	40
Age					
Under 30 years	48	46	5	54	45
30 to 44 years	48	49	2	46	53
45 to 59 years	48	49	2	48	51
60 years and over	51	47	2	46	54
Religion					
White Protestant	34	63	2	32	67
Catholic	49	47	2	47	52
Jewish	79	19	1	74	25
Marital status					
Married	44	53	2	42	57
Unmarried	57	38	4	58	40
Party Identification					
Democratic	86	11	2	89	11
Republican	8	91	1	49	48
Independent	45	47	6	6	93
Region					
East	56	39	3	56	43
Midwest	48	49	2	48	51
South	43	55	1	42	58
West	48	46	4	50	49

Sources: Data for 1952–1980 from the final pre-election Gallup survey, as summarized in *Gallup Poll Monthly* 374 (November 1996), pp. 17–20. Data for 1984–2004 from *New York Times* exit polls, as summarized in Marjorie Connelly, "How Americans Voted: A Political Portrait," *New York Times*, November 7, 2004, sec. 4, p. 4; "Exit Polls," MSNBC, available at http://www.msnbc.msn.com/id/5297138/.

	2008	
	Obama (D)	McCain (R)
National	53 %	46 %
Sex		
Men	49	48
Women	56	43
Race		
White	43	55
Black	95	4
Latino	67	31
Education		
No high school	63	35
High school graduate only	52	46
Some college	51	47
College graduate	50	48
Postgraduate	58	40
Income		
Under $15,000	73	25
$15,000–$30,000	60	37
$30,000–$50,000	55	43
$50,000 and over	49	49
Labor union household	59	39
Age		
Under 30 years	66	32
30 to 44 years	52	46
45 to 64 years	50	49
65 years and over	45	53
Religion		
White Protestant	34	65
Catholic	54	45
Jewish	78	21
Marital status		
Married	47	52
Unmarried	65	33
Party Identification		
Democratic	89	10
Republican	9	90
Independent	52	44
Region		
East	59	40
Midwest	54	44
South	45	54
West	57	40

Source: CNN.com. "Election Center 2008." http://www.cnn.com/ELECTION/2008/results/polls/#USP00p1.

	2012	
	Obama (D)	**Romney (R)**
National	51 %	47 %
Sex		
Men	45	55
Women	55	44
Race		
White	39	59
Black	93	6
Latino	71	27
Education		
No high school	64	35
High school graduate only	51	48
Some college	48	49
College graduate	47	51
Postgraduate	55	42
Income		
Under $50,000	73	25
$50,000–$100,000	60	37
$100,000 and over	44	54
Labor union household	58	40
Age		
Under 30 years	60	37
30 to 44 years	54	45
45 to 64 years	47	51
65 years and over	44	56
Population of Area		
Large city	69	29
Small city	58	21
Suburbs	48	50
Small town	42	56
Rural	37	61
Religion		
White Protestant	30	69
Catholic	50	48
Jewish	69	30
Marital status		
Married	42	56
Unmarried	62	35
Party Identification		
Democratic	92	8
Republican	7	93
Independent	45	50

Source: CNN.com. "Election Center 2012." http://www.cnn.com/election/2012/results/race/president.

Voter Turnout in Presidential Elections, by Population Characteristics, 1976–2012

1976	Persons of Voting Age (in thousands)	Persons Reporting They Voted (in thousands)	Percent Reporting They Voted	Percent Reporting They Did Not Vote
Total	146,548	86,698	59.2	40.8
Men	68,957	41,079	59.6	40.4
Women	77,591	45,620	58.8	41.2
White	129,316	78,808	60.9	39.1
Nonwhite	17,232	7,890	45.8	54.2
18–24 years old	26,953	11,367	42.2	57.8
25–34 years old	31,533	17,472	55.4	44.6
35–44 years old	22,769	14,411	63.3	36.7
45–64 years old	43,293	29,763	68.7	31.3
65 years and older	22,001	13,685	62.2	37.8
Metropolitan	99,590	58,943	59.2	40.8
Nonmetropolitan	46,959	27,755	59.1	40.9
Non-South	99,403	60,829	61.2	38.8
South	47,145	25,869	54.9	45.1
Under 9 years of school	24,947	11,010	44.1	55.9
9–11 years of school	22,216	10,481	47.2	52.8
12 years	55,665	33,058	59.4	40.6
More than 12 years	43,719	32,150	73.5	26.5
Employed	86,034	53,314	62.0	38.0
Unemployed	6,430	2,812	43.7	56.3
Not in labor force	54,085	30,573	56.5	43.5

Source: U.S. Bureau of the Census, *Current Population Reports*, Series P-20, no. 322 (March 1978).
Note: Voting age population defined as civilian noninstitutional population (including noncitizens) aged eighteen years and over.

1980

	Persons of Voting Age (in thousands)	Persons Reporting They Voted (in thousands)	Percent Reporting They Voted	Percent Reporting They Did Not Vote
Total	157,085	93,066	59.2	40.8
Men	74,082	43,753	59.1	40.9
Women	83,003	49,312	59.4	40.6
White	137,676	83,855	60.9	39.1
Nonwhite	19,409	9,211	47.5	52.5
18–24 years old	28,138	11,225	39.9	60.1
25–34 years old	35,733	19,498	54.6	45.4
35–44 years old	25,552	16,460	64.4	35.6
45–64 years old	43,569	30,205	69.3	30.7
65 years and older	24,094	15,677	65.1	34.9
Metropolitan	106,627	62,703	58.8	41.2
Nonmetropolitan	50,459	30,363	60.2	39.8
Non-South	106,524	64,963	61.0	39.0
South	50,561	28,103	55.6	44.4
Under 9 years of school	22,656	9,643	42.6	57.4
9–11 years of school	22,477	10,246	45.6	54.4
12 years	61,165	35,998	58.9	41.1
More than 12 years	50,787	37,179	73.2	26.8
Employed	95,041	58,778	61.8	38.2
Unemployed	6,893	2,838	41.2	58.8
Not in labor force	55,151	31,449	57.0	43.0

Source: U.S. Bureau of the Census, *Current Population Reports*, Series P-20, no. 370 (April 1982).
Note: Voting age population defined as civilian noninstitutional population (including noncitizens) aged eighteen years and over.

1984

	Persons of Voting Age (in thousands)	Persons Reporting They Voted (in thousands)	Percent Reporting They Voted	Percent Reporting They Did Not Vote
Total	169,963	101,878	59.9	40.1
Men	80,327	47,354	59.0	41.0
Women	89,636	54,524	60.8	39.2
White	146,761	90,152	61.4	38.6
Nonwhite	23,202	11,726	50.5	49.5
18–24 years old	27,976	11,407	40.8	59.2
25–34 years old	40,292	21,978	54.5	45.5
35–44 years old	30,731	19,514	63.5	36.5
45–64 years old	44,307	30,924	69.8	30.2
65 years and older	26,658	18,055	67.7	32.3
Metropolitan	NA	NA	NA	NA
Nonmetropolitan	NA	NA	NA	NA
Non-South	112,376	69,183	61.6	38.4
South	57,587	32,695	56.8	43.2
Under 9 years of school	20,580	8,833	42.9	57.1
9–11 years of school	22,068	9,798	44.4	55.6
12 years	67,807	39,773	58.7	41.3
More than 12 years	59,508	43,473	73.1	26.9
Employed	104,173	64,213	61.6	38.4
Unemployed	7,389	3,247	44.0	56.0
Not in labor force	58,401	34,418	58.9	41.1

Source: U.S. Bureau of the Census, *Current Population Reports*, Series P-20, no. 405 (March 1986).
Note: Voting age population defined as civilian noninstitutional population (including noncitizens) aged eighteen years and over.

1988

	Persons of Voting Age (in thousands)	Persons Reporting They Voted (in thousands)	Percent Reporting They Voted	Percent Reporting They Did Not Vote
Total	178,098	102,224	57.4	42.6
Men	84,531	47,704	56.4	43.6
Women	93,568	54,519	58.3	41.7
White	152,848	90,357	59.1	40.9
Nonwhite	25,250	11,867	47.0	53.0
18–24 years old	25,569	9,254	36.2	63.8
25–34 years old	42,677	20,468	48.0	52.0
35–44 years old	35,186	21,550	61.3	38.7
45–64 years old	45,862	31,134	67.9	32.1
65 years and older	28,804	19,818	68.8	31.2
Metropolitan	139,134	79,505	57.1	42.9
Nonmetropolitan	38,964	22,719	58.3	41.7
Non-South	117,373	69,130	58.9	41.1
South	60,725	33,094	54.5	45.5
Under 9 years of school	19,145	7,025	36.7	63.3
9–11 years of school	21,052	8,698	41.3	58.7
12 years	70,033	38,328	54.7	45.3
More than 12 years	67,878	48,173	71.0	29.0
Employed	113,836	66,510	58.4	41.6
Unemployed	5,809	2,243	38.6	61.4
Not in labor force	58,453	33,471	57.3	42.7

Source: U.S. Bureau of the Census, *Current Population Reports*, Series P-20, no. 440 (October 1989)
Note: Voting age population defined as civilian noninstitutional population (including noncitizens) aged eighteen years and over.

1992

	Persons of Voting Age (in thousands)	Persons Reporting They Voted (in thousands)	Percent Reporting They Voted	Percent Reporting They Did Not Vote
Total	185,684	113,866	61.3	38.7
Men	88,557	53,312	60.2	39.8
Women	97,126	60,554	62.3	37.7
White	157,837	100,405	63.6	36.4
Nonwhite	27,847	13,461	48.3	51.7
18–24 years old	24,371	10,442	42.8	57.2
25–34 years old	41,603	22,120	53.2	46.8
35–44 years old	39,716	25,269	63.6	36.4
45–64 years old	49,147	34,399	70.0	30.0
65 years and older	30,846	21,637	70.1	29.9
Metropolitan	144,593	88,222	61.0	39.0
Nonmetropolitan	41,091	25,644	62.4	37.6
Non-South	122,025	76,276	62.5	37.5
South	63,659	37,590	59.0	41.0
Under 9 years of school	15,391	5,406	35.1	64.9
9–11 years of school	20,970	8,638	41.2	58.8
12 years	65,281	37,517	57.5	42.5
More than 12 years:				
1 to 3 years of college	46,691	32,069	68.7	31.3
4 or more years of college	37,351	30,236	81.0	19.0
Employed	116,290	74,138	63.8	36.2
Unemployed	8,263	3,820	46.2	53.8
Not in labor force	61,131	35,908	58.7	41.3

Source: U.S. Bureau of the Census, *Current Population Reports*, Series P-20, no. 466 (April 1993).
Note: Voting age population defined as civilian noninstitutional population (including noncitizens) aged eighteen years and over.

1996

	Persons of Voting Age (in thousands)	Persons Reporting They Voted (in thousands)	Percent Reporting They Voted	Percent Reporting They Did Not Vote
Total	193,651	105,017	54.2	45.8
Men	92,632	48,909	52.8	47.2
Women	101,020	56,108	55.5	44.5
White	162,779	91,208	56.0	44.0
Nonwhite	30,872	13,809	44.7	55.3
18–24 years old	24,650	7,996	32.4	67.6
25–34 years old	40,066	17,265	43.1	56.9
35–44 years old	43,327	23,785	54.9	45.1
45–64 years old	53,721	34,615	64.4	35.6
65 years and older	31,888	21,356	67.0	33.0
Metropolitan	155,735	83,984	53.9	46.1
Nonmetropolitan	37,916	21,033	55.5	44.5
Non-South	125,571	69,467	55.3	44.7
South	68,080	35,550	52.2	47.8
Under 9 years of school	13,986	4,188	29.9	70.1
9–11 years of school	21,002	7,099	33.8	66.2
12 years	65,208	32,019	49.1	50.9
More than 12 years:				
1 to 3 years of college	50,939	30,835	60.5	39.5
4 or more years of college	42,517	30,877	72.6	27.4
Employed	125,634	69,300	55.2	44.8
Unemployed	6,409	2,383	37.2	62.8
Not in labor force	61,608	33,335	54.1	45.9

Source: U.S. Bureau of the Census, *Current Population Reports*, Series P-20, no. 504 (August 1997).
Note: Voting age population defined as civilian noninstitutional population (including noncitizens) aged eighteen years and over.

2000

	Persons of Voting Age (in thousands)	Persons Reporting They Voted (in thousands)	Percent Reporting They Voted	Percent Reporting They Did Not Vote
Total	202,609	110,826	54.7	45.3
Men	97,087	51,542	53.1	46.9
Women	105,523	59,284	56.2	43.8
White	168,733	95,098	56.4	43.6
Nonwhite	33,876	15,728	46.4	53.6
18–24 years old	26,712	8,635	32.3	67.7
25–34 years old	37,304	16,286	43.7	56.3
35–44 years old	44,476	24,452	55.0	45.0
45–64 years old	61,352	39,301	64.1	35.9
65 years and older	32,764	22,152	67.6	32.4
Metropolitan	NA	NA	NA	NA
Nonmetropolitan	NA	NA	NA	NA
Non-South	130,774	72,385	55.4	44.6
South	71,835	38,441	53.5	46.5
Under 9 years of school	12,894	3,454	26.8	73.2
9–11 years of school	20,108	6,758	33.6	66.4
12 years	66,339	32,749	49.4	50.6
More than 12 years:				
1 to 3 years of college	55,308	33,339	60.3	39.7
4 or more years of college	47,960	34,526	72.0	28.0
Employed	133,434	74,068	55.5	44.5
Unemployed	4,944	1,734	35.1	64.9
Not in labor force	64,231	35,023	54.5	45.5

Source: U.S. Bureau of the Census, *Current Population Reports*, Series P-20, no. 542 (February 2002).
Note: Voting age population defined as civilian noninstitutional population (including noncitizens) aged eighteen years and over.

2004

	Persons of Voting Age (in thousands)	Persons Reporting They Voted (in thousands)	Percent Reporting They Voted	Percent Reporting They Did Not Vote
Total	215,694	125,736	58.3	41.7
Men	103,812	58,455	56.3	43.7
Women	111,882	67,281	60.1	39.9
White	176,618	106,588	60.3	39.7
Nonwhite	39,076	19,148	49.0	51.0
18–24 years old	27,808	11,639	41.9	58.1
25–34 years old	39,003	18,285	46.9	53.1
35–44 years old	43,130	24,560	56.9	43.1
45–64 years old	71,015	47,326	66.6	33.4
65 years and older	34,738	23,925	68.9	31.1
Metropolitan	NA	NA	NA	NA
Nonmetropolitan	NA	NA	NA	NA
Non-South	138,506	82,224	59.4	40.6
South	77,188	43,512	56.4	43.6
Not high school graduate	33,293	10,132	30.4	69.6
High school graduate only	68,545	35,894	52.4	47.6
Some college	58,913	38,922	66.1	33.9
College graduate	36,591	26,579	72.6	27.4
Postgraduate	18,352	14,210	77.4	22.6
Employed	138,831	83,250	60.0	40.0
Unemployed	7,251	3,362	46.4	53.6
Not in labor force	69,612	39,124	56.2	43.8

Source: U.S. Bureau of the Census, *Current Population Reports*, Series P-20, no. 556 (March 2006).
Note: Voting age population defined as civilian noninstitutional population (including noncitizens) aged eighteen years and over.

2008

	Persons of Voting Age (in thousands)	Persons Reporting They Voted (in thousands)	Percent Reporting They Voted	Percent Reporting They Did Not Vote
Total	225,499	131,144	63.6	36.4
Men	108,974	60,729	61.5	38.5
Women	116,525	70,415	65.7	34.3
White	183,169	109,100	64.4	35.6
Black	26,528	16,133	64.7	35.3
Hispanic	30,852	9,745	49.9	50.1
Asian	10,455	3,357	47.6	52.4
18–24 years old	26,263	12,515	48.5	51.5
25–34 years old	40,240	19,501	57.0	43.0
35–44 years old	41,460	22,865	62.8	37.2
45–54 years old	44,181	27,623	67.4	32.6
55–64 years old	33,896	23,071	71.5	28.5
65–74 years old	20,227	14,176	72.4	27.6
75 years and over	17,231	11,344	67.8	32.2
Metropolitan	NA	NA	NA	NA
Nonmetropolitan	NA	NA	NA	NA
Non-South	143,097	83,608	64.3	35.7
South	82,402	47,536	62.6	37.4
Not high school graduate	30,204	9,076	39.3	60.7
High school graduate only	70,427	35,866	54.9	45.1
Some college	63,780	41,477	68.0	32.0
College graduate	40,850	29,330	77.0	23.0
Postgraduate	20,238	15,425	82.7	17.3
Civilian labor force	152,707	90,715	65.2	34.8
Unemployed	9,521	4,642	54.7	45.3
Not in labor force	72,792	40,429	60.3	39.7

Source: U.S. Bureau of the Census, *Population Division, Education and Social Stratification Branch* (July 2009).

Note: Voting age population defined as civilian noninstitutional population (including noncitizens) aged eighteen years and over.

2012

	Persons of Voting Age (in thousands)	Persons Reporting They Voted (in thousands)	Percent Reporting They Voted	Percent Reporting They Did Not Vote
Total	235,248	132,948	61.8	38.2
Men	113,243	61,551	59.7	40.3
Women	122,005	71,397	63.7	36.3
White	173,466	107,846	62.2	37.8
Black	26,915	17,183	66.2	33.8
Hispanic	23,329	11,188	48.0	52.0
Asian	9,033	4,331	47.9	52.1
18–24 years old	29,878	11,353	41.2	58.8
25–44 years old	80,770	39,942	57.3	42.7
45–64 years old	82,087	52,013	67.9	32.1
65–74 years old	24,162	17,182	73.5	26.5
75 years and over	18,352	12,459	70.0	30.0
Metropolitan	NA	NA	NA	NA
Nonmetropolitan	NA	NA	NA	NA
Non-South	148,180	84,415	62.5	37.5
South	87,068	48,533	60.7	39.3
Not high school graduate	29,206	8,297	38.3	61.7
High school graduate only	70,579	34,402	52.6	47.4
Some college	67,652	41,601	64.2	35.8
College graduate	44,436	31,192	75.0	25.0
Postgraduate	23,374	17,457	81.3	18.7
Civilian labor force	153,666	88,674	63.4	36.6
Unemployed	11,091	5,111	51.9	48.1
Not in labor force	81,582	44,275	58.9	41.1

Source: U.S. Bureau of the Census, *Population Division, Education and Social Stratification Branch* (May 2013).

Note: Voting age population defined as civilian noninstitutional population (including noncitizens) aged eighteen years and over.

Selections from the Democratic and Republican Party Platforms, 2012

DEMOCRATIC PLATFORM

Economic Policy

"We've come a long way since 2008. . . . Since early 2010, the private sector has created 4.5 million jobs, and American manufacturing is growing for the first time since the 1990s. The President knew from the start that to rebuild true middle class security, we can't just cut our way to prosperity. We must out-educate, out-innovate, and out-build the world. . . . President Obama and Democrats in Congress cut taxes for every working family, putting more money in the pockets of Americans who need it most. A typical family has saved $3,600 during his first term. We have already enacted . . . payroll tax relief, tax credits for businesses that hire veterans, and an extension of unemployment insurance that also included reforms . . . to help the long-term unemployed reconnect with the labor force and support for workers looking to become entrepreneurs. . . . The Republicans in Congress and Mitt Romney have a very different idea about where they want to take this country. To pay for their trillions in additional tax cuts weighted towards millionaires and billionaires, they'll raise taxes on the middle class and gut our investments in education, research and technology, and new roads, bridges, and airports. They'll end Medicare as we know it."

Education

"President Obama and the Democrats are committed to working with states and communities so they have the flexibility and resources they need to improve elementary and secondary education in a way that works best for students. To that end, the President challenged and encouraged states to raise their standards so students graduate ready for college or career and can succeed in a dynamic global economy. Forty-six states responded, leading to groundbreaking reforms that will deliver better education to millions of American students. . . . To help keep college within reach of every student, Democrats took on banks to reform our student loan program, saving more than $60 billion by removing banks acting as middlemen so we can better and more directly invest in students. . . . Mitt Romney has a radically different vision. He says we need fewer teachers."

Environment and Energy

"Democrats are committed to balancing environmental protection with development, and that means preserving sensitive public lands from exploration, like the Arctic National Wildlife Refuge and other irreplaceable national landscapes. . . . We can move toward a sustainable energy-independent future if we harness all of America's great natural resources. That means an all-of-the-above approach to developing America's many energy resources, including winds, solar, biofuels, geothermal, hydropower, nuclear, oil, clean coal and natural gas. . . . In the last four years, President Obama and the Democratic Party have taken concrete steps to make us more energy independent. We've supported nearly 225,000 clean energy jobs and Americans are importing less oil, breathing cleaner air, and saving money on energy costs."

Abortion

"The Democratic Party strongly and unequivocally supports *Roe v. Wade* and a woman's right to make decisions regarding her pregnancy, including a safe and legal abortion, regardless of ability to pay. We oppose any and all efforts to weaken or undermine that right. Abortion is an intensely personal decision between a woman, her family, her doctor and her clergy; there is no place for politicians or government to get in the way. We strongly and unequivocally support a woman's decision to have a child by providing affordable health care and ensuring the availability of and access to programs that help women during pregnancy and after the birth of a child, including caring adoption programs."

Gay Marriage

"We support marriage equality and support the movement to secure equal treatment under law for same-sex couples. We also support the freedom of churches and religious entities to decide how to administer marriage as a religious sacrament without government interference. We oppose discriminatory federal and state constitutional amendments and other attempts to deny equal protection of the laws to committed same-sex couples who seek the same respect and responsibilities as other married couples."

Terrorism and National Security

"Under the leadership of President Obama and the Democratic Party, the tide of war is now receding, and America is looking ahead to a new future. We have responsibly ended the war in Iraq. We have struck major blows against al-Qaeda, bringing Osama bin Laden and other senior al-Qaeda officials to justice, and putting the terrorist organization on the path to defeat. And we have reversed the momentum of the Taliban and established the conditions to draw down our forces in Afghanistan. These actions have enabled a broader strategic rebalancing of American foreign policy. After more than a decade of war, we can focus on nation-building here at home. . . . We are committed to an unrelenting pursuit of those who would kill Americans or threaten our homeland, our allies, our partners, and our interests in the world. . . . Many Republicans, including Mitt Romney, would have preferred to leave tens of thousands of U.S. troops in Iraq in an open-ended commitment, against the will of the Iraqi government and people."

Health Care

"We believe accessible, affordable, high quality health care is part of the American promise, that Americans should have the security that comes with good health care, and that no one should go broke because they get sick. Over the determined opposition of Republicans, we enacted landmark reforms that are already helping millions of Americans, and more benefits will come soon. As a result of our efforts, young Americans entering the workforce can stay on their parents' plans. Insurers can no longer refuse to cover kids with pre-existing medical conditions. Insurance companies will no longer be able to arbitrarily cap or cancel coverage, or charge women more simply because of their gender."

Immigration

"The country urgently needs comprehensive immigration reforms that brings undocumented immigrants out of the shadows and requires them to get right with the law, learn English and pay taxes in order to get on a path to earn citizenship. We need an immigration reform that creates a system for allocating visas that meets our economic needs, keeps families together, and enforces the law. But instead of promoting the national interest, Republicans have blocked immigration reform in Congress and used it as a political wedge. . . . When states sought to interfere with federal immigration law by passing local measures targeting immigrants, this administration challenged them in court."

REPUBLICAN PLATFORM

Economic Policy

"Republicans believe in the Great American Dream, with its economics of inclusion, enabling everyone to have a chance to own, invest, build, and prosper. It is the opposite of the policies which, for the past three and a half years, have stifled growth, destroyed jobs, halted investment, created unprecedented uncertainty, and prolonged the worst economic downturn since the Great Depression. . . . The best jobs program is economic growth. We do not offer another made-in-Washington package of subsidies and spending to create temporary or artificial jobs. . . . Our goal is a tax system that is simple, transparent, flatter and fair. . . . The massive federal government is structurally and financially broken. For decades it has been pushed beyond its core functions, increasing spending to unsustainable levels. Unless we take dramatic action now, young Americans and their children will inherit an unprecedented legacy of enormous and unsustainable debt, with the interest alone consuming an ever-increasing portion of the country's wealth."

Education

"Parents are responsible for the education of their children. We do not believe in a one size fits all approach to education and support providing broad education choices to parents and children at the state and local level. . . . More money alone does not necessarily equal better performance. . . . We support options for learning, including home schooling and local innovations like single-sex classes, full-day school hours, and charter schools. School choice, whether through . . . vouchers or tax credits is important for all children, especially for families with children trapped in failing schools. . . . We support the English First approach and oppose divisive programs that limit students' ability to advance in American society. . . . We affirm the right of students to engage in prayer at public school events in public schools. . . . We call on state officials to ensure that our public colleges and universities be places of learning and the exchange of ideas, not zones of intellectual intolerance favoring the Left."

Environment and Energy

"Efforts to reduce pollution, encourage recycling, educate the public, and avoid ecological degradation have been a success. However, we need a dramatic change in the attitude of officials in Washington, a shift from a job-killing punitive mentality to a spirit of cooperation with producers, landowners, and the public. . . . Many of these new rules are creating regulatory uncertainty, preventing new projects from going forward, discouraging new investment, and stifling job creation. . . . The Republican Party is committed to domestic energy independence. . . . No new nuclear generating plants have been licensed and constructed for thirty years. We call for timely processing of new reactor applications. . . . The current administration has used taxpayer dollars to pick winners and losers in the energy sector while publicly threatening to bankrupt anyone who builds a new coal-fired plant and has stopped the Keystone XL Pipeline. The current President has done nothing to disavow the scare campaign against hydraulic fracturing."

Abortion

"Faithful to the 'self evident' truths enshrined in the Declaration of Independence, we assert the sanctity of human life and affirm that the unborn child has a fundamental individual right to life which cannot be infringed. We support a human life amendment to the Constitution, and we endorse legislation to make clear that the Fourteenth Amendment's protections apply to unborn children. We oppose using public revenues to promote or perform abortion and will not fund or subsidize health care which includes abortion coverage. We support the appointment of judges who respect traditional family values and the sanctity of innocent human life."

Gay Marriage

"The institution of marriage is the foundation of civil society. Its success as an institution will determine our success as a nation. . . . We recognize and honor the courageous efforts of those who bear the many burdens of parenting alone, even as we believe that marriage, the union of one man and one woman must be upheld as the national standard, a goal to stand for, and promote through laws governing marriage. We embrace the principle that all Americans should be treated with respect and dignity."

Terrorism and National Security

"Every potential enemy must have no doubt that our capabilities, our commitment, and our will to defeat them are clear, unwavering, and unequivocal. . . . We will employ the full range of military and intelligence options to defeat Al Qaeda and its allies. . . . We will accept no arms control agreement that limits our right to self-defense, and we will fully deploy a missile defense shield for the people of the United States and for our allies. . . . The current administration's National Security Strategy reflects the extreme elements in its liberal domestic coalition. It is a budget-constrained blueprint that, if fully implemented, will diminish the capabilities of our Armed Forces. The strategy significantly increases the risk of future conflict by declaring to our adversaries that we will no longer maintain the forces necessary to fight and win more than one conflict at a time."

Health Care

"The Patient Protection and Affordable Care Act—Obamacare—was never really about healthcare, though its impact upon the nation's health is disastrous. From its start, it was about power, the expansion of government control over one sixth of our economy, and resulted in an attack on the Constitution, by requiring that U.S. citizens purchase health insurance. . . . We believe that taking care of one's health is an individual responsibility. . . . Our goal is to encourage the development of a healthcare system that provides higher quality care at a lower cost to all Americans. . . . We seek to increase healthcare choice and options, contain costs and reduce mandates, simplify the system for patients and providers, restore cuts made to Medicare, and equalize the tax treatment of group and individual health insurance plans. . . . our practical, non-intrusive reforms will promote state leadership in healthcare reform, promote a free-market based system, and empower consumer choice."

Immigration

"In an age of terrorism, drug cartels, human trafficking, and criminal gangs, the presence of millions of unidentified persons in this country poses grave risks to the safety and sovereignty of the United States. Our highest priority . . . is to secure our borders. . . . Granting amnesty only rewards and encourages more law breaking. . . . We insist upon enforcement at the workplace through verifications systems so that jobs can be available to all legal workers. . . . The current administration's approach to immigration has undermined the rule of law at every turn."

Notes

Chapter 1

1. Anthony King, *Running Scared: Why America's Politicians Campaign Too Much and Govern Too Little* (New York: Martin Kessler, 1997).

2. See Bruce Cain, John Ferejohn, and Morris Fiorina, *The Personal Vote: Constituency Service and Electoral Independence* (Cambridge, MA: Harvard University Press, 1987), p. 13; and Leon D. Epstein, *Political Parties in Western Democracies* (New York: Praeger, 1967), p. 43.

3. Richard Boyd's research suggests that heavy demands on U.S. voters may be depressing participation in any one election. In the Connecticut town he studied, he found that more people voted at some time during the year than voted in any given election: "a system that holds elections as frequently as we do in the United States must expect that even citizens who are attentive to politics and its obligations will not be at the polls every election. I would argue, then, that the frequency of elections in the United States is one explanation of the somewhat lower voting rate we experience in any given election compared to European countries." Richard W. Boyd, "Decline of U.S. Voter Turnout: Structural Explanations," *American Politics Quarterly* 9 (April 1981): 133–59. Switzerland, the other low-turnout democracy, also has frequent elections, and referendums; see David Butler and Austin Ranney, eds., *Referendums around the World: The Growing Use of Direct Democracy* (Washington, DC: AEI Press, 1994). In *Running Scared*, Anthony King argues that the U.S. pattern of frequent elections has important consequences for governing. Note also that turnout in recent European Union elections was substantially lower than national elections in most European countries; the 2004 EU election featured an overall turnout rate of under 50 percent. See Robert Anderson, Christopher Condon, and Stefan Wagstyl, "Apathy Rules among Newest Member States," *Financial Times*, June 15, 2004, p. 14.

4. See Steven J. Rosenstone and John Mark Hansen, *Mobilization, Participation, and Democracy in America* (New York: Macmillan, 1993), pp. 178–79.

5. A summary of these trends is a central topic in Steven E. Schier and Todd E. Eberly, *American Government and Popular Discontent: Stability without Success* (New York: Routledge, 2013). See also Matthew J. Hetherington, *Why Trust Matters: Declining Political Trust and the Demise of Political Liberalism* (Princeton, NJ: Princeton University Press, 2006).

6. Raymond E. Wolfinger, David P. Glass, and Peverill Squire, "Predictors of Electoral Turnout: An International Comparison," *Policy Studies Review* 9 (Spring 1990): 551–74, at 555, based on vote validated data from the 1980 National Election Studies.

7. Ibid., pp. 146–50. Americans do least well on "trust in government" questions, but respond much more positively to questions about their efficacy (rejecting such statements as "people like me have no say in what the government does") and to questions asking if a political party expresses their point of view.

8. Peverill Squire, Raymond E. Wolfinger, and David P. Glass, "Residential Mobility and Voter Turnout," *American Political Science Review* 81 (March 1987): 45–84.

9. Orley Ashenfelter and Stanley Kelley Jr., "Determinants of Participation in Presidential Elections," *Journal of Law and Economics* 18 (December 1975): 695–733. The prospect of partisan manipulation of purge laws by politicians seeking to disenfranchise likely supporters of the opposition has become an area of concern among some government watchdog groups over the past several years; see Myrna Perez, "Voter Purges," Brennan Center for Justice at New York University, September 2008, http://www.brennancenter.org/page/-/publications/Voter.Purges.f.pdf.

10. The U.S. Election Assistance Commission reported that there were 194 million registered voters as of 2012, with 23 million of these classified as "inactive" voters (probably reflecting voters who had moved or died but had not yet been purged from the voting rolls). See U.S. Election Assistance Commission, "2012 Election Administration and Voting Survey: A Summary of Key Findings," September 2013, http://www.eac.gov/assets/1/Page/990-050%20EAC%20VoterSurvey_508Compliant.pdf, p. 6. The general outline of this argument has been known for over seventy-five years. For example, Harold Gosnell wrote in 1930 that "[i]n the European countries studied, a citizen who is entitled to vote does not, as a rule, have to make any effort to see that his name is on the list of eligible voters. The inconvenience of registering for voting in this country has caused many citizens to become non-voters." Harold G. Gosnell, *Why Europe Votes* (Chicago: University of Chicago Press, 1930), p. 185. See also Raymond E. Wolfinger and Steven J. Rosenstone, *Who Votes?* (New Haven, CT: Yale University Press, 1980); G. Bingham Powell Jr., "American Voter Turnout in Comparative Perspective," *American Political Science Review* 80 (March 1986): 17–43; and Glenn E. Mitchell and Christopher Wlezien, "The Impact of Legal Constraints on Voter Registration, Turnout, and the Composition of the American Electorate," *Political Behavior* 17 (June 1995): 179–202.

11. This is presumably pegged to completion of the harvest in the colonial Northeast.

12. Stanley Kelley Jr., Richard E. Ayres, and William G. Bowen, "Registration and Voting: Putting First Things First," *American Political Science Review* 61 (June 1967): 359–79, at 374–75.

13. In Richard E. Ayres, "Registration 1960: Key to a Democratic Victory?" (unpublished senior thesis, Princeton University, 1964), cited in Kelley, Ayres, and Bowen, "Registration and Voting," p. 375, the author notes the correlation between convenience of registration and percent of the vote for the Democratic Party as proof of the Chicago Daley machine's awareness of this phenomenon.

14. Dunn v. Blumstein, 405 U.S. 330 (1972); Burn v. Forston, 410 U.S. 686 (1972); and Marston v. Lewis, 410 U.S. 759 (1973).

15. Benjamin Highton and Raymond E. Wolfinger, "Estimating the Effects of the National Voter Registration Act of 1993," *Political Behavior* 20 (June 1998): 79–104; see also Raymond E. Wolfinger and Jonathan Hoffman, "Registering and Voting with Motor Voter," *PS: Political Science and Politics* 34 (March 2001): 85–92.

16. Stephen Knack and James White, "Election-Day Registration and Turnout Inequality," *Political Behavior* 22 (March 2000): 29–44. Not all of this difference can be explained by registration laws, however; see Benjamin Highton, "Easy Registration and Voter Turnout," *Journal of Politics* 59 (May 1997): 565–75.

17. California Secretary of State Debra Bowen, "Statement of Vote, November 6, 2012, General Election," http://www.sos.ca.gov/elections/sov/2012_general/sov_complete.pdf, p. 3.

18. Figures from Michael P. McDonald, United States Elections Project, George Mason University, http://elections.gmu.edu/early_vote_2012.html.

19. The Sentencing Project, "Felony Disenfranchisement Laws in the United States," March 2010, http://www.sentencingproject.org/doc/publications/fd_bs_fdlawsinusMarch2010.pdf.

20. McDonald's figures are available at http://elections.gmu.edu/Turnout_2012G.html. See also Michael P. McDonald and Samuel L. Popkin, "The Myth of the Vanishing Voter," *American Political Science Review* 95 (December 2001): 963–74, in which the authors argue that the much-lamented decline in electoral turnout rates after the 1960s was largely due to the growth of the ineligible population.

21. Paul E. Meehl, "The Selfish Voter Paradox and the Thrown-Away Vote Argument," *American Political Science Review* 71 (March 1977): 11–30.

22. The classic statement of this view is that of Anthony Downs, whose best effort is: "The advantage of voting per se is that it makes democracy possible. If no one votes, then the system collapses because no government is chosen. We assume that the citizens of a democracy subscribe to its principles and therefore derive benefits from its continuance; hence they do not want it to collapse. For this reason they attach value to the act of voting per se and receive a return from it." Downs, *An Economic Theory of Democracy* (New York: Harper, 1957), pp. 261–62. See also John A. Ferejohn and Morris P. Fiorina, "The Paradox of Not Voting: A Decision Theoretic Analysis," *American Political Science Review* 68 (June 1974): 525–46; and William H. Riker and Peter C. Ordeshook, "A Theory of the Calculus of Voting," *American Political Science Review* 62 (March 1968): 25–42. For a perspective critical of turnout explanations based on rational calculations of voters' personal utility, see Donald P. Green and Ian Shapiro, *Pathologies of Rational Choice Theory* (New Haven, CT: Yale University Press, 1994), pp. 47–71; and Raymond E. Wolfinger, "The Rational Citizen Faces Election Day," in M. Kent Jennings and Thomas E. Mann, eds., *Elections at Home and Abroad: Essays in Honor of Warren E. Miller* (Ann Arbor: University of Michigan Press, 1994), pp. 71–91. Wolfinger quotes Gary Jacobson: "It's the California model; people vote because it makes them feel good" (p. 84).

23. Robert M. Bond et al., "A 61-Million-Person Experiment in Social Influence and Political Mobilization," *Nature* 489 (September 2012): 295–98.

24. See Rosenstone and Hansen, *Mobilization, Participation, and Democracy in America*, pp. 23, 156–58.

25. Still an excellent summary of the voting turnout and participation literature is Raymond E. Wolfinger and Steven J. Rosenstone, *Who Votes?* (New Haven, CT: Yale University Press, 1980). See also Kay Lehman Schlozman, Sidney Verba, and Henry E. Brady, "Participation's Not a Paradox: The View from American Activists," *British Journal of Political Science* 25 (January 1995): 1–36. This study asks American activists why they participate. The authors conclude: "In an era when surveys show Americans to be disillusioned about politics, distrustful of politicians, and impatient with the level of political debate, we might have expected that activists would either characterize their own political involvement in cynically self-interested terms or see themselves as spectators at an exciting, if sometimes foolish or dirty, sport. On the contrary, their retrospective interpretations of their activity are replete with mentions of civic motivations and a desire to influence policy. Of course, many participants also report selective material or social gratifications. Still, it is striking the extent to which references to doing one's share and making the community or nation a better place to live run as a thread through activists' reports of the concerns that animated their involvement and the number of participants who discuss nothing but civic motivations for their activity" (p. 32).

26. Wolfinger and Rosenstone, *Who Votes?* pp. 94–101.

27. This is one of the most venerable and most secure generalizations in the entire literature of voting behavior studies. See Angus Campbell, Philip E. Converse, Warren E. Miller, and Donald E. Stokes, *The American Voter* (New York: Wiley, 1960), pp. 120–34; and Warren E. Miller and J. Merrill Shanks, *The New American Voter* (Cambridge, MA: Harvard University Press, 1996), pp. 117–50. For variations on this interpretation, see Arthur S. Goldberg, "Social Determination and

Rationality as a Basis of Party Identification," *American Political Science Review* 63 (March 1969): 5–25; Morris P. Fiorina, *Retrospective Voting in American National Elections* (New Haven, CT: Yale University Press, 1981), pp. 89–90; Gregory B. Markus and Philip E. Converse, "A Dynamic Simultaneous Model of Electoral Choice," *American Political Science Review* 73 (December 1979): 1055–70; and Sven Holmberg, "Party Identification Compared Across the Atlantic," in Jennings and Mann, eds., *Elections at Home and Abroad*, pp. 93–121. Larry M. Bartels, "Partisanship and Voting Behavior, 1952–1996," *American Journal of Political Science* 44 (January 2000): 35–50, argues that "[i]n the current political environment, as much or more than at any other time in the past half-century, 'the strength and direction of party identification are facts of central importance' in accounting for the voting behavior of the American electorate" (p. 44; quotation from Campbell et al., *The American Voter*, p. 121). For more recent evidence that party identification is a stable component of social identity—akin, for example, to religious affiliation—see Donald Green, Bradley Palmquist, and Eric Schickler, *Partisan Hearts and Minds: Political Parties and the Social Identities of Voters* (New Haven, CT: Yale University Press, 2002).

28. William H. Flanigan and Nancy H. Zingale, *Political Behavior of the American Electorate*, 8th ed. (Washington, DC: CQ Press, 1994), give findings on the timing of voters' decisions: "In all recent elections the independents and weak partisans were more likely to make up their minds during the campaign, while strong partisans characteristically made their decisions by the end of the conventions" (p. 162). A study of voters who waited until the last two weeks before the election to choose a candidate found that "late deciders . . . are less interested in the political outcome, less subject to conventional political forces, and far less predictable than other voters." J. David Gopoian and Sissie Hadjiharalambous, "Late-Deciding Voters in Presidential Elections," *Political Behavior* 16 (March 1994): 55–78, at 76.

29. Earlier research did not differentiate among the various sorts of independents and characterized the entire population of independents as comparatively uninvolved in politics, less interested, less concerned, and less knowledgeable than party identifiers. These generalizations hold better for the truly nonpartisan subset of "pure" independents—that is, people who do not "lean" toward one party or the other. See Campbell et al., *The American Voter*, p. 143; Bernard Berelson, Paul F. Lazarsfeld, and William N. McPhee, *Voting* (Chicago: University of Chicago Press, 1954), pp. 25–27; and Bruce E. Keith, David B. Magleby, Candice J. Nelson, Elizabeth Orr, Mark C. Westlye, and Raymond E. Wolfinger, *The Myth of the Independent Voter* (Berkeley: University of California Press, 1992), pp. 65–67. For a somewhat different treatment, see Robert Agger, "Independents and Party Identifiers," in Eugene Burdick and Arthur J. Brodbeck, eds., *American Voting Behavior* (Glencoe, IL: Free Press, 1959), chap. 17.

30. Berelson, Lazarsfeld, and McPhee, *Voting*, pp. 215–33; John R. Zaller, *The Nature and Origins of Mass Opinion* (New York: Cambridge University Press, 1992). George Belknap and Angus Campbell state that "for many people Democratic or Republican attitudes regarding foreign policy result from conscious or unconscious adherence to a perceived party line rather than from influences independent of party identification." Belknap and Campbell, "Political Party Identification and Attitudes toward Foreign Policy," *Public Opinion Quarterly* 15 (Winter 1951–52): 601–23, at 623. See also Robert Huckfeldt, Paul E. Johnson, and John Sprague, "Political Environments, Political Dynamics, and the Survival of Disagreement," *Journal of Politics* 64 (February 2002): 1–21.

31. Many voting studies contain substantial discussions of this subject. See Robert E. Lane, "Fathers and Sons: Foundations of Political Belief," *American Sociological Review* 24 (August 1959): 502–11; Campbell et al., *The American Voter*, pp. 146–47; and H. H. Remmers, "Early Socialization of Attitudes," in Burdick and Brodbeck, eds., *American Voting Behavior*, pp. 55–67. V. O. Key, *Public Opinion and American Democracy* (New York: Knopf, 1961), pp. 293–314, sums up in these words: "Children acquire early in life a feeling of party identification; they have sensitive antennae and since they are imitative animals, soon take on the political color of their family" (p. 294). See also Fred I. Greenstein, *Children and Politics* (New Haven, CT: Yale University

Press, 1965), chap. 4. In a later work, Paul R. Abramson presents an interesting discussion of this familial link and the forces that later play against it; see *Generational Change in American Politics* (Lexington, MA: Lexington Books, 1975), esp. chaps. 3 and 4. See also Richard G. Niemi and M. Kent Jennings, "Issues and Inheritance in the Formation of Party Identification," *American Journal of Political Science* 35 (November 1991): 970–88.

32. "People are more likely to associate with people like themselves—alike in political complexion as well as social position." Berelson, Lazarsfeld, and McPhee, *Voting*, p. 83. See also Robert D. Putnam, "Political Attitudes and the Local Community," *American Political Science Review* 60 (September 1966): 640–54; Ada W. Finifter, "The Friendship Group as a Protective Environment for Political Deviants," *American Political Science Review* 68 (June 1974): 607–26; and Robert Huckfeldt and John Sprague, "Networks in Context: The Social Flow of Political Information," *American Political Science Review* 81 (December 1987): 1197–1216.

33. Paul F. Lazarsfeld, Bernard Berelson, and Hazel Gaudet, *The People's Choice* (New York: Duell, Sloan and Pearce, 1944), pp. 16–28.

34. Ibid.; Angus Campbell and Homer C. Cooper, *Group Differences in Attitudes and Votes* (Ann Arbor: University of Michigan Press, 1956); Julian L. Woodward and Elmo Roper, "Political Activities of American Citizens," *American Political Science Review* (December 1950): 872–75; Key, *Public Opinion and American Democracy*, pp. 99–120, 121–81; Berelson, Lazarsfeld, and McPhee, *Voting*, pp. 54–76; Robert Axelrod, "Where the Votes Come From: An Analysis of Electoral Coalitions, 1952–1968," *American Political Science Review* 66 (March 1972): 11–20; Axelrod, "Communication," *American Political Science Review* 68 (June 1974): 717–20; Axelrod, "Communication," *American Political Science Review* 72 (June 1978): 622–24; Axelrod, "Communication," *American Political Science Review* 76 (June 1982): 393–96; Axelrod, "Presidential Election Coalitions in 1984," *American Political Science Review* 80 (March 1986): 281–84; Robert A. Jackson and Thomas M. Carsey, "Group Components of U.S. Presidential Voting Across the States," *Political Behavior* 21 (June 1999): 123–51; Miller and Shanks, *The New American Voter*, pp. 212–82. See also table 2.3.

35. V. O. Key Jr., *Southern Politics in State and Nation* (New York: Knopf, 1949), pp. 25, 75–81, 223–28, 280–85. Indeed, conflict over secession was at the root of the formation of the state of West Virginia, which broke away from Virginia and was admitted as a separate state in 1863.

36. See Earl Black and Merle Black, *Politics and Society in the South* (Cambridge, MA: Harvard University Press, 1987); Raymond E. Wolfinger and Michael G. Hagen, "Republican Prospects: Southern Comfort," *Public Opinion* 8 (October/November 1985): 8–13; Earl Black and Merle Black, *The Rise of Southern Republicans* (Cambridge, MA: Harvard University Press, 2002); David Lublin, *The Republican South: Democratization and Partisan Change* (Princeton, NJ: Princeton University Press, 2004); and Byron E. Shafer and Richard Johnston, *The End of Southern Exceptionalism: Class, Race, and Partisan Change in the Postwar South* (Cambridge, MA: Harvard University Press, 2006). For an account explaining how these changes made an impact on Congress, see Nelson W. Polsby, *How Congress Evolves: Social Bases of Institutional Change* (New York: Oxford University Press, 2004).

37. See C. Vann Woodward, *The Strange Career of Jim Crow* (New York: Oxford University Press, 1966); and Woodward, *Origins of the New South* (Baton Rouge: Louisiana State University Press, 1951).

38. Nicholas Lemann says: "In 1940, 77 percent of black Americans still lived in the South—49 percent in the rural South. The invention of the cotton picker was crucial to the great migration by blacks from the Southern countryside to the cities of the South, the West, and the North. Between 1910 and 1970, six and a half million black Americans moved from the South to the North; five million of them moved after 1940, during the time of the mechanization of cotton farming. . . . For blacks, the migration meant leaving what had always been their economic and social base in America and finding a new one." Lemann, *The Promised Land* (New York: Knopf, 1991), p. 6.

39. Campbell et al., *The American Voter*, p. 160. See, more generally, James Q. Wilson, *Negro Politics* (Glencoe, IL: Free Press, 1960); and Nancy Weiss, *Farewell to the Party of Lincoln* (Princeton, NJ: Princeton University Press, 1983), esp. pp. 209–35. Republican presidential nominee Barry Goldwater, who opposed the Civil Rights Act of 1964, intensified the Democratic loyalties of black voters, who voted Democratic at about a two-to-one rate from the 1930s until 1960 and at an eight-to-one rate from 1964 onward. See Edward G. Carmines and James A. Stimson, *Issue Evolution: Race and the Transformation of American Politics* (Princeton, NJ: Princeton University Press, 1989). For more recent data on the black vote, see Miller and Shanks, *The New American Voter*, pp. 256–59.

40. The 111th Congress of 2009–2010 included thirty-nine African-American members of the House of Representatives and one African-American senator, Roland Burris of Illinois. All were Democrats—as was Barack Obama, the nation's first black president.

41. George H. Mayer, *The Republican Party, 1854–1966*, 2nd ed. (New York: Oxford University Press, 1967), pp. 221–71.

42. Mike Clary and Deborah Ramirez, "Election Lesson: Hispanic Support for Democrats Growing in Florida," Fort Lauderdale, Florida *Sun-Sentinel*, November 8, 2012, http://articles .sun-sentinel.com/2012-11-08/newsfl-hispanic-vote-florida-20121107_1_fernand-amandi -hispanic-voters-hispanic-support.

43. Maria de los Angeles Torres says: "In the late 1800s, Cuban workers migrated to the United States in search of employment. Eventually they formed the backbone and the most radical element of the independence movement against Spain. Interestingly, Cuban tobacco workers also participated in the radical wing of the American Federation of Labor. . . .

"After 1959, Cubans migrated to the United States in great numbers. This time it was not workers, but rather the middle and upper classes.

"After the revolution, the tradition of the progressive Cuban immigrant changed radically. Since those sectors most affected by the radical programs of the revolution supplied the initial post-revolutionary immigrations from Cuba, most tended to be politically conservative." Maria de los Angeles Torres, "From Exiles to Minorities: The Politics of the Cuban Community in the United States," PhD dissertation, University of Michigan, Ann Arbor, 1986, pp. 7–8.

44. While political journalists have recently devoted a great deal of attention to Republican efforts to capture a larger share of the growing Latino vote in the United States, evidence indicates that Latinos remain, with the exception of the Cuban population in southern Florida, strongly Democratic. See David L. Leal, Matt A. Barreto, Jongho Lee, and Rodolfo O. de la Garza, "The Latino Vote in the 2004 Election," *PS: Political Science and Politics* 38 (January 2005): 41–49.

45. See David Hackett Fischer, *Albion's Seed: Four British Folkways in America* (New York: Oxford University Press, 1989), p. 17; Steven Erie, *Rainbow's End: Irish-Americans and the Dilemmas of Urban Machine Politics, 1840–1985* (Berkeley: University of California Press, 1988), pp. 25–28; Duane Lockard, *New England State Politics* (Princeton, NJ: Princeton University Press, 1959); Robert A. Dahl, *Who Governs? Democracy and Power in an American City* (New Haven, CT: Yale University Press, 1961), pp. 33–51, 216–17; Elmer E. Cornwell, "Party Absorption of Ethnic Groups: The Case of Providence, R.I.," *Social Forces* 38 (March 1960): 205–10; and J. Joseph Huthmacher, *Massachusetts People and Politics* (Cambridge, MA: Harvard University Press, 1959), pp. 118–26.

46. Samuel Lubell, *The Future of American Politics* (New York: Harper, 1951), pp. 129–57; Willi Paul Adams, *The German-Americans: An Ethnic Experience*, translated and adapted by LaVern J. Rippley and Eberhard Reichmann (New York: Max Kade German-American Center, 1993).

47. For more on political socialization, see M. Kent Jennings and Laura Stoker, "Of Time and the Development of Partisan Polarization," *American Journal of Political Science* 52 (July 2008): 619–35.

48. Pew Research Center, "Young Voters Supported Obama Less, but May Have Mattered More," November 26, 2012, http://www.people-press.org/2012/11/26/young-voters -supported-obama-less-but-may-have-mattered-more/.

49. A notable study developing the implications of this notion is Downs's classic, *An Economic Theory of Democracy*.

50. Philip E. Converse, "The Nature of Belief Systems in Mass Publics," in David E. Apter, ed., *Ideology and Discontent* (New York: Free Press, 1964), pp. 206–62; William Lyons and John M. Scheb II, "Ideology and Candidate Evaluation in the 1984 and 1988 Presidential Elections," *Journal of Politics* 54 (May 1992): 573–84; M. Kent Jennings, "Ideological Thinking among Mass Publics and Political Elites," *Public Opinion Quarterly* (Winter 1992): 419–41.

51. Alan I. Abramowitz and Kyle L. Saunders, "Ideological Realignment in the U.S. Electorate," *Journal of Politics* 60 (August 1998): 634–52; Marc J. Hetherington, "Resurgent Mass Partisanship: The Role of Elite Polarization," *American Political Science Review* 95 (September 2001): 619–31.

52. See Aaron Wildavsky, "Choosing Preferences by Constructing Institutions: A Cultural Theory of Preference Formation," *American Political Science Review* 81 (March 1987): 3–22; and Michael Thompson, Richard Ellis, and Aaron Wildavsky, *Cultural Theory* (Boulder, CO: Westview Press, 1990).

53. On Eisenhower, see Campbell et al., *The American Voter*, pp. 55–57, 525–28, 537; and Herbert H. Hyman and Paul B. Sheatsley, "The Political Appeal of President Eisenhower," *Public Opinion Quarterly* 17 (Winter 1953): 443–60. On McGovern, see Arthur H. Miller, Warren E. Miller, Alden S. Raine, and Thad A. Brown, "A Majority Party in Disarray: Policy Polarization in the 1972 Election," *American Political Science Review* 70 (September 1976): 753–78; and Samuel L. Popkin, John W. Gorman, Charles Phillips, and Jeffrey A. Smith, "Comment: What Have You Done for Me Lately? Toward an Investment Theory of Voting," *American Political Science Review* 70 (September 1976): 779–805.

54. The portions of this analysis that deal with voters and issues are adapted from chap. 8, "Public Policy and Political Preference," in Campbell et al., *The American Voter*, pp. 168–87. See also Zaller, *The Nature and Origins of Mass Opinion*.

55. See Hazel Gaudet Erskine, "The Polls: The Informed Public," *Public Opinion Quarterly* 26 (Winter 1962): 669–77. This article summarizes questions asked from 1947 to 1960 of national samples of Americans in order to ascertain their information on current news topics. Similar data for 1935–1946 are contained in Hadley Cantril and Mildred Strunk, *Public Opinion, 1935–46* (Princeton, NJ: Princeton University Press, 1951). In light of this and later work, Philip E. Converse was able to conclude: "Surely the most familiar fact to arise from sample surveys in all countries is that popular levels of information about public affairs are, from the point of view of the informed observer, astonishingly low." Converse, "Public Opinion and Voting Behavior," in Fred I. Greenstein and Nelson W. Polsby, eds., *Handbook of Political Science* (Reading, MA: Addison-Wesley, 1975), volume 4, pp. 75–169, at 79. See also Michael X. Delli Carpini and Scott Keeter, *What Americans Know about Politics and Why It Matters* (New Haven, CT: Yale University Press, 1996); and Philip E. Converse, "Assessing the Capacity of Mass Electorates," *Annual Review of Political Science* 3 (June 2000): 331–53.

56. The data on which this conclusion is based refer to issues in rather general categories such as "economic aid to foreign countries," the "influence of big business in government," and "aid to education" (Campbell et al., *The American Voter*, p. 182). It is highly probable that the proportion of people meeting the requirements of having an opinion and differentiating among the parties would be substantially reduced if precise and specific policies within these general issue categories formed the basis of questions in a survey. See also Converse, "Public Opinion and Voting Behavior."

57. Campbell et al., in *The American Voter*, tentatively conclude that in the Eisenhower years, covered by their study, "people who paid little attention to politics were contributing very disproportionately to partisan change" (p. 264). Zaller, *The Nature and Origins of Mass Opinion*, confirms these findings. He shows that the greater the level of political awareness, the more likely people are to possess "cueing messages" that help them filter out information contrary to

their existing viewpoint on a given issue. Thus greater awareness results in an increasing ratio of ideologically consistent to inconsistent considerations governing opinion formation. This means that more aware liberals, for example, are more likely to support liberal positions (pp. 100–101). The implications for partisan change are clear: political awareness leads to stability in issue preferences and discourages change. Political inattentiveness, conversely, leads to unstable issue preferences and is therefore more likely to lead to partisan change.

58. Philip E. Converse, "Information Flow and the Stability of Partisan Attitudes," *Public Opinion Quarterly* 26 (Winter 1962): 578–99. John R. Zaller says: "When people are exposed to two competing sets of electoral information, they are generally able to choose among them on the basis of their partisanship and values even when they do not score especially well on tests of political awareness. But when individuals are exposed to a one-sided communication flow, as in low-key House and Senate elections, their capacity for critical resistance appears quite limited.

"The conclusion I draw from this is that the most important source of resistance to dominant campaigns . . . is countervalent information carried within the overall stream of political information." Zaller, *The Nature and Origins of Mass Opinion*, pp. 252–53.

59. According to the 2008 National Election Study, 39 percent of respondents considered themselves independents, but nearly two-thirds of these leaned toward either the Democratic or Republican Party. Only 14 percent of respondents were "pure," non-leaning independents, and many of them did not vote. See Keith et al., *The Myth of the Independent Voter*.

60. See Sidney Verba, Richard A. Brody, Edwin B. Parker, Norman H. Nie, Nelson W. Polsby, Paul Eckman, and Gordon S. Black, "Public Opinion and the War in Vietnam," *American Political Science Review* 61 (June 1967): 317–33; and Benjamin I. Page and Richard A. Brody, "Policy Voting and the Electoral Process: The Vietnam War Issue," *American Political Science Review* 66 (September 1972): 979–95.

61. Miller, Miller, Raine, and Brown, "A Majority Party in Disarray," p. 760. The issues studied included Vietnam withdrawal, amnesty for draft dodgers, reducing military spending, government health insurance, guaranteed standard of living, urban unrest, campus unrest, protecting the rights of those accused of crime, government aid to minorities, equal rights for women, abortion, legalization of marijuana, busing, and a "liberal-conservative philosophic position." For similar findings, see Jeane Kirkpatrick, "Representation in the American National Conventions: The Case of 1972," *British Journal of Political Science* 5 (July 1975): 265–322; and Kirkpatrick, *The New Presidential Elite* (New York: Russell Sage Foundation, 1976).

62. See David W. Brady, *Critical Elections and Congressional Policy Making* (Stanford, CA: Stanford University Press, 1988), pp. 85–89.

63. Donovan Slack, "RIP Positive Ads in 2012," *Politico*, November 4, 2012, http://www.politico.com/news/stories/1112/83262.html.

64. Gary C. Jacobson, *The Electoral Origins of Divided Government* (Boulder, CO: Westview Press, 1990), p. 125. For a detailed discussion of the relationship between presidential popularity and economic performance, see Richard A. Brody, *Assessing the President: The Media, Elite Opinion, and Popular Support* (Stanford, CA: Stanford University Press, 1991), pp. 91–103; for a study of the effects of economic conditions on presidential vote choice, see Richard Nadeau and Michael S. Lewis-Beck, "National Economic Voting in U.S. Presidential Elections," *Journal of Politics* 63 (February 2001): 159–81.

65. Marjorie Connelly, "How Americans Voted: A Political Portrait," *New York Times*, November 7, 2004, sec. 4, p. 4.

66. Campbell et al., *The American Voter*, p. 148.

67. V. O. Key Jr., with the assistance of Milton C. Cummings Jr., *The Responsible Electorate: Rationality in Presidential Voting, 1936–1960* (Cambridge, MA: Harvard University Press, 1966). This was the finding that led Key to his famous remark: "The perverse and unorthodox argument of this little book is that voters are not fools" (p. 7).

68. Charles H. Franklin, "Issue Preferences, Socialization and the Evaluation of Party Identification," *American Journal of Political Science* 28 (August 1984): 459–75.

69. The degree of aggregate stability in the electorate over time, and the sensitivity of the overall distribution of party identification to the performance of incumbent officeholders, is a matter of some dispute among scholars. See Donald Green, Bradley Palmquist, and Eric Schickler, "Macropartisanship: A Replication and Critique," *American Political Science Review* 92 (December 1998): 883–99; and Robert S. Erikson, Michael B. MacKuen, and James A. Stimson, "What Moves Macropartisanship? A Reply to Green, Palmquist, and Schickler," *American Political Science Review* 92 (December 1998): 901–12.

70. Janet M. Box-Steffensmeier and Renee M. Smith, "The Dynamics of Aggregate Partisanship," *American Political Science Review* 90 (September 1996): 567–80.

71. Franklin, "Issue Preferences, Socialization, and the Evaluation of Party Identification," p. 474.

72. Fiorina, *Retrospective Voting in American National Elections*, p. 84.

73. Donald R. Kinder and D. Roderick Kiewiet, "Sociotropic Politics: The American Case," *British Journal of Political Science* 11 (April 1981): 129–61; Douglas A. Hibbs Jr., with the assistance of R. Douglas Rivers and Nicholas Vasilatos, "The Dynamics of Political Support for American Presidents among Occupational and Partisan Groups," *American Journal of Political Science* 26 (May 1982): 312–32.

74. Converse, "The Nature of Belief Systems in Mass Publics"; Philip E. Converse and Gregory B. Markus, "Plus Ça Change: The New CPS Election Study Panel," *American Political Science Review* 73 (March 1979): 18–30. In view of the resistance to change of individual voters and the fact that nevertheless in aggregate there are changes, it is worth considering the idea that change occurs through processes by which old voters are replaced by new. This is strongly suggested for Canada by Richard Johnston in "Party Alignment and Realignment in Canada, 1911–1965," PhD dissertation, Stanford University, 1976. V. O. Key Jr. also supported a mobilization-of-new-voters interpretation in "A Theory of Critical Elections," *Journal of Politics* 17 (February 1955): 3–18. Arthur S. Goldberg's study of American data finds that children tend to defect from the party identification of their parents when the parents' party identification is atypical for their status and the children are relatively well-educated. See Goldberg, "Social Determinism and Rationality as Bases of Party Identification," *American Political Science Review* 63 (March 1969): 5–25. Kristi Andersen, *The Creation of a Democratic Majority, 1928–1936* (Chicago: University of Chicago Press, 1979), argues that "the surge in the Democratic vote in 1932 and 1936 came primarily from newly mobilized groups" (p. 69): those who came of political age in the 1920s but did not vote until 1928, 1932, or 1936, and those who came of age between 1928 and 1936. On the other side, see the intriguing arguments for opinion change by individual voters in Robert S. Erikson and Kent L. Tedin, "The 1928–1936 Partisan Realignment: The Case for the Conversion Hypothesis," *American Political Science Review* 75 (December 1981): 951–62.

75. Donald R. Kinder, "Diversity and Complexity in American Public Opinion," in Ada W. Finifter, ed., *Political Science: The State of the Discipline* (Washington, DC: American Political Science Association, 1983), pp. 389–425, at 410 (including footnote; emphasis in original).

76. Pew Research Center for the People and the Press. "Fewer Voters Identify as Republicans: Democrats Now Have the Advantage in 'Swing' States," 20 March 2008, available at http://pewresearch.org/pubs/773/fewer-voters-identify-as-republicans.

77. See Martin P. Wattenberg, *The Decline of American Political Parties, 1952–1996* (Cambridge, MA: Harvard University Press, 1998).

78. Keith et al., *The Myth of the Independent Voter*, p. 13.

79. Pew Research Center for the People and the Press, *Trend in Party Identification 1939–2012* (Washington, DC, 2012) http://www.people-press.org/2012/06/01/trend-in-party-identification-1939-2012/. Partisan independents—leaners—vote their party preferences less frequently than

strong party identifiers but more frequently than weak party identifiers, and pure independents do not vote very much at all. Between 1952 and 1988, an average of 67 percent of Democratic-leaning independents voted Democratic in presidential elections, as compared to 63 percent of "weak" Democrats; 86 percent of Republican-leaning independents voted for Republican candidates during the same period, as compared to 85 percent of "weak" Republicans. Keith et al., *The Myth of the Independent Voter*, p. 68. Party identification was considered strong in 1952 at a time when, according to National Election Studies data, 23 percent of the adult population declared themselves to be independents: 10 percent leaning to the Democrats, 7 percent leaning to the Republicans, and 6 percent pure independents. By 1980, the proportion of self-styled independents had risen to 34 percent: 13 percent pure, 11 percent Democratic, and 10 percent Republican. It has remained more or less stable since. Thus, while the number of pure independents has nearly doubled, they are still not a large fraction of the potential electorate. It is easy to overstate the political impact of the decline in party identifiers, in view of the fact that the increase among independents is divided between two-thirds who are in effect hidden party supporters and one-third who are mostly nonvoters. Keith et al., *The Myth of the Independent Voter*, pp. 47–51.

80. Converse, "The Role of Belief Systems in Mass Publics"; Kinder, "Diversity and Complexity in American Public Opinion"; Green, Palmquist, and Schickler, *Partisan Hearts and Minds*.

81. Connelly, "How Americans Voted."

82. CNN.com, "Election Center 2008: Exit Polls," http://www.cnn.com/ELECTION/2008/results/polls/#USP00p1.

83. CNN.com, Election Center 2012: Exit Polls," http://www.cnn.com/election/2012/results/race/president.

84. Larry M. Bartels, "The Irrational Electorate," *Wilson Quarterly*, Autumn 2008, http://www.princeton.edu/~bartels/how_stupid.pdf.

Chapter 2

1. Some years ago, David R. Mayhew noticed this pattern of difference in the congressional parties. See Mayhew, *Party Loyalty Among Congressmen: The Difference Between Democrats and Republicans, 1947-1962* (Cambridge, MA: Harvard University Press, 1966).

2. CNN.com, "Election Center 2008: Exit Polls," http://www.cnn.com/ELECTION/2008/results/polls/#USP00p1. CNN.com, "Election Center 2012: Exit Polls," http://www.cnn.com/election/2012/results/race/president.

3. This table is an adaptation and update of the work of Robert Axelrod's research on the electoral coalitions of the parties. See Robert Axelrod, "Where the Votes Come From: An Analysis of Electoral Coalitions, 1952–1968," *American Political Science Review* 66 (March 1972): 11–20; Axelrod, "Communication," *American Political Science Review* 68 (June 1974): 717–20; Axelrod, "Communication," *American Political Science Review* 72 (June 1978): 622–24; Axelrod, "Communication," *American Political Science Review* 76 (June 1982): 393–96; and Axelrod, "Presidential Election Coalitions in 1984," *American Political Science Review* 80 (March 1986): 281–84.

4. Harold W. Stanley, William J. Bianco, and Richard G. Niemi, "Partisanship and Group Support over Time: A Multivariate Analysis," *American Political Science Review* 80 (September 1986): 969–76.

5. *Gallup Poll Monthly* 374 (November 1996): 17–20.

6. Connelly, "How Americans Voted."

7. Raymond E. Wolfinger, "Dealignment, Realignment, and Mandates in the 1984 Election," in Austin Ranney, ed., *The American Elections of 1984* (Durham, NC: Duke University Press, 1985), pp. 277–96, at 290.

8. Axelrod, "Communication," June 1982, p. 395; Axelrod, "Presidential Election Coalitions in 1984"; Connelly, "How Americans Voted."

9. Antonio Gonzalez and Steven Ochoa, "The Latino Vote in 2008: Trends and Characteristics," William C. Velasquez Institution, Los Angeles, 2009, available at http://wcvi.org/data/election/wcvi_nov2008nationalanalysis_121808.pdf.

10. Secular Student Alliance, "Rise of the Godless," March 1, 2009, available at http://www.secularstudents.org/godless.

11. David A. Hopkins, "The 2008 Election and the Political Geography of the New Democratic Majority," *Polity* 41 (July 2009): 368–87.

12. See Raymond A. Bauer, Ithiel de Sola Pool, and Lewis Anthony Dexter, *American Business and Public Policy* (New York: Atherton Press, 1963), pp. 323–99, esp. p. 373. A similar argument is made in John R. Wright, "PACs, Contributions, and Roll Calls: An Organizational Perspective," *American Political Science Review* 79 (June 1985): 400–414.

13. Richard L. Berke, "Trade Vote Effect May Ebb Over Time," *New York Times*, November 23, 1993, sec. 1, p. 23; R. W. Apple Jr., "Unions Faltering in Reprisals against Trade Pact Backers," *New York Times*, February 21, 1994, p. A1.

14. Marjorie Connelly, "Portrait of the Electorate: Who Voted for Whom in the House," *New York Times*, November 13, 1994, sec. 1, p. 24.

15. See Seymour M. Lipset, Paul F. Lazarsfeld, Allen H. Barton, and Juan Linz, "The Psychology of Voting: An Analysis of Political Behavior," in Gardner Lindzey, ed., *Handbook of Social Psychology* (Cambridge, MA: Addison-Wesley, 1954).

16. Angus Campbell, Philip E. Converse, Warren E. Miller, and Donald E. Stokes, *The American Voter* (New York: Wiley, 1960), pp. 483–94.

17. CBS News/*New York Times* 1980 exit polls showed men voting 54 percent Reagan to 37 percent Carter and women 46 percent Reagan to 45 percent Carter. Everett Carll Ladd, "The Brittle Mandate: Electoral Dealignment and the 1980 Presidential Election," *Political Science Quarterly* 96 (Spring 1981): 1–25, at 16.

18. See Kathleen Frankovic, "Sex and Politics: New Alignments, Old Issues," *PS: Political Science and Politics* 15 (Summer 1982): 439–48; and Frankovic, "Women and Men: Is a Realignment Under Way?" *Public Opinion* 5 (April/May 1982): 21–32.

19. Connelly, "How Americans Voted." CNN.com, "Election Center 2012: Exit Polls," http://www.cnn.com/election/2012/results/race/president.

20. Karen M. Kaufmann, "Culture Wars, Secular Realignment, and the Gender Gap in Party Identification," *Political Behavior* 24 (September 2002): 283–307 (quote on p. 291).

21. Herbert F. Weisberg, "The Demographics of a New Voting Gap: Marriage Differences in American Voting," *Public Opinion Quarterly* 51 (Autumn 1987): 335–43; Eric Plutzer and Michael McBurnett, "Family Life and American Politics: The 'Marriage Gap' Reconsidered," *Public Opinion Quarterly* 55 (Spring 1991): 113–27; Laura Stoker and M. Kent Jennings, "Political Similarity and Influence between Husbands and Wives," in Alan S. Zuckerman, ed., *The Social Logic of Politics* (Philadelphia: Temple University Press, 2005), pp. 51–74.

22. Barbara Norrander and Clyde Wilcox, "The Gender Gap in Ideology," *Political Behavior* 30 (December 2008): 503–23 (quote on p. 521).

23. Frankovic, "Sex and Politics"; Karen M. Kaufmann and John R. Petrocik, "The Changing Politics of American Men: Understanding the Sources of the Gender Gap," *American Journal of Political Science* 43 (July 1999): 864–87.

24. Kaufmann, "Culture Wars."

25. Pamela Johnston Conover and Virginia Sapiro, "Gender, Feminist Consciousness, and War," *American Journal of Political Science* 37 (November 1993): 1079–99; Carole Kennedy Chaney, R. Michael Alvarez, and Jonathan Nagler, "Explaining the Gender Gap in U.S. Presidential Elections, 1980–1992," *Political Research Quarterly* 51 (June 1998): 311–39.

26. Indeed, some of the most vocal groups have no membership at all and exist only as lobbying organizations. See Jeffrey M. Berry, *Lobbying for the People: The Political Behavior of Public*

Interest Groups (Princeton, NJ: Princeton University Press, 1977), p. 186; and Robert D. Putnam, *Bowling Alone: The Collapse and Revival of American Community* (New York: Simon and Schuster, 2000), pp. 49–64.

27. "Why Americans Are Mad: An Interview with Rush Limbaugh," *Policy Review* 61 (Summer 1992), p. 47; "Behind the Bestsellers," *Publishers Weekly*, October 4, 1993, p. 14; Joyce Howard Price, "Scandal Rushes Limbaugh Back into Radio's Top Spot," *Washington Times*, September 27, 1998, p. A3; Dana Milbank, "My Bias for Mainstream News," *Washington Post*, March 20, 2005, p. B01.

28. Joseph E. Cantor, "PACs: Political Financiers of the '80s," *Congressional Research Service Review*, February 1982, pp. 14–16; Xandra Kayden and Eddie Mahe Jr., *The Party Goes On: The Persistence of the Two-Party System in the United States* (New York: Basic Books, 1985).

29. "Corporate Political Action Committees Are Less Oriented to Republicans Than Expected," *Congressional Quarterly*, April 8, 1978, pp. 849–54; Theodore J. Eismeier and Philip H. Pollock III, *Business, Money and the Rise of Corporate PACs in American Elections* (New York: Quorum Books, 1988), pp. 79–96.

30. Thomas J. Rudolph, "Corporate and Labor PAC Contributions in House Elections: Measuring the Effects of Majority Party Status," *Journal of Politics* 61 (February 1999): 195–206; Gary C. Jacobson, *The Politics of Congressional Elections*, 6th ed. (New York: Longman, 2004), pp. 63–75; Federal Election Commission, "PAC Contributions to Candidates, 1993–2009," http://www.fec.gov/press/press2010/20100406Pary_Files/2contribhistory2009.pdf.

31. Edwin M. Epstein, "Corporations and Labor Unions in Electoral Politics," *Annals of the American Academy of Political and Social Science* 425 (May 1976), p. 49. The Bipartisan Campaign Reform Act (BCRA) of 2002, sometimes known as the McCain-Feingold or Shays-Meehan law after its congressional sponsors, did not change the contribution limits applicable to PACs.

32. Ibid., p. 50. For more on PACs, see William J. Crotty and Gary C. Jacobson, *American Parties in Decline* (Boston: Little, Brown, 1980), pp. 100–155; Edwin M. Epstein, "PACs and the Modern Political Process," in Betty Bock et al., eds., *The Modern Corporation: Size and Impacts* (New York: Columbia University Press, 1984), pp. 399–496; Michael J. Malbin, ed., *Parties, Interest Groups, and Campaign Finance Laws* (Washington, DC: American Enterprise Institute, 1980); Elizabeth Drew, *Politics and Money* (New York: Macmillan, 1983); Theodore J. Eismeier and Philip H. Pollock III, "A Tale of Two Elections: PAC Money in 1980 and 1984," *Corruption and Reform* 1 (1986): 189–207; Anthony Corrado, *Creative Campaigning: PACs and the Presidential Selection Process* (Boulder, CO: Westview Press, 1992); David M. Hart, "Why Do Some Firms Give? Why Do Some Give a Lot? High-Tech PACs, 1977–1996," *Journal of Politics* 63 (November 2001): 1230–49.

33. This is a venerable idea. For example, see American Political Science Association, "Toward a More Responsible Two-Party System," Report of the Committee on Political Parties, 1950.

34. Frank J. Sorauf, "Parties and Political Action Committees in American Politics," in Kay Lawson and Peter Merkl, eds., *When Parties Fail* (Princeton, NJ: Princeton University Press, 1988), pp. 35–62.

35. Citizens United vs. FEC 2010, 50.

36. McCutcheon et al. vs. FEC 2013, 40.

37. These and other totals cited in this section are from https://www.opensecrets.org/pres12/.

38. This issue is also about money, mainly restricting the amount of money litigants can extract from business enterprises.

39. There are, of course, numerous ways of gaining access to public officials, but participation in their original selection is the primary avenue of access used by political parties. Our interpretation of parties is based on a rich literature: for example, Pendleton Herring, *The Politics of Democracy: American Parties in Action*, rev. ed. (New York: W. W. Norton, 1965); V. O. Key Jr., *Politics, Parties and Pressure Groups*, 5th ed. (New York: Crowell, 1964); David B. Truman, "Federalism and the Party System," in Arthur MacMahon, ed., *Federalism: Mature and Emergent* (New

York: Doubleday, 1955), pp. 115–36; Anthony Downs, *An Economic Theory of Democracy* (New York: Harper, 1957); Leon D. Epstein, *Political Parties in the American* Mold (Madison: University of Wisconsin Press, 1986); and a burgeoning literature on state and local political party organizations. See especially David B. Truman, *The Governmental Process* (New York: Knopf, 1971), pp. 262–87; Malcolm E. Jewell and Sarah M. Morehouse, *Political Parties and Elections in American States*, 9th ed. (Washington, DC: CQ Press, 2001); David R. Mayhew, *Placing Parties in American Politics* (Princeton, NJ: Princeton University Press, 1986); and Larry J. Sabato and Bruce Larson, *The Party's Just Begun: Shaping Political Parties for America's Future*, 2nd ed. (New York: Longman, 2002).

40. See Jacobson, *The Politics of Congressional Elections*, 6th ed., pp. 122–46; and Bruce Cain, John Ferejohn, and Morris Fiorina, *The Personal Vote: Constituency Service and Electoral Independence* (Cambridge, MA: Harvard University Press, 1987). For evidence that parties are beginning to reassert influence over candidate nominations, see Casey B. K. Dominguez, "Before the Primary: Party Participation in Congressional Nominating Processes," PhD dissertation, University of California, Berkeley, 2005.

41. For a more expansive view of endorsements, see Marty Cohen, David Karol, Hans Noel, and John Zaller, *The Party Decides: Presidential Nominations Before and After Reform* (Chicago: University of Chicago Press, 2008).

42. See John F. Bibby, "Party Renewal in the National Republican Party," in Gerald M. Pomper, ed., *Party Renewal in America* (New York: Praeger, 1980), pp. 102–15; and Cornelius P. Cotter and John F. Bibby, "Institutional Development of Parties and the Thesis of Party Decline," *Political Science Quarterly* 95 (Spring 1980): 1–27.

43. Herbert McClosky, Paul J. Hoffman, and Rosemary O'Hara, "Issue Conflict and Consensus among Party Leaders and Followers," *American Political Science Review* 54 (June 1960): 406–27. The authors compared large samples of Democratic and Republican leaders on twenty-four major public issues and conclude that "the belief that the two American parties are identical in principle and doctrine has little foundation in fact. Examination of the opinions of Democratic and Republican leaders show them to be distinct communities of co-believers who diverge sharply on many important issues." They add, "little support was found for the belief that deep cleavages exist among the electorate but are ignored by the leaders. One might, indeed, more accurately assert the contrary, to wit: that the natural cleavages between the leaders are largely ignored by the voters" (pp. 425–26). They found in 1956 that on most issues, the Democratic Party elite held positions not only closer to the Democratic rank and file but also closer to the Republican rank and file than those of the Republican elite. While the party elites still differed significantly from each other in 1972, the tables had turned and the "Republican elite held views that were more representative of the views and values of rank and file Democrats than were the views of Democratic delegates." Jeane Kirkpatrick, "Representation in the American National Conventions: The Case of 1972," *British Journal of Political Science* 5 (July 1975): 265–322. Differences between the party elites have increased substantially since 1972; see Warren E. Miller and M. Kent Jennings, *Parties in Transition: A Longitudinal Study of Party Elites and Party Supporters* (New York: Russell Sage Foundation, 1986); and Marc J. Hetherington, "Resurgent Mass Partisanship: The Role of Elite Polarization," *American Political Science Review* 95 (September 2001): 619–31.

44. For varying assessments of polarization, see Morris P. Fiorina and Samuel J. Abrams, *Disconnect: The Breakdown in Representation in American Politics* (Norman: University of Oklahoma Press, 2012) and Alan I. Abramowitz, *The Disappearing Center: Engaged Citizens, Polarization and American Democracy* (New Haven, CT: Yale University Press, 2010).

45. Charlotte Allen, "For Catholic Politicians, A Hard Line," *Washington Post*, April 11, 2004, p. B01.

46. John F. Bibby, Robert J. Huckshorn, James L. Gibson, and Cornelius P. Cotter, *Party Organization and American Politics* (New York: Praeger, 1984), p. 314; John F. Bibby, "State Party

Organizations: Strengthened and Adapting to Candidate-Centered Politics and Nationalization," in L. Sandy Maisel, ed., *The Parties Respond: Changes in American Parties and Campaigns*, 4th ed. (Boulder, CO: Westview Press, 2002), pp. 19–46.

47. The Supreme Court gives the national convention the right to regulate standards for admission to it, even overriding enactments of state legislatures on the subject of primary elections, and in this important respect national standards can be imposed on state party organizations. See Cousins v. Wigoda, 419 U.S. 477 (1975) and Democratic Party of the U.S. et al. v. LaFollette et al., 450 U.S. 107 (1981). See also Everett Carll Ladd Jr. with Charles D. Hadley, *Transformations of the American Party System* (New York: Norton, 1975); Austin Ranney, *Curing the Mischiefs of Faction: Party Reform in America* (Berkeley: University of California Press, 1975); William Crotty, *Party Reform* (New York: Longman, 1983); James Ceaser, *Reforming the Reforms* (Cambridge, MA: Ballinger, 1982); Gary D. Wekkin, *Democrat versus Democrat* (Columbia: University of Missouri Press, 1984); and Nelson W. Polsby, *Consequences of Party Reform* (New York: Oxford University Press, 1983).

48. Paul S. Herrnson, "National Party Organizations at the Dawn of the Twenty-First Century," in Maisel, ed., *The Parties Respond*, pp. 47–78.

49. See William S. Livingston, "A Note on the Nature of Federalism," *Political Science Quarterly* 67 (March 1952): 81–95; Mayhew, *Placing Parties in American Politics*.

50. See Ronald B. Rapoport and Walter J. Stone, *Three's a Crowd: The Dynamic of Third Parties, Ross Perot, and Republican Resurgence* (Ann Arbor: University of Michigan Press, 2005).

51. Steven J. Rosenstone, Roy L. Behr, and Edward H. Lazarus, *Third Parties in America*, 2nd ed. (Princeton, NJ: Princeton University Press, 1996), p. 19.

52. At least one study suggests that Perot's candidacy hurt Bush more than Clinton, though not enough to affect the outcome of the election; see R. Michael Alvarez and Jonathan Nagler, "Economics, Issues and the Perot Candidacy: Voter Choice in the 1992 Election," *American Journal of Political Science* 37 (August 1995): 714–44, at 737–38. Alvarez and Nagler estimate that Perot supporters would have divided about evenly between Bush and Clinton had Perot not run, while the rest of the electorate preferred Clinton to Bush 53 percent to 47 percent. In addition, Perot drew most of his support from men, who are otherwise more likely to vote Republican than are women.

53. Herbert F. Weisberg and David C. Kimball, "Attitudinal Correlates of the 1992 Presidential Vote," in Herbert F. Weisberg, ed., *Democracy's Feast: Elections in America* (Chatham, NJ: Chatham House, 1995), p. 104.

54. See Dean Lacy and Quin Monson, "The Origins and Impact of Votes for Third-Party Candidates: A Case Study of the 1998 Minnesota Gubernatorial Election," *Political Research Quarterly* 55 (June 2002): 409–37.

55. Daniel Mazmanian has shown that third-party candidates do best in years in which there is an intensely conflictual issue on the political agenda, suggesting that focusing discontent and raising issues are, for these candidates, functions most profitably performed in unison. Mazmanian, *Third Parties in Presidential Elections* (Washington, DC: Brookings Institution, 1974), p. 28.

56. See Paul R. Abramson, John H. Aldrich, Phil Paolino, and David W. Rohde, "Third-Party and Independent Candidates: Wallace, Anderson, and Perot," *Political Science Quarterly* 110 (Fall 1995): 349–67.

Chapter 3

1. The unit rule is not prescribed in the Constitution or by federal law. Instead, it is the result of individual state action that provides, in all states except Maine and Nebraska, that electors for party nominees are grouped together and elected en bloc on a "general ticket" such that a vote for one elector is a vote for all the electors on that ticket, with a plurality vote electing all electors for the state. Missouri senator Thomas Hart Benton said in 1824: "The general ticket system . . .

was the offspring of policy. . . . It was adopted by the leading men of [ten states] to enable them to consolidate the vote of the state." Thomas Jefferson had earlier pointed out that "while ten states choose either by legislatures or by a general ticket it is folly and worse than folly for the other states not to do it." In short, once a few states maximized their impact by using the unit rule, the others followed suit. See Motion for Leave to File Complaint, Complaint and Brief, Delaware v. New York, No. 28 Original, U.S. Supreme Court, October term, 1966; and Neal R. Peirce, "The Electoral College Goes to Court," *The Reporter*, October 6, 1966.

In Maine and Nebraska the electoral vote of each congressional district (two in Maine and three in Nebraska) is determined by the vote within the district, and the two electoral votes that the states have by virtue of their senators are cast according to the overall vote in the state as a whole. Here is a summary of the Maine law, taken from *Nomination and Election of the President and Vice President of the United States Including the Manner of Selecting Delegates to National Political Conventions* (Washington, DC: Government Printing Office, 1980), p. 356:

"Electors shall vote by separate ballot for one person for President and one person for Vice President. A presidential elector is elected from each congressional district and two at large. They shall convene in the Senate chamber in Augusta on the first Monday after the second Wednesday of December at 2:00 p.m. following their election. The presidential electors at large shall cast their ballots for President and Vice President of the political party which received the largest number of votes in the State. The presidential electors of each congressional district shall cast their ballots for the candidates for President and Vice President of the political party which received the largest number of votes in each congressional district."

2. Further confirmation of the view that the electoral college benefits the more populous states is provided by Steven J. Brams and Morton D. Davis, "The 3/2's Rule in Presidential Campaigning," *American Political Science Review* 68 (March 1974): 113–34; Claude S. Colatoni, Terrence J. Levesque, and Peter D. Ordeshook, "Campaign Resource Allocations under the Electoral College," *American Political Science Review* 69 (March 1975): 141–52; and John A. Yunker and Lawrence D. Longley, "The Biases of the Electoral College: Who Is Really Advantaged?" in Donald R. Matthews, ed., *Perspectives on Presidential Selection* (Washington, DC: Brookings Institution, 1972), pp. 172–203.

3. "Presidential Campaign Stops: Who's Going Where," *Washington Post* website, http://www.washingtonpost.com/wp-srv/special/politics/2012-presidential-campaign-visits/.

4. Our discussion of money in elections owes a great deal to the work of Herbert Alexander, who, over the years, built up an unequaled store of knowledge on this subject. Important legislation affecting money in politics includes the Federal Election Campaign Act of 1971, the Federal Election Campaign Act Amendments of 1974 (2 USC 431), and, more recently, the Bipartisan Campaign Reform Act of 2002 (Pub. L. No. 107-155, 116 Stat. 81). For a wide-ranging set of materials on election reform up to and including the 1971 Act, see U.S. Senate Select Committee on Presidential Campaign Activities, *Election Reform: Basic References* (Washington, DC: Government Printing Office, 1973). A compact summary of the state of the law as of 1975 is contained in U.S. Senate Subcommittee on Privileges and Elections of the Committee on Rules and Administration, *Federal Election Campaign Laws* (Washington, DC: Government Printing Office, 1975). For a useful discussion of the law's political implications, see the American Bar Association, *Symposium on Campaign Financing Regulation* (Chicago: American Bar Association, 1975); and Jo Freeman, "Political Party Contributions and Expenditures under the Federal Election Campaign Act: Anomalies and Unfinished Business," *Pace Law Review* 4 (Winter 1984): 267–96.

5. Federal Election Commission, "FEC Summarizes Campaign Activity of the 2011–2012 Election Cycle," press release, April 19, 2013, http://www.fec.gov/press/press2013/20130419_2012-24m-Summary.shtml.

6. The total amount of independent expenditures in 2012 from OpenSecrets, "Total Outside Spending by Election Cycle, Excluding Party Committees," https://www.opensecrets.org/outsidespending/cycle_tots.php.

7. Federal Election Commission, "FEC Summarizes Campaign Activity of the 2011–2012 Election Cycle."

8. Alexander and Corrado, *Financing the 1992 Election*, pp. 44–46.

9. Jodi Kantor and Nicholas Confessore, "Leading Role in Obama '08, But Backstage in '12," *New York Times*, July 15, 2012, p. A1.

10. Michael Cornfield, "Game-Changers: New Technology and the 2008 Presidential Election," in Larry J. Sabato, ed., *The Year of Obama: How Barack Obama Won the White House* (New York: Longman, 2009), p. 217.

11. Michael Toner, "The Impact of Federal Election Laws on the 2008 Presidential Election," in Sabato, ed., *The Year of Obama*, pp. 153–54.

12. Alexander and Corrado, *Financing the 1992 Election*, p. 69. See also Charles T. Royer, ed., *Campaign for President: The Managers Look at '92* (Hollis, NH: Hollis Publishing Company, 1994), pp. 83–84.

13. Matthew Mosk and John Solomon, "Clinton, Obama Top $100 Million in 2007 Donations," *Washington Post*, January 1, 2008, p. A04.

14. Richard Stevenson and Glen Justice, "Bush Took In $130.8 Million in Political Contributions in 2003," *New York Times*, January 8, 2004, p. A21.

15. "Obama Campaign Reveals Biggest Fundraisers around Election Day," CNN, March 2, 2013, http://politicalticker.blogs.cnn.com/2013/03/02/obama-campaign-reveals -biggest-donors-around-election-day/.

16. Paul Blumenthal, "Obama Bundlers Raiser $55.5 Million for President's Re-Election," *Huffington Post*, October 15, 2011, http://www.huffingtonpost.com/2011/10/15/barack-obama- bundlers-55-million-dollars-re-election_n_1011877.html.

17. Federal Election Commission, "Public Funding of Presidential Elections," brochure, April 2014, http://www.fec.gov/pages/brochures/pubfund.shtml.

18. Susan Page and Jill Lawrence, "White House Hopefuls, Activists Are Stirring," *USA Today*, February 8, 2006, p. 5A.

19. Jim Acosta, "Pro-Romney Super PAC Slams Gingrich," CNN, December 21, 2011, http:// www.cnn.com/2011/12/21/politics/romney-super-pac/; Jane Mayer, "Attack Dog," *The New Yorker*, February 13, 2012, pp. 40–51.

20. Phil Hirschkorn, "The Donors Bankrolling the 2012 Super PACs," CBS News, May 7, 2012, http://www.cbsnews.com/news/the-donors-bankrolling-the-2012-super-pacs/; Alexandra Duszak, "PAC Profile: Winning Our Future," Center for Public Integrity, May 2014, http://www .publicintegrity.org/2012/01/30/7998/pac-profile-winning-our-future.

21. Federal Election Commission, "FEC Summarizes Campaign Activity of the 2011–2012 Election Cycle."

22. This requirement, known as the "magic words" test, is in practice ineffective, as most political advertising—even that financed directly by candidates—does not use "explicit advocacy" terms such as "vote for," "elect," or "defeat" anyway. To the viewer, advertising funded by soft money from parties is therefore virtually indistinguishable from that paid for by hard money campaign donations to candidates. See David B. Magleby, "Dictum Without Data: The Myth of Issue Advocacy and Party Building," Brigham Young University, http://csed.byu.edu/ Assets/Pew/Dictum.pdf; and Michael Franz and Kenneth Goldstein, "Following the (Soft) Money: Party Advertisements in American Elections," in L. Sandy Maisel, ed., *The Parties Respond: Changes in American Parties and Campaigns*, 4th ed. (Boulder, CO: Westview Press, 2002), pp. 139–62.

23. Federal Election Commission, "FEC Reports Increase in Party Fundraising for 2000," press release, May 15, 2001, http://www.fec.gov/press/051501partyfund/051501partyfund.html.

24. For more on the party-building effects of soft money, see Ray La Raja, "Political Parties in the Era of Soft Money," in Maisel, ed., *The Parties Respond*, pp. 163–88.

25. Sunlight Foundation, "Outside Spending by Race: President," http://reporting.sunlight-foundation.com/outside-spending-2012/race_detail/P/US/00/

26. For a perspective critical of the alleged effects of campaign money on the political system, see Elizabeth Drew, *The Corruption of American Politics: What Went Wrong and Why* (Secaucus, NJ: Birch Lane Press, 1999).

27. See Edwin M. Epstein, "Corporations and Labor Unions in Electoral Politics," *Annals of the American Academy of Political and Social Science* 425 (May 1976): 33–58.

28. Herbert E. Alexander, *Financing the 1980 Election* (Lexington, MA: Lexington Books, 1983), p. 109.

29. Herbert E. Alexander and Harold B. Meyers, "The Switch in Campaign Giving," *Fortune*, November 1965, pp. 103–8.

30. Herbert E. Alexander, *Financing the 1972 Election* (Lexington, MA: Lexington Books, 1976).

31. For expenditure figures, see ibid., pp. 17–24, and for 1956 to 1976, see Herbert E. Alexander, *Financing the 1976 Election* (Washington, DC: CQ Press, 1979).

32. Jim Rutenberg, "Nearing Record, Obama's Ad Effort Swamps McCain," *New York Times*, October 18, 2008, p. A1.

33. Kathleen Hall Jamieson, ed., *Electing the President 2012: The Insiders' View* (Philadelphia: University of Pennsylvania Press, 2013), p. 145.

34. Quoted in Jamieson, ed., *Electing the President 2012*, p. 38.

35. Herbert E. Alexander, "Financing the Parties and Campaigns," in Paul T. David, ed., *The Presidential Election and Transition, 1960–61* (Washington, DC: Brookings Institution, 1961), p. 119.

36. Alexander, *Financing the 1972 Election*, p. 98; and Alexander, *Financing the 1976 Election*, p. 169.

37. Alexander, *Financing the 1976 Election*, p. 246; Alexander, *Financing the 1980 Election*; *FEC Reports on Financial Activities 1979–1980*, Final Report, Presidential Pre-Nomination Campaign (Washington, DC: Government Printing Office, October 1981).

38. Herbert E. Alexander and Brian A. Haggerty, *Financing the 1984 Election* (Lexington, MA: Lexington Books, 1987), p. 149.

39. Alexander and Bauer, *Financing the 1988 Election*, pp. 37–38.

40. Federal Election Commission, "Disbursements, Cash, and Debts of Presidential Campaigns Through February 29, 2004," http://www.fec.gov/press/bkgnd/pres_cf/atm0229/presdisbursem32004.pdf.

41. Boatright, "Campaign Finance in the 2008 Election," p. 139.

42. Federal Election Commission, "Presidential Pre-Nomination Campaign Disbursements, March 31, 2012," http://www.fec.gov/press/bkgnd/pres_cf/pres_cf_odd_doc/presdisbursm42012.pdf.

43. Roger Simon, "Turning Point," *U.S. News and World Report*, July 19, 2004, pp. 34–75.

44. Edward Wyatt, "Clark Ending His Campaign After Poor Showing in South," *New York Times*, February 11, 2004, p. A25.

45. Michael Falcone, "Clinton Is Out $13 Million She Lent Campaign," *New York Times*, December 23, 2008, p. A16.

46. Like Forbes, most self-funding candidates lose their elections, proving that wealth cannot necessarily buy votes (or at least enough votes). See Jennifer A. Steen, *Self-Financed Candidates in Congressional Elections* (Ann Arbor: University of Michigan Press, 2006).

47. For the details on the Forbes campaign, see Corrado, "Financing the 1996 Elections," pp. 143–45; and William G. Mayer, "The Presidential Nominations," in Pomper, ed., *The Elections of 1996*, pp. 36–56.

48. John C. Green and Nathan S. Bigelow, "The 2000 Presidential Nominations: The Cost of Innovation," in David B. Magleby, ed., *Financing the 2000 Election* (Washington, DC: Brookings Institution, 2002), p. 55; Howard Kurtz and Ben White, "Forbes Signals He Will Withdraw," *Washington Post*, February 10, 2000, p. A6.

49. Mark Preston, Romney Spending $85,000-Plus a Day on TV Ads," CNN.com, November 13, 2007, http://www.cnn.com/2007/POLITICS/11/13/romney.ads/index.html.

50. Tarini Parti, "More Women Gave to President Obama Than to Mitt Romney," *Politico*, December 14, 2012, http://www.politico.com/story/2012/12/more-women-gave-to-obama-than-romney-85068.html.

51. Joshua Green, "The Science behind Those Obama Fundraising E-Mails," *Bloomberg Business*, November 29, 2012, http://www.bloomberg.com/bw/articles/2012-11-29/the-science-behind-those-obama-campaign-e-mails.

52. This information is now continuously available to the public on various Internet sites, e.g., Political Money Line, http://www.fecinfo.com.

53. Buckley et al. v. Valeo et al., 424 U.S. 1 (1976). See also Daniel D. Polsby, "Buckley v. Valeo: The Special Nature of Political Speech," *Supreme Court Review*, 1976, pp. 1–43.

54. Adam Liptak, "Supreme Court Blocks Ban on Corporate Political Spending," *New York Times*, January 21, 2010, p. A1.

55. See William L. Rivers, "The Correspondents after 25 Years," *Columbia Journalism Review* 1 (Spring 1962). "In 1960," he says, "57 percent of the daily newspapers reporting to the *Editor & Publisher* poll supported Nixon, and 16 percent supported Kennedy. In contrast, there are more than three times as many Democrats as there are Republicans among the Washington newspaper correspondents; slightly more than 32 percent are Democrats, and fewer than 10 percent are Republicans" (p. 5). See also S. Robert Lichter and Stanley Rothman, "Media and Business Elites," *Public Opinion* 4 (October/November 1981): 42–46, 59–60; and S. Robert Lichter, Stanley Rothman, and Linda S. Lichter, *The Media Elite* (Bethesda, MD: Adler and Adler, 1986).

56. Pew Research Center for the People and the Press, "The State of the News Media, 2004: An Annual Report on American Journalism," report, May 23, 2004, http://people-press.org/reports/display.php3?ReportID=214.

57. Michael J. Robinson, "Just How Liberal Is the News? 1980 Revisited," *Public Opinion* 5 (February/March 1983): 55–60.

58. For a definitive, though fictitious, commentary, see Nathanael West, *Miss Lonelyhearts* (New York: Harcourt, Brace, 1933).

59. See Richard Brody and Catherine R. Shapiro, "A Reconsideration of the Rally Phenomenon in Public Opinion," in Samuel Long, ed., *Political Behavior Annual*, vol. 2 (Boulder, CO: Westview Press, 1989). See also John E. Mueller, "Presidential Popularity from Truman to Johnson," *American Political Science Review* 64 (March 1970): 18–34; Kenneth N. Waltz, "Electoral Punishment and Foreign Policy Crises," in James N. Rosenau, ed., *Domestic Sources of Foreign Policy* (New York: Free Press, 1967), pp. 263–93; and Richard A. Brody, *Assessing the President: The Media, Elite Opinion, and Popular Support* (Stanford, CA: Stanford University Press, 1991).

60. Amos Tversky and Daniel Kahneman, "Rational Choice and the Framing of Decisions," *Journal of Business* 59 (1986): 251–78.

61. Aaron Wildavsky and Karl Dake, "Theories of Risk Perception: Who Fears What and Why," *Daedalus* 119 (Fall 1990): 41–60; Aaron B. Wildavsky, *But Is It True? A Citizen's Guide to Environmental Health and Safety Issues* (Cambridge, MA: Harvard University Press, 1995); Christopher J. Bosso, "Setting the Agenda: Mass Media and the Discovery of Famine in Ethiopia," in Michael Margolis and Gary A. Mauser, eds., *Manipulating Public Opinion: Essays on Public Opinion as a Dependent Variable* (Pacific Grove, CA: Brooks/Cole, 1989), pp. 153–74.

62. Joanne M. Miller and Jon A. Krosnick, "News Media Impact on the Ingredients of Presidential Evaluations: Politically Knowledgeable Citizens Are Guided by a Trusted Source," *American Journal of Political Science* 44 (April 2000): 301–15.

63. John R. Zaller, *The Nature and Origins of Mass Opinion* (New York: Cambridge University Press, 1992), pp. 6–16. Zaller's main work in this area remains unpublished: "The Role of Elites in Shaping Public Opinion," PhD dissertation, University of California, Berkeley, 1984.

64. See Theodore H. White, *The Making of the President, 1960* (New York: Atheneum, 1961), pp. 333–38. Corroborative testimony is given by Benjamin C. Bradlee, *Conversations with Kennedy* (New York: Norton, 1975). On Barry Goldwater's press relations, see Charles Mohr, "Requiem for a Lightweight," *Esquire*, August 1968, pp. 67–71, 121–22.

65. Timothy Crouse, *The Boys on the Bus* (New York: Random House, 1973), pp. 189–90; Theodore H. White, *The Making of the President, 1972* (New York: Atheneum, 1973), pp. 251–68. See also Jules Witcover, *The Resurrection of Richard Nixon* (New York: Putnam, 1970); and Joe McGinniss, *The Selling of the President, 1968* (New York: Trident Press, 1969).

66. Daron R. Shaw and Brian E. Roberts, "Campaign Events, the Media and the Prospects of Victory: The 1992 and 1996 U.S. Presidential Elections," *British Journal of Political Science* 30 (April 2000): 259–89.

67. See Frank Luther Mott, *The News in America* (Cambridge, MA: Harvard University Press, 1952), p. 110; and Edwin Emery and Henry L. Smith, *The Press and America* (Englewood Cliffs, NJ: Prentice Hall, 1954), p. 541ff.

68. Dave D'Alessio and Mike Allen, "Media Bias in Presidential Elections: A Meta-Analysis," *Journal of Communication* 50 (September 2000): 133–56, at 148–49.

69. Project for Excellence in Journalism, "Winning the Media Campaign," report, October 22, 2008, http://www.journalism.org/node/13307.

70. Pew Research Center Journalism Project, "Winning the Media Campaign 2012," November 2, 2012, http://www.journalism.org/2012/11/02/winning-media-campaign-2012/.

71. The classic formulation is by A. J. Liebling: "With the years, the quantity of news in newspaper is bound to diminish from its present low. The proprietor, as Chairman of the Board, will increasingly often say that he would like to spend 75 cents now and then on news coverage, but that he must be fair to his shareholders." Liebling, *The Press* (New York: Ballantine Books, 1961), p. 5. Occasionally, there is evidence of an improvement in the news coverage in some communities when the papers have been taken over by the more responsible chains. Cases in point include Philadelphia and San Jose, where the Knight-Ridder chain upgraded newspapers they purchased. However, these gains have recently been jeopardized everywhere by conditions of economic decline in the newspaper business. Knight-Ridder itself was sold in 2006 under pressure from stockholders who thought their shares were undervalued. See Katharine Q. Seelye and Andrew Ross Sorkin, "Newspaper Chain Agrees to a Sale for $4.5 Billion," *New York Times*, March 13, 2006, p. A1.

72. Bernard C. Cohen, *The Press and Foreign Policy* (Princeton, NJ: Princeton University Press, 1963), presents figures from a variety of sources on foreign affairs news (chap. 4). His conclusion: "The volume of coverage is low." See also Elie Abel, ed., *What's News: The Media in American Society* (San Francisco: Institute for Contemporary Studies, 1981).

73. Elmo Roper observed that "on the civil rights issue [in 1948], Mr. Dewey draws the support of voters favoring exactly opposite things, and more than that, each side thinks Dewey agrees with them." Hugh A. Bone, *American Politics and the Party System* (New York: McGraw-Hill, 1955), p. 477. In 1968, the bulk of those voting for Eugene McCarthy in the New Hampshire primary were not Vietnam "doves," as McCarthy was, but were even more belligerent about the war than Lyndon Johnson. See Philip E. Converse, "Public Opinion and Voting Behavior," in Fred I. Greenstein and Nelson W. Polsby, eds., *Handbook of Political Science* (Reading, MA: Addison-Wesley, 1975), vol. 4, pp. 75–169, at 81.

74. When asked by the Gallup poll in 1979 to gauge how much confidence they had in newspapers, among other institutions, 51 percent of the respondents said "a great deal or quite a lot," 47 percent said "some or very little," 1 percent said "none," and 1 percent had no opinion. *The Gallup Poll: Public Opinion 1979* (Wilmington, DE: Scholarly Resources, 1980), p. 159. In 1980 only 42 percent said "a great deal or quite a lot." *The Gallup Poll: Public Opinion 1980* (Wilmington, DE: Scholarly Resources, 1981), p. 247. By 1986, the number of respondents saying "a great

deal or quite a lot" had shrunk to 37 percent. Since then, reported confidence has remained fairly steady, falling as low as 29 percent in 1994 and rising as high as 39 percent in 1990. It stood at 35 percent in 1997. Frank Newport, "Small Business and Military Generate Most Confidence in Americans," *The Gallup Poll Monthly* 383 (August 1997), pp. 21–24. A CBS News/*New York Times* poll in early 2006 reported that 15 percent of respondents had "a great deal" of confidence in the news media, compared to 48 percent who had "a fair amount" of confidence and 36 percent who had little or no confidence. CBS News, "The State of the Media," press release, February 3, 2006, http://www.cbsnews.com/htdocs/pdf/020306POLL.pdf.

75. This paragraph summarizes the major findings of researchers on what has come to be called the "two-step flow" of information, emphasizing the influence of group membership and face-to-face interaction. See Elihu Katz and Paul F. Lazarsfeld, *Personal Influence* (Glencoe, IL: Free Press, 1955).

76. Pew Research Center for the People and the Press, "Cable Leads the Pack as Campaign News Source," February 7, 2012, http://www.people-press.org/2012/02/07/cable-leads -the-pack-as-campaign-news-source/.

77. David L. Vancil and Sue D. Pendell, "The Myth of Viewer-Listener Disagreement in the First Kennedy-Nixon Debate," *Central States Speech Journal* 38 (1987), pp. 16–27. See also James N. Druckman, "The Power of Television Images: The First Kennedy-Nixon Debate Revisited," *Journal of Politics* 65 (May 2003): 559–71.

78. Adam Nagourney, "Antiwar Stance Buoys Howard Dean in Iowa," *New York Times*, March 29, 2003, p. B12.

79. *Fox News Sunday* transcript, June 12, 2011, http://www.foxnews.com/on-air/fox-news- sunday/print/transcript/tim-pawlenty-defends-his-economic-plan-attacks-obamneycare.

80. Adam Sorensen, "Tim Pawlenty's ObamneyCare Wimp Out," *Time*, December 7, 2011, http:// content.time.com/time/specials/packages/article/0,28804,2101344_2100819_2100815,00.html.

81. Kevin Hechtkopf, "Rick Perry Fails to Remember What Agency He'd Get Rid of in GOP Debate," CBS News, November 10, 2011, http://www.cbsnews.com/news/ rick-perry-fails-to-remember-what-agency-hed-get-rid-of-in-gop-debate/.

82. C. Anthony Broh, "Horse Race Journalism," *Public Opinion Quarterly* 44 (Winter 1980): 514–29.

83. See, for example, Jules Witcover's comments about reporters' attempts to deny Gerald Ford the advantage of the White House in 1976. Witcover, *Marathon: The Pursuit of the Presidency, 1972–1976* (New York: Viking Press, 1977), pp. 528–56.

84. See the list of most popular websites as measured by Alexa at http://www.alexa.com/ topsites/countries/US.

85. Mitt Romney adviser Kevin Madden as quoted in Jamieson, ed., *Electing the President, 2012*, p. 57.

86. See, e.g., Tim Craig and Michael D. Shear, "Allen Quip Provokes Outrage, Apology," *Washington Post*, August 15, 2006, p. A01; Michael D. Shear, "'Macaca Moment' Marks a Shift in Momentum," *Washington Post*, September 3, 2006, p. C01.

87. "Full Transcript of the Mitt Romney Secret Video," *Mother Jones*, September 19, 2012, http://www.motherjones.com/politics/2012/09/full-transcript-mitt-romney-secret-video.

88. Michael D. Shear and Michael Barbaro, "In Video Clip, Romney Calls 47% 'Dependent' and Overly Entitled," *New York Times*, The Caucus blog, http://thecaucus.blogs.nytimes. com/2012/09/17/romney-faults-those-dependent-on-government/?_r=0.

89. David Corn, "The Story Behind the 47 Percent Video," *Mother Jones*, December 31, 2012, http://www.motherjones.com/politics/2012/12/story-behind-47-video.

90. Philip Rucker, "Romney: '47 Percent' Remarks Were 'Completely Wrong,'" *Washington Post*, October 5, 2012, http://www.washingtonpost.com/politics/decision2012/romney-47 -percent-remarks-were-completely-wrong/2012/10/05/a346beaa-0ed8-11e2-a310 -2363842b7057_story.html.

91. Quoted in Jamieson, ed., *Electing the President 2012*, pp. 66–67.

92. Memo posted on barackobama.com, August 29, 2007. See also Zack Exley, "Obama Organizers Plot a Miracle," www.huffingtonpost.com, August 27, 2007.

93. Colin Delany, blog post, December 23, 2008, at www.epolitics.com.

94. Nelson W. Polsby, "The Democratic Nomination," in Austin Ranney, ed., *The American Elections of 1980* (Washington, DC: American Enterprise Institute, 1981), pp. 37–60; and *The Gallup Opinion Index*, Report No. 183, December 1980, p. 51. Another example occurred during the 1964 campaign, when it was announced that United States vessels in the Gulf of Tonkin had been fired upon and President Johnson took to the airwaves to promise vigorous defensive measures. In late July, just before the incident, he received favorable ratings from 59 percent of the voters, to 31 percent for Goldwater; in early August, just after the incident, the president's score went up to 65 percent, and Goldwater's declined to 29 percent. American Institute of Public Opinion Survey, released October 18, 1964. For other examples, see Nelson W. Polsby, *Congress and the Presidency*, 4th ed. (Englewood Cliffs, NJ: Prentice Hall, 1986), p. 73; and Brody, *Assessing the President*.

95. Quoted in *Campaign for President: The Managers Look at 2012*, Institute of Politics at Harvard University Kennedy School of Government (Lanham, MD: Rowman & Littlefield, 2013), p. 199.

96. Christopher Achen and Larry Bartels have demonstrated that when voters believe that conditions are worsening, they respond by punishing incumbents at the polls, even if public officials could not possibly be responsible for the causes of distress (such as a drought, or, remarkably, a series of shark attacks which ruined the vacation season for New Jersey resort towns in the summer of 1916). Christopher H. Achen and Larry M. Bartels, "Blind Retrospection: Electoral Responses to Drought, Flu, and Shark Attacks," unpublished paper, Princeton University, 2004, http://www.international.ucla.edu/media/files/PERG.Achen.pdf.

97. Howard S. Bloom and H. Douglas Price, "Voter Response to Short-Run Economic Conditions: The Asymmetric Effect of Prosperity and Recession," *American Political Science Review* 69 (December 1975): 1240–54. For a more recent discussion of the relationship between economic performance, other events, and presidential popularity, see Brody, *Assessing the President*, pp. 91–132; and Samuel Kernell, *Going Public: New Strategies of Presidential Leadership*, 4th ed. (Washington, DC: CQ Press, 2006).

98. Much of the material in this section is adapted from Nelson W. Polsby, *Political Promises: Essays and Commentary on American Politics* (New York: Oxford University Press, 1974), pp. 156–59.

99. Ray C. Fair, "Econometrics and Presidential Elections," *Journal of Economic Perspectives* 10 (Summer 1996): 89–102; Alan I. Abramowitz, "An Improved Model for Predicting Presidential Election Outcomes," *PS: Political Science and Politics* 21 (Fall 1988): 843–47. See also James E. Campbell and Thomas E. Mann, "Forecasting the Presidential Election: What Can We Learn from the Models?" *The Brookings Review* 14 (Fall 1996): 27–31; and Larry M. Bartels and John Zaller, "Presidential Vote Models: A Recount," *PS: Political Science and Politics* 34 (March 2001): 9–20.

100. Ross K. Baker, "The Second Reagan Term," in Gerald M. Pomper, ed., *The Election of 1984: Reports and Interpretations* (Chatham, NJ: Chatham House, 1985), p. 150.

Chapter 4

1. Much of the historical discussion of the nomination process in this chapter is drawn from our own observations via the mass media, the personal observations of one of us who attended the Democratic National Conventions of 1960, 1968, 1972, and 1980 and the Republican National Conventions of 1964 and 1980, and from a classic set of basic texts on American parties and elections, including Moisei Ostrogorski, *Democracy and the Party System in*

the United States (New York: Macmillan, 1910); Charles Edward Merriam and Harold Foote Gosnell, *The American Party System: An Introduction to the Study of Political Parties in the United States*, rev. ed. (New York: Macmillan, 1929); Peter H. Odegard and E. Allen Helms, *American Politics: A Study in Political Dynamics* (New York: Harper & Brothers, 1938); Pendleton Herring, *The Politics of Democracy: American Parties in Action*, rev. ed. (New York: W. W. Norton, 1965); E. E. Schattschneider, *Party Government* (New York: Farrar and Rinehart, 1942); D. D. McKean, *Party and Pressure Politics* (Boston: Houghton Mifflin, 1949); V. O. Key Jr., *Politics, Parties and Pressure Groups*, 5th ed. (New York: Crowell, 1964); Edward McChesney Sait and H. R. Penniman, *Sait's American Parties and Elections*, 4th ed. (New York: Appleton-Century-Crofts, 1948); Austin Ranney and Willmoore Kendall, *Democracy and the American Party System* (New York: Harcourt Brace, 1956); William Goodman, *The Two-Party System in the United States* (Princeton, NJ: Van Nostrand, 1960); and Gerald M. Pomper, *Nominating the President: The Politics of Convention Choice*, 2nd ed. (Evanston, IL: Northwestern University Press, 1966). We also found quite useful a more specialized literature on nominations, including Paul T. David, Malcolm C. Moos, and Ralph M. Goldman, *Presidential Nominating Politics in 1952*, vols. 1–5 (Baltimore: Johns Hopkins University Press, 1954); Paul T. David, Ralph M. Goldman, and Richard C. Bain, *The Politics of National Party Conventions* (Washington, DC: Brookings Institution, 1960); and Richard C. Bain, *Convention Decisions and Voting Records* (Washington, DC: Brookings Institution, 1960).

More recent texts on party organization and presidential nominations that a student might find useful include Samuel J. Eldersveld, *Political Parties in American Society* (New York: Basic Books, 1982); Joel L. Fleishman, ed., *The Future of American Political Parties* (Englewood Cliffs, NJ: Prentice Hall, 1982); Howard Reiter, *Selecting the President* (Philadelphia: University of Pennsylvania Press, 1985); William J. Crotty and Gary C. Jacobson, *American Parties in Decline* (Boston: Little, Brown, 1980); Gerald M. Pomper, *Elections in America: Control and Influence in Democratic Politics*, rev. ed. (New York: Longman, 1980); Nelson W. Polsby, *Consequences of Party Reform* (New York: Oxford University Press, 1983); Everett Carll Ladd Jr., with Charles D. Hadley, *Transformations of the American Party System*, 2nd ed. (New York: Norton, 1978); Leon D. Epstein, *Political Parties in the American Mold* (Madison: University of Wisconsin Press, 1986); Austin Ranney, *Curing the Mischiefs of Faction: Party Reform in America* (Berkeley: University of California Press, 1975); and William G. Mayer, ed., *In Pursuit of the White House: How We Choose Our Presidential Nominees* (Chatham, NJ: Chatham House, 1996).

2. For each party's most recent delegate selection rules, see Democratic National Committee, "Call for the 2008 Democratic National Convention," http://www.democrats.org/page/-/pdf/call2008ConventionFINAL.pdf; Republican National Committee, "Call for the 2008 Republican National Convention," http://web.archive.org/web/20080730192248/http://www.gop.com/images/2008_Call_FINAL.pdf. After the 2000 election, the Democratic National Committee revised its rules in order to allow states other than Iowa and New Hampshire to select delegates beginning in early February rather than early March, thus matching the expanded delegate selection "window" already allowed by the Republicans. This change prompted additional front-loading of the primary season as several states moved up their primaries to take advantage of the new rules. In order to prohibit a recurrence of the 2008 calendar, when severe front-loading resulted in Iowa and New Hampshire voting in early January in order to precede other states' primaries, both national party committees authorized a revised calendar for 2012 that required most states to wait until March to hold their primaries. See Molly Ball, "Pols Hope to Push Back Primaries," *Politico*, December 19, 2010, http://www.politico.com/news/stories/1210/46567.html.

3. Democrats have resisted "open" primaries in which any citizen can participate. The national Democratic Party has fought to prohibit Republicans from voting in Democratic presidential primaries. See Gary D. Wekkin, *Democrat versus Democrat* (Columbia: University of Missouri Press, 1984); see also Tashjian v. Republican Party of Connecticut, 107 S. 544 (1986). The rules of both national parties permit states to allow independents to vote in presidential

primaries, but whether they can actually do so varies according to state law. Sometimes state officials attempt to manipulate these laws in order to help their favored nominees, as when Michigan Republicans opened their 2000 primary to independent voters with the expectation that they would help George W. Bush defeat Steve Forbes. This strategy ultimately backfired, as John McCain defeated Bush in Michigan partially on the strength of support from independents. See Bruce E. Cain and Megan Mullin, "Competing for Attention and Votes: The Role of State Parties in Setting Presidential Nomination Rules," in L. Sandy Maisel, ed., *The Parties Respond: Changes in American Parties and Campaigns* (Boulder, CO: Westview Press, 2002), pp. 99–120.

4. Frank Newport and Joseph Carroll, "Key Election Trends from 2007," report for Gallup, December 28, 2007, http://www.gallup.com/poll/103495/election-summary.aspx.

5. Quoted in *Campaign for President: The Managers Look at 2012*, Institute of Politics at Harvard University Kennedy School of Government (Lanham, MD: Rowman & Littlefield, 2013), pp. 62–63, 66.

6. Quoted in *Campaign for President*, p. 108.

7. James Hohmann and Alex Isenstadt, "RNC Rolls Out 2016 Debate Schedule," *Politico*, January 16, 2015, http://www.politico.com/story/2015/01/rnc-2016-debate-schedule-114329.html.

8. One recent study argues that the "invisible primary" is in fact the key period for determining nomination outcomes, with party leaders steering support to their favored candidates during this time that is of immense assistance in winning the subsequent primaries and caucuses; see Marty Cohen, David Karol, Hans Noel, and John Zaller, *The Party Decides: Presidential Nominations Before and After Reform* (Chicago: University of Chicago Press, 2008).

9. Citizens and politicians in these states seem to care deeply about their status as first in the nation and guard it jealously. Indeed, when Arizona began to consider challenging New Hampshire by scheduling an early primary for 1996, Senator Phil Gramm was widely criticized in New Hampshire for seeming to approve of that attempt; see "Rocky Start in Granite State Knocks Gramm Off Balance," *Washington Post*, February 26, 1995, p. A18.

Our discussion of Iowa and New Hampshire borrows freely from Nelson W. Polsby, "The Iowa Caucuses in a Front-Loaded System: A Few Historical Lessons," in Peverill Squire, ed., *The Iowa Caucuses and the Presidential Nominating Process* (Boulder, CO: Westview Press, 1989), pp. 149–62. See also Squire, *The Iowa Caucuses*; Gary R. Orren and Nelson W. Polsby, eds., *Media and Momentum: The New Hampshire Primary and Nomination Politics* (Chatham, NJ: Chatham House, 1987); "Special Report: Political Odd Couple," W. John Moore, "Rural Prospecting," and Burt Solomon, "Where America Is At," all *National Journal*, September 26, 1987, pp. 2394–409; "When Iowa Becomes Brigadoon," *Economist*, January 9, 1988, pp. 21–22; "Iowa," *Congressional Quarterly Weekly Report*, August 29, 1987, pp. 1994–97; and "The Iowa Democratic Caucuses: How They Work," *New York Times*, February 7, 1988, p. 14.

10. Indeed, Henry E. Brady and Richard Johnston argue that the main educational effect of the entire primary process for voters is to inform them about candidate viability. See "What's the Primary Message? Horse Race or Issue Journalism," in Orren and Polsby, eds., *Media and Momentum*, pp. 127–86.

11. As Muskie told Theodore H. White: "That previous week . . . I'd been down to Florida, then I flew to Idaho, then I flew to California, then I flew back to Washington to vote in the Senate, and I flew back to California, and then I flew into Manchester and I was hit with this [attack]. I'm tough physically, but no one could do that." White, *The Making of the President, 1972* (New York: Atheneum, 1973), pp. 81–82.

12. "Ford's 1976 Campaign for the GOP Nomination," *1976 Congressional Quarterly Almanac* (Washington, DC: CQ Press, 1976), p. 900.

13. Elizabeth Drew writes of Carter: "Early successes and surprises were big elements in Carter's plan. . . . The basic idea was to show early that the southerner could do well in the North and could best Wallace in the South. . . . He visited a hundred and fourteen towns in Iowa, beginning in 1975 (and his family made countless other visits)." Drew, *American Journal: The Events of 1976*

(New York: Random House, 1977), pp. 143–44, 466–67. See also Jules Witcover, *Marathon: The Pursuit of the Presidency, 1972–1976* (New York: Viking Press, 1977), p. 14.

14. R. W. Apple Jr., "Carter Defeats Bayh by 2-1 in Iowa Vote," *New York Times*, January 20, 1976, p. A1. This was not the first time in 1976 that Apple had puffed Carter. Elizabeth Drew's diary of January 27, 1976 reported: "A story by R. W. Apple Jr., in the *Times* last October saying that Carter was doing well in Iowa was itself a political event, prompting other newspaper stories that Carter was doing well in Iowa, and then more news magazine and television coverage for Carter than might otherwise have been his share." Drew, *American Journal*, p. 6.

15. Nelson W. Polsby, "The Democratic Nomination and the Evolution of the Party System," in Austin Ranney, ed., *The American Elections of 1984* (Durham, NC: Duke University Press, 1985), pp. 36–65. In the eight-day gap between Iowa and New Hampshire, Gary Hart went from 10 percent in the public opinion polls to a 41 percent vote in the New Hampshire primary itself. See Peter Hart's comments in the *Presidential Campaign Hotline*, January 25, 1988, p. 19.

16. Howell Raines, "Hart Scores Upset with 41% in New Hampshire Primary," *New York Times*, February 29, 1984, p. A1.

17. R. W. Apple Jr., "Democrats' Hopes Fade as Front-Runner Slips," *New York Times*, February 11, 1992, p. A22.

18. Robin Toner, "Bush Jarred in First Primary; Tsongas Wins Democratic Vote," *New York Times*, February 19, 1992, p. A1.

19. For the timetable of these events, see Royer, *Campaign for President*, pp. 305–9.

20. Writing when Clinton was still neck-and-neck with Tsongas in New Hampshire opinion polls, R. W. Apple Jr. of the *New York Times* predicted that a Clinton loss would be "terribly damaging" (Apple, "Democrats' Hopes Fade"). By the time of the primary, Clinton had reduced media expectations to such an extent that his second-place showing was considered surprisingly strong.

21. Adam Nagourney, "In the First Mile of a Marathon, Kerry Emerges as a Front-Runner," *New York Times*, February 26, 2003, p. A14.

22. See, e.g., David S. Broder, "Dean Still Standing after Foes Take Shots," *Washington Post*, January 5, 2004, p. A06.

23. Adam Nagourney, "In Democratic Pack, the Race Is On for No. 3 and Maybe No. 4," *New York Times*, January 6, 2004, p. A18.

24. For an in-depth narrative of the events surrounding the 2004 Iowa caucus, see Roger Simon, "Turning Point," *U.S. News and World Report*, July 19, 2004, pp. 34–75.

25. See Howard Kurtz, "Reporters Shift Gears on the Dean Bus," *Washington Post*, January 23, 2004, p. C01; and Kurtz, "Trailing in the Media Primary, Too," *Washington Post*, January 29, 2004, p. A01.

26. Rachel Smolkin, "Not Too Shabby," *American Journalism Review* 28 (April/May 2004), pp. 40–45; Sheryl Gay Stolberg, "Containing Themselves: Whoop, Oops and the State of the Political Slip," *New York Times*, January 25, 2004, sec. 4, p. 1.

27. See Andres Martinez, "Will We Remember 2004 as the Year of the Dean Bubble?" *New York Times*, January 30, 2004, p. A24; and Alex Beam, "It's Game Over for Dean's Web Dreams," *Boston Globe*, February 10, 2004, p. E1.

28. Ceci Connolly, "Senator Enjoys Political Renewal," *Washington Post*, January 28, 2004, p. A13.

29. Barbara Norrander, "Democratic Marathon, Republican Sprint: The 2008 Presidential Nominations," in Janet Box-Steffensmeier and Steven E. Schier, eds., *The American Elections of 2008* (Lanham, MD: Rowman & Littlefield, 2009), p. 35.

30. Joshua Green, "The Front-Runner's Fall," *Atlantic*, September 2008, pp. 64–74.

31. Roger Simon, "Relentless: Amid the Corn," *Politico*, August 25, 2008, http://www.politico.com/news/stories/0808/12722.html.

32. Norrander, "Democratic Marathon, Republican Sprint," p. 42.

33. Simon, "Amid the Corn."

34. Dan Balz, Anne E. Kornblut, and Shailagh Murray, "Obama Wins Iowa's Democratic Caucuses," *Washington Post*, January 4, 2008, p. A01.

35. Adam Nagourney, "Obama Takes Iowa in a Big Turnout," *New York Times*, January 4, 2008, p. A1.

36. Roger Simon, "Relentless: Lost in Hillaryland," *Politico*, August 25, 2008, http://www.politico.com/news/stories/0808/12721.html.

37. Bill McInturff, McCain chief pollster, quoted in Kathleen Hall Jamieson, ed., *Electing the President, 2008: The Insiders' View* (Philadelphia: University of Pennsylvania Press, 2009), pp. 84–85.

38. Peter Cook and Greg Giroux, "Romney's Tie Costs $75 a Vote to Santorum's $10," *Bloomberg Business*, January 5, 2012, http://www.bloomberg.com/news/articles/2012-01-05/romney-s-iowa-tie-cost-75-a-vote-to-santorum-s-10.

39. If voters opting to remain uncommitted are counted, Bill Clinton actually finished fourth in the 1992 Iowa caucuses, which were uncontested that year due to the candidacy of Iowa senator Tom Harkin.

40. Richard M. Scammon and Alice V. McGillivray, *America at the Polls* (Washington, DC: Elections Research Center, Congressional Quarterly, 1988), p. 585.

41. For a wealth of information on the past, present, and future scheduling of presidential primaries and caucuses, see the Frontloading HQ website maintained by political scientist Josh Putnam at http://frontloading.blogspot.com.

42. This penalty was reversed before the convention, allowing the two states full representation.

43. Ultimately, the Michigan and Florida delegations were seated in full at the Democratic convention, after Clinton's concession meant that they would not affect the outcome of the nomination contest. See Barry C. Burden, "The Nominations: Rules, Strategies and Uncertainty," in Michael Nelson, ed., *The Elections of 2008* (Washington, DC: CQ Press, 2009), p. 39.

44. Chris Cillizza and Zachary A. Goldfarb, "Democrats Tweak the Primary Calendar," *Washington Post*, July 23, 2006, p. A04.

45. Michael Cooper and Megan Thee, "Resurgent McCain Is Florida Victor," *New York Times*, January 30, 2008, p. A1.

46. B. Drummond Ayres Jr., "McCain Rethinks the Arizona Primary," *New York Times*, February 7, 1999, p. A20.

47. Rhodes Cook, "In '88 Contest, It's What's Up Front That Counts," *Congressional Quarterly Weekly* Report, August 23, 1986, pp. 1997–2002, at 2002.

48. Ibid., at 1999.

49. Further discussion can be found in F. Christopher Arterton, *Media Politics: The News Strategies of Presidential Campaigns* (Lexington, MA: Lexington Books, 1984).

50. Royer, *Campaign for President*, pp. 79–80; Peter Goldman, Thomas M. DeFrank, Mark Miller, Andrew Murr, and Tom Mathews, *Quest for the Presidency, 1992* (College Station: Texas A&M University Press, 1994), pp. 132–35, 144–49.

51. See Tom Rosensteil, *Strange Bedfellows* (New York: Hyperion, 1993), p. 136.

52. Henry E. Brady and Michael G. Hagen, "The 'Horse-Race' or the Issues: What Do Voters Learn from Presidential Primaries?" paper presented at the Annual Meetings of the American Political Science Association, August, 1986. See also Brady and Johnston, "What's the Primary Message?" in Orren and Polsby, eds., *Media and Momentum*, pp. 127–86.

53. John G. Geer, "Voting in Presidential Primaries," paper presented at the annual meeting of the American Political Science Association, August 30–September 2, 1984, p. 6.

54. Poll results compiled by the Polling Report, http://www.pollingreport.com/wh04dem.htm.

55. Data from the poll aggregation website Huffington Post Pollster, http://elections.huffingtonpost.com/pollster/2012-national-gop-primary.

56. Cited in Geer, "Voting in Presidential Primaries," p. 15.

57. Ibid., pp. 15–21.

58. Brady and Hagen, "The 'Horse-Race' or the Issues," pp. 38–39.

59. Larry M. Bartels, "Ideology and Momentum in Presidential Primaries," paper presented at the annual meeting of the American Political Science Association, September 1982. See also Larry M. Bartels, *Presidential Parties and the Dynamics of Public Choice* (Princeton, NJ: Princeton University Press, 1988).

60. Lawrence S. Rothenberg and Richard A. Brody, "Participation in Presidential Primaries," *Western Political Quarterly* 41 (June 1988): 253–71.

61. Figures from Michael P. McDonald, George Mason University, http://elections.gmu.edu/Turnout_2008P.html. This pattern has held steady over time. See Austin Ranney, "Turnout and Representation in Presidential Primary Elections," *American Political Science Review* 66 (March 1972): 21–37, for the years 1948 to 1968; Austin Ranney, *Participation in American Presidential Nominations, 1976* (Washington, DC: American Enterprise Institute, 1977), p. 20, and James Lengle, *Representation in Presidential Primaries: The Democratic Party in the Post Reform Era* (Westport, CT: Greenwood Press, 1981), p. 10, for 1976; and Ranney, *American Elections of 1980*, pp. 353, 364, for 1980. By 2000, turnout in primaries had dropped to 18 percent, while 51 percent of the voting-age population turned out in the general election. "Report: Turnout in Primaries 2nd Lowest in Past 40 Years," *Seattle Times*, September 1, 2000, p. A5 (citing a report by the Center for the Study of the American Electorate). Turnout in 2004 was high on the Democratic side compared to previous years in states voting early in the process, such as New Hampshire, but dropped off considerably once Kerry became the presumptive nominee. Republican primary turnout was uniformly low in 2004, since President George W. Bush ran unopposed for renomination. See Anne E. Kornblut, "Democratic Turnout Seen So-So, Despite Party Assertions," *Boston Globe*, March 10, 2004, p. A3.

62. A comprehensive online resource for state delegate allocation rules and other nomination procedures is the Green Papers, http://www.thegreenpapers.com.

63. Karen Tumulty, "The Five Mistakes Clinton Made," *Time*, May 8, 2008, http://www.time.com/time/politics/article/0,8599,1738331,00.html.

64. Roger Simon, "Relentless: Looking Like Whiny Babies," *Politico*, August 25, 2008, http://www.politico.com/news/stories/0808/12720.html.

65. Ibid.

66. Thomas E. Mann, "Elected Officials and the Politics of Presidential Selection," in Ranney, *The American Elections of 1984*, pp. 100–128, at 103–5. See also David E. Price, *Bringing Back the Parties* (Washington, DC: CQ Press, 1984); Glenn, "Front-Loading the Race," p. 333; and Dennis W. Gleiber and James D. King, "Party Rules and Equitable Representation: The 1984 Democratic National Convention," *American Politics Quarterly* 15 (January 1987): 107–21.

67. Greg J. Borowski, "Superdelegates Feel the Heat," *Milwaukee Journal Sentinel*, February 11, 2008, p. A1.

68. Evan Thomas, "The Long Siege," *Newsweek Special Election Edition*, November 17, 2008, pp. 61–74.

69. David Mark, "Convention Cities Ready Bids for '04," *Campaigns and Elections*, August 2002, p. 30.

70. Jo Freeman, "The Political Culture of the Democratic and Republican Parties," *Political Science Quarterly* 101 (Fall 1986): 327–56, at 328. See also Byron Shafer, "Republicans and Democrats as Social Types: or, Notes toward an Ethnography of the Political Parties," *Journal of American Studies* 20 (1986): 341–54.

71. Freeman, "Political Culture," p. 329.

72. Ibid.

73. Kirkpatrick, "Representation in the American National Conventions: The Case of 1972," *British Journal of Political Science* 5 (July 1975): 265–322, at 285.

74. Barbara G. Farah, "Delegate Polls: 1944 to 1984," *Public Opinion* 7 (August/September 1984): 43–45.

75. M. Kent Jennings, "Women in Party Politics," prepared for the Russell Sage Foundation Women in Twentieth-Century American Politics Project, Beverly Hills, CA, January 1987, pp. 11–12.

76. For extensive documentation, see Ladd, *Transformations of the American Party System*. See also Everett Carll Ladd Jr., and Charles D. Hadley, "Political Parties and Political Issues: Patterns in Differentiation Since the New Deal," Sage Professional Paper, American Politics Series, Beverly Hills, CA, 1973, pp. 4–11; Herbert McClosky, Paul J. Hoffman, and Rosemary O'Hara, "Issue Conflict and Consensus among Party Leaders and Followers," *American Political Science Review* 54 (June 1960): 406–27; and Jeane Kirkpatrick, "Representation in the American National Conventions, p. 304.

77. John D. Huber and G. Bingham Powell Jr., "Congruence between Citizens and Policymakers in Two Visions of Liberal Democracy," *World Politics* (April 1994): 291–326; Torben Iversen, "Political Leadership and Representation in West European Democracies: A Test of Three Models of Voting," *American Journal of Political Science* 38 (February 1994): 45–74. An important early work is Maurice Duverger, *Political Parties: Their Organization and Activity in the Modern State* (London: Methuen, 1954).

78. Nolan McCarty, Keith W. Poole, and Howard Rosenthal, *Polarized America: The Dance of Ideology and Unequal Riches* (Cambridge, MA: MIT Press, 2006).

79. For the best analysis of the role of the modern convention, see Byron E. Shafer, *Bifurcated Politics* (Cambridge, MA: Harvard University Press, 1988); see also Polsby, *Consequences of Party Reform*, pp. 75–78.

80. The three big broadcast networks, in the days when they were the only sources of immediate coverage, featured "gavel-to-gavel" reporting, which meant that whenever the conventions were in session, the networks would switch from their normal programming to the convention. It did not mean that the networks necessarily broadcast whatever was happening at the podium, although they did spend plenty of time transmitting live speeches. In addition, the news teams supplied analysis, interviews with party leaders and rank-and-file delegates, and other stories of interest. For the gradual end of the "gavel-to-gavel" standard, see Shafer, *Bifurcated Politics*, pp. 226–89. On cable television, CNN comes close to the old gavel-to-gavel coverage, while C-SPAN offers full coverage of the official proceedings, which the networks never did even in the days of gavel-to-gavel. C-SPAN, with its seemingly endless supply of airtime, also airs hours of viewer call-ins, interviews with party elites and rank-and-file delegates, and feature stories in which their cameras follow individual delegates from their hometowns to the convention floor, including in 1992 a trip to the laundromat with a delegate before she boarded a bus to the Democratic convention in New York City.

81. The focus on disunity during the coverage of the 1980 convention (see Joe Foote and Tony Rimmer, "The Ritual of Convention Coverage in 1980," in William C. Adams, ed., *Television Coverage of the 1980 Presidential Campaign* [Norwood, NJ: Ablex, 1983]) did not seem to affect the public, at least immediately. Carter's convention "bounce" was a historically large ten points (Shafer, *Bifurcated Politics*, p. 234).

82. These wrap-up shows may go "late," thereby extending the time on the air, especially if a speech shown live (typically, the presidential nominee's acceptance speech) runs long. On the other hand, in 1992 the second day of the Democratic convention coincided with baseball's All-Star Game. CBS chose baseball over politics and did not even have a wrap-up show from the convention that night. "Media Coverage: Take Me Out to the Ballgame," *The Hotline*, July 15, 1992. See also Rosenstiel, *Strange Bedfellows*, pp. 201–33; Edwin Diamond, "Scaling Back the TV Coverage," *National Journal Convention Preview*, June 16, 1992, p. 19.

83. Evan Thomas and Peter Goldman, "Victory March: The Inside Story," *Newsweek Special Election Issue*, November 18, 1996, pp. 88–90, 97–98; Robert E. Denton Jr., "Five Pivotal Elements

of the 2000 Presidential Campaign," in Robert E. Denton Jr., ed., *The 2000 Presidential Campaign: A Communication Perspective* (Westport, CT: Praeger, 2002), pp. 9–10.

84. Richard Morin and Dan Balz, "Bush Support Strong after Convention," *Washington Post*, September 10, 2004, p. A01.

85. Steven E. Schier and Janet Box-Steffensmeier, "The General Election Campaign," in Janet Box-Steffensmeier and Steven E. Schier, eds., *The American Elections of 2008* (Lanham, MD: Rowman & Littlefield, 2009), p. 61.

86. See Nate Silver, "Split Verdict in Polls on Romney Convention Bounce," FiveThirtyEight. com, September 2, 2012, http://fivethirtyeight.blogs.nytimes.com/2012/09/03/sept-2-split-verdict-in-polls-on-romney-convention-bounce/ and "Polls Find Hints of Obama Convention Bounce," September 7, 2012, http://fivethirtyeight.blogs.nytimes.com/2012/09/07/sept-7-polls-find-hints-of-obama-convention-bounce/.

87. Christopher Madison, "The Convention Hall and the TV Screen," *National Journal Convention Special*, July 23, 1988, p. 1950.

88. Rosenstiel, *Strange Bedfellows*, p. 224.

89. James Bennet, "Bush's New Vantage Point, from an Island of a Stage," *New York Times*, September 3, 2004, p. P3.

90. Jim VandeHei and John F. Harris, "Kerry: 'America Can Do Better,'" *Washington Post*, Friday, July 30, 2004, p. A01.

91. In 1992, Republicans running for lower offices were dissatisfied with their allotment of time from the convention management; see Richard E. Cohen, "No Showcase for Rest of Ticket," *National Journal Convention Daily*, August 20, 1992, p. 34. Unlike the Democrats, who had one long session each day beginning in the evening, the Republicans divided into a prime-time session and a daytime session, thus (in the eyes of the daytime speakers) clearly signaling to reporters that only the prime-time session was newsworthy.

92. See Andrew Mollison, "Maestro of the Democrats," *New Leader*, June 27, 1988, pp. 3–4. On the other hand, the leader of a too-united party may need to create excitement, as George Bush apparently intended to do in 1988 by refusing to reveal his choice for vice president until the eve of the convention. James M. Perry and Ellen Hume, "Bush Aiming for Suspense as GOP Starts Convention," *Wall Street Journal*, August 15, 1988, p. 40. Lyndon Johnson attempted the same stunt in 1964.

93. Evan Thomas, "Center Stage," *Newsweek*, November 17, 2008, pp. 87–99.

94. Adam Nagourney, "Heralding New Course, Democrats Nominate Obama," *New York Times*, August 28, 2008, p. A1.

95. Michael Barbaro and Michael D. Shear, "Before Eastwood's Talk with a Chair, Clearance from the Top," *New York Times*, August 31, 2012, http://www.nytimes.com/2012/09/01/us/politics/romney-aides-scratch-their-heads-over-eastwoods-speech.html; Halimah Abdullah, "Eastwood, the Empty Chair and the Speech Everyone's Talking About," CNN, August 31, 2012, http://www.cnn.com/2012/08/31/politics/eastwood-speech/; Amy Argetsinger, "Clint Eastwood Goes Unscripted with Punchy Speech at Republican Convention," *Washington Post*, August 30, 2012, http://www.washingtonpost.com/blogs/reliable-source/post/clint-eastwood-goes-unscripted-with-punchy-speech-at-republican-convention/2012/08/30/3b2a1e02-f317-11e1-892d-bc92fee603a7_blog.html.

96. See Irving G. Williams, *The American Vice-Presidency: New Look* (New York: Doubleday, 1954); and Joel K. Goldstein, *The Modern American Vice Presidency* (Princeton, NJ: Princeton University Press, 1982).

97. Stanley Kelley Jr., "The Presidential Campaign," in Paul T. David, ed., *The Presidential Election and Transition, 1960–1961* (Washington, DC: Brookings Institution, 1961), pp. 70–71.

98. Quoted in Kathleen Hall Jamieson, ed., *Electing the President 2012: The Insiders' View* (Philadelphia: University of Pennsylvania Press, 2013), p. 123.

99. David S. Broder and Bob Woodward, *The Man Who Would Be President: Dan Quayle* (New York: Simon and Schuster, 1992), pp. 13–30; and "Bush Takes Command But Quayle Draws Fire," *Congressional Quarterly Weekly Report*, August 20, 1988, pp. 2307–9.

100. Thomas and Goldman, "Victory March," pp. 85–88.

101. Jamieson, ed., *Electing the President, 2008*, p. 30.

102. Elisabeth Bumiller, "Palin Disclosures Raise Questions on Vetting," *New York Times*, September 2, 2008, p. A1.

103. Stuart Rothenberg, "Barney Frank: A Definite No to Nunn," *The Rothenberg Report*, June 20, 2008, http://rothenbergpoliticalreport.blogspot.com/2008/06/barney-frank-definite-no-to-nunn.html.

104. Richard Brookhiser, *The Outside Story* (Garden City, NY: Doubleday, 1986), p. 155. In the event, Representative Ferraro's candidacy was mildly detrimental to the ticket. See Polsby, "Democratic Nomination and Evolution of the Party System," pp. 36–65.

105. Nicolle Wallace, senior adviser to the McCain-Palin campaign, quoted in Jamieson, ed., *Electing the President, 2008*, p. 27.

106. Gerald M. Pomper, "The Presidential Election: Change Comes to America," in Michael Nelson, ed., *The Elections of 2008* (Washington, DC: CQ Press, 2009), p. 59.

107. Roy Elis, D. Sunshine Hillygus, and Norman Nie, "The Dynamics of Candidate Evaluations and Vote Choice in 2008: Looking to the Past or Future?" *Electoral Studies* 29 (December 2010): 582–93.

108. The year 2000 was a remarkable anomaly not only because the popular majority choice did not prevail, but also because the presidency was not determined by Congress as the Constitution provides, but by the Supreme Court. See Ronald Dworkin, ed., *A Badly Flawed Election: Debating Bush v. Gore, the Supreme Court, and American Democracy* (New York: New Press, 2002).

Chapter 5

1. See Seymour M. Lipset, Paul F. Lazarsfeld, Allen H. Barton, and Juan Linz, "The Psychology of Voting: An Analysis of Political Behavior," in Gardner Lindzey, ed., *Handbook of Social Psychology* (Reading, MA: Addison-Wesley, 1954), pp. 1124–75; Paul F. Lazarsfeld, Bernard Berelson, and Hazel Gaudet, *The People's Choice* (New York: Columbia University Press, 1948), pp. 87–93; Bernard R. Berelson, Paul F. Lazarsfeld, and William N. McPhee, *Voting* (Chicago: University of Chicago Press, 1954), pp. 16–17; and Richard A. Brody, "Change and Stability in Partisan Identification: A Note of Caution," paper delivered at the annual meeting of the American Political Science Association, Chicago, September 1974.

2. David Maraniss, "Aboard the Clinton Campaign, Somewhere Over the Battleground States," *Washington Post*, November 2, 1992, p. A1.

3. For a theoretically useful elaboration of the distinction between "swing" and "battleground" states, see Darshan J. Goux, "Grading the Battleground: A New Measure of Campaign Activity in the States," paper delivered at the Annual Meeting of the American Political Science Association, Philadelphia, PA, August 2006.

4. In fact, the contemporary regional bases of the parties are, by historical standards, unusually durable from election to election, increasing the predictability of state-level electoral outcomes. See David A. Hopkins, "The 2008 Election and the Political Geography of the New Democratic Majority," *Polity* 41 (July 2009), pp. 368–87.

5. Candidate visit data from the *Washington Post*, Presidential Campaign Stops: Who's Going Where," http://www.washingtonpost.com/wp-srv/special/politics/2012-presidential-campaign-visits/. Debates and fundraisers are not considered public campaign events.

6. In Kathleen Hall Jamieson, ed., *Electing the President, 2008: The Insiders' View* (Philadelphia: University of Pennsylvania Press, 2009), p. 142.

7. Dan Balz and Amy Goldstein, "Campaigns Cross Paths in Midwest," *Washington Post*, August 5, 2004, p. A01.

8. Garry Abrams, "See How They Run: Why Do Candidates Dash Madly across the Map? Blame It on a Special Breed Called the Scheduler," *Los Angeles Times*, September 29, 1988, pt. 5, p. 1.

9. Evan Thomas, "Center Stage," *Newsweek Special Election Edition*, November 17, 2008, pp. 87–99.

10. Elizabeth Bumiller, "McCain Draws Line on Attacks as Crowds Cry 'Fight Back,'" *New York Times*, October 11, 2008, p. A12.

11. One study has found at least small effects from campaign visits; see Jeffrey M. Jones, "Does Bringing Out the Candidate Bring Out the Votes?" *American Politics Quarterly* 26 (October 1998): 395–19. Campaigns may allocate a variety of resources, including candidate visits and paid advertising, in a coordinated way, making it impossible for outside researchers or campaign managers to know which affected the voters.

12. Evan Thomas and Peter Goldman, "Victory March: The Inside Story," *Newsweek,* special election issue, November 18, 1996, p. 124.

13. In Jamieson, ed., *Electing the President, 2008*, p. 144.

14. Marjorie Connelly, "How Americans Voted: A Political Portrait," *New York Times*, November 7, 2004, sec. 4, p. 4.

15. Scott Keeter, Juliana Horowitz, and Alec Tyson, "Young Voters in the 2008 Election," Pew Research Center for the People and the Press, November 12, 2008, http://pewresearch.org/pubs/1031/young-voters-in-the-2008-election.

16. Pew Research Center for the People and the Press, "Public Dissatisfied with Democratic Leaders, But Still Happy They Won," November 7, 2007, http://people-press.org/report/368/public-dissatisfied-with-democratic-leaders-but-still-happy-they-won.

17. Dana Milbank, "True Confessions from the Trail," *Washington Post*, April 24, 2009, p. A02.

18. Transcript of presidential debates, *New York Times*, October 16, 1976. See also Angus Campbell, Philip E. Converse, Warren E. Miller, and Donald E. Stokes, *The American Voter* (New York: Wiley, 1960), pp. 44–59; and Angus Campbell, Gerald Gurin, and Warren E. Miller, *The Voter Decides* (Evanston, IL: Row, Peterson, 1954), pp. 44–45, esp. table 4-3.

19. John R. Petrocik, "Issue Ownership in Presidential Elections, with a 1980 Case Study," *American Journal of Political Science* 40 (August 1996): 825–50; Byron E. Shafer and William J. M. Claggett, *The Two Majorities: The Issue Context of Modern American Politics* (Baltimore: Johns Hopkins University Press, 1995).

20. James E. Campbell, "Why Bush Won the Presidential Election of 2004: Incumbency, Ideology, Terrorism, and Turnout," *Political Science Quarterly* 120 (Summer 2005): 219–42.

21. See Henry A. Plotkin, "Issues in the Campaign," in Gerald M. Pomper, ed., *The Election of 1984* (Chatham, NJ: Chatham House, 1985), pp. 48–52; Albert R. Hunt, "The Campaign and the Issues," in Austin Ranney, ed., *The American Elections of 1984* (Durham, NC: Duke University Press, 1985), pp. 129–65, at 142–44; William Schneider, "The November 6 Vote for President: What Did It Mean?" in Ranney, ed., *The American Elections of 1984*, pp. 203–44, at 239–42; Benjamin Ginsberg and Martin Shefter, "A Critical Realignment? The New Politics, the Reconstituted Right, and the Election of 1984," in Michael Nelson, ed., *The Elections of 1984* (Washington, DC: CQ Press, 1985), pp. 5–24; Morris P. Fiorina with Samuel J. Abrams and Jeremy Pope, *Culture War? The Myth of a Polarized America* (New York: Longman, 2004); and James Q. Wilson, "How Divided Are We?" *Commentary*, February 2006, pp. 15–21.

22. See Shafer and Claggett, *The Two Majorities*.

23. Pew Research Center for the People and the Press, "Beyond Red vs. Blue: Profiles of the Typology Groups," May 10, 2005, http://people-press.org/report/?pageid=949.

24. Larry M. Bartels, "What's the Matter with *What's the Matter with Kansas?*" *Quarterly Journal of Political Science* 1 (March 2006): 201–26.

25. For more on the Obama campaign's racial strategy, see Marc Ambinder, "Race Over?" *The Atlantic*, January/February 2009, pp. 62–65.

26. Lloyd Grove, "When They Ask If Dukakis Has a Heart, They Mean It," *Washington Post Weekly Edition*, October 17–23, 1988, pp. 24–25.

27. Curt Suplee, "Bush's Candidacy Is Being Cooled Off by His Warmth Index," *Washington Post National Weekly Edition*, July 25–31, 1988, pp. 23–24.

28. Peter Goldman, Thomas M. DeFrank, Mark Miller, Andrew Murr, and Tom Mathews, *Quest for the Presidency, 1992* (College Station: Texas A&M University Press, 1994), pp. 657–58.

29. In Jamieson, ed., *Electing the President, 2008*, p. 36.

30. Quoted in Kathleen Hall Jamieson, ed., *Electing the President, 2012: The Insiders' View*, ed. Kathleen Hall Jamieson (Philadelphia: University of Pennsylvania Press, 2013), pp. 34, 60.

31. Michael Kranish, "Mitt Romney Was Hesitant to Reveal Himself," *Boston Globe*, December 23, 2012, http://www.bostonglobe.com/news/nation/2012/12/23/the-story-behind-mitt-romney-loss-presidential-campaign-president-obama/OeZRabbooIw0z7QYAOyFFP/story.html.

32. "Our Cheesy Democracy," *New Republic*, November 3, 1986, pp. 8–9.

33. Larry J. Sabato, *The Rise of Political Consultants: New Ways of Winning Elections* (New York: Basic Books, 1981), pp. 169–70. One writer claims that the height of negativity was reached in that year when Johnson's campaign, along with the daisy ad, included an "ad (never aired) that tied Goldwater to the Ku Klux Klan, a third that featured the eastern seaboard being sawed off and cast out to sea . . . , and a fourth that showed a little girl eating an ice cream cone laced with strontium 90 and cesium 137, the presumed result of Goldwater's commitment to nuclear testing." Richard Armstrong, *The Next Hurrah: The Communications Revolution in American Politics* (New York: Beach Tree Books, 1988), p. 17.

34. Sabato, *The Rise of Political Consultants*, pp. 170–71.

35. Rich Galen, "Nail the Opposition," *Campaigns and Elections*, May/June 1988, p. 45. See also Rich Galen, "The Best Defense Is a Good Offense," *Campaigns and Elections*, October/November 1988, pp. 29–34.

36. Sabato, *The Rise of Political Consultants*, p. 166.

37. Galen, "The Best Defense Is a Good Offense," p. 30.

38. The Bush campaign tried to reap political rewards from the Swift Boat charges without being held responsible for their accuracy, or for illegal coordination with the independent ad campaign. Without directly agreeing with the claims made in the Swift Boat ads, Bush's ex-president father George H. W. Bush called them "rather compelling." See James Bennet, "Ex-President Bush Calls Charges of Swift Boat Group Compelling," *New York Times*, August 31, 2004, p. P5.

39. Lois Romano and Jim VandeHei, "Kerry Says Group Is a Front for Bush," *Washington Post*, August 20, 2004, p. A01.

40. Diana Owen, "The Campaign and the Media," in Janet Box-Steffensmeier and Steven E. Schier, eds., *The American Elections of 2008* (Lanham, MD: Rowman & Littlefield, 2009), p. 17.

41. Jill Lawrence, "McCain Seen as 'Bare-Knuckled Fighter' Who Won't Take No for Answer," *USA Today*, October 9, 2008, p. 4A.

42. Steven E. Schier and Janet Box-Steffensmeier, "The General Election Campaign," in Box-Steffensmeier and Schier, eds., *The American Elections of 2008*, pp. 64–67.

43. Helene Cooper and Michael D. Shear, "Facing Criticism, Obama Defends Ads Attacking Romney's Record at Bain Capital," *New York Times*, May 21, 2012, http://www.nytimes.com/2012/05/22/us/politics/obama-defends-attacks-on-romneys-record-at-bain.html.

44. For a study suggesting that negative advertising reduces voter turnout and lowers individuals' sense of political efficacy, see Stephen Ansolabehere, Shanto Iyengar, Adam Simon, and Nicholas Valentino, "Does Attack Advertising Demobilize the Electorate?" *American Political Science Review* 88 (December 1994): 829–38.

45. John G. Geer, *In Defense of Negativity: Attack Ads in Presidential Campaigns* (Chicago: University of Chicago Press, 2006).

46. See Richard M. Nixon, *Six Crises* (New York: Doubleday, 1962), and especially Theodore H. White, *The Making of the President, 1960* (New York: Atheneum, 1961), for a discussion of two candidates' contrasting attitudes toward their "camp" of reporters. For the 1964 election, see Theodore H. White, *The Making of the President, 1964* (New York: Atheneum, 1965). For 1968, see Theodore H. White, *The Making of the President, 1968* (New York: Atheneum, 1969), p. 327ff. For 1972, see Timothy Crouse, *The Boys on the Bus* (New York: Random House, 1973). For 1976, see Jules Witcover, *Marathon: The Pursuit of the Presidency, 1972–1976* (New York: Viking Press, 1977). For 1980, see Jack W. Germond and Jules Witcover, *Blue Smoke and Mirrors* (New York: Viking Press, 1981), pp. 213–15, 260–64. On 1984, see Martin Schram, *The Great American Video Game: Presidential Politics in the Television Age* (New York: Morrow, 1987).

47. In 1984, Mondale's backers felt President Reagan was avoiding the issues in a campaign that stuck to broad, patriotic themes. The "great communicator," they argued, was exploiting the media with his carefully staged events. Many in the media agreed and did negative stories about the Reagan campaign's manipulative tactics. Negative coverage of this sort gave the Reagan camp grounds for complaints of their own concerning an anti-Republican "spin" to nightly newscasts. See Michael J. Robinson, "Where's the Beef? Media and Media Elites in 1984," in Ranney, ed., *The American Elections of 1984*, pp. 166–202. Allegations of bias in the ABC newsroom tainted the 1992 campaign, fueled in part by the decision of anchor Peter Jennings to invite Clinton to respond to a speech President Bush gave after the Los Angeles riots. See Tom Rosenstiel, *Strange Bedfellows* (New York: Hyperion, 1993), p. 141.

48. Quoted in Jamieson, ed., *Electing the President, 2012*, p. 59.

49. Center For Media and Public Affairs, "Election Watch: Campaign Final," *Media Monitor*, Winter 2009, p. 3, http://www.cmpa.com/pdf/media_monitor_jan_2009.pdf.

50. Goldman et al., *Quest for the Presidency, 1992*, pp. 422–23.

51. Caryn James, "Where Politics and Comedy Intermingle, the Punch Lines Can Draw Blood," *New York Times*, November 4, 2000, p. B11.

52. Peter Johnson, "Worlds of Politics, Comedy Converge," *USA Today*, January 26, 2004, p. 1D.

53. Bill Carter, "Candidate Delivers a Ratings Boost," *New York Times*, October 20, 2008, p. C6.

54. Lisa de Moraes, "Will Gloves Come Off When McCain Faces Letterman?" *Washington Post*, October 16, 2008, p. C07.

55. Martha T. Moore, "Romney Avoids Entertainment TV," *USA Today*, October 25, 2012, http://www.usatoday.com/story/news/politics/2012/10/24/romney-obama-letterman-leno/1655251/; Bill Carter, "As Obama Accepts Offers, Late-Night Television Longs for Romney," *New York Times*, October 28, 2012, http://www.nytimes.com/2012/10/29/business/as-obama-accepts-offers-late-night-television-longs-for-romney.html.

56. See Matthew A. Baum, "Talking the Vote: Why Presidential Candidates Hit the Talk-Show Circuit," *American Journal of Political Science* 49 (April 2005): 213–34.

57. Jim Rutenberg, "Black Radio's Zeal for Obama Is Left's Answer to Limbaugh," *New York Times*, July 27, 2008, p. A1.

58. See Jonathan H. Bernstein, "The Expanded Party in American Politics," PhD dissertation, University of California, Berkeley, 1999.

59. See, for an early survey, Stanley Kelley Jr., *Professional Public Relations and Political Power* (Baltimore: Johns Hopkins University Press, 1956).

60. Frank I. Luntz, *Candidates, Campaigns, and Consultants* (Oxford: Basil Blackwell, 1988), p. 52.

61. Ibid.

62. Brian Stelter, "Enticing Text Messagers in a Get-Out-the-Vote Push," *New York Times*, August 18, 2008, p. A12. In the event, the news of Biden's selection leaked to the press before the Obama campaign could release the text message to supporters. See Jose Antonio Vargas, "Overload Slows Texts Announcing the No. 2," *Washington Post*, August 24, 2008, p. A10.

63. Mark Petracca, "Political Consultants and Democratic Governance," *PS: Political Science and Politics* 22 (March 1989): 11–14, at 13.

64. Ibid.

65. Luntz, *Candidates, Campaigns, and Consultants*, p. 57.

66. James Moore and Wayne Slater, *Bush's Brain: How Karl Rove Made George W. Bush Presidential* (New York: John Wiley and Sons, 2003); Lou Dubose, Jan Reid, and Carl M. Cannon, *Boy Genius: Karl Rove, the Brains Behind the Remarkable Political Triumph of George W. Bush* (New York: Public Affairs, 2003).

67. Luntz, *Candidates, Campaigns, and Consultants*, p. 51.

68. Sabato, *The Rise of Political Consultants*, p. 26.

69. Dick Kirschten and James A. Barnes, "Itching for Action," *National Journal*, June 4, 1988, p. 1478.

70. Luntz, *Candidates, Campaigns, and Consultants*, p. 72.

71. Occasionally the roles are reversed and consultants find themselves more "dovish" than their employers. In the 1972 general election campaign, George McGovern ditched Charles Guggenheim, his media adviser, because the latter refused (on pragmatic grounds) to produce negative ads. See Sabato, *The Rise of Political Consultants*, p. 121.

72. See Jonathan Bernstein, "The *New* New Presidential Elite," in William G. Mayer, ed., *In Pursuit of the White House 2000* (Chatham, NJ: Chatham House, 1999); Robin Kolodny and Angela Logan, "Political Consultants and the Extension of Party Goals," *PS: Political Science and Politics* 31 (June 1998): 155–59.

73. Luntz, *Candidates, Campaigns and Consultants*, p. 50.

74. Dan Morain and Bob Drogin, "Steve Schmidt: The Driving Force Behind John McCain," *Los Angeles Times*, October 6, 2008; Adam Nagourney, "In New Shake-Up, McCain Campaign Shifts Managers," *New York Times*, July 3, 2008, p. A1. For more on the internal workings of the McCain campaign, see Robert Draper, "The Making (and Remaking and Remaking) of the Candidate," *New York Times Magazine*, October 26, 2008, p. 54.

75. Kirk Victor, "The Braintrusters," *National Journal*, February 13, 1988, pp. 394–95.

76. Ibid., p. 397.

77. Ibid.

78. Ibid., p. 393.

79. Ibid., p. 392.

80. Ibid., p. 393.

81. Sabato, *The Rise of Political Consultants*, p. 69.

82. Quoted in Scott C. Ratzan, "The Real Agenda Setters: Pollsters in the 1988 Presidential Campaign," *American Behavioral Scientist* 32 (March/April 1989): 451–63, at 451.

83. Quoted in Paul Simon, *Winners and Losers* (New York: Continuum, 1989), p. 165.

84. Sabato, *The Rise of Political Consultants*, p. 71.

85. Ibid., p. 21.

86. Gerald M. Goldhaber, "A Pollster's Sampler," *Public Opinion*, June/July 1984, p. 50.

87. For one example of this phenomenon, see Carey Goldberg, "Political Battle of the Sexes Is Tougher Than Ever," *New York Times*, October 6, 1996, sec. 1, p. 1.

88. Richard Morin and Dan Balz, "'Security Mom' Bloc Proves Hard to Find," *Washington Post*, October 1, 2004, p. A05.

89. Ryan Lizza, "How Obama Won," *The New Yorker*, November 17, 2008, p. 46.

90. Ibid.

91. Ana Marie Cox, "McCain Campaign Autopsy." *Daily Beast*, November 7, 2008, http://www.thedailybeast.com/blogs-and-stories/2008-11-07/mccain-campaign-autopsy.

92. Quoted in *Campaign for President: The Managers Look at 2012*, Institute of Politics at Harvard University Kennedy School of Government (Lanham, MD: Rowman & Littlefield, 2013), p. 160.

93. Quoted in Jamieson, ed., *Electing the President, 2012*, p. 29.

94. Quoted in Jamieson, ed., *Electing the President, 2012*, p. 28.

95. Quoted in Jamieson, ed., *Electing the President, 2012*, p. 19.

96. Roger Simon, "Obama Pollster: Mitt Wasn't Trusted," *Politico*, November 7, 2012, http://www.politico.com/news/stories/1112/83469.html.

97. Lyndsey Layton, "Cheney Hopes Aloha Stop Sways Hawaiians," *Washington Post*, November 2, 2004, p. A08.

98. Andy Barr, "Palin Disagrees with Michigan Move," *Politico*, October 3, 2008, http://www.politico.com/news/stories/1008/14253.html.

99. Katharine Q. Seelye, "McCain Camp Finds Some Hope in Pennsylvania," *New York Times*, November 3, 2008, p. A20.

100. Rosenstiel, *Strange Bedfellows*, p. 302.

101. Levy, "Polling and the Presidential Election," p. 86.

102. Danny N. Bellenger, Kenneth L. Bernhardt, and Jac L. Goldstucker, *Qualitative Research in Marketing* (Chicago: American Marketing Association, 1976), p. 8.

103. Myril Axelrod, "10 Essentials for Good Qualitative Research," *Marketing News*, March 14, 1975, p. 10.

104. Elizabeth Kolbert, "Test-Marketing a President," *New York Times Magazine*, August 30, 1992, p. 21.

105. William D. Wells, "Group Interviewing," in *Focus Group Interviews* (Chicago: American Marketing Association, 1979), p. 2.

106. Hagstrom and Guskind, "Calling the Races," p. 1974.

107. Robert G. Kaiser, "Hearts, Not Minds," *Washington Post*, June 30, 2008, p. C1.

108. Quoted in *Campaign for President*, p. 118.

109. Goldman et al., *Quest for the Presidency, 1992*, p. 257–58.

110. Howard Kurtz, "Why Obama Went Low Key in His Democratic Convention Speech, *The Daily Beast*, September 7, 2012, http://www.thedailybeast.com/articles/2012/09/07/why-obama-went-low-key-in-his-democratic-convention-speech.html.

111. Longer ads are occasionally produced, especially for small, low-cost media markets, but prime-time is dominated by ten- and thirty-second spots.

112. Luntz, *Candidates, Consultants, and Campaigns*, pp. 83–88.

113. Sabato, *The Rise of Political Consultants*, p. 182.

114. T. W. Farnam, "The Influence Industry: Obama Campaign Took Unorthodox Approach to Ad Buying," *Washington Post*, November 14, 2012, http://www.washingtonpost.com/politics/the-influence-industry-obama-campaign-took-unorthodox-approach-to-ad-buying/2012/11/14/c3477e8c-2e87-11e2-beb2-4b4cf5087636_story.html.

115. The Nielsen Company, "Television Audience 2009," http://blog.nielsen.com/nielsenwire/wp-content/uploads/2010/04/TVA_2009-for-Wire.pdf.

116. Luntz, *Candidates, Campaigns, and Consultants*, p. 210.

117. Aaron Smith, "The Internet's Role in Campaign 2008," Pew Internet and American Life Project, April 2009, http://www.pewinternet.org/~/media//Files/Reports/2009/The_Internets_Role_in_Campaign_2008.pdf.

118. Owen, "The Campaign and the Media," in Box-Steffensmeier and Schier, eds., *The American Elections of 2008*, p. 18.

119. Earl Mazo, *Richard Nixon* (New York: Harper, 1959), pp. 21–22, 362–69.

120. See White, *The Making of the President, 1960*, pp. 282–83; Herbert A. Selz and Richard D. Yoakum, "Production Diary of the Debates," in Sidney Kraus, ed., *The Great Debates: Kennedy versus Nixon, 1960* (Bloomington: Indiana University Press, 1977), pp. 73–126; Elihu Katz and Jacob J. Feldman, "The Debates in the Light of Research: A Survey of Surveys," in Kraus, ed., *The Great Debates*, pp. 173–223.

121. See Charles Mohr, "President Tells Polish-Americans He Regrets Remark on East Europe," *New York Times*, October 9, 1976; and R. W. Apple Jr., "Economy Is Stressed by Dole and Mondale during Sharp Debate," *New York Times*, October 16, 1976.

122. See Hedrick Smith, "No Clear Winner Apparent; Scene Is Simple and Stark," *New York Times*, October 29, 1980. After the election, Terence Smith of the *Times* wrote:

"The continual emphasis on Mr. Reagan's image as a hair-triggered proponent of American military intervention—the war and peace issue as it came to be called—may have been overdone, in the opinion of some Carter aides. In June, Mr. [Jody] Powell [Carter's press secretary] was telling reporters that Mr. Reagan was 'too benign' a figure to be painted as a warmonger, a la Barry Goldwater in 1964. 'It wouldn't be believable,' he said then.

"But beginning with his Middle Western swing the day after Labor Day, Mr. Carter stressed this point above all others, warning that the election was a choice between war and peace. He did so because of private polls taken by Mr. Caddell that showed this to be the public's greatest hidden fear about the Republican candidate. The President was hoist by his own hyperbole, in the view of some Carter aides, who feel the President grossly overstated Mr. Reagan's record and aroused the public's skepticism about his argument. In the end, they feel, Mr. Reagan's cool, collected, nonthreatening performance in the debate defused the issue." See "Carter Post-Mortem: Debate Hurt but Wasn't Only Cause for Defeat," *New York Times*, November 9, 1980.

123. Gerald M. Pomper, "The Presidential Election," in Pomper, ed., *The Election of 1984*, p. 76.

124. Richard Brookhiser, *The Outside Story* (Garden City, NY: Doubleday, 1986), p. 272.

125. Hunt, "The Campaign and the Issues," in Ranney, ed., *The American Elections of 1984*, pp. 149–58.

126. Goldman et al., *Quest for the Presidency, 1992*, p. 559.

127. Ibid., pp. 572–73.

128. Marjorie Randon Hershey, "The Campaign and the Media," in Gerald M. Pomper, ed., *The Election of 2000* (New York: Chatham House, 2001), pp. 60–63.

129. Richard L. Berke and Kevin Sack, "In Debate 2, Microscope Focuses on Gore," *New York Times*, October 11, 2000, p. A1.

130. Robert V. Friedenberg, "The 2000 Presidential Debates," in Robert E. Denton Jr., ed., *The 2000 Presidential Campaign: A Communication Perspective* (Westport, CT: Praeger, 2002), pp. 135–66.

131. Jodi Wilgoren and Richard W. Stevenson, "Day after Debate, Candidates Assess the Performances," *New York Times*, October 2, 2004, p. A10; Dan Balz, "Debate Leads to Shifts in Strategy," *Washington Post*, October 3, 2004, p. A01.

132. Richard Morin, "Singling Out Mary Cheney Was Wrong, Most Say," *Washington Post*, October 17, 2004, p. A05.

133. Dan Balz and Jim VandeHei, "A Deep Divide on Domestic Front," *Washington Post*, October 14, 2004, p. A01; Elisabeth Bumiller and David M. Halbfinger, "Bush and Kerry, Feeling Like Winners, Go to Las Vegas," *New York Times*, October 15, 2004, p. A21.

134. Evan Thomas, "The Great Debates," *Newsweek Special Election Edition*, November 17, 2008, pp. 100–110.

135. Adam Nagourney and Jeff Zeleny, "Rivals Display Stark Contrasts in Clashes on Iraq, Economy," *New York Times*, September 27, 2008, p. A1.

136. Schier and Box-Steffensmeier, "The General Election Campaign," in Box-Steffensmeier and Schier, eds., *The American Elections of 2008*, p. 65.

137. Joe Klein, "Obama's Debate Strategy: Unilateral Disarmament?" *Time* Swampland bloc, October 3, 2012, http://swampland.time.com/2012/10/03/the-debate/.

138. Nate Silver, "Romney Erases Obama's Convention Bounce in Forecast," FiveThirtyEight .com, October 9, 2012, http://fivethirtyeight.blogs.nytimes.com/2012/10/09/oct-9-romney-erases-obamas-convention-bounce-in-forecast/.

139. Peter Baker, "For the President, Punch, Punch, Another Punch," *New York Times*, October 17, 2012, http://www.nytimes.com/2012/10/17/us/politics/in-second-debate-obama-strikes-back.html.

140. Brian Montopoli, "Conservatives Assail Debate Moderator Candy Crowley," CBS News, October 17, 2012, http://www.cbsnews.com/news/conservatives-assail-debate-moderator-candy-crowley/.

141. Quoted in Jamieson, ed., *Electing the President, 2012*, p. 107.

142. Quoted in Jamieson, ed., *Electing the President, 2012*, p. 114.

143. James Fallows, "Slugfest," *Atlantic*, September 2012, http://www.theatlantic.com/magazine/archive/2012/09/slugfest/309063/.

144. Sarah Huisenga and Rebecca Kaplan, "Portman to Play Obama in Romney Debate Prep," *National Journal*, August 27, 2012, http://www.nationaljournal.com/2012-conventions/portman-to-play-obama-in-romney-debate-prep-20120827.

145. See Patrick Healy, "Pact on Debates Will Let McCain and Obama Spar," *New York Times*, September 21, 2008, p. A23.

146. Kim Severson, "What's for Dinner? The Pollster Wants to Know," *New York Times*, April 16, 2008, p. F1; Steven Levy, "In Every Voter, a 'Microtarget,'" *Washington Post*, April 23, 2008, p. D01. See also Douglas B. Sosnick, Matthew J. Dowd and Ron Fournier, *Applebee's America: How Successful Political, Business, and Religious Leaders Connect with the New American Community* (New York: Simon and Schuster, 2006); Mark J. Penn with E. Kinney Zalesne, *Microtrends: The Small Forces Behind Tomorrow's Big Changes* (New York: Twelve Publishers, 2007).

147. Alan S. Gerber and Donald P. Green, "The Effects of Canvassing, Telephone Calls, and Direct Mail on Voter Turnout: A Field Experiment," *American Political Science Review* 94 (September 2000): 653–63; Alan S. Gerber and Donald P. Green, "Do Phone Calls Increase Voter Turnout? A Field Experiment," *Public Opinion Quarterly* 65 (Spring 2001): 75–85; Donald P. Green, Alan S. Gerber, and David W. Nickerson, "Getting Out the Vote in Local Elections: Results from Six Door-to-Door Canvassing Experiments," *Journal of Politics* 65 (November 2003): 1083–96; Donald P. Green and Alan S. Gerber, *Get Out the Vote! How to Increase Voter Turnout*, 2nd edition (Washington, DC: Brookings Institution, 2008).

148. Alec MacGillis, "Obama Camp Relying Heavily on Ground Effort," *Washington Post*, October 12, 2008, p. A04.

149. Zack Exley, "The New Organizers: What's Really Behind Obama's Ground Game," *Huffington Post*, October 8, 2008, http://www.huffingtonpost.com/zack-exley/the-new-organizers-part-1_b_132782.html.

150. Michael Silberman, "Welcome to the New Media Campaign Tools of 2012, "*Mother Jones*, March 13, 2009, http://motherjones.com/politics/2009/03/welcome-new-media-campaign-tools-2012-0?page=1; David Herbert, "Obama's 'Project Houdini' Revealed," *National Journal Online*, November 10, 2008, http://www.nationaljournal.com/njonline/no_20081107_4999.php.

151. Alexis C. Madrigal, "When the Nerds Go Marching In," *The Atlantic*, November 16, 2012, http://www.theatlantic.com/technology/archive/2012/11/when-the-nerds-go-marching-in/265325/.

152. See Sasha Issenberg, "Obama's White Whale," *Slate*, February 15, 2012, http://www.slate.com/articles/news_and_politics/victory_lab/2012/02/project_narwhal_how_a_top_secret_obama_campaign_program_could_change_the_2012_race_.html.

153. Adam Nagourney, "Campaigns Adjust Their Pace to Meet Short Season," *New York Times*, September 10, 2008, p. A20.

154. See Jules Abels, *Out of the Jaws of Victory* (New York: Holt, 1959).

155. Robert Alford, "The Role of Social Class in American Voting Behavior," *Western Political Quarterly* 16 (March 1963): 180–94; and Campbell et al., *The American Voter*, chap. 13.

156. For extensive recital of these critiques, see Christine M. Black and Thomas Oliphant, *All by Myself: The Unmaking of a Presidential Campaign* (Chester, CT: Globe Pequot Press, 1989).

157. David Shribman and James M. Perry, "Self-Inflicted Injury: Dukakis's Campaign Was Marred by a Series of Lost Opportunities," *Wall Street Journal*, November 8, 1988, p. 1.

158. Karen M. Paget, "Afterthoughts on the Dukakis/Bentsen Campaign," *Public Affairs Report*, January 1989, pp. 1, 4.

159. John Jacobs, "Dukakis Admits Campaign 'Mistakes,'" *San Francisco Examiner*, October 14, 1989.

160. Elisabeth Bumiller, "Palin Disclosures Raise Questions on Vetting," *New York Times*, September 2, 2008, p. A1.

161. Jeanne Cummings, "RNC Shells Out $150K for Palin Fashion," *Politico*, October 22, 2008, http://www.politico.com/news/stories/1008/14805.html.

162. Ben Smith, "Palin Allies Report Rising Camp Tension," *Politico*, October 25, 2008, http://www.politico.com/news/stories/1008/14929.html. This article was the first to use the term "going rogue" to describe Palin's increasing lack of cooperation with McCain campaign handlers (quoting an anonymous Republican official). Adopting the phrase as a flattering descriptor of her independent spirit, Palin later used it as the title of her first book.

163. Michael Cooper and Dalia Sussman, "Growing Doubts on Palin Take a Toll, Poll Finds," *New York Times*, October 31, 2008, p. A1.

164. Monica Langley, "As Economic Crisis Peaked, Tide Turned against McCain," *Wall Street Journal*, November 5, 2008, p. A1.

165. Michael Kranish, "The Story Behind Mitt Romney's Loss in the Presidential Campaign to President Obama," *Boston Globe,* December 23, 2012, http://www.boston.com/news/politics/2012/president/2012/12/23/the-story-behind-mitt-romney-loss-the-presidential-campaign-president-obama/2QWkUB9pJgVIi1mAcIhQjL/story.html; Noam Scheiber, "The Internal Polls That Made Mitt Romney Think He'd Win," *The New Republic*, November 30, 2012, http://www.newrepublic.com/blog/plank/110597/exclusive-the-polls-made-mitt-romney-think-hed-win.

166. Adam Nagourney, Ashley Parker, Jim Rutenberg, and Jeff Zeleny, "How a Race in the Balance Went to Obama," *New York Times*, November 7, 2012, http://www.nytimes.com/2012/11/08/us/politics/obama-campaign-clawed-back-after-a-dismal-debate.html.

167. John Heilemann and Mark Halperin, "The Intervention," *New York*, November 2, 2013, http://nymag.com/news/features/heilemann-halperin-double-down-excerpt-2013-11/.

168. See, for example, Samuel Lubell, *The Future of American Politics* (New York: Harper, 1951); Samuel Lubell, "Personalities and Issues," in Kraus, ed., *The Great Debates*, pp. 151–62; and Joseph Alsop, "The Negro Vote and New York," *New York Herald-Tribune* (and elsewhere), August 8, 1960. Reporting of this sort became a feature of the election-year *Washington Post* coverage. See, for example, Rowland Evans and Robert Novak, "Stronghold Lost," *Washington Post*, August 4, 1980.

169. There are several sources readers can consult about the technology and tactics of polling. Many years ago George Gallup published *A Guide to Public Opinion Polls* (Princeton, NJ: Princeton University Press, 1948). See also *Opinion Polls, Interviews* by Donald McDonald with Elmo Roper and George Gallup (Santa Barbara, CA: Center for the Study of Democratic Institutions, 1962); and Charles W. Roll Jr. and Albert H. Cantril, *Polls* (New York: Basic Books, 1972). In 1972, Representative Lucien Nedzi of Michigan held congressional hearings on the possible effects of information about polls on subsequent voting. See *Public Opinion Polls, Hearings before the Subcommittee on Library and Memorial*, Committee on House Administration, House of Representatives, 93d Cong., 1st sess., H.R. 5503, September 19, 20, 21, and October 5, 1972. A further flap occurred in 1980, as the result of Jimmy Carter's concession of defeat and the television network predictions of a Reagan victory before voting was completed on the West Coast. See Raymond Wolfinger and Peter Linquiti, "Tuning In and Turning Out," *Public Opinion*, February/March 1981, pp. 56–60; John E. Jackson, "Election Night Reporting and Voter Turnout," *American Journal of Political Science* 27 (November 1983): 615–35; *Election Day Practices and Election Projections, Hearings Before the Task Force on Elections of the Committee on House*

Administration and the Subcommittee on Telecommunications, Consumer Protection, and Finance of the Committee on Energy and Commerce, U.S. House of Representatives, 97th Cong., 1st and 2nd sess., December 15, 1981, and September 21, 1982, and Percy Tannenbaum and Leslie J. Kostrich, *Turned-On TV/Turned-Off Voters: Policy Options for Election Projections* (Beverly Hills, CA: Sage, 1983).

170. Robert Sherwood, *Roosevelt and Hopkins* (New York: Harper, 1948), p. 86. See also Archibald M. Crossley, "Straw Polls in 1936," *Public Opinion Quarterly* 1 (January 1937): 24–36; and a survey of the literature existing at that time, Hadley Cantril, "Technical Research," *Public Opinion Quarterly* 1 (January 1937): 97–110.

171. Maurice C. Bryson, "The *Literary Digest* Poll: Making of a Statistical Myth," *The American Statistician* 30 (November 1976): 184–85; Peverill Squire, "The 1936 *Literary Digest* Poll," *Public Opinion Quarterly* 52 (Spring 1988): 125–34.

172. Frederick Mosteller et al., *The Pre-Election Polls of 1948*, Bulletin 60 (New York: Social Science Research Council, 1949).

173. See the Polling Report compilation of 2004 survey data at http://www.pollingreport.com/2004.htm.

174. See Daniel J. Hopkins, "No More Wilder Effect, Never a Whitman Effect: When and Why Polls Mislead about Black and Female Candidates," *Journal of Politics* 71 (July 2009): 769–81.

175. Alexander Burns, "The GOP Polling Debacle," *Politico*, November 11, 2012, http://www.politico.com/news/stories/1112/83672.html.

176. Jan Crawford, "Adviser: Romney 'Shell-Shocked' by Loss," CBS News, November 8, 2012, http://www.cbsnews.com/news/adviser-romney-shellshocked-by-loss/; Matt Viser, "New Film Shows Flawed, Human Mitt Romney," *Boston Globe*, January 18, 2014, http://www.bostonglobe.com/news/nation/2014/01/18/mitt-romney-family-side-downplayed-campaign-revealed-documentary/0Jh53bme1OjV9SuM0Q8ytN/story.html.

177. Quoted in Jamieson, ed., *Electing the President, 2012*, p. 77.

178. On the import of early projections, see Philip L. Dubois, "Election Night Projection and Turnout in the West," *American Politics Quarterly* 11 (July 1983): 349–64. Dubois argues (against a number of other studies) that the early projections did have a significant impact on turnout. For a sophisticated analysis of the policy problems involved, see Tannenbaum and Kostrich, *Turned-On TV/Turned-Off Voters.*

179. Michael Cousineau, "Exit Poll Wrong Call in Senate Race Leaves Anger, Hurt, Red Faces," *Union Leader* (Manchester, NH), November 7, 1996, p. A1.

180. Joan Konner, "The Case for Caution: This System Is Dangerously Flawed," *Public Opinion Quarterly* 67 (Spring 2003): 5–18 (quote on p. 7). See also Paul Biemer, Ralph Folsom, Richard Kulka, Judith Lessler, Babu Shah, and Michael Weeks, "An Evaluation of Procedures and Operations Used by the Voter News Service for the 2000 Presidential Election," *Public Opinion Quarterly* 67 (Spring 2003): 32–44.

181. Matt Krantz, "Exit Poll Rumors Push Dow into Loss," *USA Today*, November 3, 2004, p. 4B.

182. See Campbell et al., *The American Voter*; and Warren E. Miller and J. Merrill Shanks, *The New American Voter* (Cambridge, MA: Harvard University Press, 1996).

183. See Paul F. Lazarsfeld, "The Use of Panels in Social Research," *Proceedings of the American Philosophical Society* 92 (November 1948): 405–10.

184. This is known as the "Hawthorne effect," named after a famous experiment in industrial psychology. See George C. Homans, *The Human Group* (New York: Harcourt, Brace, 1950), pp. 48–155.

185. Stephen Borrelli, Brad Lockerbie, and Richard G. Niemi, "Why the Democrat-Republican Partisanship Gap Varies from Poll to Poll," *Public Opinion Quarterly* 51 (1987): 115–19. See also Howard Schuman, *Questions and Answers in Attitude Surveys: Experiments on Question Form, Wording, and Context* (Thousand Oaks, CA: Sage Publications, 1996).

186. Silver's model failed to predict the 2008 electoral result only in Indiana, which was projected for McCain but ultimately supported Obama by about one percentage point in the statewide popular vote.

187. The design of the ballot in Palm Beach County probably led a number of voters intending to vote for Democratic nominee Al Gore to cast ballots instead for Reform Party candidate Pat Buchanan. This alone may have cost Gore the presidency. See Henry E. Brady, Michael C. Herron, Walter R. Mebane Jr., Jasjeet Singh Sekhon, Kenneth W. Shotts, and Jonathan Wand, "Law and Data: The Butterfly Ballot Episode," *PS: Political Science and Politics* 34 (March 2001): 59–69.

188. The U.S. Supreme Court first became involved in the Florida recount legal struggle on November 24, 2000 (*Bush v. Palm Beach County Canvassing Board*, 531 U.S. 1004). The Court granted a stay sought by Bush halting the recount of ballots ordered by the Florida Supreme Court on December 9 (*Bush v. Gore*, 531 U.S. 1046), foreshadowing its eventual 5–4 decision on the merits in Bush's favor on December 12 (*Bush v. Gore*, 531 U.S. 98). Al Gore formally conceded the election in a nationwide address the following day. All of the justices who favored Bush had been appointed by Republican presidents; two of the justices on the other side had also been Republican appointees.

189. See, for example, Howard Gillman, *The Votes That Counted: How the Court Decided the 2000 Election* (Chicago: University of Chicago Press, 2001); Cass R. Sunstein and Richard A. Epstein, eds., *The Vote: Bush, Gore and the Supreme Court* (Chicago: University of Chicago Press, 2001); and Ronald Dworkin, ed., *A Badly Flawed Election: Debating* Bush v. Gore, *the Supreme Court, and American Democracy* (New York: New Press, 2002).

190. See Henry E. Brady, Justin Buchler, Matt Jarvis, and John McNulty, *Counting All the Votes: The Performance of Voting Technology in the United States* (Berkeley, CA: Survey Research Center and Institute of Governmental Studies, 2001), http://ucdata.berkeley.edu/pubs/countingallthevotes.pdf.

191. For example, precincts in Florida using the problematic punch-card ballots were more likely to contain significant minority populations than places with other ballot types. See Josh Barbanel and Ford Fessenden, "Racial Pattern in Demographics of Error-Prone Ballots," *New York Times*, November 29, 2000, p. A25. See also Michael Tomz and Robert P. Van Houweling, "How Does Voting Equipment Affect the Racial Gap in Voided Ballots?" *American Journal of Political Science* 47 (January 2003): 46–60. Their data are from South Carolina and Louisiana.

192. Ford Fessenden and John M. Broder, "Study of Disputed Florida Ballots Finds Justices Did Not Cast the Deciding Vote," *New York Times*, November 12, 2001, p. A1.

193. Henry E. Brady, "Detailed Analysis of Punch Card Performance in the Twenty Largest California Counties in 1996, 2000, and 2003," report, University of California, Berkeley, 2003.

194. Robert Pear, "Bush Signs Legislation Intended to End Voting Disputes," *New York Times*, October 29, 2002, p. A22.

195. Richard Wolf, "Another Mess at the Polls? The Voting Equipment's New, But Problems Are Likely on Election Day," *USA Today*, October 29, 2008, p. 1A.

196. Peter Whoriskey, "Vote Disparity Still a Mystery in Fla. Election for Congress," *Washington Post*, November 29, 2006, p. A03.

197. Wolf, "Another Mess at the Polls?"

198. Verified Voting, "Key Facts for 2012," https://www.verifiedvoting.org/key-facts-2012/.

199. Associated Press, "Schwarzenegger Recasts Ballot after Voting Mishap," June 8, 2010.

200. John Colapinto, "Enter Laughing," *The New Yorker*, July 20, 2009, p. 28.

Chapter 6

1. See William Crotty, *Party Reform* (New York: Longman, 1983), pp. 40–43; Adam Clymer, "Democrats Adopt Nominating Rules for '80 Campaign," *New York Times*, June 10, 1978; Clymer,

"Democrats Alter Delegate Rules, Giving Top Officials More Power," *New York Times*, March 27, 1982; Rhodes Cook, "Democrats' Rules Weaken Representation," *Congressional Quarterly Weekly Report*, April 3, 1982, p. 750; Austin Ranney, "Farewell to Reform—Almost," in Kay Schlozman, ed., *Elections in America* (Boston: Allan and Unwin, 1987), 106; Rhodes Cook, "Democratic Party Rules Readied for '92 Campaign," *Congressional Quarterly Weekly Report*, March 17, 1990, p. 847; "Democrats Alter Nominating Rules," *Congressional Quarterly Weekly Report*, April 14, 1990, p. 148; and Democratic Party Committee on Presidential Nomination Timing and Scheduling website, http://www.democrats.org/page/s/nominating.

2. On the history of the GOP reform process from 1996 to 2012, see Caitlin E. Jewitt, "The Republican Party and the Unsuccessful 2012 Presidential Nomination Reforms," a paper prepared for the 2013 State of the Parties Conference, Akron Ohio. http://www.uakron.edu/dotAsset/79292ea0-70b6-4375-8ecd-80f79a3cff04.pdf.

3. Aaron Blake, "RNC Moves to shrink 2016 primary calendar," *Washington Post*, January 24, 2014; Zeke J. Miller, "GOP Takes Control of 2016 Primary Debates" *Time*, August 8, 2014.

4. On polarized Congressional floor voting, several scholarly studies and graphs indicating its record levels are available at "The Polarization of Congressional Parties" Voteview.com http://voteview.com/political_polarization.asp; note particularly the work by Nolan McCarty linked there. On polarization among partisans in the American public, see Pew Research Center for the People and the Press, "Political Polarization in the American Public," June 12, 2014, http://www.people-press.org/2014/06/12/political-polarization-in-the-american-public/.

5. There are many examples of the party reform school of thought. See, for example, Woodrow Wilson, *Congressional Government* (Boston: Houghton Mifflin, 1889); Henry Jones Ford, *The Rise and Growth of American Politics* (New York: Macmillan, 1898); A. Lawrence Lowell, *Public Opinion and Popular Government* (New York: Longmans, Green, 1913); William MacDonald, *A New Constitution for a New America* (New York: B. W. Huebsch, 1921); William Y. Elliott, *The Need for Constitutional Reform* (New York: McGraw-Hill, 1935); E. E. Schattschneider, *Party Government* (New York: Farrar and Rinehart, 1940); Henry Hazlitt, *A New Constitution Now* (New York: McGraw-Hill, 1942); Thomas K. Finletter, *Can Representative Government Do the Job?* (New York: Reynal and Hitchcock, 1945); James M. Burns, *Congress on Trial* (New York: Harper, 1949); Committee on Political Parties, American Political Science Association, *Toward a More Responsible Two-Party System* (New York: APSA, 1950); Stephen K. Bailey, *The Condition of Our National Political Parties* (New York: Fund for the Republic, 1959); James MacGregor Burns, *The Deadlock of Democracy: Four-Party Politics in America* (Englewood Cliffs, NJ: Prentice Hall, 1963); Lloyd N. Cutler and C. Douglas Dillon, "Can We Improve on Our Constitutional System?" *Wall Street Journal*, February 15, 1983; and Lloyd N. Cutler, "To Form a Government," *Foreign Affairs* 59 (Fall 1980): 126–43. The work of the Committee on Political Parties, representing the collective judgment of a panel of distinguished political scientists in 1950, is the statement we refer to most often. In 1971 a member of the committee published a thoughtful reconsideration of its main ideas. See Evron M. Kirkpatrick, "Toward a More Responsible Two-Party System: Political Science, Policy Science, or Pseudo Science?" *American Political Science Review* 65 (December 1971): 965–90.

6. Committee on Political Parties, *Toward a More Responsible Two-Party System*, p. 1.

7. Ibid., p. 66.

8. Ibid., p. 15.

9. A sample of this literature might include Pendleton Herring, *The Politics of Democracy: American Parties in Action*, rev. ed. (New York: W. W. Norton, 1965); Herbert Agar, *The Price of Union* (Boston: Houghton Mifflin, 1950); Malcolm C. Moos, *Politics, Presidents and Coattails* (Baltimore: Johns Hopkins University Press, 1952); Austin Ranney and Willmoore Kendall, *Democracy and the American Party System* (New York: Harcourt, Brace, 1956); David B. Truman, *The Governmental Process* (New York: Knopf, 1953); John Fischer, "Unwritten Rules of American Politics," *Harper's*, November 1948, pp. 27–36; Peter Drucker, "A Key to American Politics:

Calhoun's Pluralism," *Review of Politics* 10 (October 1948): 412–26; Ernest F. Griffith, *Congress: Its Contemporary Role* (New York: New York University Press, 1951); Murray Stedman and Herbert Sonthoff, "Party Responsibility: A Critical Inquiry," *Western Political Quarterly* 4 (September 1951): 454–86; Julius Turner, "Responsible Parties: A Dissent from the Floor," *American Political Science Review* 45 (March 1951): 143–52; William Goodman, "How Much Political Party Centralization Do We Want?" *Journal of Politics* 13 (November 1961): 536–61; and Austin Ranney, *The Doctrine of Responsible Party Government* (Urbana: University of Illinois Press, 1954).

10. Herring, *The Politics of Democracy*, p. 327.

11. Ibid., p. 420.

12. Committee on Political Parties, *Toward a More Responsible Two-Party System*, p. 19.

13. Bailey, *The Condition of Our National Political Parties*, p. 20.

14. Nelson W. Polsby and William G. Mayer, "Ideological Cohesion in the American Two-Party System," in Nelson W. Polsby and Raymond E. Wolfinger, eds., *On Parties: Essays Honoring Austin Ranney* (Berkeley: Institute of Governmental Studies Press, 1999), pp. 219–54.

15. See David B. Truman, "Federalism and the Party System," in Arthur W. MacMahon, ed., *Federalism: Mature and Emergent* (New York: Russell and Russell, 1962), pp. 115–36. This situation is deplored in Cutler and Dillon, "Can We Improve on Our Constitutional System?" One possible remedy, changing the terms of office of senators and members of Congress to coincide exactly with presidential elections, is analyzed in Nelson W. Polsby, "A Note on the President's Modest Proposal," in Polsby, *Political Promises* (New York: Oxford University Press, 1974), pp. 101–7.

16. Members of Congress with local strength not based on ideology are not at all uncommon. See, for instance, examples in Raymond A. Bauer, Ithiel de Sola Pool, and Lewis Anthony Dexter, *American Business and Public Policy* (New York: Atherton Press, 1963), chaps. 16, 18, and 19; Richard F. Fenno, *Home Style* (Boston: Little, Brown, 1978); and Bruce Cain, John Ferejohn, and Morris Fiorina, *The Personal Vote: Constituency Service and Electoral Independence* (Cambridge, MA: Harvard University Press, 1987).

17. Nelson W. Polsby, *How Congress Evolves: Social Bases of Institutional Change* (New York: Oxford University Press, 2004).

18. See Walter J. Stone, "On Party Switching among Presidential Activists: What Do We Know?" *American Journal of Political Science* 35 (August 1991): 598–607.

19. Polsby, *How Congress Evolves*.

20. Christopher Hare, Keith T. Poole, and Howard Rosenthal, "Polarization in Congress Has Risen Sharply. Where Is It Going Next?' *Washington Post*, February 13, 2014, http://www.washingtonpost.com/blogs/monkey-cage/wp/2014/02/13/polarization-in-congress-has-risen-sharply-where-is-it-going-next/.

21. Polsby, *Consequences of Party Reform*; Byron E. Shafer, *Quiet Revolution: The Struggle for the Democratic Party and the Shaping of Post-Reform Politics* (New York: Russell Sage Foundation, 1983).

22. For strong evidence on this point, see Samuel Stouffer, *Communism, Conformity and Civil Liberties* (Garden City, NY: Doubleday, 1955); and Julian L. Woodward and Elmo Roper, "Political Activity of American Citizens," *American Political Science Review* 44 (December 1950): 872–75. Two more recent studies have examined the voters' desire not to be interfered with by the government as well as the importance of their private lives to them as compared with national issues. See Paul M. Sniderman and Richard A. Brody, "Coping: The Ethic of Self-Reliance," *American Journal of Political Science* 21 (August 1977): 501–21; and Richard A. Brody and Paul M. Sniderman, "From Life Space to Polling Place: The Relevance of Personal Concerns for Voting Behavior," *British Journal of Political Science* 7 (July 1977): 337–60.

23. Evidence indicates that a sizable contingent of voters do make decisions based on this criterion. In general, perceptions of national conditions weigh more heavily than changes in voters' personal fortunes over the previous four years. See Donald R. Kinder and D. Roderick

Kiewiet, "Sociotropic Politics: The American Case," *British Journal of Political Science* 11 (April 1981): 129–61; and Gregory Markus, "The Impact of Personal and National Economic Conditions on the Presidential Vote: A Pooled Cross-Sectional Analysis," *American Journal of Political Science* 32 (February 1988): 137–54. Some argue that this type of "retrospective voting" is not rational, since it often applies even to events such as natural disasters which incumbents clearly cannot control; see Christopher H. Achen and Larry M. Bartels, "Blind Retrospection: Electoral Responses to Drought, Flu, and Shark Attacks," unpublished paper, Princeton University, 2004.

24. See, for example, Jack Citrin, Herbert McClosky, J. Merrill Shanks, and Paul M. Sniderman, "Personal and Political Sources of Alienation," *British Journal of Political Science* 5 (January 1975): 1–31; and Arthur H. Miller, "Political Issues and Trust in Government: 1964–70," along with the "Comment" by Jack Citrin, both in *American Political Science Review* 68 (September 1974): 951–1001.

25. In systems like the United States, with its extremely frequent elections, this would require a lot of voting. See Anthony King, *Running Scared: Why America's Politicians Campaign Too Much and Govern Too Little* (New York: Martin Kessler, 1997).

26. Jürgen Habermas, *Legitimation Crisis* (Boston: Beacon Press, 1975).

27. An earlier statement of main themes in this section is Aaron B. Wildavsky's "On the Superiority of National Conventions," *Review of Politics* 24 (July 1962): 307–19.

28. Everett Carll Ladd, "Party Reform and the Public Interest," *Political Science Quarterly* 102 (Autumn 1987): 355-369. See, more generally, Gary R. Orren and Nelson W. Polsby, eds., *Media and Momentum: The New Hampshire Primary and Nomination Politics* (Chatham, NJ: Chatham House, 1987).

29. Caroline J. Tolbert, David P. Redlawsk, and Daniel C. Bowen, "Reforming Presidential Nominations: Rotating State Primaries or a National Primary?" *PS: Political Science and Politics* 42 (2009), pp. 71–79.

30. A classic statement is Moisei Ostrogorski, *Democracy and the Party System in the United States* (New York: Macmillan, 1910), pp. 158–60. See also Elmo Roper, "What Price Conventions?" *Saturday Review*, September 3, 1960, p. 26.

31. Dan Balz and Perry Bacon Jr., "Clinton Backers Rebuke Pelosi for Stance on Superdelegates," *Washington Post*, March 27, 2008, p. A07.

32. See Herbert McClosky, Paul J. Hoffmann, and Rosemary O'Hara, "Issue Conflict and Consensus among Party Leaders and Followers," *American Political Science Review* 54 (June 1960): 406–27; Jeane Kirkpatrick, *The New Presidential Elite: Men and Women in National Politics* (New York: Russell Sage Foundation, 1976); and John S. Jackson III et al., "Political Party Leaders and the Mass Public: 1980–1984," paper presented at the annual meeting of the Midwest Political Science Association, Chicago, April 1987.

33. Gerald M. Pomper, *Elections in America: Control and Influence in Democratic Politics*, rev. ed. (New York: Longman, 1980), pp. 185–87.

34. Alan D. Monroe, "American Party Platforms and Public Opinion," *American Journal of Political Science* 27 (February 1983): 27-42, at 38.

35. Ibid., pp. 27–42.

36. Marty Cohen, David Karol, Hans Noel, and John Zaller, *The Party Decides: Presidential Nominations Before and After Reform* (Chicago: University of Chicago Press, 2008).

37. This argument roughly corresponds to one of the main approaches to calculating the strategic advantage of members of a coalition, pioneered by Irwin Mann and Lloyd Shapley. The argument proceeds as follows: "the Shapley value defines the power of actor A as the number of permutations (orderings) in which A occupies the pivotal position (that is, orderings in which A can cast the deciding vote) divided by the total number of possible permutations." See George Rabinowitz and Stuart Elaine MacDonald, "The Power of the States in U.S. Presidential

Elections," *American Political Science Review* 80 (March 1986): 65–87, at 66. This approach shows the large states to be the winners. Their influence is more than proportional to their size. This model is often supplemented by an analysis that attempts to determine the influence of the average voter within each state. Along these lines, Lawrence Longley and James Dana Jr. conclude that residents of California (the most advantaged state) have more than twice the "relative voting power" of the inhabitants of Arkansas (the least advantaged state). See Longley and Dana, "New Empirical Estimates of the Biases of the Electoral College for the 1980s," *Western Political Quarterly* 37 (March 1984): 157–75.

Yet these calculations assume that all patterns of state voting are equally likely. This obviously is not a realistic assumption. Some states lean strongly toward one party. Building on this insight, Rabinowitz and MacDonald utilize the results of recent elections to identify likely pivotal states and make their own calculation of relative voting power. Once again, the large states are the winners. There are differences, however, from the results of the previous model. Most large states are even more influential, but the power of the states that lean strongly toward one party is diminished. Strongly Democratic Massachusetts is the biggest loser, dropping to a mere one-seventh of its influence as determined by the Shapley model.

Which model of state electoral power is more accurate? The second, which takes into account likely voting patterns, would appear more complete. Yet pivot patterns are imperfect guides to future behavior. With Jimmy Carter at the head of the ticket in 1980, Georgia was one of the most strongly Democratic states in the nation. In 1984, Walter Mondale lost Georgia by an even larger margin than the nation as a whole. Predicting future swing states from past behavior may lead to serious errors.

One might also question the emphasis on the importance of swing states. Is a state that provides a loyal and consistent base of support for one party necessarily unimportant? Is not a solid base as important to a winning coalition as more volatile swing states?

38. There are, of course, many other plans for "reform," involving almost all possible combinations of these three alternatives. For example, President Nixon at one point recommended that the 40 percent plurality plank that usually goes with the direct election proposal be applied instead to the present electoral college setup. See David S. Broder, "Mitchell Recommends Electoral Compromise," *Washington Post*, March 14, 1969. A second example is the "federal system plan" proposed by Senators Bob Dole and Tom Eagleton in 1970, which stated the following:

1. A candidate would be elected president by (a) winning a plurality of the national vote and (b) winning either pluralities in more than 50 percent of the states and D.C., or pluralities in states with 50 percent of the voters in the election.
2. If no candidate qualified, the election would go to an electoral college where the states would be represented as they are today, and candidates would automatically receive the electoral votes of the states they won.
3. In the unlikely event that no candidate received a majority of the electoral votes, the electoral votes of states that went for third-party candidates would be divided between the two leading national candidates in proportion to their share of the popular votes in those states. *Congressional Record*, March 5, 1970, S3026.

These plans had the following characteristics: (1) they were too complicated to solve any problems of public confusion or public perception that they are not "democratic," and (2) they had no significant body of congressional support.

39. Eric R. A. N. Smith and Peverill Squire argue, following Shapley's logic, that the importance of states should be calculated according to the ease with which undecided voters can be influenced. See Eric R. A. N. Smith and Peverill Squire, "Direct Election of the President and Power of the States," *Western Political Quarterly* 40 (March 1987): 31–44.

40. George C. Edwards III, *Why the Electoral College Is Bad for America* (New Haven, CT: Yale University Press, 2004); Robert W. Bennett, *Taming the Electoral College* (Stanford, CA: Stanford University Press, 2006).

41. Darshan J. Goux and David A. Hopkins, "The Empirical Implications of Electoral College Reform," *American Politics Research* 36 (November 2008): 857–79.

42. On September 18, 1969, by a vote of 339 to 70, a direct-election plan with a 40 percent plurality runoff provision was passed by the U.S. House of Representatives. See *Congressional Record*, September 18, 1969, H8142-43; for the content of the bill, see *Congressional Record*, September 10, 1969, H7745-46. For more recent discussion of proposed reforms, see Committee on the Judiciary, U.S. Senate, *Hearings on the Electoral College and Direct Election*, 95th Cong. (Washington, DC, 1977), and Bennett, *Taming the Electoral College.*

43. In 1968, the figures were similar when George Wallace ran a strong third-party campaign in the race between Richard Nixon and Hubert Humphrey. As in 1992, a fourth candidate would have needed only 6 or 7 percent of the national total to keep either major-party candidate from having the required 40 percent (Nixon won with only 43 percent, although he had 56.2 percent of the electoral vote). The Michigan Survey Research Center finds that only 1.5 percent of the voters in 1968 felt that Senator Eugene McCarthy of Minnesota was the best man for president in the spring and still felt that way after the election. If all participants in the system had known that he was not going to be defeated and disappear but would be a serious candidate at least through the first election, it is at least possible to conjecture that he could have picked up an additional 4 or 5 percent. Philip E. Converse, Warren E. Miller, Jerrold G. Rusk, and Arthur C. Wolfe, "Continuity and Change in American Politics: Parties and Issues in the 1968 Election," *American Political Science Review* 63 (December 1969): 1083–1105, at 1092.

44. The article that deals most clearly with the electoral college in terms of its virtues of conciliation and broad coalition building is John Wildenthal, "Consensus after L.B.J.," *Southwest Review* 53 (Spring 1968): 113–30. Wildenthal argues, in part, "rather than complain about being deprived of a choice when both parties wage 'me too' campaigns, the American people should be thankful that the interests of a wide variety of Americans can be reconciled by both parties with similar programs."

45. Roscoe Drummond, "Perils of the Electoral System," *Washington Post*, November 14, 1960. An argument in some ways parallel to our own is contained in Anthony Lewis, "The Case against Electoral Reform," *The Reporter*, December 8, 1960, pp. 31–33. See also Allan Sindler, "Presidential Election Methods and Urban-Ethnic Interests," *Law and Contemporary Problems* 27 (Spring 1962): 213–33.

46. David A. Hopkins and Darshan J. Goux, "Repealing the Unit Rule? Electoral Vote Allocation and Candidate Strategy," paper delivered at the Annual Meeting of the Midwest Political Science Association, Chicago, IL, April 2008.

47. Or, even worse, the Supreme Court, fearing "chaos," might step in and put its thumb on the scale, as in 2000. See Richard A. Posner, *Breaking the Deadlock: The 2000 Election, the Constitution, and the Courts* (Princeton, NJ: Princeton University Press, 2001); Richard A. Posner, "*Bush v. Gore* as Pragmatic Adjudication," in Dworkin, ed., *A Badly Flawed Election*, pp. 187–13.

48. Hopkins and Goux, "Repealing the Unit Rule?," p. 7.

49. See Arthur Schlesinger Jr., "A One-for-All Electoral College," *Wall Street Journal*, August 19, 1988, p. 16; Arthur Schlesinger Jr., "How to Democratize American Democracy," in *A Badly Flawed Election*, ed. Dworkin, pp. 215–29.

50. Despite popular misconceptions, even the 1964 Republican platform, written by supporters of Barry Goldwater, contained explicit promises to preserve these programs.

51. David R. Mayhew argues in *Divided We Govern: Party Control, Lawmaking and Investigations* (New Haven, CT: Yale University Press, 1991) that sheer legislative productivity is not harmed by divided government, with its constraints on party responsibility.

Chapter 7

1. Morris P. Fiorina, with Samuel J. Abrams and Jeremy C. Pope, *Culture War? The Myth of a Polarized America* (New York: Longman, 2004); Herbert McClosky, Paul S. Hoffmann, and Rosemary O'Hara, "Issue Conflict and Consensus among Party Leaders and Followers," *American Political Science Review* 54 (June 1960): 406–27.

2. This parallels in many respects an argument to be found in Robert A. Dahl, *A Preface to Democratic Theory* (Chicago: University of Chicago Press, 1956).

3. Richard A. Brody and Benjamin I. Page, "Policy Voting and the Electoral Process: The Vietnam War Issue," *American Political Science Review* 66 (September 1972): 979–95. See also William Schneider, "The November 4 Vote for President: What Did It Mean?" in Austin Ranney, ed., *The American Elections of 1980* (Washington, DC: American Enterprise Institute, 1981), pp. 212–62; and Nelson W. Polsby, "Party Realignment in the 1980 Election," *Yale Review* 72 (Autumn 1982): 43–54.

4. See Dahl, *A Preface to Democratic Theory*, pp. 124–31. The famous general statement from which this application is derived is Kenneth J. Arrow, *Social Choice and Individual Values*, 2nd ed. (New Haven, CT: Yale University Press, 1963).

5. Raymond E. Wolfinger and Steven J. Rosenstone, *Who Votes?* (New Haven, CT: Yale University Press, 1980), p. 83. See also Jack Citrin, Eric Schickler, and John Sides, "What If Everyone Voted? Simulating the Impact of Increased Turnout in Senate Elections," *American Journal of Political Science* 47 (2003): 75–90; and Sides, Schickler, and Citrin, "If Everyone Had Voted, Would Bubba and Dubya Have Won?" *Presidential Studies Quarterly* 38 (September 2008): 521–39.

6. See Nelson W. Polsby, *Consequences of Party Reform* (New York: Oxford University Press, 1983).

7. Ibid. See also the argument made by Marty Cohen, David Karol, Hans Noel, and John Zaller, *The Party Decides: Presidential Nominations Before and After Reform* (Chicago: University of Chicago Press, 2008).

8. See Jack Dennis, "Trends in Public Support for the American Party System," *British Journal of Political Science* 5 (April 1975): 187–230. A recent version of this argument is found in Fiorina, *Culture War?*

9. For the story on split-ticket voting and its effects, see Gary C. Jacobson, *The Electoral Origins of Divided Government* (Boulder, CO: Westview Press, 1990). See also Morris Fiorina, *Divided Government*, 2nd ed. (Boston: Allyn and Bacon, 1996).

10. See Richard J. Ellis, *Democratic Delusions: The Initiative Process in America* (Lawrence: The University Press of Kansas, 2002); David S. Broder, *Democracy Derailed: Initiative Campaigns and the Power of Money* (New York: Harcourt, 2000).

11. See Bruce E. Cain, Sara Ferejohn, Margarita Najar, and Mary Walther, "Constitutional Change: Is It Too Easy to Amend Our State Constitution?" in Bruce E. Cain and Roger G. Noll, eds., *Constitutional Reform in California: Making State Government More Effective and Responsive* (Berkeley, CA: Institute of Governmental Studies Press, 1995), pp. 265–90, esp. pp. 284–89.

Index